Edward W. Klink III is Assistant Professor of
New Testament at Talbot School of Theology,
Biola University.

THE SHEEP OF THE FOLD

The last generation of Gospel scholarship has considered the reconstruction and analysis of the audience behind the Gospels as paradigmatic. The key hermeneutical template for reading the Gospels has
been the quest for the community that each Gospel represents. But this
scholarly consensus regarding the audience of the Gospels has recently
been reconsidered. Using as a test case one of the most entrenched
Gospels, Edward Klink explores the evidence for the audience behind
the Gospel of John. This study challenges the current Gospel paradigm
by examining the community construct and its functional potential in
early Christianity, the appropriation of a Gospel text and J. L. Martyn's
two-level reading of John, and the implied reader located within the narrative. The study concludes by proposing a more appropriate audience
model for reading John, as well as some implications for the function
of the Gospel in early Christianity.

EDWARD W. KLINK III is Assistant Professor of New Testament at
Talbot School of Theology, Biola University.

SOCIETY FOR NEW TESTAMENT STUDIES

MONOGRAPH SERIES

General Editor: John Court

141

THE SHEEP OF THE FOLD

SOCIETY FOR NEW TESTAMENT STUDIES

MONOGRAPH SERIES

Recent titles in the series

The Sheep of the Fold

The Audience and Origin of the Gospel of John

EDWARD W. KLINK III

CAMBRIDGE UNIVERSITY PRESS
Cambridge, New York, Melbourne, Madrid, Cape Town, Singapore, São Paulo

Cambridge University Press
The Edinburgh Building, Cambridge CB2 8RU, UK

Published in the United States of America by Cambridge University Press, New York

www.cambridge.org
Information on this title: www.cambridge.org/9780521875820

© Edward W. Klink III 2007

First published 2007

Printed in the United Kingdom at the University Press, Cambridge

A catalogue record for this publication is available from the British Library

Library of Congress Cataloguing in Publication data
Klink, Edward W., 1975–
The Sheep of the fold: the audience and origin of the Gospel of John / Edward W. Klink.
  p.   cm. – (Society for New Testament Studies Monograph series)
Includes bibliographical references and index.
ISBN-13: 978 0 521 87582 0 (hardback)
ISBN-10: 0 521 87582 X (hardback)
1. Bible. N. T. John – Criticism, interpretation, etc.   I. Title   II. Series.
BS2615.52.K57   2007
226.5′066–dc22
2007002297

ISBN 978-0-521-87582-0 hardback

CONTENTS

ACKNOWLEDGMENTS

This monograph is a revision of a doctoral thesis completed at the University of St. Andrews. The majority of the research and writing was undertaken during our three-year residence in St. Andrews, Scotland, from 2002 to 2005. I am indebted to my supervisor, Professor Richard Bauckham, for his visionary guidance over my research and for being an exemplary model of scholarship. Thanks are also due to Professor Ron Piper, whose secondary supervision provided a "critical" guide for my own thinking process; and to Dr. Stephen Barton and Dr. Bruce Longenecker for their judicial examination of my thesis, as well as their encouragement in its publication. I would also like to thank Johannes Beutler S.J., for his helpful remarks on my original manuscript. I am also grateful to my doctoral colleagues and their families at St. Mary's College, who provided a constant "classroom" for my own learning process, as well as a home away from home for our family.

In light of our new home in southern California, thanks are due to my colleagues and friends at Biola University and Talbot School of Theology. My department has overwhelmed us in their welcome, especially my NT colleagues, Drs. Matt Williams, Jon Lunde, Ken Berding, and Michelle Lee, who have mentored and encouraged me throughout my first year of teaching. Thanks are also due to my department chairs, Dr. David Talley and Dr. Jim Mohler, and to the deans, Dr. Dennis Dirks and Dr. Michael Wilkins, for the vision they have cast and environment they have nurtured at Talbot. I would also like to thank Patrick Saia for all his administrative assistance.

This monograph is dedicated to my beautiful wife, Laura. I am unable to express how thankful I am to share every detail of life with you. Thank you for your work with our sons, Jacob and Benjamin, and your commitment to our academic ministry. You will always be my Ecclesiastes 9:9.

ABBREVIATIONS

AA	*American Anthropologist*
AB	The Anchor Bible
ABRL	The Anchor Bible Reference Library
AES	*Archives Européennes de Sociologie*
AGAJU	Arbeiten zur Geschichte des antiken Judentums und des Urchristentums
AJBI	*Annual of the Japanese Biblical Institute*
AJT	*American Journal of Theology*
ANTC	Abingdon New Testament Commentaries
ARP	*Annual Review of Psychology*
ASAM	Association of Social Anthropologists Monographs
ASNTU	Acta Seminarii Neotestamentici Upsaliensis
ASR	*American Sociological Review*
ATANT	Abhandlungen zur Theologie des Alten und Neuen Testaments
BBB	*Bonner biblische Beiträge*
BBET	Beiträge zur biblischen Exegese und Theologie
BD	Beloved Disciple
BEAK	*Bis zur Entstehung der alkatholischen Kirche*
BETL	Bibliotheca Ephemeridum Theologicarum Lovaniensium
BENT	Beiträge zur Einleitung in das Neue Testament
BFCT	Beiträge zur Förderung christlicher Theologie
BH	Bibliothèque historique
BI	*Biblical Interpretation*
BIS	*Biblical Interpretation Series*
BJRL	*Bulletin of the John Rylands Library*
BJS	Brown Judaic Studies
BJSoc	*British Journal of Sociology*
BL	*Bibel und Leben*
BLS	The Bible and Liberation Series

BN	*Biblische Notizen*
BNTC	Black's New Testament Commentaries
BS	The Biblical Seminar
BTB	*Biblical Theology Bulletin*
BTS	Biblisch-Theologische Studien
BZATW	Beihefte zur Zeitschrift für die alttestamentliche Wissenschaft
BZNTW	Beihefte zur Zeitschrift für die neutestamentliche Wissenschaft
CB	Coniectanea biblica
CBNTS	Coniectanea biblica, New Testament Series
CBQ	*Catholic Biblical Quarterly*
CBSS	The Continuum Biblical Studies Series
CCT	Challenges in Contemporary Theology
CGT	Culture, Gender, Theory
CFTL	Clark's Foreign Theological Library
CH	*Church History*
CI	*Critical Inquiry*
CIBR	*Currents in Biblical Research*
CPLE	Critical Perspectives on Literacy and Education
CR	*Classical Review*
CS	*Current Sociology*
CSCD	Cambridge Studies in Christian Doctrine
CSHJ	Chicago Studies in the History of Judaism
CSSHSup	Comparative Studies in Society and History: Supplements Series
CTM	*Concordia Theological Monthly*
CV	*Communio Viatorum*
DR	*Downside Review*
EH	Europäische Hochschulschriften
EMZ	*Evangelische Missions-Zeitschrift*
ESGL	*Eirene: Studia Graeca at Latina*
ESSR	Essays in the Scientific Study of Religion.
EvQ	*Evangelical Quarterly*
EvT	*Evangelische Theologie*
ExpT	*Expository Times*
FBBS	Facet Books Biblical Series
FCNT	Feminist Companion to the New Testament and Early Christian Writings
FE	Fourth Evangelist
FFF	*Foundations and Facets Forum*

FFNT	Foundations and Facets: New Testament
FG	Fourth Gospel
FMAS	Foundations of Modern Anthropology Series
FRC	The Family, Religion, and Culture
FRLANT	Forschungen zur Religion und Literatur des Alten und Neuen Testaments
GA	General Audience
GAC	*The Gospels for All Christians*
GBS	Guides to Biblical Scholarship
GBSNTS	Guides to Biblical Scholarship New Testament Series
HFF	Hermenia: Foundations and Facets
HJ	*The Heythrop Journal*
HJL	*Heidelberger Jahrbücher der Literatur*
HR	*History of Religions*
HTCNT	Herders Theological Commentary on the New Testament
HTR	*Harvard Theological Review*
HTS	*Hervormde Teologiese Studies*
HTSS	Hervormde Teologiese Studies Supplementum
HTStud	Harvard Theological Studies
HZ	*Historische Zeitschrift*
IBRB	Institute for Biblical Research Bibliographies
IBS	*Irish Biblical Studies*
ICC	The International Critical Commentary
IEJ	*Israel Exploration Journal*
IJST	*International Journal of Systematic Theology*
ISBL	Indiana Studies in Biblical Literature
IST	Issues in Systematic Theology
ITL	International Theological Library
ITQ	*Irish Theological Quarterly*
JAAR	*Journal of the American Academy of Religion*
JBL	*Journal of Biblical Literature*
JBLMS	Journal of Biblical Literature Monograph Series
JComm	Johannine Community
JLCR	Jordan Lectures in Comparative Religion
JLT	*Journal of Literature and Theology*
JR	*Journal of Religion*
JRA	*Journal of Roman Archaeology*
JRH	*Journal of Religious History*
JSHJ	*Journal for the Study of the Historical Jesus*
JSNT	*Journal for the Study of the New Testament*

JSNTSup	Journal for the Study of the New Testament: Supplement Series
JSOT	*Journal for the Study of the Old Testament*
JSOTSup	Journal for the Study of the Old Testament: Supplement Series
JSPSSup	Journal for the Study of the Pseudepigrapha: Supplement Series
JSSR	*Journal for the Scientific Study of Religion*
JTS	*Journal of Theological Studies*
KCSS	Key Concepts in the Social Sciences
KEKNT	Kritisch-exegetischer Kommentar über das Neue Testament
KI	Key Idea
KJNTL	*Kritisch. Journ. d. neuest. theol. Lit.*
LCBI	Literary Currents in Biblical Interpretation
LEC	Library of Early Christianity
LHA	Local, Heterogeneous Audience
LXX	Septuagint
MNTS	McMaster New Testament Studies
MTZ	*Münchener Theologische Zeitschrift*
NICNT	The New International Commentary on the New Testament
NIDNTT	New International Dictionary of New Testament Theology
NovT	*Novum Testamentum*
NovTSup	Novum Testamentum, Supplements
NT	New Testament
NTC	The New Testament in Context
NTG	New Testament Guides
NTL	The New Testament Library
NTR	New Testament Readings
NTS	*New Testament Studies*
NTT	New Testament Theology
NTTS	New Testament Tools and Studies
OBS	Oxford Bible Series
OT	Old Testament
PBTS	Paternoster Biblical and Theological Studies
PCTSA	*Proceedings of the Catholic Theological Society of America*
PE	*Pro Ecclesia*
PNTC	Pillar New Testament Commentary

PTMS	The Pittsburgh Theological Monograph Series
RevExp	*Review and Expositor*
RHPR	*Revue d'histoire et de philosophie religieuses*
RNT	Regensburger Neues Testament
RPS	Religious Perspectives Series
RRT	*Reviews in Religion and Theology*
RSR	*Religious Studies Review*
RTT	Research in Text Theory
SA	*Sociological Analysis*
SR	*Social Research*
SB	Stuttgarter Bibelstudien
SBB	Stuttgarter Biblische Beiträge
SBL	Society of Biblical Literature
SBLMS	Society of Biblical Literature Monograph Series
SBLDS	Society of Biblical Literature Dissertation Series
SBLRBS	Society of Biblical Literature Resources for Biblical Study
SBLSBS	Society of Biblical Literature Sources for Biblical Study
SBLSP	*Society of Biblical Literature Seminar Papers*
SBLSS	Society of Biblical Literature Semeia Studies
SBLSymS	Society of Biblical Literature Symposium Series
SBG	Studies in Biblical Greek
SBT	Studies in Biblical Theology
SC	*Second Century: A Journal of Early Christian Studies*
SCC	Studies in Creative Criticism
SCH	Studies in Church History
SCL	Sather Classical Lectures
SECT	Sources of Early Christian Thought
SHR	Studies in the History of Religion
SHS	The Scripture and Hermeneutics Series
SJLA	Studies in Judaism in Late Antiquity
SJT	*Scottish Journal of Theology*
SNTSMS	Society for New Testament Studies Monograph Series
SNTU	*Studien zum Neuen Testament und seiner Umwelt*
SNTW	Studies of the New Testament and Its World
SP	*Studia Patristica*
SPB	Studia Post-Biblica
SPP	Studies in Philosophical Psychology
SPSH	Scholars Press Studies in the Humanities
SR	*Studies in Religion*
SSD	Studies in Social Discontinuity

SSEJC	Studies in Scripture and Early Judaism and Christianity
ST	*Studia Theologica*
SVC	Supplements to Vigiliae Christianae: Texts and Studies of Early Christian Life and Language
SVSGTR	Sammlung gemeinverständlicher Vorträge und Schriften aus dem Gebiet der Theologie und Religionsgeschichte,
TB	*Tyndale Bulletin*
TDNT	Theological Dictionary of the New Testament
TEH	Theologische Existenz heute
ThB	*Theologische Beiträge*
ThR	*Theologische Rundschau*
ThStud	*Theologische Studien*
ThZ	*Theologische Zeitschrift*
TJ	*Trinity Journal*
TPINTC	Trinity Press International New Testament Commentaries
TS	*Theological Studies*
TTL	Theological Translation Library
TTS	Theologische Texte und Studien
TU	Texte und Untersuchungen
USQR	*Union Seminary Quarterly Review*
UUA	Uppsala Universitets Årsskrift
VT	*Vetus Testamentum*
WBC	Word Biblical Commentary
WD	*Wort und Dienst*
WMANT	Wissenschaftliche Monographien zum Alten und Neuen Testament
WTJ	*The Westminster Theological Journal*
WUNT	Wissenschaftliche Untersuchungen zum Neuen Testament
ZAW	*Zeitschrift für die Alttestamentliche Wissenschaft*
ZNW	*Zeitschrift für die neutestamentliche Wissenschaft*
ZWT	*Zeitschrift für Wissenschaftliche Theologie*

1

THE AUDIENCE AND ORIGIN OF THE GOSPELS: INTRODUCTION AND METHOD

Introduction

It has long been recognized that any study of the Gospels must incorporate to some degree a detailed understanding of the origins and traditions of early Christianity, whether explicitly or implicitly. The modern commentary almost always begins by discussing the introductory material before discussing the text proper. This approach is simply assumed. The end result is certainly affected in principle by the starting point. This is not to say that any understanding of the text is predetermined a priori and that the text itself is left helpless to the scholar's dissecting and analyzing tools; on the contrary, the text is often used as the very tool itself by which one draws theories by which it need be analyzed. Thus, any attempt to understand the Gospels and their meaning must consider thoroughly the means by which an understanding of what they are and how they came to be directly affects how one discovers what they mean.

The danger with the above is obvious: where one starts can undoubtedly determine where one will end. Too often a particular understanding of Christian origins can malign a text so that it no longer reveals the meaning most appropriate to early Christian belief and the text within which it dwells.[1] In order to prevent such a mishap, it seems appropriate to step back from the detailed aspects of current research to see if the picture being painted by modern scholars is appropriately describing the texts as we now have them. When this is done to the Gospels, a corrective appraisal of the current view of their origin and historical background is much in need. Fortunately, such a critique has already been suggested. A trend has sprouted in a significant part of recent Gospel research that challenges the current understanding of a Gospel's audience and origin, specifically in

---

[1] Hugh Anderson, *Jesus and Christian Origins* (New York: Oxford University Press, 1964), p. 16, summarizes well the complexity of the study of Christian origins by saying, "Every form of inquiry into the rise of Christianity, environmental-historical and theological as well as dogmatic is confronted with the dilemma of where to start and what to choose."

1

relation to the historical environment in which and for which the Gospels were created.[2] It gives an appraisal of the current picture of the Christian beginnings which, by necessity, coerces one's interpretive outlook on the Gospel text itself. A detailed look at the problem and its correlative aspects is now in order.

Problem to be addressed: its recent development

The discussion of the introductory and foundational issues of the Gospels abounds. The complexity of establishing certainty in these issues need not be explained, for it is well assumed. Within these discussions, however, a great variety of differences exists between the various results of scholarly research. But what has become almost unanimously assumed in current research is the audience for whom the Gospels were written. The current consensus assumes that the Gospels were written for a specific, geographically located audience in contrast to a general audience. Any survey of current literature on Gospels scholarship reveals how dominant audience or "community" reconstructions have become for interpretive method.[3]

Recently, this general scholarly consensus was questioned in an attempt to correct what some have called the unproven and hermeneutically determinative assumptions used to reconstruct the current understanding of Christian origins. This critique was proposed in the 1998 book

---

[2] This recent trend is rooted primarily in the English-language academic community. Not all methodological approaches to the Gospels have been so tied to the historical audience. For example, since the dissertations of Birger Olsson, *Structure and Meaning in the Fourth Gospel: A Text-Linguistic Analysis of John 2:1–11 and 4:1–42*, CB 6, trans. Jean Gray (Lund: CWK Gleerup, 1974) and Horacio E. Lona, *Abraham in Johannes 8: ein Beitrag zur Methodfragen*, EH 65 (Bern: H. Lang, 1976), a synchronic reading of the FG in particular has become more accepted. Also prominent is the "Swiss School" of exegesis which focuses on the relation between texts, instead of the reconstruction of authors and their communities. See, for example, Andreas Dettwiler, *Die Gegenwart des Erhöhten: Eine exegetische Studie Zu den johanneischen Abschiedsreden (Joh. 13,31–16,33) unter besonderer Berücksichtigung ihres Relectere-Charakters*, FRLANT 169 (Göttingen: Vandenhoeck & Ruprecht, 1995).

[3] Some recent and popular examples include the following: Colleen M. Conway, "The Production of the Johannine Community: A New Historicist Perspective," *JBL* 121 (2002), pp. 479–95; David C. Sim, *The Gospel of Matthew and Christian Judaism: The History and Setting of the Matthean Community* (Edinburgh: T. & T. Clark, 1998); David L. Balch (ed.), *Social History of the Matthean Community* (Minneapolis: Fortress Press, 1991); J. Andrew Overman, *Church and Community in Crisis: The Gospel According to Matthew* (Valley Forge, Pa.: Trinity Press International, 1996); Anthony J. Saldarini, *Matthew's Christian-Jewish Community* (Chicago: University of Chicago Press, 1994); Gary M. Burge, *The Anointed Community: The Holy Spirit in the Johannine Tradition* (Grand Rapids: Eerdmans, 1987); Philip F. Esler, *Community and Gospel in Luke-Acts* (Cambridge: Cambridge University Press, 1987).

The Gospels for All Christians: Rethinking the Gospel Audiences (*GAC*), edited by Richard Bauckham and contributed to by several other British scholars.[4] A summary of this book's critical thesis is now in order.

The most crucial and well-received essay in *GAC* is the initial chapter by the editor himself, Richard Bauckham.[5] Arguably this is the case because Bauckham sets forth the thesis proper while the rest of the essays simply support its various aspects, establishing a cumulative argument. Bauckham's thesis is to challenge and refute the current consensus in Gospels scholarship which assumes that the Gospels were written for a specific church or group of churches. Bauckham proposes that it is more probable that the Gospels were written for general circulation around the churches and envisaged a very general Christian audience. "Their implied readership is not specific but indefinite: any and every Christian community in the late-first-century Roman Empire."[6] Bauckham's thesis is argued in five cumulative parts, each of which we should now summarize.

First, the assumption that a more specific audience is intended is simply assumed; in fact, as Bauckham argues, whereas the Christian background of the audience is often given extensive support and argumentation in its discussion, the question of the specific or general nature of the audience is remarkable for having never been discussed in print.[7] Bauckham hopes to "sow an initial seed of possibility" against nearly all the literature of the last few decades that has increasingly built large and sophisticated arguments upon the assumption of a specific audience, "as though no alternative could ever have occurred to anyone."[8]

Second, Bauckham briefly summarizes the history of the Gospel-community interpretation.[9] He argues that this view of the Gospel communities goes as far back as the end of the nineteenth century in British

[4] Richard Bauckham (ed.), *The Gospels for All Christians: Rethinking the Gospel Audiences* (Grand Rapids: Eerdmans, 1998).

[5] While the other essays are helpful, their existence can be seen as supportive arguments for the thesis which Bauckham presents. In his critique of *GAC*, David C. Sim, "The Gospels for All Christians: A Response to Richard Bauckham," *JSNT* 84 (2001), p. 5, states, "Without doubt the most important contribution in this volume is the first essay, 'For Whom Were Gospels Written?,' by Richard Bauckham himself. It is this offering that presents the most sustained attack on the consensus position and the most detailed account of the alternative hypothesis."

[6] Bauckham, "Introduction", in *GAC*, pp. 1–2. As we will discuss below, the phrase "any and every" will need to be more clearly defined. The audience is certainly not wholly indefinite.

[7] Bauckham, "For Whom Were the Gospels Written?," in *GAC*, p. 10.   [8] *Ibid.*, p. 11.

[9] A more complete history of the community-hypothesis in Gospels scholarship will be given below.

scholarship. With the discussion having begun in the origins discussions at the turn of the nineteenth century, it was soon considered common practice to discuss the developing idea of the Gospels' *Sitze im Leben*, which became a prominent theme just after the Second World War, and in such discussions to focus on a particular Gospel community in contrast to a more general audience. Then, in the 1960s and 1970s, after form criticism had already become a standard tool of Gospels scholarship, some major works on the Gospels and their communities were produced using a relatively new method called redaction criticism. "The redaction critics often complained that form criticism, despite its professed emphasis on the Christian community as the *Sitz im Leben* of the Gospel traditions, always considered the community in highly general terms . . . The redaction critics were intent on much more specificity."[10] Thus, Bauckham claims, many community interpretations of each of the four Gospels began to appear on the scholarly horizon. The result of this has led to a more allegorical reading of the Gospels in the service of reconstructing both the character and history of the community behind the Gospel, but also an increasingly sophisticated use of social-scientific methods to assist with the reconstructing process.[11]

Third, Bauckham questions whether the assumption being practiced in current Gospels research is in any way confirmed by the fact that multiple conclusions and results have been built upon it. For Bauckham, the results that are derived are simply the results of applying a particular reading strategy to the text, not of showing that this particular reading strategy does "better justice to the text than another reading strategy."[12] While not disproving the methodology behind this untested reading strategy, Bauckham argues that the relative success, or amount of detailed reconstructions, does not prove at all that a reading strategy based on a different, or even contrary, assumption, would not be equally or even more successful.[13]

Fourth, it seems more appropriate to assume, based on historical evidence, that someone writing a Gospel in the late first century would have envisaged a more general audience.[14] This seems to be an appropriate counter-assumption to the community reconstructions simply by comparing the Gospels with the Pauline epistles. Bauckham argues this aspect on two fronts: first, the difference in genre between Paul's epistles and the Gospels implies a different type of reading, hence a different or broader

---

[10] *Ibid.*, p. 18.   [11] *Ibid.*, pp. 19–22.   [12] *Ibid.*, p. 22.

[13] *Ibid.*, p. 26. This is not to say that the use of a heuristic method is inappropriate simply because it is unproven. What Bauckham is questioning is the use of a heuristic model as the starting point from which the rest of the inquiry takes place.

[14] *Ibid.*

readership. Second, the more basic but important question of why would anyone put in writing this information in the genre of *bios* and yet expect it to be treaded like the epistolary genre. In many ways, the simplicity of this question forces us to deal with the more basic assumptions of the creative use of the Gospels.

Fifth, Bauckham argues that the general character of the early Christian movement should not be pictured as "a scattering of isolated, self-sufficient communities with little or no communication between them, but quite the opposite: a network of communities with constant, close communication among themselves."[15] This aspect of the early church is not an assumed reconstruction but is supported by the historical evidence we have concerning the late first and early second centuries of Christianity.

It seems as if the ground was ripe for the broader audience promoted by *GAC*. While several prominent "community" interpretations had already begun to lessen their stance on the specificity of description of the particular community, other NT scholars argued against the trend as a whole. This is especially evident since *GAC* where entire sections within conferences[16] have dealt with what may be called the "Gospel community debate." Since this author has recently provided an extended discussion of the evidence of both pre-*GAC* warnings and the post-*GAC* debate in "The Gospel Community Debate: State of the Question," only a summary of the current situation will be given here.[17]

The Gospel community debate is much larger than *GAC* and its recent critique of the current approach to Gospel audiences. The Gospel community debate is connected to several historical and hermeneutical developments going back as far as the late 1970s. At the same time it is has been through the "rethinking" of the Gospels' origin and audience by *GAC* that the debate has been brought into focus. In light of the discussion of Gospel audience and origin since *GAC*, it has become evident that the way forward for the Gospel community debate centers upon four areas of definition.

The first area that needs definition is the use of the term "community." A good example of an ambiguous understanding of the term "community" can be seen in the recent work on the FG by Andrew Lincoln. As Lincoln explains in relation to his own work:

[15] *Ibid.*, p. 30.

[16] Society of Biblical Literature Annual Meeting, Johannine Literature section, November 2002; Life in Abundance: An International Conference on the Gospel of John: in Tribute to the Life of Raymond E. Brown, October 2003; Society of Biblical Literature Annual Meeting, Synoptic Gospels section, November 2003.

[17] Edward W. Klink III, "The Gospel Community Debate: State of the Question," *CIBR* 3 (2004), pp. 60–85.

this study takes care to distinguish between this group, from which the Gospel emerged, and either the implied readers or intended audience that it addresses. The former may well be included in, but certainly does not exhaust, the latter. In other words, in the view posited here, although the narrative is shaped by and addresses the needs of the group from which it emerged, it also gives clear indications in its final form that its perspective transcends any particular experiences of this group and is addressed to a wider audience . . . We do not, however, need to banish all discussion of communities behind particular Gospels and any consideration of the hermeneutical significance that the enquiries behind such a discussion might have.[18]

Lincoln's proposed handling of the *Sitz im Leben* of the FG is too vague to be of any help. How does he plan to differentiate between the "community" that created the Gospel and the "community(ies)" for which the Gospel was intended? If he does not want to banish the discussion of communities, a more appropriate definition is needed. Even then, there are inherent dangers when one applies formative terms such as Gospel "community," "group," or "sect" to the discussion of the audience of the Gospels. Only by defining the contours of a "community" will the use of community terminology become useful.

The second area that needs definition is the nature of the Gospel genre. As Graham Stanton has warned, a Gospel is not a letter and cannot be read like one.[19] The work on Gospel genre by Richard Burridge has helped define what a Gospel *is*;[20] what is needed is further discussion of what a Gospel can *do*. Questions concerning Gospel referentiality need to be asked of the Gospel narratives.[21] How one understands the nature of the *bios* is not of more importance than how one understands the referential function of narrative and the reading assumptions of first-century readers. Thus, it is not just a matter of the type of genre, but the function of genre.

[18] Andrew T. Lincoln, *Truth on Trial: The Lawsuit Motif in the Fourth Gospel* (Peabody: Hendrickson, 2000), p. 265.

[19] Graham N. Stanton, "Revisiting Matthew's Communities," *SBLSP* (1994), pp. 9–23. Of course, Stanton is not aligning himself with the position held by *GAC*. For a response to Stanton's "loose network of communities" see Bauckham, "For Whom Were the Gospels Written?," pp. 26–27, n. 29, and pp. 45–46.

[20] Richard A. Burridge, *What Are the Gospels? A Comparison with Graeco-Roman Biography*, 2nd edn (Grand Rapids: Eerdmans, 2004); and Richard A. Burridge, "About People, by People, for People: Gospel Genre and Audiences," in *GAC*.

[21] See Hans-Josef Klauck, "Community, History, and Text(s) – a Response" (paper presented at Life in Abundance: An International Conference on the Gospel of John: A Tribute to Raymond Brown. Baltimore, October 16–18, 2003). See also Klink, "The Gospel Community Debate," pp. 64, 78–79.

The third area that needs definition is the use and function of the Gospels in the early Christian movement. Part of Bauckham's argument in *GAC* was intended to critique a consensus that seems to depend on a view of an early Christian "community" as a "self-contained, self-sufficient, introverted group, having little contact with other Christian communities and little sense of participation in a worldwide Christian movement. Identity, issues, and concerns, it seems to be presupposed, are thoroughly local."[22] Two major critiques of *GAC* challenge Bauckham on his counter-depiction of the early Christian movement.[23] The most detailed critique was an article by Margaret Mitchell involving patristic evidence.[24] According to Mitchell, far from being unconcerned with a local audience, the patristic writers were very concerned with the local origins of each of the Gospels. The patristic evidence points to numerous local audience traditions that were interested in the historical and local origins of the Gospels. In fact, according to Mitchell, these Gospel origins acted as a "hermeneutical key" for later readers of the Gospels.[25] But could the same evidence be read in a different way? What, for example, does Mitchell mean by "hermeneutical key?" Two questions seem most pertinent here. First, do the patristic writers actually possess knowledge of the specific historical circumstances of the individual Gospels? Related to this is the formation and use of tradition in the early church. The second question is connected to the first: to what extent do these traditions reflect their own agendas (i.e. different from the modern historical critical understanding)? Related to this is the use of the Gospels in worship and as scripture,[26] the interrelation between the Gospels,[27] and the

[22] Bauckham, "For Whom," pp. 30–31.

[23] See Philip F. Esler, "Community and Gospel in Early Christianity: A Response to Richard Bauckham's Gospel for All Christians," *SJT* 51 (1998), pp. 235–48, who critiques Bauckham's picture of the early Christian movement from a social-scientific perspective. Bauckham gives a specific response to his colleague in the same journal which is titled "Response to Philip Esler," *SJT* 51 (1998), pp. 249–53. See also Sim, "A Response to Richard Bauckham," who critiques Bauckham's picture of the early Christian movement from a historical perspective. Cf. Klink, "The Gospel Community Debate," pp. 69, 72–73.

[24] Margaret M. Mitchell, "Patristic Counter-Evidence to the Claim that 'The Gospels Were Written for All Christians,'" *NTS* 51 (2005), pp. 36–79, originally presented at the annual meeting for the Society for Biblical Literature in Atlanta, Ga., November, 22–25, 2003.

[25] *Ibid.*, p. 17.

[26] See Oscar Cullmann, *Early Christian Worship*, trans. A. Stewart Todd and J. B. Torrance, SBT 10 (London: SCM Press, 1963); Martin Hengel, *The Four Gospels and the One Gospel of Jesus Christ: An Investigation of the Collection and Origin of the Canonical Gospels*, trans. John Bowden (London: SCM Press, 2000).

[27] See the discussions between Bauckham, "John for Readers of Mark," in *GAC*, and Wendy E. Sproston North, "John for Readers of Mark: A Response to Richard Bauckham's Proposal," *JSNT* 25 (2003), pp. 449–68.

four-fold Gospel.[28] As Mitchell has reminded us concerning the Gospel community debate, the path forward cannot ignore the voices from the past.[29]

The fourth area that needs definition is the role of "community" reconstructions in Gospel hermeneutics. Twenty-five years ago Luke Timothy Johnson argued that the use of "community" reconstructions in the interpretation of the Gospels was a dangerous enterprise.[30] For Johnson, even if we assumed that a community existed behind a Gospel, we would not be certain how to apply the information from the text to the specific community. He uses the example of the discussion of prayer in Luke: are we to suppose that Luke stresses praying because his community does not pray (or that some in the community do not pray)? Or are we to assume he is correcting an inappropriate view on prayer; one that requires a theological lesson?[31] For Johnson, anything but a general description of Luke's readers does injustice to the text; it destroys the text's intended literary meaning. Since Johnson, several similar hermeneutical "warnings" have also been given,[32] even by some who support the reconstruction of Gospel "communities."[33] Finally, the most thorough hermeneutical critique of "community" reconstructions was recently presented by Dwight Peterson, looking specifically at the Gospel of Mark.[34] Peterson

---

[28] See Oscar Cullmann, "The Plurality of the Gospels as a Theological Problem in Antiquity: A Study in the History of Dogma," in A. J. B. Higgins (ed.), *The Early Church: Oscar Cullmann*, trans. A. J. B. Higgins and S. Godman (London: SCM Press, 1956), pp. 39–54; and Graham Stanton, "The Fourfold Gospel," *NTS* 43 (1997), pp. 317–46.

[29] This area might also include an examination of the extra-canonical Gospels, as has recently been done by Thomas Kazen, "Sectarian Gospels for Some Christians? Intention and Mirror Reading in the Light of Extra-Canonical Gospels," *NTS* 51 (2005), pp. 561–78.

[30] Luke Timothy Johnson, "On Finding Lukan Community: A Cautious Cautionary Essay," *SBLSP* (1979), pp. 87–100.

[31] *Ibid.*, p. 91.

[32] See Edwin Judge, "The Social Identity of the First Christians: A Question of Method in Religious History," *JRH* 11 (1980), pp. 201–17; Dale Allison, "Was There a Lukan Community?," *IBS* 10 (1988), pp. 62–70; Bengt Holmberg, *Sociology and the New Testament: An Appraisal* (Minneapolis, Fortress Press, 1990), pp. 124–25; and Stephen Barton, "The Communal Dimensions of Earliest Christianity: A Critical Survey of the Field," *JTS* 43 (1992), pp. 399–427, especially 425. For a fuller discussion see Klink, "The Gospel Community Debate."

[33] See Jack Dean Kingsbury, "Conclusion: Analysis of a Conversation," in Balch (ed.), *Social History of the Matthean Community*, pp. 259–69. While offering concluding remarks at the end of the essays, Kingsbury gives a surprise warning to such a methodological practice. "To move from text to social situation by simply invoking the principle of transparency is, owing to the high degree of subjectivity involved and the paucity of independent evidence for corroborating one's findings, hazardous indeed" (262).

[34] Dwight N. Peterson, *The Origins of Mark: The Markan Community in Current Debate*, BIS 48 (Leiden: Brill, 2000).

approaches the community-hypothesis by studying the hermeneutical principles used by proponents of such an interpretive method. According to Peterson, the purpose of his book is to show that the concept of "The Markan Community . . . is the product of highly speculative, viciously circular and ultimately unpersuasive and inconclusive reading."[35] The circular nature of such a method, whereby the text is used as a window to see the originating aspects of an early Christian community so that the text can be understood, is a circular and illegitimate practice and is based upon a faulty hermeneutical methodology.

But the recent critiques of "community" reconstructions in Gospel hermeneutics are not merely due to observed flaws in methodology. The entire postmodern critique of modernity's historical-critical emphasis is also related to the Gospel community debate. Robert Kysar has recently suggested that the "Whither" of the Gospel community is connected to the postmodern critique of the dominance of the historical-critical method.[36] The rise of postmodern interpretive methods that press upon the old paradigm is beginning to forge the way ahead. The alternative approaches to the text are taking their stand against the old redaction critical method of seeing in every word and phrase in the Gospels an image standing behind it. Postmodern interpretation's denial that the text is merely a means to an end presents a radical challenge to the way a "text," specifically a Gospel text, is read. Such approaches are not divorced from the Gospel community debate.

The above discussion of the four most pressing areas in the Gospel community debate that are in need of definition gives both direction and credence to this book. The only full monograph concerning the Gospel community debate, *The Origins of Mark* by Dwight Peterson, was actually completed with all but revisions as a doctoral dissertation without any knowledge of *GAC*.[37] That the field of Gospel scholarship is ripe for continued research concerning Gospel audience and origin is evident from the continued debate.

---

[35] *Ibid.*, p. 196.

[36] Robert Kysar, "The Whence and Whither of the Johannine Community" (paper presented at Life in Abundance: An International Conference on the Gospel of John: A Tribute to Raymond Brown. Baltimore, October 16–18, 2003). Now published under the same title in John R. Donahue (ed.), *Life in Abundance: Studies of John's Gospel in Tribute to Raymond E. Brown* (Collegeville: Liturgical Press, 2005), pp. 65–81.

[37] Peterson only cites *GAC* on two occasions, the first of which appears to be only a footnote adding comprehensiveness to the introduction of his original work. The conclusion, which may have been added during revision for publication, also deals briefly with *GAC*.

Historical survey: the quest for the Gospel community

Before we can further the Gospel community debate we must trace the history of "community" reconstructions in the history of Gospel interpretation.[38] The areas of NT scholarship that we are going to use to trace the concept of "community" through are massive; each alone could warrant a historical study in its own right. Thus, in order to focus on the appropriate task, we shall only seek the origin and methodological use of the "community" concept and its gradual development into the community reconstructions currently used in Gospel research. The purpose of this survey is to trace the developing definition of the term "community" and its use as the interpretive grid by which the Gospel audience and origin are determined.

Source criticism: the geographic origin of community

The history of community reconstructions does not present a clear and precise understanding of the view that each Gospel was written in and for its own community. In fact, the concept of "community" only gradually developed as various historical-critical methods were employed to the text of the Gospels. It is this gradual development that has led to an improper and untested hermeneutical methodology, as well as the inaccurate historical picture that such a view creates. Thus, as we move through the stages of historical interpretation over the last century, it is important to note that the term "community" has not always had the same meaning or implication as it does today. Only a survey of the development will make this clear.

A survey of the introductions to the NT of a century or more ago will reveal that different questions were asked of the text. The general discussion of Gospel authorship, date, and provenance reveals their interests and indifference to the problems raised since then. The terms they used and titles given to aspects of early Christian history and theology carried a different meaning for that era in biblical scholarship. Thus, when we begin to look for the community reconstructions in Gospels scholarship we need not look too far, for such a development is relatively recent.

It seems as if the first to present the view that the evangelist wrote for his own community were British scholars.[39] Possibly the first to make

---

[38] Although both Bauckham, "For Whom," and Peterson, *The Origin of Mark*, refer to its general historical development, a fuller treatment of the concept of "community" is needed.

[39] Cf. Bauckham, "For Whom," p. 13.

mention that a Gospel was written "in and for" a specific community was Henry Barclay Swete.[40] Swete, in reference to Mark's place and time of writing states, "According to the prevalent belief of the ancient church St. Mark wrote his Gospel in Rome and for the Roman Church." Swete draws this conclusion from patristic evidence which need not yield such an interpretation.[41] But following this comment on Mark's assumed intended reader, Swete goes no further.[42] Swete immediately moves on to the next introductory question of Mark, the time it was written. The hermeneutical principle of using the intended "community" as the grid and basis of interpretation is absent from the exegetical and historical discussion. In fact, a general survey of introductions in commentaries around the time of Swete finds little discussion of "community." The questions of that sort were yet to be asked.

The primary impetus in British scholarship that supposed each Gospel had a specific "community" was established by Burnett Hillman Streeter.[43] While this is certainly true, we must pay careful attention to the exact understanding of Gospel "community" that Streeter uses. Streeter introduces his work by claiming to unite in this work the various and specialized branches of research such as textual criticism, source-analysis, and the background of the NT.[44] This is the major point from which all of Streeter's methodological principles depart. Thus, when he discusses the four Gospels selected by early Christianity and the "idea" of a NT canon, his picture of the origin of Christianity argued that each Gospel was accepted into the canon amidst all the comparative difficulties brought with it because, "at the time when the Canon was definitely settled, each of the four had acquired such a degree of prestige that no one of them could be excluded . . ."[45] Streeter continues, then, to draw conclusions about each of the Gospels based upon this understanding of the origin of the Gospels, an understanding based heavily upon manuscript traditions known in the early church. Streeter states:

---

[40] Swete, *The Gospel According to Mark* (London: Macmillan, 1898). Cf. Bauckham, "For Whom," p. 13.

[41] Bauckham, "For Whom," pp. 13–14. According to Bauckham, Swete is basing this specifically on the accounts of Clement of Alexandria (*ap.* Eusebius, *Hist. Eccl* 6.14.6–7). See especially n. 7 for Bauckham's discussion of what Clement implied in reference to the distribution of Mark in Rome.

[42] The evidence of the commentary itself is important here. This is where one would expect to find the exegetical results of the definition of evidence.

[43] Streeter, *The Four Gospels: A Study in Origins* (London: Macmillan, 1924). Cf. Bauckham, "For Whom," p. 11.

[44] *Ibid.*, p. xxxvii.   [45] *Ibid.*, p. 11.

> Certain of the divergences between the Gospels . . . are of such a
> character that it is difficult to believe that these books originated
> in the same church, or even in the same neighbourhood. The
> contrast between the Jewish atmosphere of Matthew and the
> even more markedly Gentile proclivities of Luke is enhanced
> by a still more notable contrast between the divergent cycles of
> tradition on which they draw.[46]

For Streeter the geographical area in which the Gospels were created had
to have been the major influence in their literary emphasis and in their
overall approval in early Christianity. In this way Streeter can announce,
"Thus we are led on to the view that the Gospels were written in and
for different churches, and that each of the Gospels must have attained
local recognition as a religious classic, if not yet as inspired scripture,
before the four were compiled into a collection recognized by the whole
church."[47] According to Bauckham, the statement that the Gospels were
written "in and for" different churches encapsulates the axiom of the
current consensus of Gospel origins and audiences.[48]

Thus, the beginnings of community-based interpretations were under
way. Obviously the differences between Streeter's understanding of
Gospel "community" and current Gospel scholarship is great,[49] but this
basic understanding of a Gospel's creation, the geographical influence
in particular emphases, and the overall picture of early Christianity had
found for itself a birthday. From this time forward, admittedly with a still
developing understanding, the idea of a Gospel "community" would soon
become a common term in Gospel scholarship.

Form criticism: the tradition of the community

Around the same time Streeter was developing his major source-critical
work German scholarship was formulating an understanding of Gospel

---

[46] *Ibid.*

[47] *Ibid.*, p. 12. Streeter summarizes his opinion later by stating, "Inevitably this inde-
pendence resulted in local diversity – in regard to doctrinal emphasis, Church organization,
the religious literature most valued, and also, as we shall see, in regard to the manuscript
tradition of such books as they had in common. Thus the history of Catholic Christianity
during the first five centuries is very largely the history of a progressive standardization of
a diversity the roots of which were planted in the sub-Apostolic age" (p. 15).

[48] Bauckham, "For Whom," p. 15.

[49] Streeter, using the foundations forged by textual criticism, believed the Gospels
to have been formed within the major geographical centers that supported them in the
early church. Current Gospel community reconstructions, with no ties in any way to text-
critical assumptions, base their community reconstructions on the assumed community
existence of each Gospel, apart from any concrete historical evidence.

origins that would carry even further the concept of "community." It was in the early part of the twentieth century that *Formgeschichte* became the common tool with which the process of historical-critical readings could be carried out on the text and tradition of the Gospels. Surveys of form criticism and its origins are legion, and no attempt will be made to repeat such an exercise here.[50] Our purpose is to show how the concept of "community" gradually developed within Gospels scholarship and soon became the standard by which historical criticism interpreted the text of the Gospels.

Questions concerning the difference between tradition, legend (*Sagen*) and history in the Hebrew and Christian Scriptures have been active since the nineteenth century. As early as 1865, the existence of "forms" in literature had become commonly recognized, although undefined.[51] But it was not until nearly thirty years later that the prominent Julius Wellhausen, in his historical-critical study of the OT, began taking notice and defining such an enterprise. Wellhausen refused to see in the Hebrew writings a tradition of antiquity but rather that the stories, in Genesis for example, were a mere reflection of life and religion in the era of the Monarchy projected back into the pre-Mosaic times.[52] Wellhausen's fame is attributed to his source-critical "documentary theory" which used as a basic methodological criterion the literary form of the Hebrew text; but his prophetic insight into related research in NT studies was also present.[53]

[50] For a good discussion of the nature and practice of form criticism see E. V. McKnight, *What is Form Criticism?* GBSNTS (Philadelphia: Fortress Press, 1969); and Craig L. Blomberg, "Form Criticism," in Joel B. Green, Scot McKnight, and I. Howard Marshall (eds.), *Dictionary of Jesus and the Gospels* (Downers Grove, Ill.: Intervarsity Press, 1992). For a good discussion of the historical development of form criticism see W. G. Kümmel, *Introduction to the New Testament*, trans. Howard C. Kee (Nashville: Abingdon, 1975); and Stephen Neill and N. T. Wright, *The Interpretation of the New Testament, 1861–1986*, 2nd edn (Oxford: Oxford University Press, 1988). For a well-known critique of form criticism see E. Güttgemanns, *Candid Questions concerning Gospel Form Criticism: A Methodological Sketch of the Fundamental Problematics of Form and Redaction Critics*, trans. William G. Doty, 2nd edn PTMS 26 (Pittsburgh: Pickwick Press, 1979).

[51] Heinrich Ewald, *History of Israel*, trans. Russell Martineau (London: Longmans and Green, 1869–86), vol. II, p. 139, traced "The history of the style (form) of commandments." A little later Franz Overbeck, "Über die Anfänge der patristischen Literatur," *HZ* 12 (1882), p. 429, reprinted 1954, p. 12, could write that "A literature has a history in its forms; hence a proper history of literature will be a history of forms." Cf. Klaus Koch, *The Growth of the Biblical Tradition: The Form-Critical Method*, trans. S. M. Cupitt (London: Adam and Charles Black, 1969), pp. 3–5.

[52] See Wellhausen, *Prolegomena to the History of Israel*, trans. J. Sutherland Black and Allan Menzies (Edinburgh: Adam & Charles Black, 1895), especially the introduction, for his own methodological starting point in reference to the Hebrew Scriptures.

[53] See especially his work in the Gospels: *Das Evangelium Matthaei* (Berlin: Georg Reimer, 1904); *Das Evangelium Marci* (Berlin: Georg Reimer, 1903); *Das Evangelium*

This idea of a literary understanding in application to the Scriptures received its foremost impetus and definition in the work of Herman Gunkel.[54] Gunkel, with the work of Wellhausen and others in the background, pioneered the form-critical branch of literary research. But it was Gunkel specifically who argued that the biblical writings originated not so much from individual writers, as from the complex working of "communities."[55] This becomes most obvious when we compare Gunkel's *The Legends of Genesis: The Biblical Saga and History*[56] with the work that soon developed in Gospels scholarship in the beginning of the twentieth century.

William Wrede, influenced by the work of Wellhausen, challenged the assumption in NT scholarship that Mark was more historical and less theological than the other three Gospels.[57] With a blow of this magnitude to Mark, the Gospel assumed to be more historical and less theological than the other three, all the Gospels and their historical validity were affected. Wrede, doing redaction years before the criticism itself would begin, argued that Mark and his "community" believed that Jesus was the Messiah but had to confront a tradition of Jesus in which he never claimed the Messianic identity for himself. According to Wrede, this is why Mark reworked, so to speak, the tradition about Jesus in order to serve the purposes of the theological interests of the "community."[58] In reference to the reworking of the Jesus tradition Wrede stated:

> I should never for an instant lose sight of my awareness that I have before me descriptions, the authors of which are later Christians, be they ever so early-Christians who could only look at the life of Jesus with the eyes of their own time and who

Lucae (Berlin: Georg Reimer, 1904); *Das Einleitung in die drei ersten Evangelium* (Berlin: Georg Reimer, 1905). According to Rudolf Bultmann, *The History of the Synoptic Tradition*, trans. John Marsh (Oxford: Basil Blackwell, 1963), p. 2, the most far-reaching and important work in the field of synoptic Gospels research since Wrede has been done by Wellhausen.

[54] Koch, *The Growth of the Biblical Tradition*, p. 3. According to Koch, even at the end of the nineteenth century Gunkel introduced form-critical methods of biblical scholarship, although he used different terminology: *Gattungsforschung* (research into literary types) or *Literaturgeschichte* (history of literature). In fact, it was L. Koehler, *Das formgeschichtliche Problem des N. T.* (Leiden: Brill, 1924), p. 7, who spoke of form criticism as the "child of Gunkel's spirit." Cf. Vincent Taylor, *The Formation of the Gospel Tradition* (London: Macmillan, 1933), p. 11.

[55] For a discussion of Gunkel's work and the "community" theory in Johannine origins see Thomas L. Brodie, *The Quest for the Origin of John's Gospel: A Source-Oriented Approach* (New York: Oxford University Press, 1993), pp. 35, 144–45.

[56] Gunkel, *The Legends of Genesis: The Biblical Saga and History*, trans. W. H. Carruth (New York: Schocken Books, 1964).

[57] Wrede, *The Messianic Secret*, trans. J. C. G. Greig (London: James Clark, 1971).

[58] See the related discussion by Peterson, *The Origins of Mark*, pp. 10–11.

described it on the basis of the belief of the community, with all the view-points of the community, and with the needs of the community in mind . . . For Mark's notion of Jesus' mode of teaching did not grow out of the impression made by transmitted sayings and discourses of Jesus. More congenial to the Gospel would be the idea of the imparting of divine truths such as were for Mark and the community of his day the essentials of the Christian faith.[59]

From this point on the initial "community" reconstructions were fully underway. But before redaction criticism would have its day, a fully developed criticism that could handle the pre-Gospel Jesus tradition was needed. Its need was met in NT form criticism.

Between 1919 and 1921, three major works of NT form criticism revolutionized the way scholars undertook historical criticism.[60] The work of Martin Dibelius,[61] Karl L. Schmidt,[62] and Rudolf Bultmann[63] greatly promoted the "community's" role in the origin of the Gospels. In essence what Wellhausen and Gunkel had given birth to in the OT was brought to fruition in NT form criticism. The term *Formgeschichte* first appeared in the work of Dibelius.[64] Dibelius started with the activity of the early church, studied the various tradition forms in the Gospels, and analyzed them and traced their individual history right to the Gospel form itself. It was Dibelius who helped to define *Sitz im Leben*[65] and describe the multi-faceted unliterary nature of the "Church," which for him eventually gave forth the Gospels in their literary form. Bultmann, in contrast to Dibelius, started with the Gospels themselves and worked back from the material to the earlier forms of it that can be traced from a prior tradition. Bultmann states that the work of Wrede annihilated the seemingly clear picture of historical development in Mark. Hence our work is now as follows:

---

[59] Wrede, *The Messianic Secret*, pp. 5, 79.

[60] See Erich Fascher, *Die formgeschichtliche Methode: Eine Darstellung und Kritik, Zugleich ein Beitrag zur Geschichte des Synoptischen Problems*, BZNTW 2 (Berlin: Alfred Töpelmann, 1924), pp. 1–51, for a good survey of form criticism's historical development from the perspective of German scholarship.

[61] Dibelius, *From Tradition to Gospel*, trans. Bertram Lee Woolf (London: Ivor Nicholson, 1934). The original German title was *Die Formgeschichte des Evangeliums* (Tübingen: J. C. B. Mohr, 1919).

[62] Schmidt, *Der Rahmen der Geschichte Jesu* (Berlin: Trowitzsch & Sohn, 1919).

[63] Bultmann, *The History of the Synoptic Tradition*, trans. John Marsh (Oxford: Basil Blackwell, 1963). The original German title *Die Geschichte der synoptischen Tradition* (Göttingen: Vandenhoeck & Ruprecht, 1921).

[64] Koch, *The Growth of the Biblical Tradition*, p. 3.

[65] According to Dibelius, *From Tradition to Gospel*, p. 7, the *Sitz im Leben* is "the historical and social stratum in which precisely these literary forms were developed."

> Mark is the work of an author who is steeped in the theology of
> the early Church, and who ordered and arranged the material that
> he received in the light of the faith of the early Church . . . and
> the task which follows for historical research is this: to separate
> the various strata in Mark and to determine which belongs to the
> original historical tradition and which derived from the work of
> the author.[66]

Bultmann helped form criticism define the idea of "community" and its
secondary nature. With Bultmann, terms like "community," "primitive
Christianity," and "early Church," amalgamated into the source of the
life-setting in which and by which the Gospel material took its shape and
found its home. In essence, the early Christian "communities" took and
used the Jesus tradition for their own polemical and communal needs;
this is what we find in varying ways in each of the Gospels.[67] Schmidt
focused on the framework of the Gospel narratives and showed that the
Gospels were put together by an evangelist who used small units of traditional material and fitted them loosely together as his interests and
purposes led him.[68] His work shows that a distinction is to be made
between the traditional material and the editorial material. The work of
Schmidt was similar to Wrede's in that it foresaw the work of redaction
criticism.

Although the main impetus of NT *Formgeschichte* was begun by the
three German scholars mentioned above, it was not long before form criticism was a common exegetical tool in the English-speaking world. In his
work *The Formation of the Gospel Tradition*, Vincent Taylor introduced
form criticism to Britain, admittedly with some critique. This book, published in 1933 and based upon eight lectures given at the University of
Leeds in 1932, allows us to see both the development of form criticism
over a decade after the work of Schmidt, as well as its English reception.
What is most interesting for our purposes is how Taylor supports form
criticism's emphasis on the "community" and its role in using and establishing the Jesus tradition material, but is wary of asserting its radical use.
According to Taylor:

---

[66] Bultmann, *The History of the Synoptic Tradition*, p. 1.

[67] As Bultmann, *The History of the Synoptic Tradition*, p. 4, explains, "The *Sitz im Leben*
is not . . . an individual historical event, but a typical situation or occupation in the life of a
community."

[68] Norman Perrin, *What is Redaction Criticism* (London: SPCK, 1970), pp. 14–15.

[Form criticism] is almost bound to result in scepticism. In dealing with popular forms it is natural to stress the activity of a community, and, while this cannot be ignored even in relation to the sayings-tradition, the tendency is to ignore the creativity of the original speaker. This danger might perhaps be avoided by a Form-Criticism conscious of its limitations . . .[69]

Taylor argues against Bultmann's presentation of the "community" as follows:

As Bultmann sees it, the primitive community exists *in vacuo*, cut off from its founders by the walls of an inexplicable ignorance. Like Robinson Crusoe it must do the best it can. Unable to turn to anyone for information, it must invent situations for the words of Jesus, and put into his lips sayings which personal memory cannot check.[70]

What is important to note is that while Taylor criticizes the radical nature of form critics' use, or abuse, of the early Christian community or communities, he did not deny that such a "community" existed behind the formation of the Gospels. Thus, while less radical than his German counterparts, Taylor carries forward the idea that a "community" stands behind each of the Gospels.[71]

Form criticism took pains to identify in the Gospel texts the various forms of the traditional material that would have been known and used by the evangelists.[72] Then, following a definition of the form, the specific material of the tradition would be assigned an appropriate *Sitz im Leben* in the early church. If the history that the evangelist presented could no longer be trusted, thanks much to the work of Wrede, then the historical nature of the texts themselves would be made manifest in the life-settings from which they would have originated. Each unit of the Gospels would have originated in a typical setting in the early church. In this way the various forms are like windows into the life and ministry of the early church. In essence, form criticism carried on what literary and source criticism could not do: form criticism broadened the picture of the early church into a sociological movement of multiple traditions and concepts. Thus, once form criticism appeared in Gospels scholarship:

---

[69] Taylor, *The Formation of the Gospel Tradition*, p. 31.   [70] *Ibid.*, p. 41.
[71] Taylor is not thinking of a specific "community" as is common in today's assumption, but he does carry forward the terminology.
[72] The current rekindling of interest in orality puts form criticism on the agenda again.

The individual persons, such as the authors of the gospel had been considered to be, began to move into the background and to fade away the moment the synoptic gospels began to be regarded as the outcome of a pre-literary work of collection, undertaken by Christian communities.[73]

The change of focus from literary document to literary creation, then from literary creation to literary creation in the life-setting of a "community," became axiomatic for form critics. The simplistic idea that a single evangelist had created each of the Gospels had become naïve, now the focus was the early Christian "communities" and their various *Sitze im Leben*. To the form critic the term "community" is still quite vague; it simply refers to the group of Christians who owned some part of the Jesus tradition. The true creativity of the "community" was yet to be discovered.[74]

Redaction criticism: the creative depiction of the community

Once it was assumed that the various traditions were in direct relations with a specific context, the creative aspects of primitive Christianity were soon to be noticed. As was mentioned above, a few scholars had already given hints of what would soon become redaction criticism.[75] Already the specifics of the origin of the Gospels and their created environments, namely their originating communities, had begun to take the focus of Gospel production. But the creative depiction of the "communities" behind the Gospels came to the forefront when redaction criticism became the norm in Gospel scholarship. From the work of the form critics, followed by the focus of interpretation to be derived from the exact *Sitz im Leben* of each Gospel, now the primary interpretive intention

---

[73] Joachim Rohde, *Rediscovering the Teaching of the Evangelists*, trans. Dorothea M. Barton (London: SCM Press, 1968), p. 3.

[74] This is not to say that Bultmann's form-critical work lacked creativity. The difference is that with redaction criticism the "community" became more specific and this creativity extended to the evangelist/redactor.

[75] Also important here is the work of R. H. Lightfoot, *History and Interpretation in the Gospels* (London: Hodder and Stoughton, 1934) and G. D. Kilpatrick, *The Origins of the Gospel According to St. Matthew* (Oxford: Clarendon Press, 1946). In the stages between form and redaction criticism, both continued emphasizing the life-settings of the early church and their effect on the Gospel texts. As Kilpatrick explains, "While we may not say that the Gospel [of Matthew] was created by a community, yet it was created in a community and called forth to meet the needs of a community. This will require us to reconstruct something of the context of Christian religion and Church life in which the book came into being" (p. 2).

has shifted from some ideal-construct of an unknown primitive community to a more exact delineation of the "community" of the evangelist itself. "Redaction criticism investigates the evangelist and his community, the one in which he is standing and for whom he is writing, unlike form criticism, which enquires about the Sitz im Leben of the individual pericopes."[76] This came in part because redaction critics considered the Gospel milieu defined by form criticism to be too vague.[77] While some redaction critics were hesitant to label the entire creative force of the Gospel as dependent on corporate rather than individual authorship, the majority agreeds that they still "require for their *Sitz im Leben* a church where such sophisticated discussion might be expected to meet with a sympathetic response on the part of at least some of the members."[78] Valid historical research, then, must establish the context (i.e. "community") of origin in order to truly interpret the Gospels. Thus, after the Second World War, the scholarship world was ripe for a more defined "community" context.

Redaction criticism was quite varied in its initial years. Some used redactional study simply to highlight the particular theological emphases of the evangelist or Gospel, whereas others tended to focus more specifically on the context in which the Gospel arose.[79] In a similar way to form criticism, three scholars were the impetus for redaction criticism, each in a different Gospel: Günther Bornkamm[80] in Matthew, Hans Conzelmann[81] in Luke, and Willi Marxsen[82] in Mark. Bornkamm's work in Matthew takes as its starting point the completed work of form criticism, namely, that the content and form of the Gospels are determined not by historical biography, but by the faith of the church in Jesus Christ. Although Bornkamm admits that some of the Gospel material was simply collected

[76] Rohde, *Rediscovering the Teaching of the Evangelists*, p. 22.

[77] Krister Stendahl, *The School of Matthew and Its Use of the Old Testament*, ASNTU 20 (Uppsala: Almquist & Wiksells, 1954), p. 12. Stendahl, working heavily on a corrected form of Kilpatrick's work on Matthew, argued that the undefined preaching as labeled by the form critics was better to be seen as language that reveals a "school" atmosphere as the origin behind the Gospel tradition and formation.

[78] R. T. France, *Matthew: Evangelist and Teacher* (Exeter: Paternoster Press, 1989), p. 114.

[79] Bauckham, "For Whom," p. 17.

[80] Günther Bornkamm, Gerhard Barth, and Heinz Joachim Held, *Tradition and Interpretation in Matthew*, trans. Percy Scott (London: SCM Press, 1963). The most famous work was originally done by Bornkamm, "The Stilling of the Storm in Matthew."

[81] Conzelmann, *The Theology of St. Luke*, trans. Geoffrey Buswell (New York: Harper & Brothers, 1960).

[82] Marxsen, *Mark the Evangelist: Studies on the Redactional History of the Gospel*, trans. James Boyce, Donald Juel, and William Poehlmann (Nashville: Abingdon Press, 1969).

by the evangelist and arranged by thematic equivalents, in the stilling of the storm in Matthew 8.23–27 he notices how Matthew's use of that specific tradition (probably Mark) reveals a theological intention in the evangelist's purpose.[83] This theological intention is made clearer in the work on Luke by Conzelmann and Mark by Marxsen. Conzelmann explicitly differentiates between the traditional material and the context for which it was redacted. As Conzelmann explains:

> Form criticism has shown to what extent the community projected its own problems and answers back into the reports of the life of Jesus. It is true that limits were set to this projection both by belief and by the traditional material itself. But it is not until Luke that this demarcation, this distinction between then and now, the period of Jesus and the period of the Church, between problems of yesterday and those of today, becomes fully conscious. The period of Jesus and the period of the church are presented as different epochs in the broad course of saving history, differentiated to some extent by their particular characteristics.[84]

For Conzelmann this distinction between then and now is vital to an appropriate reading of the Gospels.[85] This distinction is made even clearer by Marxsen, who developed further the conclusions of form criticism and separated their conclusions from those of redaction criticism. For Marxsen, calling the evangelist a mere collector does not do justice to his work as an author.[86] Although there are similarities between form and redaction criticism, there are differences that need to be noted, specifically their *Sitz im Leben* differences. Marxsen was the first to introduce three unique life-settings for the study of the Gospels. The first life-setting is the unique situation of Jesus' activity (i.e. the historical Jesus). The second life-setting is the situation of the primitive church (i.e. form criticism). The third life-setting is the unique situation of the evangelist's creation of the Gospel (i.e. redaction criticism).[87] Thus, in reference to our understanding of Gospel origins Marxsen states, "This third life-situation is thus thoroughly differentiated, though it is not as complex as the second, since we have three (or four) fixed points in our extant gospels. And if we

---

[83] Bornkamm, "The Stilling of the Storm," p. 57.

[84] Conzelmann, *The Theology of St. Luke*, p. 13.

[85] While it is true that Conzelmann believed Luke to be aware of three epochs, for our purposes his distinction between the original tradition and the later "community" is important. For the introduction of two *Sitze im Leben* see Joachin Jeremias, *The Parables of Jesus*, trans. S. H. Hooke (London: SCM Press, 1954), p. 18.

[86] Marxsen, *Mark the Evangelist*, p. 18.   [87] *Ibid.*, p. 23.

examine the development from one to the other, a very vivid picture of the history of the early church results."[88] Thus, the beginning of the quest for the third *Sitz im Leben* was now underway. A thorough definition of the third life-setting of the Gospel, the detailed "community" context in which and for which the Gospel arose, was needed.

Following the work of these early and founding redaction critics, the late 1960s and 1970s saw the production of works on the Gospels that were specifically concerned with the unique "community" situation of each of the Gospels.[89] Using the Gospel of Mark as an example, the work of Theodore Weeden[90] exemplifies this approach. For Weeden, the clues to interpreting Mark are to be found in the situation for which he is writing; clues which can only be deduced from the text itself. Thus, one must read the text with eyes of a first-century reader,[91] denoting all the instances where pure (if possible) Jesus tradition material is not redacted and contrast it with the redacted Jesus material utilized for Mark's "community" and its issues. Since Mark portrays a Christological dispute within the pages of his Gospel, and since no such dispute is known in early Christian history, then, "the only way to account for Mark's consuming interest in it is that it has some existential importance for the situation in his own community."[92] A similar procedure, also in Mark, can be found in the work of Howard C. Kee.[93] The premise of his argument is that the Gospel of Mark is written to address the pressing needs of the Markan community as the delay of the Parousia is becoming problematic. Kee argues that full delineations of the "community" context of the Gospels have been wholly absent from Gospels scholarship. He states:

> To the extent that the historical setting of Mark has been considered by its interpreters, scholars have been almost wholly content to utilize stereotypes of the situation in Judaism and in the period down to AD 70. But most interpreters of Mark have not been concerned with much beyond the theology of Mark, as though theological affirmations were formed during the early decades of the church's existence by a process of intellectual debate –

---

[88] *Ibid.*, p. 25.   [89] Bauckham, "For Whom," p. 17.

[90] Theodore J. Weeden, *Mark – Traditions in Conflict* (Philadelphia: Fortress Press, 1971).

[91] In chapter 3 we will challenge the approach of Weeden and others who assume that a modern redaction-critical approach allows the interpreter to "read with the eyes of a first-century reader."

[92] *Ibid.*, p. 69.

[93] Kee, *Community of the New Age: Studies in Mark's Gospel* (London: SCM Press, 1997).

like a present-day seminar. The crucial factors of the kind of community with which the author was identified, the social and cultural forces which shaped his existence, consciously and unconsciously, are almost wholly left out of account. In short, no serious effort is made to determine the horizon of the author of our earliest gospel.[94]

In a similar fashion to Weeden, Howard Clark Kee defines the process by which the interpreter of the Gospels can successfully establish this background to the Gospel and thus be more fully able to interpret its text:

> What was the *Sitz im Leben* from which and for which Mark's gospel was written? To answer that question responsibly it is not sufficient to attach a general label to Mark – such as Hellenistic-Jewish-Christian, or Palestinian-Jewish-Christian. By analysis of the text itself, but with the aid of paradigms for the study of eschatological communities as well as historical analogies with apocalyptic communities close in space and time to primitive Christianity in the first century, it should be possible to trace the contours of the Markan community.[95]

Thus, for the interpretation of Mark the community behind the Gospel has become the locus of interpretation. As Kee asserts above, it was no longer appropriate to simply place the Gospels in the midst of first-century Jewish-Christian culture and read the Gospel texts. What was needed was a precise placement of the Gospels in their context; a context simply assumed to be a unique and particular Christian "community." The Gospels of Luke and Matthew have been led to the same trough to drink.[96] It is simply assumed that such a methodology is not only appropriate but required. Therefore, any study in the Synoptic Gospels in the last thirty years will almost certainly begin with the reconstructed context of a Gospel "community" as its interpretive locus.

The survey given above establishes the growing consensus of a "community" behind each of the four Gospels up to the 1960s. In the 1960s and 1970s each Gospel began to take a "community" life of its own as the brief examples mentioned above make clear. The FG is no exception.[97]

---

[94] *Ibid.*, p. 9.   [95] *Ibid.*, p. 77. See also Bauckham, "For Whom," p. 18.

[96] For examples see Klink, "The Gospel Community Debate."

[97] Although the FG is certainly related to the source, form, and redaction movements discussed above, it has always maintained some distinction, especially in its role in redaction criticism and its relation to the Synoptics.

In fact, it is likely that the Gospel of John has had more reconstructions made concerning its "community" origins than any of the other Gospels, and has clearly kept pace, if not surpassed, the work done on the other three.[98] The reasons for this and examples will be discussed more thoroughly below since we will use the FG as our test case.

Social-scientific criticism: the articulation of the community

Since the 1960s, the reconstructions of "communities" have become more elaborate and technical. The Gospel communities have needed to be more clearly articulated in order for a fuller understanding of the texts to occur. Interestingly, Willi Marxsen had already hinted at such a procedure in 1956 when he stated:

> Thus we inquire into the situation of the community in which the gospels arose. The community ought not to be unqualifiedly viewed as located in a specific place, though we shall keep in mind the possibility of defining it exactly. Our concern is much more with what is typical in this community, its views, its time, perhaps even its composition. Hence, a sociological element is present throughout.[99]

This "sociological" element has certainly arrived. In chapter 2 we will discuss in full the current methodological procedures involved in the application of sociological methods to the Gospels and their "communities."

Conclusion

Our survey has shown the progressive development of the concept of "community" throughout the last one hundred years of Gospel scholarship. It began as scholars searched for the sources behind the Gospels and the British view that prevailed, linked in many ways to the text-critical conclusions of local text-types, argued that the Gospels grew out of local fame in major geographic centers of early Christianity. With the onslaught of form criticism, and with it the preliminary death of the historical Jesus, the early "communities" became the focus of secondary and purposeful adaptation. Then, through redaction criticism, the theological purpose and

---

[98] See Bauckham, "For Whom," pp. 18–19, for his discussion of JComm reconstructions in comparison to the Synoptics.

[99] Marxsen, *Mark the Evangelist*, p. 24.

intent of the evangelists and their "community" contexts became established. Since then the evangelist and his "community" have been used as a tool, or window, to see the "community" context in a more clear and articulated way. This has been greatly advanced by sociological theory. Thus, the "community" reconstructions in current Gospel scholarship are an undeniably primary method of understanding the origin and context of the Gospels in order to interpret them with accuracy. It is this development and understanding of the picture of Christian origins that this text is attempting to critique.

The fourth Gospel and "community"

The historically enigmatic nature of the FG has led it to become probably the most frequent Gospel with a community reconstructed behind it. Although the discussion above focused much on the Synoptic Gospels, in part due to the relative distance commonly placed between John and the Synoptics, the parallel work done in the discovery of the JComm is well noted.[100] Although Gospel scholarship has separated the two endeavors, "community" reconstructions have been doing similar work to them both. A survey of the development of the reconstructions of the JComm is now in order.

It is impossible to separate the reconstructions of the JComm from the authorship, source, and origin issues of the Gospel, or in fact, from all of the Johannine literature.[101] The often used term "riddle" for the Johannine writings is fitting, for John has caused many to propose creative theories about its origin and creative sources. Hence, the developed concept of a "community" that stands behind the Gospel, as the other Gospels seem to support, has seemed to make perfect sense to many. The focus of study can then be placed on finding and describing the obviously unique character of the "community," which then describes the unique nature of the Gospel itself. While "community" discussion came to Johannine scholarship in a similar manner as it did the Synoptics, around the time of the work and influence of B. H. Streeter and his geography-focused source hypothesis, John's oddities in comparison with the Synoptics have lent themselves to a more communal creation. It can also be argued that John was the first Gospel to have "community" concepts used to explain and describe its unique and uncertain origin.

---

[100] See Bauckham, "For Whom," pp. 18–19.
[101] See below for our methodological approach to the FG and the rest of the Johannine literature.

The most comprehensive history of JComm reconstructions was done by R. Alan Culpepper in *The Johannine School*.[102] Culpepper noted that many Johannine scholars used terms like "community," "circle," or even "school," to describe the creative environment in and for which the FG was written. He argued that a more detailed delineation of such terms was required, and his hypothesis, based on comparing John with other known ancient schools, was that the term "school" most thoroughly covers the creative milieu in which John originated.[103] Of course, Culpepper was not arguing *if* these terms were appropriate, but *which* of these terms was most appropriate. What is useful for our purpose is his detailed tracing of the development of "school" or "community" language over the last four hundred years of Johannine scholarship.[104]

In Johannine scholarship, once it was held that John the apostle may not be the author, as was traditionally believed, then a wave of varying theories were presented in its place, leading to the current reconstructions of the JComm. Initially it was believed that if it were not the apostle, at least one of his close companions completed the work from his memoirs.[105] This thesis was held and adapted so that it was assumed that the apostle was not the author, but one after him, a disciple of his most probably.[106]

---

[102] Culpepper, *The Johannine School: An Evaluation of the Johannine-School Hypothesis Based on an Investigation of the Nature of Ancient Schools*, SBLDS 26 (Missoula, Mont.: Scholars Press, 1975). Originally a Ph.D. dissertation at Duke University in 1974 under the supervision of D. Moody Smith, the same supervisor as Dwight Peterson, *The Origins of Mark*.

[103] Culpepper, *The Johannine School*, p. 1.

[104] Our survey only traces the Johannine origin question in reference to the community-hypothesis, and only after the late nineteenth century. For a good survey of Johannine origins prior to 1874 see Christoph E. Luthardt, *St. John the Author of the Fourth Gospel* (Edinburgh: T. & T. Clark, 1875), pp. 15–25; this book was enlarged, revised, and translated by C. R. Gregory, who added an important appendix, "Literature of the Disputed Origin of the Fourth Gospel from 1792 to the Present"; James Drummond, *An Inquiry into the Character and Authorship of the Fourth Gospel* (London: Williams and Norgate, 1903), pp. 67–71; Paton J. Gloag, *Introduction to the Johannine Writings* (London: James Nisbet and Co., 1891), pp. 123–30; and Vincent H. Stanton, *The Gospels as Historical Documents*, Part III: "The Fourth Gospel" (Cambridge: Cambridge University Press, 1920), pp. 1–16. For a list of commentaries on John published between 1517 and 1875 and a list of books on John dating from 230–1878 CE see Christoph E. Luthardt, *St. John's Gospel: Described and Explained According to Its Peculiar Character*, trans. C. R. Gregory, 3 vols. (Edinburgh: T. & T. Clark, 1876–78). See also David Friedrich Strauss, *Das Leben Jesu für das deutsche Volk bearbeitet* (Leipzig: F. A. Brockhaus, 1864), pp. 90–114, for a survey of the history of Johannine scholarship from Bretschneider to Baur.

[105] Jacob C. R. Eckermann, "Uber die eigentlich sichern Gründe des Glaubens an die Hauptthatsachen der Geschichte Jesu, und über die wahrscheinliche Entstehung der Evangelien und der Apostelgeschicht," *ThB* 2 (1976), pp. 106–256.

[106] Karl G. Breschneider, *Probablia de evangelii et epistolarum Joannis Apostoli, indole et origine* (Leipzig: University Press, 1820); Ludwig A. Dieffenbach, "Über einege

Culpepper claims that although it was C. Hermann Weisse[107] who was the first to conclude that a group of followers or disciples of the apostle wrote the Gospel using notes which the apostle left when he died, it was Ludwig Baumgarten-Crusius[108] who first used the idea of a Johannine "circle" in defense of John's authenticity.[109] In the late 1800s both Michel Nicholas[110] and Carl H. von Weizsäcker[111] argued that the FG was written by a pupil of John or a member of the Ephesian church, the location where it was assumed John originated.[112] Thus, from as early as 1860, the disputed origin of John made the ground ripe for the establishment of a group of Johannine disciples from which one was to be the understood author of the FG.

The next century brought forth a growing consensus that the FG was in some way a creation of a Johannine "circle," that is, the work and ideas of the disciples of the Apostle. In discussing the relation between the Gospel of John and the Johannine letters, James Moffatt's 1918 NT introduction summarizes the current understanding of Johannine literature by stating the general position many scholars had come to agree upon. He states, "Their relationship on the disjunctive hypothesis is accounted for by the common language of a group or school in Asia Minor . . ."[113] Although Culpepper narrows his focus to the use of the term "school" in reference to this Johannine circle, such specific connotations seem not to be present in the descriptions of the scholars themselves. Their intention, it seems, was to use a term that would denote the relationship between the Apostle and his later followers, thus seeing a relationship between the Apostle and the text. To assume that the use of the term "school" in 1863

wahrscheinliche Interpolationen im Evangelium Johannis," *KJNTL* 5 (1816), pp. 1–16; Heinrich E. G. Paulus, "Bretschneider de Origine Ev. Et Epist. Joann.," *HJL* (1821), pp. 112–42. The above were all cited by Gregory, "Literature of the Disputed Origin," pp. 292–95.

[107] Weisse, *Die evangelische Geschichte kritisch und philosophisch bearbeitet*, 2 vols. (Leipzig, Dörffling und Franke, 1838), vol. II, pp. 225–300, cited by Drummond, "An Inquiry into the Character and Authorship of the Fourth Gospel," p. 404.

[108] Baumgarten-Crusius, *Theologische Auslegung der johanneischen Schriften*, 2 vols. (Thuringen: Jenai, 1843–45).

[109] Culpepper, *The Johannine School*, pp. 2–3.

[110] Nicholas, *Études critiques sur la Bible: Noveau Testament* (Paris: Michel Lévy Frères, 1864), pp. 127–221.

[111] Weizsäcker, *Untersuchungen über die evangelische Geschichte ihre Quellen und den Gang ihrer Entwicklung*, 2 vols., 2nd edn (Tübingen: J. C. B. Mohr, 1901), vol. I, iii, pp. 220–302.

[112] Culpepper, *The Johannine School*, p. 3.

[113] James Moffatt, *An Introduction to the Literature of the New Testament*, ITL (New York: Charles Scribner's Sons, 1918), p. 389. Moffatt gives a full list of agreeing scholars following this general summary (pp. 389–90).

is anything like its use today is assuming too much.[114] Thus, through the first six decades in the twentieth century, the discussion in NT scholarship focused on the enigma of the FG and its relationship to the other Johannine writings. The more "orthodox" defended the authorship of the Apostle, the less "orthodox" assumed some type of Johannine group as the responsible party for some or, more probably, all of the Johannine writings. The Johannine oddities and the various proposals concerning the background of the Gospel presented by these causes, not unlike current Johannine scholarship, were certainly present.[115] In the 1920s, the influence of form criticism and its picture of the origin of the Gospels also played a role. As discussed above, the concept of "community," even in John, seemed to fit well the understanding of the Gospel's origin and the notable Johannine oddities, although the "community" was as vague as it was in the Synoptics. The uncertainty of the origin, authorship, and sources of the Gospel of John, and its relation to the other Johannine writings, made the JComm reconstructions appear to many to be a most plausible explanation.

It was in the 1960s, in the high point of redactional activity in all four of the Gospels, that the face of JComm reconstructions was drastically affected. In 1968, the first edition of *History and Theology in the Fourth Gospel* was presented by J. Louis Martyn.[116] John Ashton states in reference to Martyn's book, "for all its brevity [it] is probably the most important single work on the Gospel since Bultmann's commentary."[117] Martyn combined two growing conclusions into this one work: the Jewish nature of the Gospel as its background and origin and the reality that John

---

[114] See Culpepper, *The Johannine School*, p. 4, for the beginning of his detailed focus on the term "school" in describing the assumed group that authored John. The date 1863 reveals what to Culpepper was the first occurrence of the term "school" to refer to the Johannine group of disciples; it was used by Ernest Renan, *Vie di Jésus*, 9th edn (Paris: G. Paetz, 1864), pp. xxii–xxxii.

[115] See Culpepper, *The Johannine School*, pp. 4–34, for the most detailed treatment, albeit biased, of the use of the term "school."

[116] Martyn, *History and Theology in the Fourth Gospel*, 3rd edn, NTL (Louisville: Westminster John Knox Press, 2003). The second revised and enlarged edition was published in 1979. A third edition, unchanged from the second, was recently published in 2003; this third edition is the text from which all subsequent discussion will take place.

[117] Ashton, *Understanding the Fourth Gospel* (Oxford: Clarendon Press, 1991), p. 107. Also cited by Bauckham, "For Whom," p. 19, who refers also in n. 18 to the comment of D. Moody Smith, "The Contribution of J. Louis Martyn to the Understanding of the Gospel of John," in R. T. Fortna and B. R. Gaventa (eds.), *The Conversation Continues: Studies in Paul and John*, J. L. Martyn Festschrift (Nashville: Abingdon Press, 1990), p. 293, n. 30: "Martyn's thesis has become a paradigm, to borrow from Thomas Kuhn. It is a part of what students imbibe from standard works, such as commentaries and textbooks, as knowledge generally received and held to be valid."

was a book of many compositional levels.[118] Martyn himself states his purpose in his introduction:

> Our first task . . . is to say something as specific as possible about the actual circumstances in which John wrote his Gospel. How are we to picture daily life in John's church? Have elements of its peculiar daily experiences left their stamp on the Gospel penned by one of its members? May one sense even in its exalted cadences the voice of a Christian theologian who writes *in response to contemporary events and issues* which concern, or should concern, all members of the Christian community in which he lives?[119]

Thus, Martyn sets the stage to present his picture of the powerful message hidden within the innermost passages of the text of the FG.

According to Martyn, the text of John needs to be read on two levels: one that reflected the tradition of the church and the other that was involved in the contemporary issues of the particular community.[120] For Martyn, each writer in the NT handled these two issues and their relationship in different ways. This is in part because although each drew from a similar cistern of tradition, each had unique social and religious circumstances which they faced. In this way Martyn can say, "Consequently, when we read the Fourth Gospel, we are listening both to tradition and to a new and unique interpretation of that tradition."[121] Methodologically, then, according to Martyn, one could compare how different writers of the NT adapted the common tradition to their specific circumstances; thus, the different application denotes something of the historical circumstance in which each "community" lived and ministered.

For Martyn, this could be done quite easily with the Gospels. Martyn takes passages that have counterparts in both the Synoptics and John, traditional stories, and applies his method to them. In this way Martyn claims:

> It is just possible, then, that careful attention to *style* and to accents characteristic of the discourses will enable us to distinguish . . . between (a) traditional materials and (b) passages in which elements of John's own interests and experiences are more or less clearly reflected.[122]

---

[118] Ashton, *Understanding the Fourth Gospel*, pp. 106–07.
[119] Martyn, *History and Theology*, p. 29.   [120] *Ibid.*, pp. 30–31.
[121] *Ibid.*, p. 30.   [122] *Ibid.*, p. 32.

To denote the traditional material Martyn uses the German term *Einmalig*, since even with help he could not find "a suitable English equivalent." By this term Martyn means to imply "back there" as opposed to "now and here."[123] Thus, Martyn traces through key pericopae in John with the following methodological principle:

> In what follows, therefore, we will have to keep constantly in mind that the text presents its witness on two levels: (1) It is a witness to an *einmalig* event during Jesus' earthly lifetime . . . (2) The text is also a witness to Jesus' powerful presence in actual events experienced by the Johannine church.[124]

In this way, Martyn has not only assumed a Johannine "community," but has even provided a method by which interpreters may take a "glimpse"[125] through a once clouded window into the actual historical circumstances that were faced by the JComm that authored, for itself and by itself, the text of the Gospel of John.

The influence from Martyn's first edition in 1968 to the current day is massive. Since then it has been the common assumption that the FG was written in and for a specific "community." Following in Martyn's trail there have been many and various proposals given to delineate the exact nature, circumstances, and historical development of the "community" in which the text of the FG was written.[126] A brief chronological survey of other Johannine "community" reconstructions and their particular methodological emphases is now in order.[127]

Although Martyn had the earliest impact on "community" interpretation in John, he was not actually the first example of the recent JComm reconstructions. In 1966 the first volume of Raymond Brown's magisterial commentary in John was published. In his discussion of the composition

---

[123] *Ibid.*, p. 40, n. 22.   [124] *Ibid.*, p. 40.

[125] The term "glimpse" is taken from a later essay on the JComm by Martyn: "Glimpses into the History of the Johannine Community." This essay was originally published in *L'Evangile de Jean: Sources, redaction, théologie*, ed. M. de Jonge, BETL 44 (Gembloux: Duculot, 1977), pp. 259–99. It has since been republished in Martyn's *The Gospel of John in Christian History: Essays for Interpreters* (New York: Paulist Press, 1978), pp. 90–121.

[126] See also Brown, *The Community of the Beloved Disciple: The Life, Loves, and Hates of an Individual Church in New Testament Times* (New York: Paulist Press, 1979), pp. 171–82, and Brodie, *The Quest for the Origin of John's Gospel*, pp. 15–21, for surveys of JComm reconstructions.

[127] According to Kysar, "Whence and Whither," p. 67, the expression "Johannine community" was first used in its modern sense by Jan Adolph Bühner, *Der Gesandte und sein Weg im vierten Evangelium: Die kulturund religionsgeschtliche Grundlagen der johanneischen Sendungschristologie sowie ihre traditionsgeschichtliche Entwicklung*, WUNT 2/2 (Tübingen: J. C. B. Mohr, 1977), p. 1.

of the Gospel, Brown sketches as a "working hypothesis" his now famous five stages in the production of the document. He only hints at different events or conditions in the community for whom the Gospel was intended.[128] This initial publication of Brown's view of the JComm was to become much more explicit in his *The Community of the Beloved Disciple* published in 1979. This work is by far the most comprehensive and thorough explanation of the individual stages of the community and the many groups, for and against the authoring Johannine group, that were related in some way to the JComm. Some of his later works also incorporate his "community" reconstruction and add flesh to its earlier portrayal.[129] It is worth noting that Brown's proposed reconstruction is "wrapped up" in the other introductory issues involved in the FG. His appeal to a single "community" to which the Gospel was directed is intended to handle the peculiar features of the document by references to several events in the life of the community. In essence, "the community concept grew out of Brown's efforts to explicate the peculiarities of the Gospel."[130]

This leads us into the two primary methodological approaches to the excavation of the JComm. The reconstructions of Brown and Martyn are rooted in the introductory questions of the FG, as evidenced by Brown. An understanding of the historical context in which the Gospel was written facilitates one's understanding of the text of the Gospel. The reconstructed context and the received text are in a reciprocal hermeneutical relationship. But a second type of "community" reconstruction also began shortly after Martyn. This second approach was initiated by Wayne Meeks' article "The Man from Heaven in Johannine Sectarianism," published in 1972. Using the methods of sociology of knowledge Meeks examines the descent/ascent motif in the FG and argues that it comprises a myth by which the Johannine Christians understood and strengthened their status as a sectarian counter-culture "group." Once the audience behind John was assumed to be a recognizable "group," various approaches were used to define its functional make-up. Meeks' provocative article did much to fashion a view of the JComm that has dominated scholarship for years to come. While debate raged over the use of the term "sect" or "sectarian" to describe the "community,"[131] the view of the Johannine Christians as a minority group in their culture and their emphasis on the

---

[128] Kysar, "Whence and Whither," p. 67.

[129] For example, in his work in his *The Epistles of John*, AB 30 (London: Geoffrey Chapman, 1982), pp. 70–71, 94–97, Brown incorporates a later period in the community's life when, he believes, the church is divided over its interpretation of the Gospel.

[130] Kysar, "Whence and Whither," p. 68.

[131] See, for example, Brown, *The Community of the Beloved Disciple*, pp. 14–17, 88–91.

in-group/out-group distinction became a basic assumption of later scholarship.[132] As Kysar explains, "Meeks' ingenious proposal was the spark that ignited a wide range of social-scientific investigations of the reconstructed Johannine community."[133] We will discuss these other sociological approaches later in the chronological survey.

In 1975, in the historical-critical tradition of Martyn and Brown, further definition was brought to the use of "community" terminology by R. Alan Culpepper in his *The Johannine School*. For Culpepper, the various terms applied to the "group" of Johannine Christians needed definition. Culpepper compared the Johannine "group" to ancient Greco-Roman schools and argued that the term "school" should be applied to the whole of what we have been calling the JComm. The term never gained wide acceptance. Brown criticized the use of "school" over "community" and Culpepper's emphasis on the "community's" writing of the Gospel. According to Brown, although there is a Johannine communality of discipleship that gives credence to Culpepper's position, he goes too far in making the community the author of the Gospel. "The evangelist . . . was the author, not the community, whence the need to distinguish between school and community."[134] Thus, most Johannine reconstructions sided with Brown: the term "community" applied to the wider Johannine "group," although a "school" of followers closer to the Beloved Disciple was certainly active within the wider JComm.[135]

Following in the work of these major "community" interpretations, the next few years saw a remarkable increase of interest in the history and situation of the JComm, all of which conducted their research from the historical-critical perspective. In 1975 Georg Richter proposed a reconstruction of the JComm's history that was diametrically opposed to Martyn's.[136] While Martyn's guiding principle was that the Gospel reflected one "group" that experienced several different circumstances, Richter finds in the FG traces of several different "groups." His history is not one "community" that adapts to new situations, but several conflicting "theologies" that reflect several different "communities." In 1976 Oscar Cullmann published his full reconstruction of the JComm in

---

[132] Kysar, "Whence and Whither," p. 69.   [133] *Ibid.*

[134] Brown, *The Community of the Beloved Disciple*, p. 101, n. 196. Cf. Brown, *An Introduction to the Gospel of John*, ed. Francis J. Moloney, ABRL (New York: Doubleday, 2003), p. 197.

[135] Brown, *The Community of the Beloved Disciple*, p. 102.

[136] Richter, "Präsentische und futurische Eschatologie in 4. Evangelium," in P. Fiedler and D. Zeller (eds.), *Gegenwart und kommendes Reich* (Stuttgart: Katholisches Bibelwerk, 1975), pp. 117–52. For a good English summary see Andrew J. Mattill, "Johannine Communities behind the Fourth Gospel, Georg Richter's Analysis," *TS* 38 (1977), pp. 294–315.

The Johannine Circle.[137] Although Cullmann had published several articles on the JComm, he had never provided an overall and detailed picture of the "community" history as he understood it. In the historical-critical tradition, Cullmann tried to describe the "group" behind the text, its theological emphases, its ethnic and geographic make-up, and its relation to the text of the FG. In 1977 Marie-Emile Boismard published probably the most elaborate study of the JComm and its environment in his *L'Evangile de Jean.*[138] Boismard focuses on the various stages of composition; he describes not so much the history of a community but of the changing ethos surrounding the various writers (three) who over a period of two generations produced the Gospel. Also in 1977, Wolfgang Langbrandtner argued that the FG was originally a basic Johannine composition (*Grundschrift*) written by an author that had a Gnostic, dualistic outlook.[139] The Gospel as we now have it was completely reshaped by a later redactor who was anti-Gnostic. These two redactions reflect a major struggle that occurred over a period of about forty years in the JComm. Finally, in 1981 Klaus Wengst attempted to describe the general make-up of the "community" (not one "group" but several small and scattered "groups") and several possible geographic locations in the early Christian movement.[140]

In 1988 Jerome Neyrey published the first social-scientific "community" interpretation entitled *An Ideology of Revolt.*[141] Neyrey examines the Christology of the FG by inquiring "into the social dynamics of the community which authored it."[142] Neyrey admits that the perspective of his book was shaped by Meeks' 1972 article on Johannine sectarianism.[143] Like form-critical methods, Neyrey is asking questions concerning the social context and experience found within the text. What is new, in the tradition of Meeks, is "the explicit appeal to formal social-science models and concepts . . ."[144] Also in 1988 David Rensberger published

---

[137] Cullmann, *The Johannine Circle: Its Place in Judaism, among the Disciples of Jesus and in Early Christianity: A Study in the Origin of the Gospel of John* (London: SCM Press, 1976).

[138] Boismard and Arnaud Lamouille, *L'Evangile de Jean: Synopse des quatre évangiles*, 3 vols. (Paris: du Cerf, 1977), vol. III.

[139] Langbrandtner, *Weltferner Gott der Liebe: Die Ketzerstreit in der johanneischen Kirche*, BBET 6 (Frankfurt: Lang, 1977).

[140] Wengst, *Bedrängte Gemeinde und verherrlichter Christus: Der historische Ort des Johannesevangeliums als Schlüssel zu seiner Interpretation*, BTS 5 (Neukirchen-Vluyn: Neukirchener Verlag, 1981).

[141] Neyrey, *An Ideology of Revolt: John's Christology in Social Scientific Perspective* (Philadelphia: Fortress Press, 1988).

[142] *Ibid.*, p. xi. The amount of weight Neyrey places on the situation in which the Gospel was created is evidenced by the phrase "the community authored it [the Gospel]."

[143] *Ibid.*   [144] *Ibid.*, p. 6.

his contribution to the reconstruction of the JComm entitled *Johannine Faith and Liberating Community*.[145] Rensberger's work is an interesting example of using aspects of both models: the historical-critical and the sociological. Rensberger premises his combined and more *ad hoc* method by claiming that NT scholarship has entered a "new era in Johannine interpretation."[146] Yet Rensberger is careful to clarify that he does not consider his work as "sociological" in a proper sense, since he is not explaining "his observations on the basis of a theoretical model or models."[147] Rather, his aims are simply "descriptive [rather] than explanatory, attempting to enrich our understanding of John's purpose and theology by paying attention to the social circumstances surrounding the community for whom the gospel was written."[148]

In 1989 Martin Hengel played his hand at the JComm with his *The Johannine Question*.[149] Hengel is firmly rooted in the historical-critical method in his approach to the Johannine question. In many ways Hengel's work is a response to the overemphasis on the "community," for Hengel makes clear that he begins with the premises that the FG is the work of a "great theologian."[150] Hengel begins his inquiry in the second-century "church" since he believes "that the broad witness of Christian writers of the second century to . . . the Fourth Gospel deserves more attention than it is usually given . . ."[151] Hengel's inquiry leads him to develop a hypothesis concerning the "Johannine school," the person and character of "the elder," who is the focal point of the "school," and through him a general history of the tradition behind the Gospel culminating in a figure who was a witness to the death of Jesus. Hengel loosely cites modern reconstructions and focuses his attention on the more traditional Johannine questions.[152] In a sense, Hengel's dialogue partner is more Adolf von Harnack than Martyn, Brown, or Culpepper.

In 1991 John Painter published his massive reconstruction of the JComm entitled *The Quest for the Messiah*.[153] Similar to Rensberger but more advanced, Painter's goal is "to bring together the historical,

---

[145] Rensberger, *Johannine Faith and Liberating Community* (Philadelphia: Westminster, 1988).
[146] Hence, the title of his first chapter.
[147] Rensberger, *Johannine Faith and Liberating Community*, p. 30.   [148] *Ibid.*
[149] Hengel, *The Johannine Question*, trans. John Bowden (London: SCM Press, 1989).
[150] *Ibid.*, p. x.   [151] *Ibid.*, p. ix.
[152] For example, although Hengel is using the "school" model promoted by Culpepper, *The Johannine School*, he only refers to Culpepper in a footnote and neither defends the "school" model nor places it in the current discussion.
[153] Painter, *The Quest for the Messiah: The History, Literature and Theology of the Johannine Community*, 2nd edn (Edinburgh: T. & T. Clark, 1993).

literary, social and theological dimensions," thus attempting to set out "a synthesis in which certain new insights provide the basis for understanding the fundamental unity of the Johannine tradition."[154] Painter's amalgam of methodologies focus on the FG's portrayal of the JComm's long and specific history in which they take part in a "quest for the Messiah."

Finally, Bruce Malina has been a major contributor to the reconstruction of the JComm, even though he himself has provided no overall theory.[155] Rather, in the sociological tradition of Meeks, Malina employs insights from speech accommodation theory, antilanguage perspectives, and sociolinguistics to try to establish the general lines of the Johannine association that might assist in a more adequate interpretation of the FG. By using speech accommodation theory Malina believes that the FE reveals who the author assumed his audience was and what sort of language they would understand. Malina argues that by looking at the convergence and divergence within the Gospel of John, we are able to see how John (or John's "group") established inter-group boundaries.[156] By arguing that John's language is an antilanguage Malina is stating that the JComm is an anti-society. As Richard Rohrbaugh explains, "As an anti-society, then, the Johannine community has a language all its own. It is an anti-language, an original tongue. Any new member of the community . . . assumed a new identity, one which could stand over against 'this world' and the 'Judeans.'"[157] The JComm, according to Malina and others, is a sectarian movement that has separated from the "world" and "the Jews" by forming a symbolic construction of identity. By using insights from the sociology of knowledge, and by applying a sectarian model related to those insights, Malina and others believe that they have found a more appropriate way to read the FG.[158]

We have surveyed the development of the JComm from its origin in critical scholarship to the Gospel community debate. Most pertinent are the two primary methodological approaches utilized in recent reconstructions of the Johannine "community." The first, in the tradition of Martyn and Brown, is rooted in the traditional introductory questions about the FG and

---

[154] *Ibid.*, p. 1.

[155] Malina, "John's: The Maverick Christian Group: The Evidence of Sociolinguistics," *BTB* 24 (1994), pp. 167–82.

[156] *Ibid.*, pp. 169–70.

[157] Rohrbaugh, "The Gospel of John in the Twenty-First Century," in Fernando F. Segovia (ed.), *"What is John?,"* vol. II: *Literary and Social Readings of the Fourth Gospel,* SBLSymS 7 (Atlanta: Scholars Press, 1998), p. 262.

[158] See also Bruce J. Malina and Richard L. Rohrbaugh, *Social-Science Commentary on the Gospel of John* (Minneapolis: Fortress Press, 1998). We will discuss Malina's approach more fully in chapter 2.

attempted reconstruction through historical-critical means. The second, in the tradition of Meeks, is rooted in the more recent advances in sociological approaches to both literary texts and the "groups" behind them. But, as we saw above, some "community" interpreters use both methods in combination: applying a sociological "bent" to the historical-critical tools. It is important to note that all of these recent reconstructions of the JComm begin with the same assumption that we have traced throughout this chapter: the FG is directly connected to a specific "group" standing behind the text. Even though the "group" cannot be understood without the text, so also the text cannot be understood without the "group," at least in the sense of a historical or sociological account.[159] As we discussed above, these reconstructions are not without serious problems, as the Gospel community debate has made clear. These more recent "community" reconstructions will be discussed and critiqued throughout the remainder of this book.

Methodology

The above survey of the development of the term "community" as applied to the context in which and for which the Gospels were created has prepared us to look in detail at one Gospel in particular to see if such a methodological approach is legitimate. The Gospel which will be our test case is the Gospel of John. Although one may speak of a Gospel community debate, the issues are just now beginning to be made manifest. The various historical and hermeneutical issues involved in the initial stage of the debate are in need of further research. Thus, in testing the origin and audience of the FG, we shall center much of our discussion on the four areas of definition discussed above.

In chapter 2 we will focus our attention on the problems of definition in the Gospel community debate. Several problematic areas will be investigated. The first area to be examined will be the external definition of "community." The use of the term "community" as a category for audience and origin is simply unhelpful, since it has several possible uses and meanings. Its abstract sense has allowed it to be a catch-all for Gospel audiences. After investigating the various "community models" we will argue for a more complex model for understanding "community" in the early Christian movement. The second area to be examined will be the "community" language internal to the text. Once critics made common

---

[159] For certainly a purely narrative approach could be divorced from a historical or sociological context.

the reference to Gospel "communities," various approaches to the Gospel "language" as self-referential became an important issue. We will examine and critique the "sectarian" nature of the FG by testing the nature and function of its language. The third area to be examined will be the external evidence of Gospel "communities." Looking at the patristic writings, we will interact with and critique a recent proposal that the patristic writings reveal the hermeneutical importance of Gospel "communities."

In chapter 3 we will focus our attention on the problems of Gospel genre in the Gospel community debate. Our problems of definition are not completed by chapter 2. If the patristic writings do not reveal the hermeneutical importance of Gospel "communities," then the answer must be found in the literary nature of the Gospel texts themselves. In this sense we are asking two questions of the Gospel text. First, how does a Gospel text reveal its audience? It has been argued that the genre of the Gospels affects the assumed audience. But does a text's genre reveal if the text was intended for a local or general audience? It is this that we will attempt to clarify. Second, how would the earliest Christians have read the Gospels? This question is searching to see if the Gospel genre and its narrative form give clues to how the Gospel would have been "read" by first-century readers/hearers. How would a first-century reader have understood the story? What type of narrative referentiality can we discern in the Gospels? We will argue that the genre of the Gospels both limits the range of use of the text and allows us to see how it may have been understood by its original readers. In essence, our assumption is that the historical character of the Gospel genre and its first-century appropriation give it a more precise hermeneutical nature and its interpreters a more certain hermeneutical responsibility. Much time will be spent critiquing the reading strategy proposed by J. L. Martyn. Our goal in this chapter is to define more precisely an appropriate reading strategy for the FG.

In chapter 4 we will focus our attention on the problems of Gospel audience by searching for the "implied reader" in the FG. Over the last decade several studies in the FG have integrated literary and historical methods to the text of John. Beginning with the assumption that the narrative sheds light on the real world in which it was written and that the implied reader is assumed to know certain things that original readers would have known, we will use the concept of the "implied reader" as a heuristic device to answer one primary question: would the various explanations or comments (or lack of) befit a text written for the author's specific, geographically local community? If our comparison is between "community" and non-"community" readings of the Gospels, then part of this chapter's assumption will be to evaluate the knowledge assumptions for a local, heterogeneous group in light of its hypothetical "community" context. Thus, by using the implied reader as a heuristic device and placing the text setting in a potential "community" in the latter part of the first century, we will attempt to discover which type of audience the FG expects.

After defining early Christian "community," "Gospel," and "reader," in chapters 2 through 4, we will propose in chapter 5 our own reading of the FG in light of the Gospel community debate. The "community" readings have become totalizing in the last several decades. Until now the entire debate has been theoretical. The various conferences and article interchanges have only dealt with the exegetical principles and not exegetical practice. The newness of the debate has required more in depth discussion and clarification, as this thesis has attempted to do in the first four chapters. But now we must turn to exegetical practice. After summarizing our proposed reading strategy, we will examine five related test cases in order to show that the FG was intended to be read by a general or indefinite reading audience. The five test cases involve the following areas of debate: representative figures, the lack of contextual importance of the "expulsion from the synagogue" passages, the purpose of the FG, the mission motif in the FG, and early Christian relations. Our discussion of these test cases will involve two aspects. First, we will argue that these test cases reveal how a non-community reading is more appropriate to the narrative of the FG and its exegesis. Second, we will analyze how current "community" interpretations of various pericopae are internally inconsistent and frequently tangential to the narrative. In sum, this chapter examines the function of the FG in light of the Gospel community debate. It is in this chapter that the methodological issues related to the Gospel community debate discussed in the previous four chapters will come to fruition.

Finally, in chapter 6 we will conclude the study by summarizing our research regarding the Gospel community debate and the FG. In light of our own research, several fresh conclusions concerning the audience and origin of the FG will be suggested. Since the Gospel community debate is a continuing discussion concerning the audience and origin of the Gospels, areas in need of further research will also be highlighted.

The fourth Gospel as a test case

The Gospel that we will use for our test case will be the Gospel of John. The frequently reconstructed JComm makes the FG the preferred candidate as a test case for this book. But, unlike the Synoptic Gospels, the

FG has also been traditionally tied to the whole corpus of the Johannine literature. A brief discussion of our use of John in relation to the rest of the Johannine literature is now in order.

The enigmatic nature of the Johannine literature has caused much confusion in understanding both their historical origin and literary relationship. There is no widespread agreement on the origin of the Johannine literature; neither the order of the writings nor their shared or distinct authorship has been determined.[160] Thus, while it is common for such obscurity to provide an impetus in the construction of a developing JComm, such a case has never been proven. This text will neither attempt to prove any relationship between the Johannine literature, nor feel obliged to use the whole Johannine corpus in any methodologically necessary way.

The relationship between the canonical Johannine literature, though not unrelated to this text, is not going to be a matter of discussion.[161] Although it is common for "community" interpreters to use the Johannine letters in collaboration with the FG to reconstruct the experience and nature of the JComm, that shall not be our focus here for three reasons.[162] First, several of the most important reconstructions of the JComm

[160] For an excellent summary of the relationship between John and the Johannine letters in light of the JComm see Brown, *The Epistles of John*, pp. xi–x, 14–35, 86–102, 140–43. In reference to the necessity of using both the FG and the Johannine letters to reconstruct the JComm, Brown states, "My understanding that it is important to relate the Epistles to GJohn [Gospel of John] goes beyond the obvious. I maintain that the struggle in I and II John between the author and his opponents is centered on two contrary interpretations of the Johannine Community's tradition as known to us in GJohn . . . Thanks to the Epistles, we discover that the profound and innovative Christology of GJohn also contained dangers, so that a drama of community history, religious sociology, and theological development unfolds before our eyes" (xi). See also David Rensberger, *1 John, 2 John, 3 John*, ANTC (Nashville: Abingdon Press, 1997), pp. 17–29, 42–43; and Wendy E. Sproston, "Witnesses to what was ἀπ' ἀρχῆς: 1 John's Contribution to our Knowledge of Tradition in the Fourth Gospel," in Stanley E. Porter and Craig A. Evans (eds.), *The Johannine Readings*, BS 32 (Sheffield: Sheffield Academic Press, 1995), pp. 138–60.

[161] The complex issues involving the FG alone warrant their own study; locating the hypothetical relationship of all Johannine literature would seem to be the second stage of the process, rooted in the findings of this study.

[162] See specifically Brown, *The Community of the Beloved Disciple*, pp. 23–24, and Ben Witherington, *John's Wisdom: A Commentary on the Fourth Gospel* (Cambridge: Lutterworth Press, 1995), p. 28, who avoids dealing with a reconstruction of the JComm in full because he claims that the letters and the Gospel are writing to two different aspects of the community's situation, the Gospel against the world and the letters against a faction within the community itself. He also states his overall methodological theory concerning reconstructions of the JComm when he states, "While I think there *are* a few hints in the Gospel's text that tells us something about the Johannine community, I am basically skeptical of the ability of scholarship to successfully excavate the mound known as the Fourth Gospel and make nice distinctions between earlier and later layers of Johannine tradition, *and then correlate them with the stages in the development in the Johannine community*" (p. 6).

derive their reconstruction from the Gospel alone. For example, in John Ashton's description of the JComm, no mention of a connection to the Johannine letters is made.[163] He even entitles his chapter on the reconstruction of the JComm "The Community and its Book";[164] the singular reveals his emphasis on drawing out the "community" from the Gospel alone. Second, even those who do reconstruct the JComm by using all or part of the Johannine letters do so in a secondary manner. For example, although David Rensberger posits some connection between the Gospel and the Johannine letters, he is hesitant to make direct links between them. According to Rensberger, "the Fourth Gospel is a closed system, so that even the Johannine epistles . . . are of limited comparative usefulness."[165] Rensberger's hesitation leads us to our third reason. Although using the Johannine letters may be considered a common practice,[166] its own methodological merit has not been proven legitimate. The initial complexity is attempting to relate the social location of an epistolary genre with a biographical genre. If their content were overtly similar, some contextual comparison could possibly be attempted, though not verified. This leads us to another problem. Although there are obvious similarities between the Gospel and the letters,[167] there are also obvious differences. The differences were enough to force Bultmann to conclude that "the Gospel of John and 1 John are directed against different fronts."[168] A conclusion of difference is stated more poignantly by Schnackenburg:

> The comparison of the two writings yields one positive result. It is impossible to regard the epistle merely as a companion piece to [the Gospel of] John. It is a completely independent product.

---

[163] Ashton only mentions a pericope from the Johannine letters seven times in the entire six hundred-page volume. Most of the references are simply showing a related theological or lexical idea.

[164] Ashton, *Understanding the Fourth Gospel*, p. 160.

[165] Rensberger, *Johannine Faith and Liberating Community*, p. 113.

[166] According to Judith Lieu, *The Second and Third Epistles of John: History and Background*, SNTW (Edinburgh; T. & T. Clark, 1986), p. 166, this consensus is due to the assumption that a "community" exists behind the Gospel. In turn, this confidence in a "community" behind the Gospel has contributed to the confidence with which phrases like "Johannine community" or "Johannine Christianity" are discussed in modern scholarship.

[167] These similarities and thus a historical and "community" connection between John and the letters is certainly overestimated by Stephen S. Smalley, *1, 2, 3, John*, WBC 51 (Waco, Tx.: Word Books, 1984), pp. xxii–xxxii, who posits an amazingly smooth transition between Gospel and letters, even though he admits that the literary focus and situational context between them has changed dramatically.

[168] Bultmann, *The Johannine Epistles: A Commentary on the Johannine Epistles*, trans. R. Philip O'Hara, Lane C. McGaughy, and Robert W. Funk (Philadelphia: Fortress Press, 1973), p. 1. Cf. Ernst Haenchen, "Neuere Literatur zu den Johannesbriefe," *ThR* 26 (1960), pp. 1–43, 267–91, and more recently, Johannes Beutler, *Die Johannesbriefe: Übersetz und erklärt*, 3rd edn, RNT (Regensburg: Friedrich Pustet, 2000), pp. 18–20.

It neither presupposes the existence of the written Gospel, nor does it leave the reader to expect such a work dealing with the earthly life of the Son of God to follow.[169]

These differences require methodological gymnastics whenever the two are given any historical comparison concerning audience and origin. The various hermeneutical problems are highlighted by Judith Lieu who, although not opposed to linking the Gospel and the letters, finds the entire enterprise highly dubious.[170] Including the Apocalypse of John to the discussion adds even more confusion to the equation. Although Stephen Smalley wants to involve all the Johannine literature in his discussion of the JComm, he is forced to admit it is a debated deduction and something that cannot be proven.[171]

Therefore, for the purpose of this book, which is taking place in the context of the Gospel community debate, using only the FG as a test case is deemed appropriate. In fact, due to the loose historical or contextual connection between the Gospel and the rest of the Johannine literature, our critique of the "community" audience of the FG may dramatically affect our understanding of the audience(s) of the Johannine literature.[172] In light of the debate's focus on the Gospels, an examination of the FG must necessarily precede the rest of the Johannine corpus.

The purpose of this study

The history of interpretation of the concept of the "communities" that stand behind the Gospels reveals that the common template in scholarship places the key hermeneutical principle for interpretation as the quest for the community that each Gospel represents. In light of the Gospel community debate, this book will argue that such a hermeneutical approach is

---

[169] Rudolf Schnackenburg, *The Johannine Epistles: Introduction and Commentary*, trans. Reginald and Ilse Fuller (Tunbridge Wells: Burns & Oates, 1992), p. 39.

[170] Lieu, *The Second and Third Epistles of John*, pp. 205–16. In fact, for Lieu the entire discussion of the relationship between the Gospel and the letters returns to our ability to "excavate" the "community" behind the Gospel (p. 213). For as Lieu points out concerning this excavation, "In the absence of any external 'control' [by which she is referring to the "extremely unlikely" identification of the *Birkat ha-Minim*], the approach must depend on intrinsic force of argument . . . This is not to deny that John does reflect the community's own circumstances; it is to question whether those circumstances or past history can be 'read off' directly from distinctively Johannine passages" (p. 214). Lieu's methodological questions have highlighted the importance and task of this study.

[171] Stephen S. Smalley, *The Revelation to John: A Commentary on the Greek Text of the Apocalypse* (Downers Grove, Ill.: Intervarsity Press, 2005), p. 4.

[172] We will discuss these potential conclusions and related avenues for further research in chapter 6.

problematic. At present the study of the Gospel text is almost a secondary concern; the primary effort is spent attempting to unveil the Gospel "community" which, it is claimed, is to be found within the collection of Jesus material we call a Gospel. By attempting to provide further definition to various aspects of the Gospel community debate, and by using the FG as a test case, we will argue that the FG never was intended for a local, geographic "community" or network of "communities." The Gospel reveals a large early Christian audience, in contrast to the current "community" reconstructions which assume that each Gospel was written by and for a specific Gospel "community."

2

EARLY CHRISTIAN COMMUNITY: A STUDY OF THE COMMUNITY CONSTRUCT AND ITS FUNCTIONAL POTENTIAL IN EARLY CHRISTIANITY

The quest for the early Christian "community"

The quest for the historical Jesus that occupied much of the nineteenth century largely gave way to the quest for the early church in the twentieth century.[1] As we saw in chapter 1, the focus on the communities of the early church, though undefined, was considered by the initial form critics to be the only historical remnant left to be sought. The historical results determined by the form critics were in many ways sociological in nature. The basic methodology used by Bultmann and the other early form critics was an idea taken from the sociology of literature, namely that certain types of literature or genres (*Gattungen*) are bound to and shaped by specific types of social life-settings (*Sitze im Leben*).[2] Literary genre is a social category of communication;[3] the questions being asked of the text were sociological. The communities in which the Gospel texts were created had various functions which determined the forms and overall use of the Jesus tradition and its eventual Gospel text form.

Although the initial sociological emphasis in form criticism looked promising, the sociological potential was never developed. Thomas Best argues that, "it cannot be denied that even form criticism, with all its talk of the *Sitz-im-Leben* (life-setting) of the text, was a literary and theological[4] discipline which produced hardly any concrete historical, social, or economic information about the traditions which it studied."[5] Whether it should be attributed to the world wars[6] or the theological

---

[1] See a good discussion of the quest for the early church in reference to the origin of the Gospel of John by Brodie, *The Quest for the Origin of John's Gospel*, pp. vii–viii, 5–21, 137–52.

[2] Holmberg, *Sociology and the New Testament*, pp. 1–2.

[3] We will discuss the implications of Gospel genre in chapter 3.

[4] See Watson, "Toward a Literal Reading of The Gospels," in *GAC*.

[5] Best, "Sociological Study of the New Testament: Promise and Peril of A New Discipline," *SJT* 36 (1983), pp. 181–82.

[6] Holmberg, *Sociology and the New Testament*, p. 2.

revival of the 1920s,[7] the use and application of the social sciences to the text of the Gospels would have to wait. Even redaction criticism focused on the religious milieu of the evangelists and their particular theological emphasis rather than on the social situation.

Since the 1970s, and in light of the almost fifty-year absence of social history and sociological perspectives, what could be called a reform movement within historical criticism took place and has been broadly called social-scientific criticism.[8] Social-scientific criticism has offered what it believes to be new and improved questions to the Gospels.[9] In place of the traditional questions of occasion and purpose of the Gospel text, which are ideational or theological terms, situation and strategy are being offered.[10] Situation refers to the social circumstances and interaction that motivated the writing of a text. Examples of causality commonly used include social disorder or conflict, threats to group cohesion and commitment, problems with group boundaries, conflicts over legitimate authority, events to be celebrated, and communities to be galvanized to action.[11] Strategy, on the other hand, refers to the fact that the text is specifically designed by its producer not simply to communicate ideas but to move a specific

[7] Robert Morgan and John Barton, *Biblical Interpretation*, OBS (Oxford: Oxford University Press, 1988), pp. 145–46. See also the discussion by Robin Scroggs, "The Sociological Interpretation of the New Testament: The Present State of Research," *NTS* (1980), pp. 164–65, where the theological "pendulum," as Scroggs called it, had been taken from the liberals as unfashionable and been given to the Neo-orthodoxy emphasis upon theology and the word.

[8] It is important that we recognize the distinction between sociological and social-scientific criticism. Although they have related beginnings, they have developed into two distinct sub-disciplines. A history of sociological and social-scientific criticism is well beyond the scope of this book. For an excellent and comprehensive survey of social-scientific criticism see John Elliott, *What is Social-Scientific Criticism?* GBSNTS (Minneapolis: Augsburg Fortress, 1993). For sketches that highlight the trends of sociological criticism as it was developing see Edwin A. Judge, *The Social Pattern of Christian Groups in the First Century: Some Prolegomena to the Study of New Testament Ideas of Social Obligation* (London: Tyndale, 1960); Leander E. Keck, 'On the Ethos of Early Christians," *JAAR* 42 (1974), pp. 435–52; Jonathan Z. Smith, "The Social Description of Early Christianity," *RSR* 1 (1975), pp. 19–25; Gerd Theissen, *Studien zur Soziologie des Urchristentums*, WUNT 19 (Tübingen: Mohr Siebeck, 1979); Robin Scroggs, "The Sociological Interpretation of the New Testament," pp. 164–79; Gerd Theissen, *The Social Setting of Pauline Christianity: Essays on Corinth*, ed. and trans. John H. Schütz (Philadelphia: Fortress Press, 1982).

[9] Although social-scientific questions are not new, as its relation to form criticism showed above, the overall methodological approach that is attempting to apply pure social-scientific models on the text of the Gospels is itself an innovative enterprise.

[10] Elliott, *What is Social-Scientific Criticism?*, pp. 54–55. The concepts "situation" and "strategy" were first used by Elliott in his *A Home for the Homeless: A Sociological Exegesis of 1 Peter, Its Situation and Strategy* (Philadelphia: Fortress Press, 1981).

[11] Elliott, *What is Social-Scientific Criticism?*, p. 54. See also the earlier discussion by Klaus Berger, *Exegese des Neuen Testaments: neue Wege vom Text zur Auslegung*, Uni-Taschenbücher 658 (Heidelberg: Quelle & Meyer, 1977), pp. 111–27.

audience to some form of action.[12] "Social-scientific criticism thus aims at discovering how a given document was designed as an author's motivated response to a specific situation and how it was composed to elicit a specific social response on the part of its audience."[13]

It is in this way that the term "community" becomes used to denote the group situation in which and for which a document's strategy is functioning. The classical use of "community" was in a more general sense, denoting the earliest "Christians"[14] and the group movement that they began following Jesus' departure. In this more general sense it can refer to the most ancient membership of the Christian religion. "Chronologically, it refers to Christian beliefs and practices of the first three or four decades after the crucifixion, and it partially overlaps Pauline Christianity."[15] Several of the older studies reflect this understanding of "community,"[16] many of which focus on Paul (Acts 15; Gal. 2).[17] Of course, the more recent understanding of "community" is not the general early movement, but the various "groups" affiliated with belief in Jesus in the first century. In this more specific sense the term is used to describe a group of "Christians" in a specific, geographic location, or, as it is used with the biblical texts, a group of Christians who are reflected in a NT document. It is in this sense that we have returned to our discussion in chapter 1 concerning the developing concept of "community." While Paul was the primary "community" focus in the older studies, modern research has commonly assumed that for the post-Pauline era the Gospels, and maybe the Deutero-Pauline letters and some of the Catholic letters, are our primary sources, not to mention bits of information from non-Christian sources[18] or the sparse and questionable information to

[12] Elliott, *What is Social-Scientific Criticism?*, p. 54.
[13] *Ibid.* In this sense there is also a rhetorical thrust that can be deduced.
[14] The use of the term "Christian" is not meant to impose institutionalization upon the first-century "Jesus movement," as if by "Christian" we imply the homogeneous institution later called the "church." Rather, we will use the term to refer to the "communities" in the first-century movement that centered themselves, in whatever fashion, upon Jesus of Nazareth.
[15] Joseph B. Tyson, *A Study of Early Christianity* (New York: Macmillan, 1973), p. 273.
[16] A good example of this procedure can be found in Adolf Harnack, *The Expansion of Christianity in the First Three Centuries*, 2 vols., trans. James Moffatt, TTL 19 (London: Williams & Norgate, 1904), vol. I, pp. 54–55. See also A. J. Mason, "Conceptions of the Church in Early Times," in H. B. Swete (ed.), *Essays on the Early History of the Church and the Ministry*, 2nd edn (London: Macmillan, 1921), pp. 3–56.
[17] Johannes Weiss, *Earliest Christianity: History of the Period A.D. 30–150*, 2 vols., trans. Frederick C. Grant (New York: Harper & Brothers, 1959), vol. I, p. 1. This is supported more recently by Frederick J. Cweikowski, *The Beginnings of the Church* (Dublin: Gill and Macmillan, 1988), p. 100.
[18] Although Judge, *The Social Pattern of Christian Groups in the First Century*, p. 16, argues that the non-Christian sources are all plagued with a "Roman slant."

be gleaned by Christian authors in the early to mid-second century. It is primarily the Gospels, though, that are being used to discover the nature and issues within the various Christian communities. Thus for historical critics, who claim that the meaning of any text is dependent on the historical circumstance in and for which it was written, the "community" behind the Gospel texts became as hermeneutically important as the texts themselves. But a problem already exists in reference to the study of early Christianity and its "communities": the paucity of sources.

The success of such an enterprise is only as likely as the sources that are available. The difficulty in grasping the occurrences of the period and the "groups" in which things occurred is compounded by the lack of directly relevant material. In many ways, the historian of early Christianity is researching a movement that is "shrouded in historical darkness."[19] Martin Hengel summarizes it best:

> All too often we are only left with traces: names of people without specific details, isolated events, sporadic accounts or obscure legends – as from Talmudic literature, except where suddenly larger fragments emerge, resting on individually lucky discoveries. We constantly come up against gaps and white patches on the map; our sources are uncertain and we have to content ourselves with more or less hypothetical reconstructions. All this is true of ancient history in general and even more of the history of early Christianity in particular, above all its first 150 years.[20]

Even the sources we do have are only the creation of Christians themselves; their own internal literature created for their own purposes.[21] What has become apparent is that the limited sources reduce our access to the "world" behind the Gospels, including the audience for whom they were created. Once a specific audience was assumed, the text was scavenged for clues to the nature and circumstances of this "community." Using insights from form and redaction criticism modern scholars began to evaluate the material to differentiate between the authentic and

---

[19] Taken from Elisabeth Schüssler Fiorenza, *In Memory of Her: A Feminist Theological Reconstruction of Christian Origins* (London: SCM Press, 1983), p. 160.

[20] Hengel, *Acts and the History of Earliest Christianity* (Philadelphia: Fortress, 1979), pp. 4–5. A similar despair is given by Burton L. Mack, *A Myth of Innocence: Mark and Christian Origins* (Philadelphia: Fortress Press, 1988), pp. 3–4.

[21] Wayne Meeks, *The First Urban Christians: The Social World of the Apostle Paul* (New Haven: Yale University Press, 1983), p. 1. Meeks considers the hermeneutical key of interpreting the Gospels to be getting inside their social-functioning worldview that is apparent in their sectarian literature.

inauthentic material; the traditional material and the redacted or inter-preted material. Such a procedure allows one to see the intentional data, supposed in the communication, as well as the unintentional data, made manifest by the context in and for which it was created.[22] Thus, with the onslaught of form criticism, and with it the preliminary death of the historical Jesus and the historically pure Gospels, the primitive Chris-tian church and its various and dispersed communities became the focus of interpretation. These later groups in the early Christian movement are seen as the co-authors of the Christian scriptures, having not merely passed on the Jesus Tradition, but intentionally adapted[23] it for the sake of their own contextually determined needs.[24]

This returns us to the Gospel community debate and the appraisal of the Gospel community reconstructions by this book. Several problems arise with an approach that attempts to discover the specific "commu-nity" in and for which a Gospel was written. First, there is a problem in establishing what is exactly meant by the term "community." The use of the term "community" as a category for audience is unhelpful since, as was discussed in chapter 1, it has several possible uses and meanings. The use of a "community" model is not inappropriate, but it must be defined and defended. Its abstract sense has allowed it to be a catch-all term for Gospel audiences; unfortunately, this catch-all has become an assumption one begins with when reading the Gospels. This chapter will argue that the current "definition" of the term has been applied too loosely. Are we to assume that a "community" was a sectarian or isolated audience? Or is it simply in reference to a local audience in a specific geographic location? Is there any historical evidence of a real JComm? Thus, if the term itself

---

[22] Marc Bloch, *The Historian's Craft*, trans. Peter Putnam (Manchester: Manchester University Press, 1954), pp. 60ff. See also the discussion by Harvey, *The Historian and the Believer* (New York: Macmillan, 1966; repr. Urbana: University of Illinois, 1996), pp. 214–21.

[23] The authority to adapt the Jesus tradition is usually assumed to have been given by the Spirit. In the context of the early church, according to Gary M. Burge, *The Anointed Community: The Holy Spirit in the Johannine Tradition* (Grand Rapids: Eerdmans, 1987), p. 224, "the Spirit was known as a revelatory aid . . . recalling the words of Christ (anamnesis) and leading into new frontiers of truth."

[24] According to Meeks, *The First Urban Christians*, p. 2, "Since we do not meet ordinary Christians as individuals, we must seek to recognize them through the collectives to which they belonged and to glimpse their lives through the typical occasions mirrored in the texts. It is in the hope of accomplishing this that a number of historians of early Christianity have recently undertaken to describe the first Christian groups in ways that a sociologist or anthropologist might. Without wishing to abandon previous accomplishments in philology, literary analysis, history of traditions, and theological insight, these scholars have sought in social history an antidote to the abstractions of the history of ideas and to the subjective individualism of existential hermeneutics."

is difficult to grasp, the actual historical circumstances of the early "communities" are even more elusive. This first issue, then, is external to the Gospel text, for it requires the application of models.

The second issue is internal: there is a dangerous circularity involved in defining the audience behind the text without anything but the text. Once the form critics made common the reference to Gospel "communities," various approaches to the Gospel "language" as self-referential became an important issue. The limited purview of the Gospel authors has allowed community interpreters to place limits on the reference of Gospel language. The Gospels were speaking on behalf of their individual communities, just as the individual communities can be seen as speaking through the Gospels. At that point "the one document per community fallacy," as James Dunn describes it,[25] wedded the external (community formation) and the internal (community language) issues into a single hermeneutical approach.

Therefore, this chapter will assess both of these issues and argue that the entire approach is problematic. We will accomplish this in three parts. First, concerning the external definition of community, we will investigate the various "models" used in assuming a "community" audience for the Gospels and will argue for a more complex model for understanding "community" in the early Christian movement. Second, in reference to the community language internal to the text, we will examine the "sectarian" nature of the Gospel of John by testing the nature and function of its "language." Third, we will conclude our quest for a definition of an early Christian "community" by examining the evidence for Gospel "communities" in the patristic writings, using specifically the evidence and argument presented by Margaret Mitchell against *GAC*.

Definition of the early Christian community: its variation and type

In the exegetical method we are appraising, where a Gospel community is reconstructed from the text and placed within a first-century context, the definition of "community" is simply too loose to be of any explanatory value. Since we have no evidence of what these so-called "communities" looked like, we are limited in ascertaining their function. As with all reconstructions, models must be used in order to establish the potential form and function of these "communities." This is central to the Gospel

---

[25] James D. G. Dunn, *Christianity in the Making: Vol. 1: Jesus Remembered* (Grand Rapids: Eerdmans, 2003), pp. 150–51.

community debate. Recent research has advanced our understanding not only of potential "community" forms, but also their functional potential through sociological analysis.[26] This research has attempted to view groups and their societal relations from a new perspective, critiquing the objective categories normally applied to these movements. This research will be especially helpful in our discussion below concerning the sectarian nature of Christian groups, but for now it will help us apply judicature between the various "subjective" descriptions of group form. Since the possible early churches or "communities" are assumed to be derivative of other known and existing social and group formations, it will be valuable to begin there. Thus, our goal is to attempt to define more closely the term "community" and its possible form in the early Christian movement.

Models of "community" in the early Christian movement

The information within the NT reveals the existence of many and variously located communities in the early Christian movement. Although around thirty Christian groups are mentioned in Acts and the Pauline letters, many other groups may also be implied.[27] Certainly these supposed Gospel "communities"[28] varied depending on group size, location, and resources. Our most immediate problem is that we have no idea what the Gospel "communities" would have looked like; everything between a single, isolated "community" and a network of "groups" has been posited.[29] Problems exist in the vague terminology currently used to describe the early Christian groups. Although recent research has attempted to define these possible audiences by looking at known group formations in the first century, such a procedure gives little pure data concerning the specific Gospel "communities." For example, in

---

[26] Most helpful here is John M. G. Barclay, *Jews in the Mediterranean Diaspora: From Alexander to Trajan (323 BCE–117 CE)* (Edinburgh: T. & T. Clark, 1996) and Philip A Harland, *Associations, Synagogues, and Congregations: Claiming a Place in Ancient Mediterranean Society* (Minneapolis: Fortress, 2003).

[27] Judge, *The Social Pattern of Christian Groups in the First Century*, p. 12. Although it is beyond the scope of this work to look specifically at the definition and usage of Christian ἐκκλησία, we are assuming it existed as a sociological and functional entity. For a discussion of the term ἐκκλησία and its pre-Christian and Christian understanding see Robert Banks, *Paul's Idea of Community: The Early House Churches in their Historical Setting* (Exeter: Paternoster, 1980), pp. 34–37, 43–51; Meeks, *The First Urban Christians*, pp. 74–110; K. L. Schmidt, TDNT, vol. III, pp. 501–36; L. Coenen, NIDNTT, vol. I, pp. 291–307.

[28] Several terms are used synonymously in scholarly literature to describe the audiences of the Gospels or the "church(es)" they represent. Thus, we will use terms like group, congregation, association, and "community" in a synonymous manner.

[29] For the purpose of the Gospel community debate, the hermeneutical difference between a single group and a network of groups is minimal; the assumption is the same: one document is representative of one audience.

order to determine the sociological form of the early Christian communities, various models of ancient group formation have been drawn on for comparison:[30] the ancient household,[31] the synagogue,[32] clubs, voluntary associations, and religious cults,[33] and philosophical schools.[34] Interestingly, the school model has been the most well-known model applied to the FG.[35] Although it is appropriate to assume that the early Christians

[30] The most recent and comprehensive work on the social history of early Christianity is by Ekkehard W. Stegemann and Wolfgang Stegemann, *The Jesus Movement: A Social History of Its First Century*, trans. O. C. Dean, Jr. (Minneapolis: Fortress Press, 1999).

[31] There is evidence in the NT that the early Christians met in one another's homes (Acts 10:1ff.; 16:15, 32ff.; 18:8ff.; 1 Cor. 1:14, 16; 16:15–19; Rom. 16:5, 23; Col. 4:15). For research on house churches see Floyd V. Filson, "The Significance of Early House Churches," *JBL* 58 (1939), pp. 105–12; Hans-Joseph Klauck, *Hausgemeinde und Hauskirche im Frühen Christentum* (Stuttgart: Katholisches Bibelwerk, 1981); C. Osiek and David L. Balch, *The Family in the New Testament: Households and House Churches*, FRC (Louisville: Westminster John Knox, 1997).

[32] It is generally assumed that between 70 and 135 CE Christianity became a religion based very largely on the geography and organization of the Hellenistic synagogue. See Martin Hengel, "Die Synagogeninschrift von Stobi," *ZNW* 57 (1966), pp. 145–83; Wayne A. Meeks, *The First Urban Christians*, pp. 80–81.

[33] For research on Greco-Roman associations see Edwin Hatch, *The Organization of the Early Christian* Churches, 4th edn, Brampton Lectures for 1880 (London: Longman & Green, 1892), pp. 26–55; Georg C. F. Heinrici, "Die Christengemeinde Korinths und die religiösen Genossenschaften der Griechen," *ZWT* 19 (1876), pp. 464–526; Judge, *The Social Pattern of Christian Groups in the First Century*, pp. 40–48; Robert L. Wilkin, "Toward A Sociological Interpretation of Early Christian Apologetics," *CH* 39 (1970), pp. 1–22; Abraham J. Malherbe, *Social Aspects of Early Christianity*, 2nd and enl. edn (Philadelphia: Fortress, 1983), pp. 87–91.

[34] The comparison of the "school" model to the Christian communities was made as early as the second century by Justin Martyr who presented Christianity as a "true philosophy," followed similarly by other apologists of the second and third centuries. At the same time, Tertullian was strictly opposed to such a designation for the Christian organization (*Apol.* 38–39). According to Stegemann and Stegemann, *The Jesus Movement*, pp. 273–74, Tertullian combined various concepts that could have been used with other Roman associations as well as with schools of philosophers. Nevertheless, Tertullian was attempting to prove the harmlessness of the Christian groups and, when doing so, specifically denies that Christian communities were identical with the *collegia* or philosophical schools. See Wilkin's understanding of the Christian defense in school-like terms in Robert L. Wilkin, "Collegia, Philosophical Schools, and Theology," in Stephen Benko and John J. O'Rourke (eds.), *The Catacombs and the Colosseum* (Valley Forge: Judson, 1971), pp. 268–91.

[35] The "school" model is different in degree from the other primary community models, which are based upon a community of location and organization. The difference is that behind the documents stands a teacher, whose scholastic influence is primary and who, for all purposes, is the school. The geographic community model is less hierarchical, less established around one individual, and is more tradition based, often assumed to be the tradition of a local church group. The concept of the JComm by Martin Hengel, *The Johannine Question*, for example, is based upon the school model. For Hengel, behind all the Johannine documents stands one head, "an outstanding teacher who founded the school . . . in Asia Minor and developed a considerable activity extending beyond the region and who – as an outsider – claimed to have been a disciple of Jesus, indeed – in the view of the school – a disciple of a quite special kind" (p. 80). Culpepper, *The Johannine School,*

would have organized themselves in a way consonant with their tradition and cultural distinctives, it is impossible to know exactly how they did so.

Although several models might be helpful in revealing ancient analogies to "community" forms, none of them is able to explain what any one of the Gospel "communities" may have been. Even if we were to argue that the household model was the initial phase of community building, especially in the Jewish context, and when available, more substantial synagogue-like and permanent structures for meeting would be established, we would not be able to place any of the Gospels in that development. The various "communities" would have probably used aspects from each of the four models, depending on their geographic location, their missionary undertakings, their local activities and fellowship needs, and their connection with other groups of Christians. The early Christian communities, as recorded in our sources, amalgamated various aspects of the numerous group models in their culture to the needs of their own specific Christian "community." But our analysis of the concept of a Gospel "community" must move beyond analogy.

The above discussion has helpfully laid out the potential groups or associations found in the early Christian movement. But that alone is not sufficient. No one model can be proven coterminous with the "community" (audience) behind a Gospel; nor can any description of that "community" be accomplished from an objective, external perspective.[36] It is at the point of external description that the definition of a Gospel "community" normally ends. A local group (or network) is assumed as a Gospel "community," fitting some or all aspects of the models mentioned above, and is then "filled-out" from data found in the Gospel texts. Using an analogy from scientific hypotheses, once the community interpreters have "determined" their constant (a local, physical group or network of groups) then the variables (community history, members represented) can be defined by using textual data. But such a procedure has already inappropriately assigned an external model as the constant when no such definition of "community" can be verified. What is needed, then, is a reevaluation of this "constant." This will require a more complex model that takes an internal approach to "community" form. This is not to deny

pp. 261–89, has a similar model: the JComm is a school founded by a dominant leader (the Beloved Disciple). To extend the "school" model too directly eradicates the many similarities the Gospel "communities" probably had with other models, especially the household and Jewish model.

[36] Even the social-historical work of Stegemann and Stegemann, *The Jesus Movement*, p. 274, reveals the problem in defining an early Christian group from an "outside view."

that external models are helpful, only that in this case such an approach is limited in analytical value. As Meeks admits, "the associations offer as little help as does the household in explaining the extralocal linkages of the Christian movement."[37] What is lacking is an attempt to weigh the significance of each Gospel's own portrayal of their form – an assessment which involves internal perceptions without assuming an external model as constant. Thus, we now turn from external analogies to internal perception.

Definition of Gospel "community": a new proposal

In the essay entitled "Can we Identify the Gospel Audiences?" in *GAC*, Stephen Barton discusses the problematic nature of defining the notoriously ambiguous term "community."[38] Barton claims that although social scientists are trained to use the term with caution, NT scholars are more liberal in their use. The term "community," according to its use by social scientists, is one of the most elusive terms to define. The social anthropologist Anthony Cohen states the case plainly, "'Community' is one of those words – like 'culture,' 'myth,' 'ritual,' symbol' – bandied around in ordinary, everyday speech, apparently readily intelligible to speaker and listener, which, when imported into the discourse of social science, however, causes immense difficulty."[39] Cohen warns that past understandings of community have been "based entirely upon a highly particularistic and sectarian definition."[40] The definition of community is not to be understood from an external perspective (first-century models), it is defined from the inside; its boundaries are marked by their symbolic meaning for the participants.[41] In reference to this Cohen states:

---

[37] Meeks, *The First Urban Christians*, p. 80.

[38] Barton, "Can We Identify the Gospel Audiences?," in *GAC*, pp. 173–94.

[39] Anthony Cohen, *The Symbolic Construction of Community*, KI 1 (London: Routledge, 1985), p. 11. Cohen is also referred to by Barton, "Can We Identify the Gospel Audiences?" See also Pierre Bourdieu, *Language and Symbolic Power*, ed. John B. Thompson, trans. Gino Raymond and Matthew Adamson (Cambridge: Polity Press, 1991), especially pp. 220–51, for a more theoretical discussion of the difficulty of defining sociological and anthropological terms.

[40] Cohen, *The Symbolic Construction of Community*, p. 12. Cohen argues that such an understanding has been a misinterpretation of the earlier writers like Durkheim, Weber, Tönnes, and Simmel.

[41] Concerning community and group identity see T. Schwartz, "Cultural Totemism: Ethnic Identity Primitive and Modern," in G. De Vos and L. Romanucci-Ross (eds.), *Ethnic Identity: Cultural Continuities and Change* (Palo Alto: Mayfield, 1975), pp. 106–31; and J. A. Boon, *Other Tribes, Other Scribes: Symbolic Anthropology in the Comparative Study of Cultures, Histories, Religions, and Texts* (Cambridge: Cambridge University Press, 1980). We will deal with this "symbolic meaning" for the participants in the so-called JComm when we deal with John's antilanguage.

> the community is not approached as a morphology, as a structure
> of institutions capable of objective definition and description.
> Instead, we try to understand "community" by seeking to cap-
> ture members' experience of it. Instead of asking, "what does
> it look like to us? What are its theoretical implications?", we
> ask, "What does it appear to mean to its members?" Rather than
> describing analytically the form of the structure from an external
> vantage point, we are attempting to penetrate the structure, to
> look *outwards* from its core.[42]

What was axiomatic in the past is that the supposed structure of the
community implied certain functions and results. While it is true that the
borders of the community, its differentiation from the other groups that
allows it to be its own entity, define the community's essence, the process
of establishing the border must occur from the inside, not the outside.[43]

Recent sociological research on the symbolic construction of community can assist us as we attempt to establish a method that allows a group
behind the text to define the nature of its community. In broad categories
the term "community" has two major uses: territorial and relational. The
territorial concept points to a context of location, physical territory, and
geographic continuity. The relational concept points to the quality or
character of human relationships, without reference to location.[44] In both
the social sciences and the Gospel "community" reconstructions, the two
concepts are not sharply exclusive. Although it is rarely discussed in NT
scholarship, the nature of community is related to the historically difficult
tension between community and society. But as we will see below, most
"community" reconstructions assume a relational concept, a symbolic
construction of community (and world). It is this concept that we will
define more closely.

As we noted above in our discussion of community models, the term
"Gospel community" does not describe any group known to exist in history. There is absolutely no evidence of a specific Gospel community
standing behind the Gospels; we have created the Gospel "community"
model for the sake of analysis.

> They are analytical and not empirical terms; concepts invented
> to help the analyst think about change and human associa-
> tions. As such, they are products of human imagination and not

---

[42] Cohen, *The Symbolic Construction of Community*, p. 20.   [43] *Ibid.*, pp. 50–63.
[44] Joseph R. Gusfield, *Community: A Critical Response*, KCSS (Oxford: Basil Blackwell,
1975), pp. xv–xvi.

descriptions of a real world. No permanent human association can be found which contains all the attributes of community. . . [45]

The use of such models goes back to Max Weber's ideal types.[46] The various terms used to describe the Gospel "communities" in the history of its use – group, school, circle, church – are forms of that first-century type. As Gusfield makes clear, "One of the great dangers in the use of ideal-types is *reification* – treating an abstract, analytical term as if it were descriptive and empirical . . . In this process the type (an idea) has been transformed into a thing."[47] This applies directly to the current definitions of Gospel "communities." The text is only allowed to reveal what the community ideal type behind the Gospel allows, as was determined by its assumed structure and functional ability. Thus, in reference to the community reconstructions, the question needs to be asked: Who is defining the boundaries of the assumed Gospel communities? If the boundaries of the Gospel communities are defined by an inappropriate, externally imposed grid of understanding, confusion and distortion will most certainly exist. The amount of community constructions for each of the Gospels seems to imply that there is widespread uncertainty concerning the boundaries of these "communities."

This book is proposing that the current "ideal type"[48] of Gospel community is mistaken. The notoriously ambiguous term, to use Barton's terminology, has produced ambiguous results. For the sake of analysis, and in light of the fact that no known "group" is known to have lived behind the Gospels, a more preferred determination of the Gospels' own audience, as viewed from the inside, would define "community" in its relational sense, in contrast to its geographical sense. Since the concept of community denotes a quality of human relations rather than a quantity of population, we need to describe the kind of social bonding that exists. Gusfield tells a joke that explains well this social interaction:

> The story is told of a dying Jew who in his last hour asks to be converted to Christianity. His sons plead against it but the old man wins out, is converted and given the last rites of the Church. The children cannot understand why their father, always a devout and Orthodox Jew, should renounce his life-long faith and they

[45] *Ibid.*, p. 11.
[46] Max Weber, *The Methodology of the Social Sciences*, trans. Edward A. Shils and Henry Finch (New York: Free Press, 1949).
[47] Gusfield, *Community*, p. 13 (emphasis original).
[48] The term "type" is singular instead of plural since the various community reconstructions all define "community" in a geographic sense.

prevail on him to explain. With his dying breath the old man rises up in bed and shouts, "Better one of them should die than one of us."[49]

Two aspects of the story are useful for our definition of "community." The first is the exclusivity of the dying man's loyalties. The distinction between "them and us" is sharp. It is the intrinsic nature of his being "one of us" that makes his death-bed conversion so strange. The humor of the joke comes when one realizes that the dying man's wish remained consistent with his participation as "one of us." The second useful aspect is the dying man's attempt to define himself as something other than what he has been – to create communal membership through symbolic construction.[50] It reveals how people identify themselves and others as belonging to one or another association. The fact that the dying man's sons, and for the joke to be understood the readers, assumed that the transition from Jew to Christian would have been real and not hypothetical shows the reality of such a symbolic construction. There was no need for physical evidence – that the man had never been in a Christian church, or been baptized, or that the man was Jewish by birth – all that was assumed to be needed was mental conversion (a symbolic construction).

A symbolic-constructed community places one in several areas of communal interaction. It is too simple to define a community member by only one aspect of community, let alone by a geographical location. "Community" is not an organized group of associates; it is an analytical category used by observers for description. "It becomes a 'class for itself' when organization develops and a self-consciousness emerges among members and they come to act collectively toward mutual [community] goals."[51] This fits well with the definition Cohen argued for above: "We try to understand 'community' by seeking to capture its members' experience of it."[52] In this way we can begin to see the one-sided nature of the terms Johannine community, or Markan community, or Matthean community, or Lukan community. The "community" reconstruction model only defines a Gospel community as one "type" of community: an enclosed, particular, even sectarian "group" of Christians in which the Gospel document arose and remained. Such a definition is too limited to provide adequate analysis; not to mention the complete lack of historical evidence for such a "community." Although it provides a helpful external model, it

[49] Gusfield, *Community*, p. 23.   [50] *Ibid.*, p. 24.

[51] *Ibid.*, p. 26. See the related discussion of Jewish "community" by Barclay, *Jews in the Mediterranean Diaspora*, p. 414.

[52] Cohen, *The Symbolic Construction of Community*, p. 20.

fails to take into account internal aspects of "community" and potential interaction with other "communities." Thus, there are other aspects of a "community" that a geographic definition cannot explain.

Post-World War II research on the establishments of national units in the retreat of colonial powers and the focus of attention on efforts of new governments to promote and develop a consciousness of nationhood provides a helpful link to our discussion of the early Christian concept of community. As Gusfield explains, "The crucial quality of communal interaction is the recognition that a common identity of communal membership implies special claims which members have on each other, as distinct from others."[53] In reference to the concept of nation, another notoriously ambiguous term,[54] Benedict Anderson has proposed the following definition: "It is an imagined political-community – and imagined as both inherently limited and sovereign."[55] As Anderson explains: "It is imagined because the members of even the smallest nation will never know most of their fellow-members, meet them, or even hear of them, yet in the minds of each lives the image of their communion."[56] But even the largest nation is limited, because it has finite, even if elastic, boundaries beyond which lie other nations. In this sense a nation is a type of "community." Again, Anderson explains:

> it is imagined as a community, because, regardless of the actual inequality and exploitation that may prevail in each, the nation is always conceived as a deep, horizontal comradeship. Ultimately it is this fraternity that makes it possible, over the past two centuries, for so many millions of people, not so much to kill, as willing to die for such limited imaginings.[57]

And later,

> The idea of a sociological organism moving calendrically through homogenous, empty time is a precise analogue of the idea of the nation, which also is conceived as a solid community moving steadily down (or up) history. An American will

---

[53] Gusfield, *Community*, p. 29.

[54] Hugh Seton-Watson, *Nations and States: An Inquiry into the Origins of Nations and the Politics of Nationalism* (Boulder, Col.: Westview Press, 1977), author of the best and most comprehensive English-language text on nationalism, explains: "Thus I am driven to the conclusion that no 'scientific definition' of the nation can be devised; yet the phenomenon has existed and exists" (p. 5).

[55] Anderson, *Imagined Communities: Reflections on the Origin and Spread of Nationalism*, rev. edn (London: Verso, 1991), p. 6.

[56] *Ibid.*   [57] *Ibid.*, p. 7.

never meet, or even know the names of more than a handful of his . . . fellow Americans. He has no idea of what they are up to at any one time. But he has complete confidence in their steady, autonomous, simultaneous activity.[58]

We have used the concept of "nation" as an analogy for the concept of "community" in order to show the potential for defining the Gospel communities in light of an internal perspective. Rather than reading the Gospels as documents for one of several Christian "communities," a reading strategy that applies a territorial model that limits the receiving audience to a geographic and special location, we propose to apply a relational model, one of a symbolic construction, as the primary mode of thinking and assuming involvement in an early Christian "community." This "community," rather than existing as one local group or networked group, often viewed as sectarian in nature, is much more connected than normally assumed. It is not an isolated "communal world" of its own but part of a much larger social system. Like a nation, the early Christians saw themselves as related to one another, as horizontal comrades. They may not have even known one another, for their group was ever-growing and thus elastic, as well as spread over a huge geographic region, but they had an imagined connection that was symbolically constructed.

Such a proposal is not difficult to reconcile with the diversity and conflict normally perceived to have existed in early Christianity. As Cohen explains, the "commonality" which is found in community need not be uniformity.[59] An important explanation by Cohen is worth quoting in full:

> It does not clone behaviour or ideas. It is a commonality of forms (ways of behaving) whose content (meanings) may vary considerably among its members. The triumph of community is to so contain this variety that its inherent discordance does not subvert the apparent coherence which is expressed by its boundaries. If the members of a community come to feel that they have less in common with each other than they have with the members of some other community then, clearly, the boundaries have become anomalous and the integrity of the "community" they enclose has been severely impugned. The important thrust of this argument is that this relative similarity or difference is not a matter for "objective" assessment: it is a matter of feeling, a matter which resides in the minds of the members themselves. Thus, although they recognize important differences among themselves, they also suppose themselves to be more like

---

[58] *Ibid.*, p. 26.   [59] Cohen, *The Symbolic Construction of Community*, p. 20.

each other than like the members of other communities. This is precisely because, although the meanings they attach to the symbols may differ, they share the symbols. Indeed, their common ownership of symbols may be so intense that they may be quite unaware or unconcerned that they attach to them meanings which can differ from those of their fellows.[60]

Thus we find the potential for difference within commonality. Gusfield is helpful here. In a section entitled, "Pre-Conditions of Community," Gusfield explains that too often suggested pre-conditions for communal development do not result in communal formation, in fact, in some cases different and even opposite sources can be associated with communal emergence.[61] A homogeneous culture, for example, has often been posited as a mark of community. Languages, moralities, and common histories are assumed to produce a sense of being unique and different in comparison to other groups. This common perception, however, does not specify the boundaries of homogeneity. As Gusfield notes:

> Why don't Europeans develop strong communal ties, since they possess much of a common history and customs as compared to non-Europeans? Why did American Jews of German origin develop a strong communal identity with American Jews of Russian origin when their "cultures" were so opposite? What appears crucial are the situations in which the culture does or does not appear homogeneous; the perception among an aggregate of people that they constitute a community. This "consciousness of kind" is not an automatic product of an abstract "homogeneity."[62]

The second area often posited as a mark of community is common territory. "It has so frequently been posited as an essential condition for community that the term is sometimes coterminous with territory, as in the 'local community,' 'community studies,' 'community power structure.'"[63] According to this text, the concept of community is part of a system of symbols used by members and observers as a way of explaining or justifying a member's behavior. "It is the behavior governed by criteria of common belonging" that established the community, not the geographic region in which it occurs.[64]

---

[60] *Ibid.*, pp. 20–21.   [61] Gusfield, *Community*, p. 31.   [62] *Ibid.*, p. 32.   [63] *Ibid.*
[64] *Ibid.*, p. 33. Admittedly, the relation between territorial size and communalism remains a central issue in social theory. For our purposes, it is only important to state that the symbolic construction of early Christianity was assumed to spread much further than the borders of one Christian "group."

This understanding of difference within commonality makes sense of the evidence we have in other NT documents. Early Christianity was not devoid of a universal Christian sense or awareness. Three times Paul alleviates tension between what would seem to be different groups functioning under the symbolic Christian construction (1 Cor. 12:13; Gal. 3:28; Col. 3:11). Elsewhere Paul urges his readers to have concern for members in other areas within "church," even those whom they may not know personally (1 Cor. 8–9). This in no way implies that there was no intra-group conflict, just that it was intra-group and not inter-group. While we must be careful in our description of what first-century Christians saw as common between themselves in a comprehensive way, or how they dealt with their differences (which is why some prefer to speak of Christianities), this does not imply that the various versions within Christianity were any less Christian or that they saw other "Christians" as equal to a completely other religious system (e.g. Gentiles, or even Jews).[65] A recent collection of essays by Judith Lieu also confirms the more complex model of early Christianity.[66] According to Lieu, "the creation, at least rhetorically, of a self-conscious and distinctive identity is a remarkable characteristic of early Christianity from our earliest sources and from Christianity's equally characteristic literary creativity."[67] After critiquing the use of external models to denote various "communities," Lieu argues that such models are incapable of accounting for the evidence both within and outside the NT documents.[68] Although our understanding of the exact "identity" of early Christians must remain opaque, it seems that "Christians" may have viewed themselves as a new *genus*, a third "race."[69] In fact, Paul's theoretical construct of a new ἄνθρωπος (Col. 3:10) is the ultimate pattern and goal of all Christians. As Lieu explains, Paul's "letters bear eloquent testimony to the practical context, the creation of new communities both out of individuals and out of existing

---

[65] This more nuanced understanding of difference within commonality also makes sense of the patristic evidence we have concerning defenders of the early church, issues of heresy, and a universal gospel.

[66] Judith Lieu, *Neither Jew Nor Greek? Constructing Early Christianity*, SNTW (London: T. & T. Clark, 2002).

[67] *Ibid.*, p. 171. Averil Cameron, *Christianity and the Rhetoric of Empire: The Development of Christian Discourse*, SCL 45 (Berkeley: University of California Press, 1991), p. 21, argues similarly: "But if ever there was a case of the construction of reality through text, such a case is provided by early Christianity . . . Christians built themselves a new world. They did so partly through practice – the evolution of a mode of living and a communal discipline that carefully distinguished them from their pagan and Jewish neighbours – and partly through a discourse that was itself constantly brought under control and disciplined."

[68] Lieu, *Neither Jew Nor Greek?*, pp. 172–82.   [69] *Ibid.*, pp. 183–84.

networks or households of both Jewish and non-Jewish background without, theoretically, giving priority to either."[70] The research of Lieu and others shows how a more complex model of identity and "community" fits well with this text and its critique of the "communities" behind the Gospels.

Such a proposal also fits well with Peter Berger's description of a "plausibility structure" (symbolically constructed world) in his *The Sacred Canopy*: a work commonly used to describe the "group" consciousness of a Gospel "community." Although Berger makes a general distinction between an entire society which serves as a plausibility structure and situations in which only a sub-society serves as such, he never provides definitions to the forms or functions in which a "sub-society" might exist.[71] Certainly individual groups could have their own plausibility structure, but, as we have argued, the Gospels do not reflect such a use, as the use of other Gospels makes clear. Thus, when Philip Esler claims, in reference to the model presented by Berger, that "The importance of this model for New Testament criticism *depends on the view* that the New Testament documents were, by and large, written *for particular* early Christian communities and that *these communities may be regarded as social worlds* of the kind Berger describes," he has misapplied Berger's model.[72] Berger never shows how to make a distinction between a sub-society, which would certainly be characteristic of the early Christian movement, and particular early Christian communities that are "part of" that sub-society. Such a move by Esler is a misuse of Berger's "plausibility structure" model.[73]

Finally, recent research in Jewish "communities" reveals a striking similarity to our proposed definition of "community." John Barclay, in a monograph devoted to *Jews in the Mediterranean Diaspora*, argues that a more complex analysis of "Judaism" is needed than has traditionally been suggested. Barclay argues that recent research has reacted against the generalizations spawned by previous generations of scholars.[74] What is interesting for our purposes is Barclay's portrayal of the unity of Diaspora Judaism, even amidst all the diversity in the different locations

---

[70] *Ibid.*, p. 184. Lieu admits that "The fragility of the construct, both practically and theoretically, is equally clear."

[71] Berger, *The Sacred Canopy: Elements of A Sociological Theory of Religion* (Garden City, NY: Doubleday, 1967), pp. 48–49.

[72] Esler, *The First Christians in their Social Worlds: Social Scientific Approaches to New Testament Interpretation* (London: Routledge, 1994), p. 6 (emphasis added).

[73] See a similar critique by Stephen Motyer, *Your Father the Devil? A New Approach to John and "the Jews,"* PBTS (Carlisle: Paternoster, 1997), pp. 30–31.

[74] Barclay, *Jews in the Mediterranean Diaspora*, p. 400.

catalogued earlier in the monograph. According to Barclay although "Jewish identity could be presented differently according to context . . . such varying Jewish profiles do not necessarily represent different 'Judaisms': one and the same socio-religious phenomenon can wear many masks."[75] The reason for this is two-fold: ethnic bonds and social and symbolic resources; the latter of which is especially pertinent to our study. According to Barclay, these "social and symbolic resources" allowed Diaspora Jews to bond at the local community level, but also at the wider level of "networks which joined Jews of *diverse communities* together."[76] What is most surprising in this regard is how well Barclay's findings mesh with Martyn's proposal for a unified Judaism that was organized enough to produce the *Birkat ha-Minim*, that is, the systematic excommunication of Jewish-Christians from Jewish synagogues.[77] According to Martyn, "clearly [this] is a formal agreement or *decision* reached by some *authoritative Jewish group* . . . We are not dealing with an *ad hoc* move on the part of the authorities . . ."[78] Of course, even though Martyn's proposal is rarely accepted in total, as we will discuss in chapter 3, the very idea that Martyn's Judaism was able to view itself as a single unit, even after centuries of strife, causing some scholars to prefer the term "Judaisms," makes his following assumption, that the Christians were isolated, closed "communities," extremely difficult to reconcile. For such a "formal decision" to have occurred, it would not only have required that Judaism had come to recognize "Christianity" as diametrically opposed to itself, but more importantly that Judaism had come to recognize "itself," with all its diversity both ideologically and geographically, as a unified movement with various "groups" working in some synthesized fashion, having communication and general agreement between them. And all of this, or at least its recognition and response to Christianity, would have had to occur in less than seventy years, since "Christianity" had come into existence, the last thirty of which were after the core and center of the Jewish faith, the temple, had been destroyed. Why, if Judaism could have been so organized and unified, according to Martyn, could not Christianity have had a similar recognition of identity? If Jewish sources can

---

[75] *Ibid.*, p. 401. Barclay is not alone in his dislike of "Judaisms." See E. P. Sanders, *Jewish Law from Jesus to the Mishnah. Five Studies* (London: SCM Press, 1990), pp. 255–56; and Richard Bauckham, "The Parting of the Ways: What Happened and Why?," *ST* 47 (1993), pp. 135–41. According to Barclay, it would appear that models drawn implicitly from Christian denominations or from contemporary varieties in Judaism have led the historian astray at this point (p. 401, n. 2).

[76] Barclay, *Jews in the Mediterranean Diaspora*, p. 413 (emphasis added).

[77] Martyn, *History and Theology in the Fourth Gospel*, pp. 46–66.   [78] *Ibid.*, p. 47.

be viewed as depicting the larger Jewish movements and thought-world, then in principle the Christian sources can as well.

Returning to the unity of Judaism, Barclay discusses several unifying resources, each of which we will discuss and relate to early Christianity. The first Jewish resource is the link with Jerusalem, the "homeland," and the temple. Both before 70 CE and certainly after the temple was primarily a conceptual reality for Diaspora Jews. But it was a significant concept, for it was the "base" of Judaism, as can be witnessed by the annual collection of dues required for the temple prior to 70 CE. Although some in early Christianity may have seen Jesus as a replacement for the temple (John 2:21), Jerusalem was still an important "base" for early Christians. The fact that Paul went to Jerusalem more than once (Gal. 2:1) implies a wide recognition of the functional centrality of a Christian leadership. A second Jewish resource is the Law/Scriptures. The importance of "the Scriptures," as evidenced by the unequivocal use of the term γραφή, is no less important to early Christians. The use of the Jewish Scriptures (OT) and a devout spreading of an oral tradition about Jesus and his disciples are evident in the early movement, even in local worship.[79] The third Jewish resource is the figure of Moses. Certainly the figure of Jesus in early Christianity is of equal if not greater standing than Moses is to Judaism (see John 9:28). The existence of four Gospel *bioi* about Jesus makes this abundantly clear. Even some of the earliest followers of Jesus were forced (honored) to bear his name: "Christians."[80] Finally, the fourth Jewish resource is practical distinctions. Barclay describes how regular practices in daily life focused Jews on their distinctiveness, and hence their unity. For Jews this can be seen in their rejection of alien, pluralist, and iconic cults, the separatism at meals, the circumcision of males, and the Sabbath observance.[81] Early Christians also had found unity in their rejection of other "religious" groups' perspectives; in fact, it might be argued that "the Jews" were one of the groups that were rejected. The important Christian meal became the Eucharist, which also had separatist components (1 Cor. 11:17–34). The NT makes clear that circumcision of the "heart" became of great importance, which was symbolized in Christian baptism. In conclusion, we have argued that taken cumulatively, there were several symbolic resources for early Christians that incorporated them into a "community" much larger than their own local community. Just as Jews in the Mediterranean Diaspora were able to form a "web of social and

[79] See the classic discussion of this by Oscar Cullmann, *Early Christian Worship*, trans. A. Stewart Todd and James B. Torrance, SBT 10 (London: SCM Press, 1953).
[80] This probably occurred only in Greek- and Latin-speaking contexts.
[81] Barclay, *Jews in the Mediterranean Diaspora*, pp. 428–42.

religious commitments"[82] that allowed interconnection amidst diversity, so also the Christian "communities" could see beyond their geographic borders to a reality greater than their own.

Of course, this does not imply a complete unity between different geographic communities, for certainly individual boundaries defined themselves over and against other communities. Again, what is needed is a more complex analysis. Although there may never have been a single, identifiable "Christian" identity; that does not imply that each "community" was its own "Christianity." Certainly Christian "communities" can not simply be defined by their individual ideological stances, as if they never saw themselves as part of a larger "community." Thus, for each group one needs to determine in what ways they viewed themselves as part of the broader "Christian" community, and in what ways they attempted to correct it (and other "deviant" forms of Christianity). Thus, using the FG as an example, certainly John saw a boundary that some groups might have extended beyond (John 15; cf. 1 John 2), yet he also maintains some general flexibility that would agree with several "communities." Again, turning to an earlier essay by John Barclay we find similar evidence within Judaism:

> individual Jewish communities could clearly take some definitions for granted and a certain unity of mind is sometimes perceptible *both within individual communities and across geographical and temporal bounds.* Philo tells us his own opinion on who has "deserted the ancestral customs," but also indicates the viewpoint of "the masses" in the Jewish community in Alexandria with which he is largely in accord. We can also discern certain topics (e.g. engagement in "idolatrous" worship and eating unclean foods) on which there appears to have been a fair degree of unanimity across different Jewish communities in our period. Thus *we need not suppose that every case of "deviating" behavior had to be negotiated from scratch in the community* as to its "deviant" or "non-deviant" status.[83]

This is not to deny that early Christianity's highly fluid conditions had less "taken-for-granted norms," as Barclay describes it, than a more established Judaism, and that the future of Christianity was determined by

[82] *Ibid.*, p. 442.
[83] Barclay, "Deviance and Apostasy: Some Applications of Deviance Theory to First-Century Judaism and Christianity," in Philip F. Esler (ed.), *Modeling Early Christianity: Social-Scientific Studies of the New Testament in its Context* (London: Routledge, 1995), p. 119 (emphasis added).

power contests, as no historian can deny, but it does imply that these struggles were not fought only by individual "communities" and without a concept of a larger "Christian" movement.[84] Thus, far from seeing John or any of the Gospels as attempting to completely supplant the other Gospels ideologically, as if the only relationship that can exist between these documents (and their "communities") is either complete acceptance or rejection, one may begin to see areas of common "unity of mind" and other areas of differing boundaries. The very fact that we even have a "Synoptic problem" would seem to point in this direction. Each Gospel does provide a definition of "Christianity" that is unique, but it is not in complete isolation or disagreement with other "versions" of other early Christians. The very fact that some evangelist would use large sections of Mark for their own presentations would seem to argue against a reading of each Gospel as representative of a limited audience. A more complex model is needed, one that accounts for the use of two or more "Gospels" for any given audience.

Definition of community: conclusion

This book is proposing that a more complex model be applied to the assumed audiences of the Gospels. Rather than defining a Gospel audience based upon a territorial or ideological model of community, we propose to define the audience based upon a relational model of community. This would, in the words of Bauckham, make the Gospels intended for "any and every Christian" reader in the first century. The key word for our purposes is not "any and every," but "Christian." Using a relational model, the Gospels would have been appropriate reading material for several geographic communities throughout the Roman Empire. Readers who were not even aware of the other's existence could participate together in the story told by the Gospels, based upon their related symbolic construction. "People who do not know each other nevertheless see themselves in the same category and share the same friends and enemies."[85] For the early Christians, the Gospels were a story that many, if not most, could share. Even amidst the diversity, and often a redefining of friends and enemies, they all saw themselves as partakers in the same story.[86]

---

[84] *Ibid.*, p. 125.   [85] Gusfield, *Community*, p. 49.

[86] This concept of a more worldwide church goes against the sectarian division model used by several interpreters, including David Sim, "The Gospels for All Christians? A Response to Richard Bauckham," who presented a major critique against Bauckham and

A community that is sectarian: John the sectarian document?

One of the hermeneutical siblings of "community" terminology in the interpretation of the Gospels is "sectarian" terminology. A full discussion of sectarianism and the early Christian movement is beyond the scope of this book. This book will argue that the model and definition of "community" we proposed above works against the sectarian model frequently applied to Gospel audiences. Our goal in this section is to critique the use of sectarian terminology as a model for interpretation, as well as to examine one influential application of the model in the FG.

Early Christianity as sectarian

Two of the earliest attempts in applying social concepts and models to a sectarian understanding of early Christianity, both published in 1975, used the comparative method.[87] The one compared early Christianity to millenarian movements using the social scientific tradition of anthropological research;[88] the other compared early Christianity to the sectarian

GAC in this area. But Sim's critique against the interconnectedness of the first-century church was not based on conceptual understanding, the symbolic construction of community, but on historical evidence of travel. For our purposes, all that is required is that there is enough evidence to conclude that the early Christian movement saw itself as broader than its own geographic region. All that is needed is cognitive recognition, not literal contact. Two later essays in GAC provide further support for this. Michael B. Thompson, "The Holy Internet: Communication between Churches in the First Christian Generation," especially pp. 68–70, argues that between 30 and 70 CE the churches had the motivation and the means to communicate often and in depth with each other. Later, Loveday Alexander, "Ancient Book Production and the Circulation of the Gospels," argues that a study of ancient book production reveals "that the writing down of the Gospels itself implies the crossing of an invisible boundary between the implicitly limited audience of an oral performance and the wider audience that can be reached by a written text" (p. 100). Even Wayne Meeks, *The First Urban Christians*, p. 107, argues that "the local groups of Christians not only enjoyed a high level of cohesion and group identity, they were also made aware that they belonged to a larger movement, 'with all who invoke the name of the Lord Jesus Christ in every place' (1 Cor. 1:2)." Although Meeks does not see what he calls a "unique network of institutions" taking place until later in the movement, he admits that our earliest sources show both aspects of a double identity (particular Christian community and universal Christianity) already at work (pp. 107–08).

[87] The millenarian model was used by John Gager, *Kingdom and Community: The Social World of Early Christianity* (Englewood Cliffs: Prentice-Hall, 1975); the sectarian model was used by Robin Scroggs, "The Earliest Christian Communities as Sectarian Movement," in Jacob Neusner (ed.), *Christianity, Judaism and Other Greco-Roman Cults. Studies for Morton Smith at Sixty*, 4 vols., SJLA 12 (Leiden: Brill, 1975), vol. II, pp. 1–23.

[88] Gager used primarily the research of Kenelm Burridge, *New Heaven, New Earth: A Study of Millenarian Activities* (Oxford: Blackwell, 1969); but Gager also used the research of Ian Charles Jarvie, *The Revolution in Anthropology* (Chicago: Henry Regnery, 1967);

movements based upon early research in sociology of religion. In both these models the assumption is that it was specific social forces that led to the rise of Christianity, created a social identity, and led to the social organization of the first believers. A brief description of these two interrelated models is needed.

Since Gager, it has become common to describe early Christianity as a millenarian movement. In 1979, Wayne Meeks argued that Pauline Christianity can rightfully be called millenarian.[89] From his detailed analysis of how apocalyptic language is used in some of Paul's letters, Meeks concludes that the concept of millenarianism is a useful model in describing Pauline communities.[90] In 1986, Robert Jewett describes how the church in Thessalonica was millenarian.[91] Using Gager's "pathbreaking" millenarian model, Jewett uses it only on one congregation and not on the entire Christian movement.[92] More recent examples include the discussion by Philip Esler on the application of millenarian research within the social sciences to Jewish and Christian literature[93] and Dennis C. Duling's thorough survey of the literature that applies millenarianism to early Christianity.[94] Thus, for many NT interpreters, the world of the early Christians is seen through the grid of a millenarian movement that is directly related to their social situation and a worldview of deprivation.

Related to the millenarian grid for reading early Christianity is the sociology of sectarianism. The classic typology of "church" and "sect" originated in the work of Max Weber. His student, Ernst Troeltsch, developed further a typology which took into account much of the descriptive

Yonina Talmon, "Pursuit of the Millennium: The Relation between Religious and Social Change," *AES* 3 (1962), pp. 25–48; repr. in W. Lessa and E. Vogt (eds.), *Reader in Comparative Religion: An Anthropological Approach*, 2nd edn (New York: Harper & Row, 1965), pp. 522–57; and Peter Worsley, *The Trumpet Shall Sound: A Study of "Cargo" Cults in Melanesia* (New York: Schocken Books, 1968).

[89] Meeks, "Social Functions of Apocalyptic Language in Pauline Christianity," in David Hellholm (ed.), *Apocalypticism in the Mediterranean World and the Near East: Proceedings of the International Colloquium on Apocalypticism: Uppsala: August 12–17, 1979* (Tübingen: Mohr, 1983), pp. 687–706.

[90] See the detailed discussion in Holmberg, *Sociology and the New Testament*, pp. 81–83.

[91] Jewett, *The Thessalonian Correspondence: Pauline Rhetoric and Millenarian Piety* (Philadelphia: Fortress, 1986).

[92] *Ibid.*, p. 162, n. 10. According to Holmberg, *Sociology and the New Testament*, p. 85, Jewett's application of Gager's model is clearly an improvement, most notably due to the more specific target group and the more detailed sociological definition given.

[93] Esler, *The First Christians in their Social Worlds*, pp. 92–109.

[94] Duling, "Millennium," in Richard L. Rohrbaugh (ed.), *The Social Sciences and New Testament Interpretation* (Peabody: Hendrickson, 1996), pp. 183–205.

material from the history of the Christian church.[95] For Troeltsch, the "church" accepts the world and society in which it lives, is conservative, and supports the values of the ruling class. It recruits and accepts everyone in principle and includes them into its salvific system. The "sect" is the opposite: a small group of intensely religious people, into which one enters by a conscious act of conversion and remains by adhering to a demanding group ethos and group behavior. The sect is usually indifferent to or critical of the world outside; often it has started as a protest movement against the "church," which it considers as worldly and degenerate.[96]

The initial social-scientific work that made the sectarian model popular as a comparison to early Christianity was by Robin Scroggs in "The Earliest Christian Communities as Sectarian Movement." Scroggs, using the work that had been done in sociology of religion by Weber and Troeltsch, as well as the well-defined sociological model of sectarian religion offered by Werner Stark,[97] gave a sociological interpretation of the sectarian nature of the early Christian communities. According to Scroggs the religious sect has seven characteristics, all of which fit "the earliest church directly stemming from the mission of Jesus."[98] For Scroggs, the same NT data that are so often viewed from an over-theologized perspective can now be seen in a fresh light. He states, "We now have a basically different *Gestalt* from which to view the data."[99] Using Mark as an example Scroggs states: "Recent work on the redaction history of Mark, combined with the awareness that the church was sectarian, open the door toward a new understanding based on the lived realities of the people rather than on some theological slogan."[100] In this way, Scroggs attempts to make visible the hidden sociological situation behind the Gospel texts.

Since Scroggs, it has become common to describe early Christianity as a sectarian movement. Already in 1972 Wayne Meeks made a somewhat implicit reference to the JComm as a sect in his "The Man from Heaven

---

[95] Troeltsch, *The Social Teachings of the Christian Church*, trans. Olive Wyon (London: George Allen & Unwin, 1931). Originally published in German as *Die Soziallehren der christlichen Kirchen und Gruppen* (Tübingen: Mohr, 1912).

[96] Adapted from the discussion by Holmberg, *Sociology and the New Testament*, pp. 86–87. For a survey of the research history of this sociology of religion category see Meredith B. McGuire, *Religion: The Social Context* (Belmont, Calif.: Wadsworth, 1981), ch. 5, "The Dynamics of Religious Collectives." See also the more critical perspective of James A. Beckford, "Religious Organization," *CS* 21 (1973), pp. 1–170, especially 12–18.

[97] Stark, *Sociology of Religion: A Study of Christendom*, vol. II, "Sectarian Religion" (London: Routledge & Kegan Paul, 1967).

[98] Scroggs, "The Earliest Christian Communities as Sectarian Movement," p. 7.

[99] *Ibid.*, p. 21.   [100] *Ibid.*, p. 22.

in Johannine Sectarianism." Although the title reveals as much, Meeks merely states that the community is sectarian without providing any justification for the classification.[101] In 1981 John Elliott, taking his starting point from the sectarian investigation of Robin Scroggs and Bryan Wilson, argues that there is a close relationship between the characteristics of a sect and the situation of the recipients of 1 Peter.[102] In 1985 Christopher Rowland argues that Christianity should be viewed as one of many Jewish sects in pre-70 Judaism.[103] For Rowland it is impossible to speak of Judaism as a well-defined orthodoxy against which Christianity stood out as evidently heretical; belief in a messiah and in the claim that the Scriptures had actually been fulfilled were not unique to Christianity.[104] In 1987 Philip Esler applies Troeltsch's church-sect model to the early Christian communities and, with the help of Bryan Wilson's typology of sectarian responses to the world, argues that the Christian congregation behind Luke-Acts had a separate and sectarian existence apart from the Judaism they were once part of.[105] Since these studies various other sectarian models have been applied to the NT documents to help explain the relationship of the Christian movement organizationally to the world in which it arose.[106] Thus, for many interpreters the world of the early Christians is seen through the grid of a sectarian movement that is directly related to their progressively schismatic relationship between their Jewish heritage and their new-found faith. The tension between the new Christians and the Jews is what the NT documents are reflecting and are, perhaps, specifically created to help the early Christians find their way in a new "world."

[101] Meeks, "The Man From Heaven in Johannine Sectarianism," *JBL* 91 (1972), p. 70; similarly, see his later essay "Breaking Away: Three New Testament Pictures of Christianity's Separation from the Jewish Communities," in Jacob Neusner and Ernest S. Frerichs (eds.), *"To See Ourselves as Others See Us": Christians, Jews, "Others" in Late Antiquity* (Chico, Calif.: Scholars Press, 1985), p. 103, n. 27.

[102] Elliott, *A Home for the Homeless*, pp. 73–78.

[103] Rowland, *Christian Origins: An Account of the Setting and Character of the Most Important Sect of Judaism* (London: SPCK, 1985), p. xvii.

[104] *Ibid.*, pp. 65, 263. Meeks, "Breaking Away," p. 93, argues that it is inappropriate to assume that every observant Jew would have been a member of some sect, "any more than a majority of non-Jews were Stoics, Platonists, or Epicureans."

[105] Esler, *Community and Gospel in Luke-Acts*, specifically pp. 6–12, for a good summary of Esler's social-science methodology.

[106] Further examples include Rodney Stark, "The Class Basis of Early Christianity: Inferences from a Sociological Model," *SA* 47 (1986), pp. 216–25; Francis Watson, *Paul, Judaism, and the Gentiles: A Sociological Approach* (Cambridge: Cambridge University Press, 1986); Margaret Y. MacDonald, *The Pauline Churches: A Socio-historical Study of Institutionalization in the Pauline and Deutero-Pauline Writings* (Cambridge: Cambridge University Press, 1988).

Although the millenarian and sectarian models have been popular, they have not been completely well received. Referring to the millenarian model, Thomas Best claims:

> it is not clear that a model derived from Melanesian culture is appropriate for understanding a movement among generally urban, relatively sophisticated men and women in the Hellenistic world. And why use as a model a group which awaited Jesus in splendid isolation upon a mountain-top, when withdrawal from the world was precisely what Paul forbade his churches to do (1 Cor 5:9–10)?[107]

The sectarian model is no different. While some scholars have tried to argue that comparison with a sectarian movement outside of the Judeo-Christian tradition is invalid, others have even been more defeating to the comparison by arguing that these so-called distant comparisons are not so distant after all.[108] According to Jonathan Smith, even the models used by social anthropologists were not used independently of Christian evidence.[109] Thus, the comparisons cannot even be used fairly to judge the Christian evidence, since their own criteria were assisted by related evidence. In the end, the use of the millenarian and/or sectarian model can be accused of simplifying complex realities in the attempt to depict the apocalyptic tenor of early Christianity.[110]

The focus of this book is not on the inappropriate nature of the entire sectarian model[111] per se, although our discussion leads in that direction. Rather, we want to argue that the sectarian model has been uncritically applied to Gospel audiences. The sectarian model is unable to hold together (and separate) both the complex individuality of various groups within the early Christian movement, as well as the inter-connectedness of the movement as a whole. For our purposes, then, and based upon

---

[107] Best, "The Sociological Study of the New Testament," p. 189.

[108] According to Christopher Rowland, "Reading the New Testament Sociologically: An Introduction," *Theology* 88 (1985), pp. 358–64, especially p. 360, the entire millenarian model comparison should not be attempted with millenarian movements outside the Judeo-Christian tradition; preferable examples would come from movements like that of Jewish messiah Sabbatai Sevi. But, as has been pointed out by Holmberg, *Sociology and the New Testament*, Rowland is only placing the researcher in the opposite difficulty: a too great proximity. "Similarities between sixteenth-century Christian movements and the early church can be more readily explained as attempts by the later Christians to emulate the New Testament ideal than as the influence of some universal millenarian pattern" (p. 80).

[109] Smith, "Too Much Kingdom, Too Little Community," *Zygon* 13 (1978), pp. 127–28.

[110] As has been argued by Derek Tidball, *An Introduction to the Sociology of the New Testament* (Exeter: Paternoster, 1983), p. 40.

[111] Our focus on the sectarian model here is due to its popularity among current Gospel "community" reconstructions.

the model we presented above, several specific objections can be labeled against the sectarian model.[112]

The first objection against the sectarian model is that it is unable to describe correctly the whole of the early Christian movement. Scroggs states in a later article that his sectarian analysis cannot be applied without alterations to the urban churches of the Hellenistic mission.[113] It could be questioned whether even the picture painted of early Palestinian Christianity is accurate. Günther Baumbach has pointed out that although the sectarian definition may fit the Essene communities, when applied to the early Christians it is easy to note several differences.[114] Just the use of the term "sect" over against the term "church" as its opposite gives one the connotation of a group opposition or deviance from the official church or religion. Yet although "identity" issues between Jews and Christians were certainly at the center of much debate, "this terminology tends to import a distortive characterization into the allegedly neutral, ideal-typical classification."[115]

A second objection against the sectarian model is its cultural limitation.[116] Troeltsch's categorization of church-sect was primarily intended for comparing and contrasting concrete historical developments in the Christian church, not for creating a universal classification scheme.[117] In fact the use of such a model, even one that has supposedly been made less culture-bound, often defines "religion" unconsciously by the picture of the later Christian church, so that sects are often measured by their degrees of organizational or doctrinal formalization. Bryan Wilson, concerning the misuse of his own sectarian research, states:

> But the conscious creation of formal and systematic organizations is in large measure a phenomenon that is culturally specific to western society . . . Perhaps the most important defect of the characterization of sects by doctrinal divergence from orthodoxy is that, like characterization in terms of organization, it puts too much emphasis on specifically Christian preoccupations.[118]

---

[112] We are not attempting to state that the use of the sectarian model has no validity, we are simply pointing out several weaknesses with the model, especially in relation to the issues involved in reading the Gospels.

[113] Scroggs, "The Sociological Interpretation of the New Testament," p. 172, n. 26.

[114] Baumbach, "Die Anfänge der Kirchwerdung im Urchristentum," *Kairos* 24 (1982), pp. 17–30.

[115] Holmberg, *Sociology and the New Testament*, p. 91. Taken from Baumbach, "Die Anfänge der Kirchwerdung im Urchristentum," pp. 21–22.

[116] The following objections are adapted from Holmberg, *Sociology and the New Testament*, pp. 108–14.

[117] Roland Robertson, *The Sociological Interpretation of Religion* (Oxford: Oxford University Press, 1972), pp. 116–17.

[118] Wilson, *Magic and the Millennium*, pp. 13, 16.

In reality the use of the sectarian model, even with the advances of its application, is really a process of circular reasoning where the Christian sects of later ages are used to analyze and explain the very movement that they all wanted to imitate.[119]

A third objection is its analytical limitation. The initial problem concerns gross oversimplification.

> On the one hand, the idea of sect itself is described in a very general way, so that it is hardly surprising that the early church can be described as sectarian, especially when one begins to suspect that the characteristics of the ideal type have been taken from early Christianity in the first place! On the other hand, early Christianity is described also in a general and monolithic way as a peasant protest movement reacting against oppression and marginalization from an equally undifferentiated body called "the establishment." . . . So, as a tool of analysis, the sect model . . . seems to be a very blunt one indeed.[120]

There have been several critiques of the church-sect distinction.[121] One of the most comprehensive is by James Beckford, who shows that there exists a logical structure of contrasting dualities that runs through most of the conventional usages of church and sect.[122] This reveals that there is an abundance of dual alternatives which offers innumerable possibilities of confusion, and often the variables that are used are neither logically

---

[119] Best, "The Sociological Study of the New Testament," pp. 188–89; Holmberg, *Sociology and the New Testament*, pp. 109–10. This is not to deny that our model is circular, for all models must be externally imposed upon a text and its reading. But if it can be helped, such radically circular methods of interpretation should be avoided.

[120] Barton, "Early Christianity and the Sociology of the Sect," p. 144.

[121] Peter L. Berger, "The Sociological Study of Sectarianism," *SR* 21 (1954), pp. 467–85; Benton Johnson, "On Church and Sect," *ASR* 28 (1963), pp. 539–49; Erich Goode, "Some Critical Observations on the Church-Sect Dimension," *JSSR* 6 (1967), pp. 69–77; Nicholas J. Demerath III, "In a Sow's Ear: A Reply to Goode," *JSSR* 6 (1967), pp. 77–84; Demerath, "Son of a Sow's Ear," *JSSR* 6 (1967), pp. 257–77; Alan W. Eister, "Toward a Radical Critique of Church-Sect Typologizing: Comment on 'Some Critical Observations on the Church-Sect Dimension,'" *JSSR* 6 (1967), pp. 85–99; Eister, "H. Richard Neibuhr and the Paradox of Religious Organization: A Radical Critique," in Charles Y. Clock and Phillip E. Hammond (eds.), *Beyond the Classics? Essays in the Scientific Study of Religion* (New York: Harper & Row, 1973), pp. 355–408; J. Kenneth Benson and James H. Dorsett, "Toward a Theory of Religious Organizations," *JSSR* 10 (1971), pp. 138–51; James E. Dittes, "Typing the Typologies: Some Parallels in the Career of Church-Sect and Extrinsic-Intrinsic," *JSSR* 10 (1971), pp. 375–83; and Hans G. Kippenberg, "Ein Vergleich jüdischer, christlicher und gnostischer Apokalyptik," in David Hellholm (ed.), *Apocalypticism in the Mediterranean World and the Near East: Proceedings of the International Colloquium on Apocalypticism: Uppsala, August 12–17, 1979* (Tübingen: Mohr, 1983), pp. 751–68.

[122] Beckford, "Religious Organization," *CS* 21 (1973), pp. 92–104.

nor factually connected with each other, but vary independently.[123] In some cases, the use of such loaded terminology with powerful rhetoric may blind us to other data and other possibilities of interpretation.[124] In the end, according to Holmberg, "Because of its historical and cultural limitations, the lack of precision in the construction of types, and the inherent tendency to static reification of the typology, the church-sect categorization of religious groups seems to be a rather doubtful instrument of analysis."[125] This has been confirmed more recently by Philip Harland who, after examining the evidence of interaction between "groups" in ancient Mediterranean society, argues that sectarian studies correctly note the differences between a certain "group" and society, but are not complex enough to see the areas where the NT documents accept and even promote cultural values, conventions, and practices of civic life.[126] According to Harland,

> The problem is that many scholars do not pay adequate attention to the concrete and complex ways in which local associations, synagogues, and assemblies found a place in polis and empire. When scholars do address the subject of group-society interaction . . . quite often they focus on issues of tension and sectarianism without sufficient regard for other evidence concerning positive interaction . . . The evidence . . . suggests the strong possibility that some Christians were maintaining multiple affiliations of memberships within social groupings other than just the Christian assemblies.[127]

Evidence of this sort forces one to question the application of a sectarian model to "groups" within the Christian movement, especially with whom we have no actual "group" evidence.[128] Harland's comments support our proposed concept of community.

[123] *Ibid.*, pp. 93–97.
[124] Barton, "Early Christianity and the Sociology of the Sect," p. 144. In such cases, the ideological emphasis or bias of the interpreter will influence the outcome.
[125] Holmberg, *Sociology and the New Testament*, p. 112.
[126] Harland, *Associations, Synagogues, and Associations: Claiming a Place in Ancient Mediterranean Society* (Minneapolis: Fortress Press, 2003), pp. 8–15, 180–269.
[127] *Ibid.*, pp. 14, 184.
[128] A recent example of the futility of the model in Johannine studies can be found in a recent monograph on John and sectarianism in Kre Sigvald Fuglseth, *Johannine Sectarianism in Perspective: A Sociological, Historical, and Comparative Analysis of Temple and Social Relationships in the Gospel of John, Philo, and Qumran*, NovTSup 119 (Leiden: Brill, 2005). Fuglseth's response to the general audience theory proposed by *GAC* is that it is "a vague and imprecise notion for a gospel like John. . . ." and "fails to explain the peculiarities of John" (p. 69). Yet, as Fuglseth is forced to admit on numerous occasions, there is no evidence for the sectarian "group" he is still willing to propose: "Unfortunately,

A fourth objection, and one most pertinent to this study, is its limitation of explanatory power.[129] If it is possible to conclude that early Christianity of just about every hue was sectarian – Matthean as well as Markan and Lukan, Johannine as well as Pauline and Petrine – we are forced to conclude that the term "sect" has only relatively weak explanatory power.[130] Even then, there is nothing close to a scholarly consensus on the distinction between the various sectarian groups in early Christianity. Some make no distinction at all and see the entire movement as sectarian (Gager[131] and Rowland[132]); some see the earliest movement in Palestine as having sectarian characteristics, but none that prevailed in the later movement (Scroggs[133]); some consider Pauline Christianity to be a clear example of a sect (Meeks[134]), even arguing that it is the first example of a sect in the early Christian movement (Watson[135]); some focus on various, more specific examples of sects like Lukan Christianity (Esler[136]) or the messianic sect seen in 1 Peter (Elliott[137]), while one scholar considers the entire period 50–140 CE as a characteristically Pauline sect (MacDonald[138]). The diversity reveals that just the use of such a model in a vague sense does little to classify the early Christian movement; it

the number of statements giving us prosopographic and sociographic information . . . is few" (p. 70); "there are no references to an author or group in the Fourth Gospel that may be compared to . . . community life found in the New Testament letters" (p. 70); "All constructive conclusions therefore remain weak in nature" (p .73); even the ecclesiological allusions and metaphors are unable to provide "conclusive arguments for the existence of a community of Johannine Christians" (p. 81); Fuglseth claims that his proposal "seems to be a well-founded thesis, but it is still an inference from allusions and a meta-perspective and cannot in itself be conclusive for the quest of the Johannine community . . ." (p. 82); and finally, "There are in fact few texts that bear witness to the existence of a community that cannot also be taken as referring to a general reader or all Christians" (p. 83). Only after Fuglseth assumes a "group" behind the FG is he able to do his comparative analysis with other "analogous movements or groups" (p. 84). But has he really defined the Johannine group, the one he cannot find sufficient evidence for in the Gospel itself? His modified sectarian model ("cultic"), though a nice heuristic device, is unable to deal with the complexity of John.

[129] Holmberg, *Sociology and the New Testament*, p. 79.
[130] Barton, "Early Christianity and the Sociology of the Sect," p. 158.
[131] Gager, *Kingdom and Community*.
[132] Christopher Rowland, *Christian Origins: An Account of the Setting and Character of the Most Important Messianic Sect of Judaism* (London: SPCK, 1985).
[133] Scroggs, "The Earliest Christian Communities as Sectarian Movement."
[134] Meeks, *The First Urban Christians*, pp. 84–107; "Breaking Away: Three New Testament Pictures of Christianity's Separation from the Jewish Communities," in J. Neusner and E. S. Frerichs (eds.), *"To See Ourselves as Others See Us": Christians, Jews, "Others" in Late Antiquity* (Chico, Calif.: Scholars Press, 1985), pp. 93–115.
[135] Watson, *Paul, Judaism, and the Gentiles*.
[136] Esler, *Community and Gospel in Luke-Acts*.
[137] Elliott, *A Home for the Homeless*.   [138] MacDonald, *The Pauline Churches*.

only clutters our understanding of it.[139] Holmberg explains it well when, in reference to the diverse conclusions, he states, "This may, of course, be due to the fecundity of scholarly imagination, but it may also point to the same conclusion as above: when looking at the 'sectarian' character of early Christianity, scholars are actually investigating rather different aspects of their object."[140] Thus, the sectarian model can really only be regarded as interesting illustrative material, but not as a model with explanatory force. The use of sectarian terminology does little to explain, but actually raises more questions; especially of the differences between the presumption of one document's audience and the connection between that document (and its audience) and the rest of the early Christian movement.[141]

One of the key aspects of both millenarian and sectarian[142] approaches to "groups" and their documents is the distinction the "group" makes between "them and us." Since human reality and human relationships are socially constructed, a "group's" document allows one to see into their "world." Of course, this is much easier for groups whose external conflicts and contexts are known so that the symbolic language can be explained by the specific social-historical context. But where a context is unknown, let alone the specific make-up of the "group," the task is more difficult. It

---

[139] The term "sect," like the term "community," is too loaded to leave undefined. The fact that sociologists have difficulty defining the term, let alone using it, should signal warning to its use by scholars trained in biblical literature. The term "parties" may be more appropriate. For example, is a Christian group a "sect" in relation to wider society or to a mainline religious group? If the latter, how can Christian Jews who still attended and participated in the temple be truly sectarian? Even if they were removed from the Synagogue, would not that imply that they saw themselves as conjoined to Judaism, not removed from it? Their symbolic construction would be more holistic than sectarian. If the former, all Christianity was sectarian to the world in a loose sense. How are we able to assume John is fully sectarian to the world, in the sense of a completely negative view, when Paul could speak of the world in both negative and positive light, depending on his audience and his perception of their "boundary" needs? Cf. Edward Adams, *Constructing the World: A Study in Paul's Cosmological Language*, SNTW (Edinburgh: T. & T. Clark, 2000), pp. 239–47.

[140] Holmberg, *Sociology and the New Testament*, p. 114.

[141] Interestingly, Raymond Brown, *The Community of the Beloved Disciple*, pp. 16–17, refuses to use the sectarian concept, although it is certainly related to his method, because the term "sect" in application to the FG is too often given "radical interpretations" and because "there is enough evidence on either side of the issue to make them unconvincing and to point toward a more nuanced interpretation of Johannine Christology and ecclesiology. At any rate, there is little to be gained by debating once more such points." Brown never pre-determines the nature of the JComm, but lets the two "levels" in John, using Martyn, *History and Theology in the Fourth Gospel*, and redaction criticism, tell the life and story of the community, whatever its social formation.

[142] Since current discussion centers upon the term "sectarian," we will use it as our primary term.

is here where we find the NT documents. John's Gospel is well traversed by sociologists who attempt to determine the audience's context by the language used. It is to John and its language that we now turn.

Antilanguage: John's sectarian audience and speech accommodation

It is not enough to apply a different model to the Gospel audience. What is needed is to show that a different model does better justice to the text at hand. Although a full testing of our proposed reading of John will not occur until chapter 5, for now it is appropriate to evaluate a common hermeneutical move in the FG; a move that sees within the language of John a code of communication that expresses more than the "plain" words of the narrative. This language communicates out of a specific context. It is here that the sectarian model, when applied to the context and language, called antilanguage because of its root in a sectarian, anti-world context, is made understandable. What is needed is a critique of this recent concept of antilanguage and its influence on the interpretation of the FG.

It was Wayne Meeks who first approached John with tools of the sociology of knowledge in his 1972 article, "The Man from Heaven in Johannine Sectarianism." After a careful description of the central descent/ascent motif in the Gospel, Meeks concludes that the whole Gospel is a closed system of metaphors which must be accepted totally or will not be understood at all.[143] In this way Meeks can argue that "one of the primary functions of the book, therefore, must have been to provide reinforcement for the community's social identity, which appears to have been largely negative. It provided a symbolic universe which gave religious legitimacy, a theodicy, to the group's actual isolation from the larger society."[144]

Meeks' method is rooted in a methodology that attempts to find correlations between expressions of faith and the underlying social situation or

---

[143] More recently, Jerome Neyrey, *An Ideology of Revolt*, advances Meeks' focus on Jesus ascent/descent to full Johannine Christology using "an explicit social-science model from the works of Mary Douglas as a coherent and extensive device for assessing the social location of John, a model that offers greater precision than the elusive definition of a 'sect' employed in Meeks's essay" (p. 117). According to Neyrey, John's high Christology reveals a group ideology of revolt (pp. 207–12). Cf. Mary Douglas, *Purity and Danger* (London: Routledge & Kegan Paul, 1996); *Essays in the Sociology of Perception* (London: Routledge & Kegan Paul, 1982); and *Natural Symbols: Explorations in Cosmology* (New York: Pantheon Books, 1982).

[144] Meeks, "The Man from Heaven in Johannine Sectarianism," p. 70. The terminology here is borrowed from Berger and Luckmann's theory of the sociology of knowledge and may be the first use of these sociological perspectives in NT studies.

structure by using insights from the sociology of knowledge.[145] According to this theory, beliefs form a social location of thought, a substructure on which the superstructure of ideology or belief is said to rest.[146] As Robin Scroggs explains it:

> This perspective teaches us that the world we live in, the world we think, or assume, has ontological foundations, is really socially constructed and is created, communicated and sustained through language and symbol . . . language, including theological language, is never to be seen as independent of other social realities. Thus, theological language and the claims made therein can no longer be explained without taking into account socio-economic factors as essential ingredients in the production of that language.[147]

Scholars have applied the theory of social location from the sociology of knowledge to the Gospel documents by using them as justification for the claim that theological language is directly and positively revelatory of the community for which the language was written. This has especially been seen as beneficial in Gospel scholarship, all of which is founded on the form critical tradition, which as we discussed at the beginning of this chapter is very sociological in nature.[148] This has been claimed to be especially fruitful in the FG. The most influential aspect of this approach for the FG is the proposal that John exhibits a sectarian, or anti-society, language called an antilanguage.

Although Meeks was the first to see in John's riddles and irony a deeper message – a language within the language – he was not the last. Meeks admitted that NT scholars "have not yet learned to let the symbolic language of Johannine literature speak in its own way."[149] Recently Bruce Malina has tried to fill that gap by attempting to define the same

---

[145] Peter L. Berger and Thomas Luckmann, *The Social Construction of Reality: A Treatise in the Sociology of Knowledge* (Harmondsworth: Penguin Books, 1966). See also Berger's *The Sacred Canopy*. According to Esler, *Community and Gospel in Luke-Acts*, p. 16, the model used by Berger and Luckmann may most usefully be regarded as a model of the genesis and maintenance of society and social institutions.

[146] Richard L. Rohrbaugh, "'Social Location of Thought' as a Heuristic Construct in New Testament Study," *JSNT* 30 (1987), pp. 103–19, especially p. 105.

[147] Scroggs, "The Sociological Interpretation of the New Testament," pp. 175–76.

[148] See, for example, Philip Esler, *Community and Gospel in Luke-Acts*, pp. 2–16.

[149] Meeks, "The Man from Heaven in Johannine Sectarianism," p. 47. Craig R. Koester, *Symbolism in the Fourth Gospel: Meaning, Mystery, Community* (Minneapolis: Fortress Press, 1995), p. xi, also admits the difficulty in understanding Johannine symbolism and tries to do so not just within the confines of the historical-critical approach, but also by considering literary, social-historical, and theological aspects of the text.

symbolism using speech accommodation theory.[150] By looking at the three-tiered nature of language, soundings and spellings, realize wordings, and realize meanings, Malina tries to show that all language is a socially significant feature in which meanings come from and in fact constitute the social system.[151] According to Malina, meaning is derived from a specific social system; in all communication authors accommodate their language to their audiences.[152] Thus, by using speech accommodation theory, which assumes that communicators adjust or accommodate their linguistic styles to their audiences as a strategy for gaining various social goals, Malina believes that the FE reveals who he thought his audience was and what sort of language they would understand. Malina argues that by looking at the convergence and divergence within the FG we are able to see how John (and the JComm) established inter-group boundaries. Such a procedure is moving beyond speech accommodation theory and applying the theory of social identity and studies of in-group bias.[153] This, in part, explains both John's distinctive or symbolic writing and his divergence from the Synoptics. "If John's language and style were so distinctive, that is because John's group was quite distinctive, hence set apart and divided from all other contemporary groups: Christian, Israelite, and Hellenistic."[154]

Malina goes even further. By comparing John's divergence or distinctive development Malina believes that John uses known symbols in a new way. In essence, John is relexicalizing and overlexicalizating language.[155] The consistent relexicalization and overlexicalization reveals that John is using what linguists call antilanguage. Antilanguage is the language of an anti-society, "a society that is set up within another society as a conscious alternative to it. It is a mode of resistance, resistance which may take the form either of passive symbols or of active hostility and even destruction."[156] Thus, for Malina, the FG was written to/within an anti-societal group because it is written in an antilanguage. In essence:

---

[150] Malina, "John's: The Maverick Christian Group: The Evidence of Sociolinguistics," *BTB* 24 (1994), pp. 167–82.

[151] *Ibid.*, p. 167.   [152] *Ibid.*, p. 168.

[153] *Ibid.*, pp. 169–70.   [154] *Ibid.*, p. 170.   [155] *Ibid.*, p. 174.

[156] Michael A. K. Holliday, *Language as Social Semiotic: The Social Interpretation of Language and Meaning* (Baltimore: University Park, 1978), p. 171. See the related discussion of antilanguage by Holliday, "Anti-languages," *AA* 78 (1976); pp. 570–84, and John Howard Yoder, *The Priestly Kingdom: Social Ethics as Gospel* (Notre Dame, Ind.: University of Notre Dame Press, 1984), pp. 50–54. For other discussions of antilanguage in John see Norman R. Petersen, *The Gospel of John and the Sociology of Light: Language and Characterization in the Fourth Gospel* (Valley Forge, Pa.: Trinity Press International, 1993); Malina and Rohrbaugh, *Social-Science Commentary on the Gospel of John*, pp. 7–14, 46–48, 59–61; Neyrey, *An Ideology of Revolt*; Neyrey, "The Sociology of Secrecy and the Fourth Gospel," in Fernando F. Segovia (ed.), *"What is John?,"* vol II: *Literary and Social Readings of the Fourth Gospel*, SBLSymS 7 (Atlanta: Scholars Press, 1998), pp. 79–109;

Antilanguage is not simply a specialized variety of language such as technical variety of ordinary language used in a special way or in particular, technical contexts . . . Rather, an antilanguage arises among persons in groups espousing and held by alternative perceptions of reality; reality as experienced and set up in opposition to some established mode of conception and perception. Consequently, an antilanguage is nobody's "mother tongue," nor is it a predictable "mother tongue" derivative. Rather antilanguage exists solely in a social context of resocialization.[157]

And of course, this resocialization of the Johannine group was in relation to "the world" and the "Jews" to whom the Gospel so frequently refers.

Malina is not alone in assigning John's antilanguage to an anti-society perspective.[158] As Rohrbaugh explains, "As an anti-society, then, the Johannine community has a language all its own. It is an anti-language, an original tongue. Any new member of the community . . . assumed a new identity, one which could stand over against 'this world' and the 'Judeans.'"[159] The JComm is, according to Malina and others, a sectarian movement that has separated from the "world" and "the Jews" by forming a symbolic construction of identity. This "community" sees society at large, the world and its members (the Jews) around them as an affront to what they believe and to the essence of who they are. By using insights from the sociology of knowledge, and by applying a sectarian model related to those insights, Malina and others believe they have found a more appropriate way to read the FG. Unfortunately, several problems occur with the use of such models. The first has to do with the use of antilanguage, a form of the sociology of knowledge, in its application to the social formation and location of a document's audience. The second has to do with the application of an antilanguage to the text of the FG.

Symbolic construct and antilanguage: the need for a new proposal

After explaining how theological language must take into account the socio-economic cultural factors in its own production, Scroggs admits

---

Rohrbaugh, "The Gospel of John in the Twenty-First Century," pp. 260–62; and Robert H. Gundry, *Jesus the Word According to John the Sectarian: A Paleofundamentalist Manifesto for Contemporary Evangelicalism, especially Its Elites, in North America* (Grand Rapids: Eerdmans, 2003), pp. 56–57.

[157] Malina, "John's: The Maverick Christian Group," p. 176.

[158] See especially Peterson, *The Gospel of John and the Sociology of Light*, and Rohrbaugh, "The Gospel of John in the Twenty-First Century," pp. 260–62.

[159] Rohrbaugh, "The Gospel of John in the Twenty-First Century," p. 262.

that "The difficult questions for the sociologists are, in concrete instances, how to move between language and social realities, and which social realities are to be related to which linguistic structure?"[160] This is the key question that must be asked of scholars who apply the sociology of knowledge to the text of the Gospels. Our appraisal will not be dealing specifically with the influential work of Berger and Luckmann, although critiques of their theory do exist.[161] Rather, we will be dealing with the application of insight from the sociology of knowledge to the Gospels.

The first warning of applying sociology of knowledge to the Gospels, according to Gerd Theissen, is that it is difficult to elicit information from analytical conclusions, that is, conclusions from different types of indirect information, especially symbols of religious belief, because it is impossible to decide at the outset whether there exists symmetry or asymmetry between symbol and social reality.[162] For example, when the apostle Paul uses the body as the symbol for the church, it has to be interpreted simultaneously as an indicative and an imperative. "This means that this symbol is both a description of a tight-knit community (evidence of a symmetry between symbol and reality) and an exhortation to be and become a community (some lack of symmetry between symbol and reality)."[163] But there is nothing evident within the symbol itself to tell us on which aspect we should put the emphasis, the symmetrical or the asymmetrical. The same can be said of the metaphorical language found in Jesus' parables, which gives us a wealth of information of the socio-economic background of this tradition. Yet to draw conclusions from

---

[160] Scroggs, "The Sociological Interpretation of the New Testament," p. 176.

[161] For an epistemological critique of Berger and Luckmann, *The Social Construction of Reality*, see B. C. Thompson, *Making Sense of Reification: Alfred Schultz and Constructionist Theory* (London: Macmillan, 1982); Robin Gill, *Theology and Social Structure* (London: Mowbrays, 1977), pp. 18–20; David Cairns, "The Thought of Peter Berger," *SJT* 27 (1974), pp. 181–97; Robin Gill, "Berger's Plausibility Structures: A Response of Professor Cairns," *SJT* 27 (1974), pp. 198–207. For similar discussion see also Robert N. Bellah, "Christianity and Symbolic Realism," in Robert Bellah (ed.), *Beyond Belief: Essays on Religion in a Post-Traditional World* (New York: Harper & Row, 1970), pp. 236–59; Robert A. Segal, "The Social Sciences and the Truth of Religious Belief," *JAAR* 48 (1980), pp. 403–13; Thomas Robbins, Dick Anthony, and Thomas E. Curtis, "The Limits of Symbolic Realism: Problems of Emphatic Field Observation in a Sectarian Context," *JSSR* 12 (1973), pp. 259–71; Robert N. Bellah, "Comment on 'The Limits of Symbolic Realism,'" *JSSR* 13 (1974), pp. 487–89; and Dick Anthony and Thomas Robbins, "From Symbolic Realism to Structuralism," *JSSR* 14 (1975), pp. 403–14.

[162] Theissen, "Die soziologische Auswertung religiöser Überlieferungen: Ihre methodologischen Probleme am Beispiel des Urchristentums," *Kairos* (1975), pp. 284–99, especially pp. 290–91.

[163] Holmberg, *Sociology and the New Testament*, p. 135.

this general background to the social location of the speaker, or even the tradition-carriers, is much more difficult. Thus, there are few definite conclusions that can be drawn from the symbols within a Gospel text; hence the large amount of reconstructions for each of the Gospels. We will discuss this more fully below when we examine Malina's depiction of the "world" in the FG.

The second warning of applying sociology of knowledge to the Gospels is that theological traditions or belief complexes often function in several different contexts.[164] Work in apocalyptic literature has revealed that the apocalyptic genre can be used by persons in very different social situations.[165] This research has shown that the corresponding relationship between apocalyptic tradition and social situation is not patterned in any uniform way. Work in the social functions of the crucifixion and resurrection has revealed similar results: one original social situation can lead to several different results because the intervening factors need not be the same. The same end result can have been reached by several different and varying routes. As Holmberg argues, "It seems inevitable that, once we leave the primitive idea of strong, direct correlation between ideas and social basis of an almost deterministic kind, we are bereft of the possibility to say anything much about correlations at all."[166]

The third warning is, surprisingly, from Richard Rohrbaugh who, in his 1987 article, "'Social Location of Thought' as a Heuristic Construct in New Testament Study," gives an important analysis of some basic concepts and postulates of the sociology of knowledge and how these affect the attempts of interpreters to find correlations between texts and their social contexts. Rohrbaugh argues that although social structures and belief are certainly related, they are so in a complex and apparently unsystematic way.[167] "The result is that a specific social location is frequently difficult to define, often overlapping with other locations, and thereby difficult to correlate with particular ideas or beliefs."[168] This social location is a plausibility structure; a mental construct and not a set of social conditions. As Rohrbaugh explains:

---

[164] Christopher M. Tuckett, *Reading the New Testament: Methods of Interpretation* (London: SPCK), pp. 361–63.

[165] Paul D. Hanson, *The Dawn of Apocalyptic: The Historical and Sociological Roots of Jewish Apocalyptic Eschatology* (Philadelphia: Fortress, 1979); Wayne A. Meeks, "Social Functions of Apocalyptic Language in Pauline Christianity."

[166] Holmberg, *Sociology and the New Testament*, p. 139.

[167] Rohrbaugh, "'Social Location of Thought' as a Heuristic Construct in New Testament Study," p. 104.

[168] *Ibid.*, p. 105.

> The social base is not the cause of other ideas, but the context in which other ideas are interpreted and understood as realistic possibilities. Few contemporary sociologists of knowledge would assume it is possible to locate causal origins of particular ideas as if a social location accounts for ideas that emerge in it . . . Even Marxists, who routinely assume a correlation between the ideas of a group and that group's social interests, shy away from rigid notions of causality. Social locations are heuristic constructs, not explanatory ones.[169]

Thus, lines of demarcation begin to blur: "how are we to know what counts as a group? How are we to handle the complexities created by the overlapping character of group participation?"[170] With this Rohrbaugh is not trying to prohibit drawing correlations between early Christian belief and its social context, but admitting that a complete concept of the group's formation is impossible to derive with certainty. A similar argument has been made by Motyer who argues that even Berger and Luckmann warned that only a macro-sociological background is ever derivable from a text's internalized consciousness.[171] According to Motyer, "The vital conclusion is that *observers cannot infer the social 'location' of any particular group merely from a study of its mentality.*"[172] Since we know nothing concerning the audience of the FG, moving from text to social location is virtually impossible, at least with any verifiable accuracy.

For our purposes the complexity of social locations through the insights of the sociology of knowledge, and especially the warning given by Rohrbaugh and Motyer, allows us to present our proposal of the "community" symbolically constructed by early Christians, even Johannine Christians, as a preferable reading. The community model we presented, which is not limited to one geographic location of ideological conflict but is allowed to assume a relational connection with several potential audiences, provides a reading of John that does not force conflicting evidence to "fit" a specific, symbolically assumed, geographic location. Our reading is able to provide a better reading of the composition and reception of the text as a whole. A full examination of our model to the text of John will be presented in chapter 5.

Therefore, with this in mind we return to John and his antilanguage. The question we need to ask is the level at which this language is to be seen as creating an "us versus them" distinction. But based upon

---

[169] *Ibid.*, p. 114.   [170] *Ibid.*, p. 106.
[171] Motyer, *Your Father the Devil?*, pp. 30–31.   [172] *Ibid.*, p. 31.

the more complex model we have proposed, the "us" may include more than just an isolated geographic "community." Even ideological disagreements need not imply another distinct exclusion. For John, as he himself states, there is one primary exclusionary factor: "that you [the reader] may believe that Jesus [as portrayed by John] is the Christ [as believed by John]." Although the descriptions of Jesus and belief might adjust according to the document, one would be hard-pressed to find evidence that such a statement was not basic to the early Christian "sub-society" (using Berger's language). Our proposal, then, argues that all of Christianity was forming its identity in relation to other forces and previous beliefs, not just some Johannine "group." In light of our proposal a few criticisms are pertinent in reference to Malina's use of antilanguage in John.

First, although it is certainly true that all ancient texts once did realize meanings from a (particular) social system, it is impossible for current interpreters to claim they have found a single location that explains the details of a document's explicated social system. Even if we were to assume that the "JComm" was anti-society and relatively confined, there is no way to be certain that the language used, language common to both the tradition they came from and the general culture in which they lived, would have been understood in the antilanguage way that Malina proposes. Malina claims too much when he states:

> John's vocabulary would mirror the lexical selections in vogue among his associates. The distinctiveness of this vocabulary would indicate that other Christian associations did not converge in this regard. As a matter of fact, given what the author of 1 John writes, it would seem that that document emerged as a sort of linguistic broker. 1 John was written to compensate for the apparent lack of understanding of what John was about and to promote solidarity and empathy.[173]

But John's vocabulary is hardly as "distinctive" as Malina has claimed. As Stephen Barton explains,

> Are metaphors like logos, light, bread, living water, good shepherd, true vine, Son of God, and so on – each of them with deep roots in the biblical and Jewish traditions and not without a certain currency in the wider Hellenistic milieu, either – as opaque as [some interpreters make] them out to be? If they are not, and

---

[173] Malina, "John's: The Maverick Christian Gospel," p. 169.

if we recall in addition the strong, universalizing missionary thrust of John, then a further crack appears in . . . sociological interpretation.[174]

For example, with all the Jewish imagery attached to "lamb" in the OT and Second Temple Judaism it is striking that Malina links the title "Lamb of God" in 1:29 with the constellation Aries; a title which was labeled by Romans after the FG was already written.[175] Such a move by Malina is problematic for two reasons. First, it implies that later Romans would have been able to read John 1:19 as equally as the "JComm," even without being anti-societal (for they were the society). Second, and related to the first, if our only access to the "meanings" of phrases or words comes from non-anti-society texts, how can we even assume to know what an anti-society reading of the FG would have looked like? It would appear that any non-anti-society reading would be out of the question for an anti-society text. Several other examples could be provided that show how Malina is required to highlight one nuance or aspect of a word or phrase, almost always from a non-anti-society, when several other plausible interpretations are available. In fact, these other plausible interpretations would have been available to the readers of the FG as well![176] Was John's antilanguage created within and confined to his own supposed community that had its own, isolated system of communication, or was Johannine language part of the social system of the wider Mediterranean world? As we have tried to show above, the attempt to fit John's language into a specific anti-societal "community" that is speaking an antilanguage is methodologically circular and unable to explain the text of John as a whole. Our proposal, that the community is an indefinite symbolic construction that correlates with much of the early Christian movement and its general cultural milieu, works just as well with the theory of speech accommodation that Malina uses for his anti-society model.[177]

Second, the one-to-one correspondence between the author and the audience is hardly proportional. If John was writing to a "community," maybe a group of which he was a leading or teaching member, he could

---

[174] Barton, "Early Christianity and the Sociology of the Sect," in Francis Watson (ed.), *The Open Text: New Directions for Biblical Studies?* (London: SCM Press, 1993), p. 148. We will discuss John's missionary thrust in chapter 5.

[175] Malina and Rohrbaugh, *Social-Science Commentary on the Gospel of John*, pp. 50–51.

[176] For another good example see the discussion of "gate" in Malina and Rohrbaugh, *Social-Science Commentary on the Gospel of John*, pp. 178–80.

[177] Where Malina emphasizes intergroup tension, we would emphasize intragroup identity formation.

have easily written in a way that not all the members would immediately be able to appreciate. In fact, some of the best literature is highly ambiguous in parts, while still communicating effectively. Barton's critique of Meeks is pertinent here:

> Doubt may . . . be cast on Meek's claim that the Fourth Gospel shows all the signs of being a "book for insiders," since "only a very rare outsider would get past the barrier of its closed metaphorical system." This strikes me as a *tour de force*. On this view, it is a wonder that anyone made it into the Johannine community at all![178]

Recently, a similar argument has been made by Alexander Jensen in his examination of Johannine language.[179] In a section on the sociological background of the Johannine text, Jensen argues, contrary to Malina, that Johannine language would have been comprehensible to the general, uninitiated reader:

> Johannine language is not an arcane language incomprehensible to the uninitiated. On the contrary, it is an open system of language, drawing concepts and symbols from the Christian and non-Christian environment and combining them in a poetic way. Therefore, the language of John's Gospel would have been, and still is comprehensible for anybody familiar with its contemporary thought . . .[180]

---

[178] Barton, "Early Christianity and the Sociology of the Text," p. 148.

[179] Jensen, *John's Gospel as Witness: The Development of the Early Christian Language of Faith* (Aldershot: Ashgate, 2004).

[180] *Ibid.*, p. 59. Although Jensen allows for a broader use of the Gospel, he critiques what he calls the extreme position presented in *GAC*. According to Jensen, "on historical and linguistic grounds it is possible to recognize distinct traditions at work behind or within John's Gospel" (p. 59). Although "it is legitimate to say that Gospel of John is a text which evolved from a particular group within the early church, and which was written within a context of a distinct theology and spirituality"; it is also possible to see how the FG "invited the reader or listener to enter the world which is brought about through its language. John's Gospel is not a document of a group which separated itself from the church, but it is an offer to the church, and which the wider church finally accepted" (p. 59). "In sum, we must see John's Gospel somewhere in-between sectarianism and universal communication" (p. 62). But Jensen's middle position, though helpful, has confused origin with audience. It is not self-evident that a document written by a specific "group" is necessarily intended for that same "group," the one that created the document. Jensen is correct to see how John's Gospel would have behind it a specific tradition or perspective of early Christianity; but he is wrong to assume that this view was self-perpetuating and not intended for the broader Christian movement. Especially when, as he admits, its theological language was invitational in nature and would have been understood "by Christians as well as everyone familiar with its contemporary religious thought" (p. 59).

In the same way, our model suggests that the text could assume different "levels" or "types" of readers. A full discussion of different types of readers and the heuristic use of the concept of the implied reader in John will be discussed in chapter 4.

A good example of the misuse of antilanguage in the FG is Malina and Rohrbaugh's description of κόσμος in John. Malina and Rohrbaugh argue that although the term κόσμος in the Hellenistic period normally means the inhabited world in which one lives, in John it only has that meaning four times.[181] For the remaining uses κόσμος is a subject of personal activity and the object of interpersonal relations; κόσμος refers to humanity, to human beings.[182] Since Malina and Rohrbaugh already assume that the FG is written to an anti-society "group" in conflict, they are required to assume that the relational sense of κόσμος is diametrically opposed to the JComm. That is, if the JComm (the in-group) is one geographically located "group," then κόσμος (the out-group) must be referring to a conflicting out-group known to this (small) band of readers.[183] From the perspective of John, then, κόσμος is the "Jews" with whom the JComm has conflict; they constitute the κόσμος (out-group) of John. But two major problems face this symbolic reading of κόσμος. First, and most problematic to this text, one is required to assume not only that John was written to a specific "group," but also that this "group" was anti-society. The term κόσμος can easily have a broad relational reference in Hellenistic literature. Second, assuming κόσμος means "Israelite/Jew" in every occurrence (except for 11:9; 17:5; 24; 21:25) creates a confusing reading of certain passages.

The example they use is itself difficult to reconcile with their reading of the JComm versus "the Jews." In 3:16 God so loved the "Israelites/the Jews" is supposed to mean that he gave only to the people of Israel his Son (in the flesh). But how would they reconcile this reading with the very next verse which claims that God will not judge "Israel/the Jews," for he wants none "of Israel/the Jews" to perish (3:17). Maybe John is inviting "the Jews" into its fellowship, rather than contrasting itself with the Jews. But this makes no sense if the JComm is in immediate "group" conflict with "the Jews." Even earlier, in 1:29, does Jesus really take away the "sins of the Jews?" Are they no longer to be considered the out-group? Is there no longer any conflict between the Jews and the JComm? What may

---

[181] Malina and Rohrbaugh, *Social-Science Commentary on the Gospel of John*, pp. 245–46.

[182] *Ibid.*, p. 246.

[183] *Ibid.*, p. 247. Note the influence of Martyn's thesis for reading John.

be even more striking is the Johannine irony in 12:19 where the Pharisees proclaim that "the world has gone after him [Jesus]." If we assume Malina and Rohrbaugh's reading of κόσμος as referring to "the Jews," then the Pharisees are themselves speaking as within an anti-society. They are placing themselves over against both Jesus and "the Jews!"[184] By placing κόσμος within a specific "community" interpretation, Malina and Rohrbaugh have distorted the text.

Interestingly, though attained through different means, a similar conclusion is made by Raymond Brown. Although he realizes the complexity of κόσμος in the FG, Brown still reads it as functioning for a specific "community."[185] Brown reads the term diachronically through the Gospel assuming that its more frequent use in the latter half of the book implies that the JComm became more involved in Gentile missions; a stage beyond its initial Jewish conflict.[186] In this way, Brown is still closely related to Malina and Rohrbaugh in his understanding of its social and relational function. Brown assumes that since the "Jews" dominate chapters 5–12 and κόσμος dominates chapters 14–17, the Gospel must be revealing the developmental stages of the "community." The κόσμος must be reflecting a Gentile "group" that had interaction and conflict with the JComm. In this way Brown sees John's use of κόσμος as stretched linearly so as to depict the various world-like "groups" that the JComm had symbolically constructed. But Brown is forced to make the developing data comply with a single social location of thought; a geographically located[187] "community" and its experiences. Yet nothing in chapters 14–17 gives indication that κόσμος is to be taken as referring to Gentiles in contrast to Jews, thus fitting his linear proposal. In fact, the opposite can be claimed for some references. For example, 16:28, which is in the section Brown claims portrays a Gentile κόσμος ("I came from the Father and have come into the world"), is reminiscent of 1:9–11, where it claims that Jesus came "into the world," that is, he "came to his own" but "his own did not accept him." Even in his commentary Brown admits that this

---

[184] It is this use of κόσμος in 12:19, one that is broadly relational in an idiomatic sense, that most commentaries promote. See C. K. Barrett, *The Gospel According to St. John*, 2nd edn (London: SPCK, 1978), p. 420; Leon Morris, *The Gospel According to John*, NICNT (London: Marshall, Morgan & Scott, 1972), p. 589.

[185] Raymond Brown, *The Gospel According to John*, 2 vols., AB 29, 29a (Garden City: Doubleday, 1966, 1970), vol. I, pp. 508–10.

[186] Brown, *The Community of the Beloved Disciple*, pp. 63–66.

[187] I use this term in order to cover Brown's idea of a "community" that moved geographically.

coming "to his own" (i.e. the "world") is certainly Israel (the "Jews").[188] Thus, although it could be said that the presentation of κόσμος in chapters 14–17 is less anti-Jewish than chapters 5–12, it cannot be said that κόσμος is completely Gentile, reflecting relations with only Gentiles. Only a more complex model of "community" can handle the nuances of κόσμος in the FG. We will present our preferred reading of κόσμος in chapter 5.

In conclusion, we have spent a good amount of space critiquing a symbolic-constructed world (plausibility structure) and antilanguage and their application to the FG. We have argued that the model Malina proposes limits the plausibility structure that the text portrays concerning the "us versus them" distinction. Even more, Malina only reinforces the interpretation he had already chosen;[189] an interpretation we have argued is circular in nature and distorts a holistic reading of John. In contrast, our proposed model of "community" is a more explanatory model; one that seeks to define the various complexities of "us versus them" through John's own perception of belief; perceptions not based on problematic audience assumptions of geographic "community" and anti-society.

Conclusion: a community that is sectarian?

This study is attempting to argue that the sectarian model is limited in its ability to access the social-historical context of first-century Christianity and the symbolically constructed social locations of individual "groups" within its early movement. Our proposed model of the early Christian movement explains better the evidence of the general Christianity revealed in the NT documents; documents that revealed both unity and diversity as well as both "group" and "inter group" documents in the same religious movement.[190] Our model also provides a more appropriate

---

[188] Brown, *John*, vol. I, p. 10.

[189] A similar critique was made of Meek's "The Man from Heaven in Johannine Sectarianism" by Christopher M. Tuckett, *Reading the New Testament: Methods of Interpretation* (London: SPCK, 1987), pp. 145–47.

[190] This was also the conclusion of James D. G. Dunn, *Unity and Diversity in the New Testament: An Inquiry into the Character of Earliest Christianity*, 2nd edn (London: SCM Press, 1990), p. 369: "I think it can justly be said that we have discovered a *fairly clear and consistent unifying strand* which from the first both marked out Christianity as something *distinctive* and different and provided the *integrating centre* for the diverse expressions of Christianity. That unifying element was the unity between the historical Jesus and the exalted Christ . . ." Cf. C. F. D. Moule, *The Birth of the New Testament*, 2nd edn, BNTC 1 (London: Adam and Charles Black, 1966), p. 10: "In a word, the apostolic proclamation about Jesus was the unifying factor; or, more deeply defined, it is to the Spirit of God himself, through Jesus Christ our Lord, that the unity-in-diversity of the New Testament is to be traced." See also, more recently, Larry Hurtado, *Lord Jesus Christ: Devotion to*

reading of the Gospels themselves, as we will attempt to show more fully in chapter 5. The FG reveals an audience that was connected to a broader section of early Christianity and its culture at large than sectarian and antilanguage readings are able to demonstrate.[191] To limit John to a sectarian "group" or to a "group" in intense conflict with the "Jews" forces the interpreter to do gymnastics to explain the parts of the text that speak to a different end. We now turn to the patristic evidence of a "community" assumption for the FG.

Patristic exegesis and the Gospels

Our focus on Gospel audience in early Christianity would be incomplete if it did not entail an examination of the evidence from the post-apostolic period through the second century. The documents written for the church at that time "provide significant and often unparalleled glimpses of and insights into the life of Christians and the Christian movement during a critical transitional stage in its history."[192] Our intent here is not to provide a comprehensive study of second-century assumptions about the Gospels and their original audiences, but to see if these writings assist us to define more clearly the type of audience the Gospels, or at least their readers, might have expected.[193] In order to assess the evidence we will use as our point of entry a recent article engaging the Gospel community debate by Margaret M. Mitchell entitled "Patristic Counter-evidence to the Claim that 'The Gospels Were Written for All Christians.'"[194] Our discussion

---

Jesus in Earliest Christianity (Grand Rapids: Eerdmans, 2003), p. 650: "in spite of the diversity, it is equally evident that Jesus was *central* in all the forms of earliest Christianity, proto-orthodox and others, that we can describe with any confidence."

[191] Although John makes some statements that some assume create a distinction between his readers and others, as Brown, *The Community of the Beloved Disciple*, pp. 88–91, has warned, other evidence in John shows that these readers (who he assumes are a single "group") did not break communion with other "Christians" whose characteristics are found in many NT works of the late first century. The Johannine Christians, Brown explains, looked on other Christians as "belonging to Jesus' own to whom they were bound by the commandment: 'As I have loved you, so must you love one another'" (p. 90).

[192] Michael Holmes (ed.), *Apostolic Fathers: Greek Texts and English Translations*, rev. edn (Grand Rapids; Baker Books, 1999), p. 1.

[193] We must admit that the second-century writers we consult are themselves the audience of the Gospels. They do not exist outside of their influence nor were they formed without their guidance. This is, of course, either part of the problem we are trying to resolve or a clue to our answer.

[194] Margaret M. Mitchell, "Patristic Counter-Evidence to the Claim that 'The Gospels Were Written for All Christians,'" *NTS* 51 (2005), pp. 36–79. Originally presented as a paper by the same title at the annual meeting of the Society of Biblical Research, Atlanta Georgia, November 22, 2003.

will focus specifically on Mitchell's discussion of patristic evidence of the Gospel audiences.[195]

Audience and origin of the Gospels: the evidence from patristics

According to Mitchell the supposition that the Gospels were grounded in a local audience and context is not a new debate. "I think it is most important to resituate the debate Bauckham has claimed to be the product of the excesses of modern critical methodologies as actually yet another instance of a very old and enduring hermeneutical problem in the exegesis of Christian literature: the relationship between the particularity and universality of the gospels."[196] The patristic exegetes were "very self consciously and complexly working at the fulcrum between the universality and particularity of the gospels (including at times an insistence upon their original local audiences)."[197] According to Mitchell:

> The gospels ultimately were read as addressing "all Christians" in that they were regarded as having communicated a universal divine truth. That they could so effectively be read this way was in fact their genius and was a major factor in the rise and missionary success of the Christian cult. But recognition of the universal readership did not concomitantly require later Christian readers . . . to disregard circumstances of original, specific, local origin. Patristic authors . . . found many creative ways to hold in tension the gospels' historical particularity and theological universality.[198]

Mitchell admits that the Gospels were intended to be universal, but not from their outset, or at least not according to the patristic interpreters who made frequent mention of the Gospels and their originating locations. Thus we are forced to deal with the contention Mitchell presents: the patristic writers never separated the universality of the Gospel message

---

[195] Although this is her primary goal, Mitchell also spent nearly ten pages critiquing logical and methodological issues in *GAC*. Since our thesis as a whole is moving the entire Gospel community debate forward, most of her proposed difficulties are consumed in the remainder of this study and will not be examined here. It is important to note that this section is only able to deal with Mitchell's general critique of the thesis of *GAC* and not with all the patristic evidence (or avenues) presented by Mitchell. Our goal is to show the possibility of a different reading of the patristic traditions Mitchell uses as counter-evidence.

[196] *Ibid.*, p. 38.   [197] *Ibid.*, p. 46.   [198] *Ibid.*

(its divine heritage) from the specific location that created the Gospels. Or, as Mitchell explains it, "Can the patristic (and later) sources which specify a local audience for any or all of the gospels be so cavalierly dismissed?"[199] It is to this specific issue and Mitchell's evaluation of it within the patristic material that we now turn.

Mitchell begins by discussing the famous tradition about the occasion of Mark's Gospel by Eusebius. According to Eusebius:[200]

> Again, in the same books Clement set forth, in the following manner, a tradition of the early elders about the order of the gospels: Clement said that those of the gospels which contain genealogies have been written first, but that the Gospel according to Mark had this *oikonomia*:[201] after Peter had preached the word publicly in Rome, and expressed the gospel by the spirit, those who were present, being many, urged Mark, since he had followed Peter from way back and remembered what had been said [by him], to write down what was said. After doing so, Mark imparted the gospel to those who were asking him for it. When Peter learned of this, he used his powers of persuasion neither to hinder nor to encourage it.[202]

For Mitchell this statement tells nothing of the circulation of the Gospel, nothing of copies, in fact, it appears that "Mark's gospel does not move

---

[199] *Ibid.*, p. 48.

[200] For the sake of discussion all translations will be those that Mitchell provides unless otherwise stated.

[201] Mitchell only transliterates this word because she claims it is "such an important and multi-valent term" in early Christian literature (p. 49, n. 38). According to Mitchell the term can mean "accommodation to circumstances" (see G. W. H. Lampe, *Patristic Greek Lexicon* [Oxford: Clarendon Press, 1961], *s.v.* p. 942, D.2) or perhaps "had this opportune occasion," or "providential appearance" (p. 941, C.6), or, less clearly, but more literally, "management, supervision" (pp. 940–41, A.1, 2, 4). It would seem that the initial three definitions Mitchell provides, definitions that are necessarily based upon context, lend more support for her understanding of this passage that places Mark's occasion as required in and for a specific locale ("accommodation to circumstances; opportune occasion"). But it would appear that contextually the term is simply telling of the "position" in which Mark stood, a position in relation to the other Gospels, and not emphasizing the position in relation to the readers. For example, H. G. Liddell and R. Scott, *A Greek-English Lexicon*, rev. by H. S. Jones, 9th edn (Oxford: Clarendon Press, 1996), p. 1204, II.3, even use the terms "arrangement" or "steps." In other words, rather than being "opportune" for the Roman readers, Mark is appropriately positioned, even an opportune literary position, in relation to the other Gospels. Cf. J. H. Moulton and G. Milligan, *Vocabulary of the Greek New Testament* (Peabody, Mass.: Hendrickson, 1997), *s.v.* p. 3622.

[202] Eusebius, *Hist. Eccl.* 6.14.5–7.

beyond the Roman Christians who asked him to write it, who are presented as a rather specific group who in turn receive the document from him."[203] This, she claims, is contrary to Bauckham's claim that "the idea of writing a Gospel purely for the members of the writer's own church or even for a few neighboring churches is unlikely to have occurred to anyone."[204]

But Mitchell's assumption is not self-evident. The focus of the text is on the *oikonomia* of the Gospel of Mark in relation to the other Gospels, not the Roman readers. Although this text "hardly represents an enthusiastic authorial or patronal dissemination of the gospel to the people beside those at Rome,"[205] neither does it state that the Gospel was only intended for the Roman audience, or that the Roman audience was only *from Rome*. The text only describes the audience who heard Peter preach "in public" (δημοσίᾳ) as "those who were present," and not as Roman. In such a major city, and with a personal sermon by the apostle Peter, a man with "powers of persuasion," it would not be unexpected if many in the audience were not natives of Rome. The very fact that the sermon was "in public" (δημοσίᾳ) alludes to the more general nature of the occasion and not some specific Christian group or house church. The audience's desire for Mark "to write down what was said" by Peter need not imply that the impetus for the creation of the Gospel of Mark was solely based upon the audience's "urging." As we will argue later, the Gospels were written to meet the *needs* of the early Christian movement. This text simply alludes to the fact that one of the groups that recognized this need was the one who heard Peter in Rome, and one of the results was the Gospel of Mark.[206] Finally, one wonders if the concluding comment, "When Peter learned of this, he used his powers of persuasion neither to hinder nor to encourage it," was meant more to honor the apostle Peter, or to excuse him from the responsibility of the "lack" of order in Mark, than to describe his lack of concern concerning its further spread.

A further issue against Mitchell's reading of this tradition can be raised. Stephen Carlson has challenged the traditional translation of the word

---

[203] Mitchell, "Patristic Counter-Evidence," p. 50.

[204] Bauckham, "For Whom Were the Gospels Written?," p. 44.

[205] Mitchell, "Patristic Counter-evidence," p. 15.

[206] This would seem to fit the other texts that have what Mitchell, "Patristic Counter-evidence," p. 15, n. 49, calls "audience request traditions." In fact, the text Mitchell mentions concerning the impetus behind the Gospel of John (Clement of Alexandria, *frag.* 8.13; cf. Eusebius, *Hist. Eccl.* 6.14.7) seems to show more of the initial impetus resting in the mind of John himself ("recognizing that the bodily matters had been recorded in the gospels . . . wrote a spiritual gospel"), than in the people who hoped to receive it. In other words, John saw the need and it was confirmed to him by others ("persuaded by men of note").

"first" in the same text: "Clement said that those of the gospels which contain genealogies have been written first . . ."[207] According to Carlson, the traditional explanations make Clement's statement difficult to reconcile with other traditions about the origin of the Gospels. All the previous proposals that construe προγράθειν in a temporal sense (i.e. "first" or "written before") are "theoretically possible, but only at the expense of taking Clement's statement out of its context and into the realm of speculation."[208] An examination of the classical usage of the term reveals that it was used for the written notice of official acts and decrees of the state. When this meaning is given to the tradition cited above, one that might be translated as "writing publicly," many problems are resolved. As Carlson explains:

> If προγεγραφθαι is taken in the sense of writing publicly, Clement's statement would mean: "He said that those gospels having the genealogies were published openly", with an implication that their publication was official. In contrast with the standard chronological interpretation, this sense provides a better fit with its literary context and poses no difficulty for Origen's ordering of the gospels. Finally, Clement's statement under this proposal suits its context in Eusebius.[209]

Carlson brings his findings into the debate initiated by *GAC* and claims the following "patristic support for the thesis provocatively introduced by Bauckham": "In terms of its textual and historical contexts, therefore, the best interpretation of Clement's statement is that the gospels with the genealogies were written before the public, as gospels for all Christians."[210] Mitchell only deals with Carlson's thesis in a footnote, and simply assumes that the locative meaning of the term is possible.[211]

Another text from Eusebius needs to be dealt with; one with which Mitchell contests the theory that the Gospels had a more intentional universal audience. According to Eusebius:

> The light of piety shone so greatly on the minds of the hearers of Peter that they were not satisfied to rest content with a single hearing, nor with an unwritten teaching of the divine proclamation. With all sorts of entreaties they persisted in asking Mark, whose Gospel is published, since he was a follower

---

[207] Stephen C. Carlson, "Clement of Alexandria on the 'Order' of the Gospels," *NTS* 47 (2001), pp. 118–25.
[208] *Ibid.*, p. 121.   [209] *Ibid.*, p. 123.   [210] *Ibid.*, p. 125.
[211] Mitchell, "Patristic Counter-Evidence," p. 49, n. 37.

of Peter, to leave a written record of the teaching that had been handed down to them orally, and by this they became the cause of the writing/scripture called the gospel according to Mark. And they say that the apostle, upon learning what had been done, after the spirit revealed [it] to him was pleased at the fervent desire of these men, and confirmed the writing for reading in the churches.[212]

Mitchell admits that at first glance this text might seem congenial to the wider audience theory, but claims that on closer look there are significant problems for such a hypothesis. For Mitchell, "this testimony contradicts the assumption that those who have the oral word do not require a written text, such that an evangelist would not write a gospel to address a community where he was present."[213] Mitchell claims that Bauckham's statements concerning the lack of need for a written document in a specific Gospel-creating community is overstated, especially based upon evidence found in this text, where the community "persisted in asking Mark . . . to leave a written record of the teaching that had been handed down to them orally . . ."[214]

But does this "community" really fit the concept of community that Bauckham suggests? The type of "community" that Bauckham is arguing against would seem to be a single, coherent body of believers that forms either one church or a few close-knit churches in a symbiotic relationship.[215] This is not the picture of a community we get from this text. There is nothing in this text that defines the audience who urged Mark to leave a written record of the apostle's teaching, the Gospel. The fact that they were the "cause" of the writing tells us nothing about who "they" were. The "hearers of Peter" could have been members of several different groups and regions. The written copy of the Gospel may have been for the use of several groups and house churches, not just the one where Peter spoke according to this tradition. This would especially be the case if Peter traveled and spoke at several geographic locations and churches. The fact that Eusebius refers to Mark as the one "whose gospel is published" leads us to believe that the published gospel was meant to be read by more than a single community; publication would imply a more general audience or less specific ownership. Even Eusebius' reference to Mark defining

---

[212] Clement of Alexandria, *frag.* 9.4–20; cf. Eusebius, *Hist. Eccl.* 2.14.1–2.
[213] Mitchell, "Patristic Counter-evidence," p. 51.
[214] Bauckham, "For Whom Were the Gospels Written?," p. 44, "surely the idea of writing a Gospel purely for the members of the writer's own church or even for a few neighboring churches is unlikely to have occurred to anyone."
[215] This is related to the definition of "community" we discussed above.

Mark to his own implied reader as the one who had already published a Gospel, fits our proposed reading of this tradition. Loosely translated the phrase would read: "Mark, the author of the published Gospel that should be familiar to you."

For Mitchell, the fact that the cause (αἰτίοι)[216] of the Gospel was not the evangelist and that the text "does not . . . say that Peter approved or disseminated this text to '*all* the churches,' or anything like the 'any and every church' of Bauckham's formulation" shows that the Gospel tradition was certainly assumed[217] to be connected to a local geographic area or community.[218] Mitchell assumes that the local reference could variously refer to the "churches at Rome," or to "the churches" (some unspecified entity beyond Rome), although, she admits, that text is silent as to specifics.[219] Mitchell states the importance of her argument this way:

> Most importantly, the fact that such a tradition arose at all . . . is indicative of the hermeneutical awareness in the early church of the multi-dimensional addressees of the gospel literature. Like the letters of Paul, though locally situated in their inaugural voyages, these texts are here presented as having made a *transition to a universal readership*. This fragment from Clement is one way of accounting for the post-compositional shift from more limited authorial design to eventual general usage, and it is a part of the larger, insistent paradoxes that govern patristic gospel interpretation between the human and divine authorship of these texts, and the particular witness of each gospel in relation to the unified testimony of them all.[220]

But this text does not do for Mitchell what she claims it does: "bridge the gap between local and more wide-spread readership."[221] In fact, no bridge was required. In reference to the written and published document of the Gospels, she makes a distinction between their meaning and significance: the Gospel had a specific meaning for the original audience alone and only later developed a more universal significance. According to Mitchell this text "describes an original local audience for Mark's gospel among the Roman churches, *even as its ultimate purpose is to*

---

[216] Mitchell notes that word αἰτίοι in ancient literary criticism is used for the historical occasion that called forth a document.

[217] Mitchell, "Patristic Counter-evidence," p. 51, admits that her attempt "is not to argue that this tradition is historically accurate, but to insist that it does represent what some early church readers *thought* about the origins of the gospels."

[218] *Ibid.*, pp. 51–52.   [219] *Ibid.* p. 51.   [220] *Ibid.*, p. 52.   [221] *Ibid.*, p. 51.

show how their historical ownership of this text was later to be super-seded."[222] But the tradition makes no such move from specific to general. The Gospel message that the apostle Peter proclaimed to the Christians in Rome[223] was called "divine proclamation" full stop; no mention of situational application was even implied. No broadening of this specifically located proclamation is required. The tradition's loose description of the audience ("hearers of Peter," "they," and "them") should have made clear to Mitchell that the tradition is focused on the important *origin* of the hearing and not the *situation* of the hearers; an importance we will explain below. The fact that the hearers wanted Mark to "leave a written record of the teaching" implies that it was something he was taking with him, a general message, not a message that was located in the specific circumstances of that audience. Why would they even have to ask him for something that was only theirs to begin with? As the previous Eusebius passage explains, if even the authorship of the Gospel is implied to be broader than Peter ("Peter . . . preached the word . . . and expressed the gospel *by the spirit* . . ."), should we not also assume that the message of the spirit's gospel is broader than the Roman Christians? This tradition, then, gives no support to the idea that the Gospel of Mark had original meaning only for Roman Christians and only later was given universal significance.[224]

Another area of discussion for Mitchell is the place of Gospel audiences in patristic exegesis. Mitchell states her concern well:

> Contrary to the impression one might receive from Bauckham's essay, these traditions about . . . authorship, which extend from Papias to Irenaeus to Clement to Origen to Eusebius, are not odd, minority voices, but they become the dominant way of thinking about gospel origins in the early church (and for much of the later interpretation in the west). Once enshrined in the Eusebian masterwork, *historia ecclesiastica*, and the writings of Jerome

---

[222] *Ibid.*, p. 52 (emphasis added).

[223] Again, this need not imply that every member of the audience was from Rome.

[224] For a good discussion of the literary concepts of meaning and significance see Kevin J. Vanhoozer, *Is There a Meaning in This Text? The Bible, the Reader, and the Morality of Literary Knowledge* (Grand Rapids: Zondervan, 1998), pp. 259–63, 421–24. Cf. E. D. Hirsch, "Meaning and Significance Reinterpreted," *CI* 11 (1984), pp. 202–24, who refined his meaning-significance distinction and now thinks that authors regularly intended to address future readers and so transcend their original situation. According to Hirsch, "Literature is typically an instrument designed for broad and continuing future applications" (p. 209).

in the west, their influence was pervasive and enduring from late antiquity up through modernity.[225]

Mitchell chastises Bauckham's dismissive footnote to the contrary: "Even if the four Gospels originally had the prestige of being local Gospels of particular major churches, there is no evidence at all that this factor was operative in the second century, when the survival of all four to form the four-Gospel canon was at stake."[226] For Mitchell this statement, responding to Streeter's theory that each of the four Gospels started with a local dominance, is

> set in serious doubt by the evidence we have already considered, is further disconfirmed by many more examples from among the ancient canon-lists, gospel prologues, and ὑποθέσεις, the essential purpose of which, in accord with literary criticism generally, was to direct and condition reading. By including such short plot summaries and often κεφάλαια or chapter lists in manuscripts, early Christians established cultures of reading and reception for their literature, using the bibliographic techniques of the late-antique library and schoolroom.[227]

Thus, according to Mitchell, the issue of Gospel audiences becomes a hermeneutical issue in patristic exegesis. The historical occasion of each Gospel was considered to be an important piece of information readers should have before encountering the text. This focus never denied the divine authorship, but saw the two working in tandem. The amount of interest in the biographical details of the evangelists, admittedly influenced by ancient encomiastic traditions, was universal. It is for this reason that Mitchell is surprised at the stark contrast between Bauckham's portrayal of the Gospel's audiences and the evidence she has presented.[228] How could Bauckham see the Gospels as communicating from "generic" evangelists and to a "generic" readership, "any and every" Church in the "Christian movement" in the Mediterranean world, when the patristic sources show such great hermeneutical interest in biographical details of authorship and historical details of origin? Or as Mitchell asks, "Why would such complex and elaborative narrative traditions grappling with the historical particularities that occasioned each have even been necessary?"[229]

---

[225] Mitchell, "Patristic Counter-evidence," p. 54.
[226] Bauckham, "For Whom Were Gospels Written?," p. 15, n. 10.
[227] Mitchell, "Patristic Counter-evidence," p. 55.   [228] *Ibid.*, p. 55.   [229] *Ibid.*, p. 61.

The function of Gospel narrative traditions in patristic exegesis

Before we can answer the question concerning the patristic interest in particularity and Bauckham's proposal for universality, we must define what the patristic exegetes meant hermeneutically by the historical particularity they ascribed to each of the Gospels. Mitchell admits that these particulars, these "audience request traditions," are not necessarily historically reliable, but describe what was occurring in the exegetical process. Mitchell explained it this way:

> The point for our purposes . . . is not to argue that this tradition is historically accurate, but to insist that it does represent what some early church leaders *thought* about the origins of the gospels . . . Most important for the question of the gospel audiences, this tradition [the Eusebius tradition concerning Mark cited above] . . . seems designed precisely to bridge the gap between local and more wide-spread readership . . . the fact that such a tradition arose at all . . . is indicative of the hermeneutical awareness in the early church of the multi-dimensional addressees of the gospel literature.[230]

Based upon this explanation, Mitchell assumes that we can know what some of the early church leaders "thought" about the origins of the Gospels. It is surprising to see Mitchell's confidence in ascertaining the cognitive process of the early church leaders in a field of study that has attempted to remove discussion of authorial intention from biblical interpretation. If we cannot be certain what Matthew intended, when we have a complete and unified document from which to work, let alone Paul from whom we have several documents, how can we assume to know the "thoughts" of the early church leaders concerning one topic mentioned in different ways in different documents? In agreement with Mitchell, we can confirm that there did exist various "traditions" about the origins of the Gospels, but nothing which would imply a "thought" by the early church leaders, as if the tradition was from the leaders themselves, let alone how the traditions were used in the hermeneutical process. We will discuss more on the definition of tradition below.

One also wonders what Mitchell implies by "this tradition . . . seems designed precisely to bridge the gap between local and more wide-spread readership." The problem of the gap between local and more widespread

---

[230] *Ibid.*, pp. 51–52.

readership was only concerning the Pauline epistles, not the Gospels.[231] The plurality of the Gospels was a problem,[232] not the locations from which they arose. It would seem that if the Gospels had come from specific locations, locations that helped to define their contextual purpose, then the plurality of the Gospels might have been less problematic. The early church could have seen the original use of each Gospel and simply explained them theologically for a more widespread audience. The fact that this did not occur might imply that their meaning was not located in a specific situation.

Finally, are these traditions really "indicative of the hermeneutical awareness in the early church of the multi-dimensional addressees of the gospel literature?" Again, unlike the Pauline epistles, the Gospels never needed to be explained away from the particular to the universal. One is hard-pressed to find in these traditions a "transition to a universal readership."[233] The Gospels never seem to need such assistance. True, these "traditions" imply an originating location, but never is that location made the interpretive key that Mitchell desires. It is rarely used to explain the difficult portions of the Gospels or to explain some aspect of the evangelist's *Sitz im Leben*. The "hermeneutical awareness of multi-dimensional addressees" was not from particular to universal, but more universal from the start.[234] The origins of the Gospels were important, but not for the sake of hermeneutics. To this we now turn.

---

[231] As Mitchell has already made mention. See N. A. Dahl, "The Particularity of the Pauline Epistles as a Problem in the Ancient Church," in A. N. Wilder *et al.* (eds.), *Neotestamentica et patristica, eine Freundesgabe, Oscar Cullmann zu seinem 60 Geburtstag*, NovTSup 6 (Leiden: Brill, 1962).

[232] See Oscar Cullmann, "The Plurality of the Gospels as a Theological Problem in Antiquity: A Study in the History of Dogma," in A. J. B. Higgins and S. Godman (eds.), *The Early Church: Oscar Cullmann* (London: SCM Press, 1956).

[233] Mitchell, "Patristic Counter-evidence," p. 52.

[234] We use the phrase "more universal" because our argument is not that the Gospels were written literally for "all" but potentially for all. The difference in nuance is important. Our argument is that the evangelists did assume that a readership broader than their own geographic location ("community") would read their Gospels and they designed their Gospel, used its genre, accordingly. In a personal response to Margaret Mitchell's 2003 paper, Richard Bauckham argues the following: "there is a clear logical distinction between an indefinite category as the audience and a specific audience. It is the difference between (e.g.) writing a book for theological students, wherever they may be, whether or not I know anything more about them than I know about all theological students as such, and on the other hand writing a class handout for the thirty-two students who are taking my course this year. In the first case, one could introduce further characterizations of the audience (theological students who are Christian believers, theological students who are training for the ministry, beginning students or students who already know quite a lot etc.) but it remains an indefinite category. It extends to students in institutions I've never heard of and places I've never thought about. In the second case, one could increase the size of the audience – a lecture class of 200 students – but they are still a specific group, one that could in principle

In dealing with the place of Gospel audiences in patristic exegesis we must define what is meant by "tradition." The term "tradition" can be employed to mean several things, but in this context it most certainly refers to a piece of historical information independent of scriptural sources handed down from an early period in the church.[235] This tradition that Mitchell utilizes in establishing any particularity in the origins of the Gospels is certainly oral tradition; the diverse and contradictory nature of the traditions makes this clear. As oral tradition, therefore, it is subject to the laws of history.[236] It cannot continue to be preserved indefinitely in an oral form without succumbing to corruption or distortion. It would seem that Mitchell would agree with this statement. She would not argue that the traditions are historically accurate, but that they reflect the "thought" of the patristic exegetes. As Mitchell explains, the historical occasion "of each gospel was considered an important piece of information readers should have before encountering the text."[237] Using the recent definition of *historia* by Frances Young, Mitchell explains further what the patristic exegetes considered historical: "*Historia* is the enquiry that produces as much information as possible with respect to the elements, actions, characters or background of the text."[238] Although the term *historia* can be defined as such, the definition in no way explains the historical method used by the patristic exegetes. Earlier in the same work Frances Young explains:

> Quintilian's word, *historike*, again represents a technical vocabulary, but to jump to the conclusion that *to historikon* is some kind of historico-critical exegesis is misplaced: I submit that too many discussions of patristic exegesis have jumped to conclusions about historical interest where such terminology is used, for it does not necessarily imply what we mean by historical.

be specified as a list of names of individuals. In these senses, 'Jewish Christians' is an indefinite category, 'the Christian communities in a wide area around Antioch' is a specific audience" (personal letter to Margaret Mitchell, April 2004, p. 2). It is this understanding of a "universal" or "general" audience that this paper is attempting to advance.

[235] Adapted from R. P. C. Hanson, *Tradition in the Early Church* (London: SCM Press, 1962), p. 7.

[236] As explained by Loveday Alexander, "Fact, Fiction, and the Genre of Acts," *NTS* 44 (1988), p. 390, "The readers, in other words, are being asked to accept the story . . . as largely fiction – but fiction sanctioned by being classified as a 'story of antiquity.'" That is, the stories have a moral value, not necessarily a historical-critical one.

[237] Mitchell, "Patristic Counter-evidence," p. 55.

[238] Frances Young, *Biblical Exegesis and the Formation of Christian Culture* (Cambridge: Cambridge University Press, 1997), p. 87. Cited by Mitchell, "Patristic Counter-evidence," p. 20, n. 60.

Historia in the first place has to do with enquiry, the knowledge acquired by investigation, and in some contexts at least it is more likely to have that kind of meaning than to imply any claim to historical factuality in our sense. Indeed, it is acknowledged that ancient literary criticism had no true historical sense.[239]

Young explains well the pitfall of equating patristic historical "thought" with the historical exegesis assumed today. Although her linking *historia* with inquiry might at first seem to support Mitchell's argument, a further look reveals it does not. The type of inquiry the patristic exegetes were interested in was not the behind-the-text issues but the textual issues themselves. Unlike modern historical criticism that "uses" the behind-the-text issues to interpret the text, such would not have been seen as necessary in pre-critical interpretation. Even the issue of the origin of the text, the point of concern here, would not have explained the text, but *verified* it. A later comment on *historia* by Young is helpful here:

> It is true that *historia* meant *pragmata* (deeds) or *res gestae* (things that happened); stories given this epithet were meant to be "true," not *res fictae* or *res fabulosae* – that was the expectation raised in readers' minds by the genre. But the distinctive thing about historical writing was not "single-minded pursuits of facts" but their presentation as morally significant, their interpretation in terms of "virtue" and "vice" and "fortune." No Antiochene could have imagined the kind of critical stance of the Biblical Theology movement, explicitly locating revelation not in the text, events to which we only have access by reconstructing them from the texts, treating the texts as documents providing historical data.[240]

The "audience request traditions" that Mitchell uses to show a hermeneutical interest do not seem to fit with the *historia* described by Young. The audience request traditions had an important significance, even a moral significance, but it was not the hermeneutical key to interpreting the text. Rather, these traditions verified to the reader that the texts and their stories were reliable and connected to a true source. These traditions did

---

[239] Young, *Biblical Exegesis and the Formation of Christian Culture*, p. 79. The same appraisal is made by D. A. Russell, *Criticism in Antiquity* (London: Gerald Duckworth, 1981), p. 159: "There can be little doubt that the historical study of literature in antiquity was very rudimentary by modern standards."

[240] Young, *Biblical Exegesis and the Formation of Christian Culture*, pp. 166–67.

not provide a *method* of reading but an *endorsement* for reading. Therefore, these traditions endorsed two things to the readers of the Gospels:
antiquity and apostolicity.

Patristic exegesis and the endorsement of tradition

The traditions about the origins of the Gospels are not hermeneutical
keys for the interpretation of the Gospel texts, but certifiers that the text
is apostolic and connected to the early history of the church.[241] Our goal
here is to see if a reading of these patristic texts not as hermeneutical keys
but as apostolic tradition will yield different results. Before looking at
some example texts, a brief explanation is in order.

Studies that examine biblical interpretation in the early church are often
forced to use source material used in the context of doctrinal debates.[242]
Looking at Irenaeus, for example, we find that since he had no explicit
hermeneutical principles of his own,[243] he often attacked the Gnostics'
interpretation of Scripture at the level of content rather than at the level
of exegetical theory.[244] But even when arguing against the Gnostic content, they use as their base the authority of the apostolic tradition, or as
Irenaeus refers to it, "the tradition of the apostles."[245] As Manlio Simonetti explains, "The Catholic Church alone is the touchstone of truth in
the interpretation of Scripture in that it is the storehouse of authentic
apostolic tradition."[246] The same appeal to the church's authority of tradition is made by Tertullian.[247] The same can be said of the third-century
exegetes. That Hippolytus believed in a tradition deriving from the apostles is evidenced by the very existence of his work, *Apostolic Tradition*.
Cyprian's comment concerning tradition is worth repeating: "For if ever
we turn to the fountain and source of divine tradition, human error ceases
and, once the purport of the heavenly mysteries is perceived, whatever

---

[241] The difficulty of defining patristic exegesis testifies to this. See Young, "Exegetical
Method and Scriptural Proof: The Bible in Doctrinal Debate," *SP* 19 (1989), pp. 291–
304.

[242] See Manlio Simonetti, *Biblical Interpretation in the Early Church: An Historical
Introduction to Patristic Exegesis*, trans. John A. Hughes (Edinburgh: T. & T. Clark, 1994),
pp. 1–33.

[243] Of course, it might be said that the use of the "rule of faith" (apostolic doctrine) is a
hermeneutical theory. Scripture, it is assumed, must be interpreted in accordance with the
"rule of faith."

[244] *Adv. Haer.* 2.20–25. See also Simonetti, *Biblical Interpretation in the Early Church*,
p. 24.

[245] *Adv. Haer.* 3.1.

[246] Simonetti, *Biblical Interpretation in the Early Church*, p. 24.

[247] *Praescr.* 20–21.

was lying hid under a fog and cloud of darkness is brought out into the light."[248] Although Martin Hengel's reconstruction of the early church's tradition deposit (i.e. Rome) is problematic, his understanding of the need for authoritative tradition in patristic exegesis is helpful:

> The relevant information about each writing, its author and its origin were kept in the Roman church archive; this was important for reading them aloud in worship, since people had to know what they were reading there and also had to convey this to the community. Anonymous public readings were hardly tolerable because *each reading needed an "authoritative" or even "inspired" text, and author.*[249]

Far from promoting the hermeneutical key that Mitchell suggests, Hengel shows the importance of the connection between the Gospel texts and their apostolic origins for readers in Christian antiquity. Finally, one would think that the same "thought" process that allowed the NT writings to be welcomed into the eventual canon would remain an important element of their interpretation. The apostolic origin of a book, real or putative, provided a presumption of authority that validated the writings.[250] Understood in this way, the audience traditions did not describe the initial reading/hearing audience to future readers/hearers, but confirmed to the church that it could feel comfortable becoming an audience of the text in the present.

Mitchell spends several pages giving examples of Gospel prologues that she claims were hermeneutically significant to their readers. After having argued for a different reading perspective above, one that is not hermeneutically relevant but authoritatively relevant, we can now turn to the audience traditions and attempt to apply this new reading perspective. The first example we are going to look at comes from the Muratorian Canon which mentions a legend about the origin of the Gospel of John:

> The fourth of the Gospels, that of John (one) of the disciples. When his fellow-disciples and bishops urged [him], he said: fast with me today for three days and, what will be revealed to each

---

[248] *Ep.* 74.10.2; translation from Hanson, *Tradition in the Early Church*, p. 99.

[249] Hengel, *The Four Gospels and the One Gospel of Jesus Christ*, p. 37 (emphasis added). Hengel's proposal is problematic in that it relies on more recent traditions and applies them to a first-century Christian movement. Certainly community interpreters who see different and sectarian "groups" behind the various NT documents would consider Hengel's proposal implausible.

[250] Bruce M. Metzger, *The Canon of the New Testament: Its Origin, Development, and Significance* (Oxford: Clarendon Press, 1987), p. 253.

one, let us relate to one another. In the same night it was revealed to Andrew, one of the Apostles, that, whilst all were to go over (it), John in his own name should write everything down. And therefore, though various rudiments (or: tendencies?) are taught in the several Gospel books, yet that matters nothing for the faith of believers, since by the one and guiding (original?) Spirit everything is declared in all . . .[251]

Although this text certainly implies that the early church was intent on being aware of the origins of the Gospels, it hardly represents the hermeneutical key that Mitchell would want. As we suggested above, the importance of the *historia* presented here is that the FG is based upon apostolic tradition; tradition that was rooted not just in the FE, but in several evangelists and church leaders in a type of apostolic committee. Such a tradition would give the Gospel a regulative authority in the churches where it was located and used in worship.[252]

Other traditions seem to give the specific purpose behind the Gospels. Two examples are worth discussing here. The first deals again with the Gospel of John:

John . . . last of all wrote a gospel, when he had been asked by the bishops of Asia [to write] against Cerinthus and the other heretics, and especially against the teaching of the Ebionites that was resounding. The latter say that the Christ did not exist before Mary, for which reason he [the evangelist] was compelled to speak about his divine generation.[253]

Mitchell admits that this tradition is an "imagined scene" of a specific Gospel audience, but still maintains that the prologue was a hermeneutical key for interpreting the Gospel: "Of utmost significance, this reconstruction of the local audience is used as *an exegetical principle that helps explain features of the text* of the gospel – in this case, the distinctive incipit of John, which is said to have been written to combat these precise heretical Christologies."[254] This specific use of the Gospel, rather than promoting Mitchell's argument, lends credence to our proposal. For the

---

[251] Translation from Wilhelm Schneemelcher, *New Testament Apocrypha. Volume One: Gospels and Related Writings*, rev. edn, trans. R. McL. Wilson (Louisville: Westminster John Knox Press, 1991), pp. 34–35.

[252] This tradition might have also been concerned with the diversity of the Gospels and tried to show how they agreed on essentials.

[253] Text from the collection by Hermann F. von Soden, *Die Schriften des Neuen Testaments*, 4 vols. (Berlin: Dunckler, 1902), vol. I, pp. 309–10.

[254] Mitchell, "Patristic Counter-evidence," p. 59 (emphasis added).

author of this tradition on John, Cerinthus and the Ebionites were not heretics that concerned him in his own situation, let alone the original situation of the FG, but belonged to the apostolic age – the age in which he writes. The author is offering a canonical explanation of a feature of the Gospel. Such a maneuver is temporally specific, but not necessarily geographically. If the author who is responding to these heretics would not have been considered as addressing a purely local audience, how can Mitchell assume that the Gospel was addressing a specific "group" context? Of course, if the author of this tradition had known of a Johannine "group" that had similar ideological battles, he could have used them as an analogy for his apostolic-age readers; but no such analogy is provided. Rather than providing support for a local audience, this tradition reveals the assumption of a broad audience – any and every location where conflict between Christians and heretics was taking place.

The second tradition deals with the Gospel of Luke:

> Luke is a Syrian from Antioch, a healer by craft, one who was a disciple of the apostles, and later followed Paul until his martyrdom, having served the Lord without distraction, wife-less, child-less, reaching 84 years he dies in Boetia, filled with the holy spirit. Although gospels were previously in existence – that according to Matthew having been written in Judea, that according to Mark in Italy, incited by the holy spirit when in the regions around Achaia, he composed this entire gospel, making clear in his introduction the very fact that others had been written before his, and that it was necessary to set forth for the believers from the Gentiles the accurate narrative of the story of salvation in order that they not be distracted by Jewish mythic accounts, nor deceived by heretical and vain imaginings to miss the mark of the truth.[255]

This tradition, like the one above, locates the Gospel in apostolic roots, placing its author in the very spirit-led ministry of Paul. The fact that this tradition placed Luke in the hands of a Gentile audience is not surprising since Luke was the companion of Paul, the missionary to the Gentiles. Helpful here is Richard Burridge's analysis of Gospel genre and its relation to the Gospel community debate. Burridge has shown that it was normal for a Greco-Roman biography to be used in a "less limited" way;

---

[255] Text from Kurt Aland, *Synopsis Quattuor Euangeliorum: Locis parallelis evangeliorum apocryphorum et partum adhibitis*, 13th edn (Stuttgart: Württembergische Bibelanstalt, 1985), p. 533.

a *bios* would only rarely be used for a closed or sectarian "group." For Burridge it is better to think of *bioi* as having certain types of people (audiences) in mind when writing, which is more like our modern concept of "market," rather than just one narrow "community."[256] A Jewish or Gentile audience as the primary audience fits well with the patristic traditions we have already examined.[257]

In summary, the following can be argued: there is no evidence in the patristic exegetical traditions provided by Mitchell that the Gospels were seen as historically determined by a particular context and only later made universal by principles of divine authorship.[258] In fact, even the patristic traditions cannot be limited to a specific context, but are befitting to a wide Christian audience in the apostolic age. The narrative traditions of the origin and audience of the Gospels assisted this hermeneutical process not by providing a method of reading the Gospels but by providing an endorsement for reading the Gospels.

Conclusion: patristic exegesis and Gospel origins

Mitchell's thorough discussion of patristic evidence provides a needed component of the Gospel community debate. Our interaction with her 2005 article forced us to provide definition to the terminology and logical structure of the argument that the Gospels were written for a broad audience. Our critique of Mitchell brought us to the following conclusion: the

---

[256] Burridge, "About People, by People, for People: Gospel Genre and Audiences," especially p. 132. Burridge is suggesting that instead of imagining hypothetical "communities" as intended by the Gospels, we should assume a wider readership that may have had emphases for certain "types" of readers. See, for example, Mary Ann Tolbert, *Sowing the Gospel: Mark's World in Literary-Historical Perspective* (Minneapolis: Fortress, 1989), pp. 59–79, 303–06, who has suggested that Mark was written for a wider readership among both Christians being persecuted and for others interested in the faith. See also May Ann Beavis, *Mark's Audience: The Literary and Social Setting of Mark: 4.11–12*, JSNTSup 33 (Sheffield: Sheffield Academic Press, 1989), p. 171, who has argued for a "more general audience of early Christian missionary teaching/preaching." We will discuss this more fully in chapter 3.

[257] This is similar to Bauckham's description of "Jewish Christians" as an indefinite category of audience.

[258] We are not denying that the Gospels were created in different locations, surrounded by different audience influences, and requested by different pressures to the evangelists. The fact that the Gospels arose in different locations, or at least were used in some locations before others or as the "primary" Gospels in certain regions above others is not opposed to our argument. We want to argue, with the assistance of Burridge, that the biographical genre of the Gospels made them more universal than particular. This is what made the plurality of the Gospels a problem. If the Gospels were not seen as harmonious with one another, if they were viewed as having different intentions and purposes that were geographically located, the differences might have been both explainable and more acceptable.

patristic evidence certainly does provide a hermeneutical key for reading the Gospels. But contrary to Mitchell, this hermeneutical key is not a method of reading, one which utilizes the Gospels' original social-historical context, but an endorsement for reading, confirmed in the apostolicity and antiquity of the Gospels themselves. The various traditions connect the Gospels to the apostolic roots of founding Christianity, thus making the Gospels authoritative and reliable. In the midst of various heretical readings of Jesus and the Gospels, along with the other Jesus books in early Christianity, these prologues and audience request traditions provided stability and approval for the four Gospels that eventually became canonical. Our goal, therefore, has been to show that the patristic evidence Mitchell assumes contradicts a more indefinite Gospel audience can be given a different reading; a reading that we have argued is more appropriate to the nature of the *historia* and the pre-critical (pre-Enlightenment) hermeneutic the patristic exegetes would have assumed. The indefinite social-historical audience of the Gospels, then, allowed them to be used canonically in several different hermeneutical situations in the early church, to which the various traditions allude.[259]

Early Christian community: conclusion

The Gospel community debate concerns several social-historical and hermeneutical issues. These issues require definition. This chapter has

---

[259] The newness of the Gospel community debate forces us to limit our range of discussion. It would have been helpful, and is eventually necessary, to deal with several issues that are related to the debate. First, the four-fold Gospel collection. Rather than seeing the Gospels as locally founded and as representing a different type of the Christian sect, we should see this collection as, according to Hurtado, *Lord Jesus Christ*, p. 580, "clear evidence that these particular texts already had a wide circulation and high standing." As Graham Stanton, "The Fourfold Gospel," *NTS* 43 (1997), pp. 317–46, explains concerning the development of the four-fold Gospel, "A political explanation has often been advanced. The fourfold Gospel is said to have been a compromise worked out between different regional preferences. However it is difficult to find any evidence for a second-century equivalent to the European parliament! The older view that individual gospels circulated only in limited geographical areas is no longer tenable: the papyri, both Christian and non-Christian, indicate that there was a great deal of contact between different regions around the Mediterranean" (p. 336). Cf. Hans von Campenhausen, *The Formation of the Christian Bible*, trans. John Austin Baker (London: Adam and Charles Black, 1974), p. 123; and Charles E. Hill, *The Johannine Corpus in the Early Church* (Oxford: Oxford University Press, 2004). Second, the Gospel titles. The very title of the Gospels, all four beginning with "according to," shows an awareness in the early church that fits within our model. Cf. Hengel, *The Four Gospels and the One Gospel of Jesus Christ.* Third, the interrelation between the Gospels. Our model brings out several related issues of the interrelations between the Gospels and how they formulate a broad, both unified and diversified, Christian identity.

attempted to do just that. We have examined three important areas that needed definition. The first area was the definition of the term "community." We argued that community need not be defined territorially, but relationally. The relational model of community is able to be more comprehensive in its appraisal of the Gospels' potential audience, one that seems to fit the evidence within the early Christian movement. The second area was the sectarian nature of early Christianity. We argued that although the sectarian model is helpful, it is too limiting to the evidence and is itself difficult to define for appropriate heuristic use. The model we proposed, based upon the relational concept of community, allows a fuller reading of the Gospels in light of early Christian evidence. Even the recent sociology of knowledge research in the FG, especially the concept of anti-language promoted by Bruce Malina, can be redefined and understood more appropriately in light of our model. The third area was the patristic evidence for Gospel communities and Gospel audiences. We argued, based upon the important paper by Margaret Mitchell, that although the patristic exegetes were interested in the origin of the Gospel documents, and discussed various locations of origin, they did not assume that the local origin of the Gospels implied a limited use of the Gospels, nor was it a hermeneutical key in the sense of modern historical-critical exegesis. Mitchell has "read" the patristic writings and their implicit interpretive strategy with a post-Enlightenment hermeneutic, which has forced her to misapply several Gospel origin and audience traditions to the original Gospel audiences. The traditions of the Gospels' origins were meant to confirm that the Gospels were rooted in the apostles and in the antiquity of the church.[260] But our work of definition is not complete; more questions need to be asked in certain areas. If the prologues do not provide the hermeneutical keys to the text, what does? How did the earliest "Christians" know how to read the Gospels? To answer this question we must examine the literary nature of the Gospel texts themselves in chapter 3.

---

[260] As we stated above, these traditions were also used to explain the diversity of the Gospels. These two things, diversity and apostolicity, were quite closely related, because if the Gospels were considered incompatible with each other, they could not be apostolic.

3

EARLY CHRISTIAN GOSPEL: GOSPEL GENRE AND A CRITIQUE OF THE TWO-LEVEL READING OF THE GOSPEL OF JOHN

No discussion of the interpretation of the Gospels can avoid discussing the Gospels as text. But the text does not exist in isolation; the Gospels were created in a social and religious milieu. For the form critic, the social environment controlled the literary creation and influenced the meaning of the text. Form criticism was sociological in its very nature and literary genre was considered a social category of communication. But as we have seen thus far, it is difficult to derive the socio-historical background of the Gospels. Not only can the sociological background only be determined in vague ways, but the text itself must be considered as its own living entity. This is stated most clearly by the social historian Abraham Malherbe:

> Our major sources for the social reconstruction of early Christianity are literary. We may expect to gain insights elsewhere – for example, from archeological data and modern social theory; but eventually we are driven back to literary sources. With that in mind we must stress the obvious, namely that sociological study of early Christianity cannot slight literary criticism. We must persist in seeking to determine the character and intention of different types of literature if we hope to discern how they functioned in relation to the communities with which they were associated. When that is done they can more properly be assessed as witnesses to particular communities.[1]

In this way it becomes imperative that we look at the Gospel text itself and the type of communication called "Gospel." For our purposes, two questions need to be asked of the Gospel text. First, how does a first-century Gospel text reveal its audience? This question is searching for clues in the form and structure of the Gospel narrative as a whole to see if anything concerning its "expected" audience can be retrieved. Does the genre of the Gospels delimit the size of the audience? Could

---

[1] Malherbe, *Social Aspects of Early Christianity*, p. 15.

a local, geographic "community" write a Gospel narrative for its own use, or does the form of the narrative imply a more general audience? As we will discuss below, it has been argued that the genre of the Gospels affects the assumed audience. But does a text's genre reveal if the text was intended for a local or general[2] audience? It is this that we will attempt to clarify. Second, how would a first-century audience have appropriated a Gospel text? This question is searching to see if the Gospel genre and its narrative form give clues to how the Gospel would have been "read" by first-century readers/hearers. How would a first-century reader have understood the story?[3] What type of narrative referentiality can we discern in the Gospels? These questions attempt to critique the current "community" readings of the Gospels. As we hope to show, the genre of the Gospels both limits the range of use of the text and allows us to see how it may have been understood by its original readers. In essence, our assumption is that the historical character of the Gospel genre and its first-century appropriation give it a more precise hermeneutical nature and its interpreters a more certain hermeneutical responsibility. It is to these two questions that we now turn.

Gospel genre and Gospel audience

Recent discussions in the Gospel community debate have shown the importance that literary genre plays in the interpretation of a text's audience. We already discussed in chapter 1 Graham Stanton's reminder of the importance of establishing the literary genre in order to do appropriate interpretive work. In reference to Matthew, Stanton says that a Gospel is not a letter; since a letter does not give a clear window onto the social situation of the recipients, a Gospel must then be treated with even more caution. "Matthew's gospel should not be expected to provide us with *detailed* information about the social setting of the first recipients. I am convinced that Matthew's choice of literary genre and the evidence of the text of the gospel itself both point in this direction."[4] We will discuss

---

[2] We use the term "general" audience and not "broad" or "wide" because our argument is not that the Gospels were written for "all," but potentially for all. Certainly the evangelists did not know where their complete audience was located, but they did assume that a readership broader than their own geographic "community" would read their Gospels and they designed their Gospel accordingly.

[3] Our concern is with the first-century readers, not later readers or appropriations of the Gospel text.

[4] Stanton, "Revisiting Matthew's Communities," p. 11. Later Stanton states, "Matthew's gospel should not be read as if it were a Pauline letter. We should stop supposing that the gospel reflects the evangelist's close relationship with one group of Christians in one house church in one particular urban geographical location" (p. 11).

this more below when we deal with the redactional specificity of Gospel interpretations. More recently Hans-Josef Klauck, responding to a paper in a section entitled "The Whence and Whither of the Johannine Community" at an international conference on the Gospel of John, argues that the discussion partly depends on the genre of Gospels and their referentiality. Klauck lists several important questions concerning referentiality:

> Do texts only refer to themselves and function as a closed system (structural and narrative criticism)? Do they, beyond that, only refer to other texts and textual worlds (intertextuality)? Do they, if they open up at all, only open up to the readers who create the meaning (reader-response criticism, reception history, and, in some ways, rhetorical criticism, too)? Or do they refer also to extra-textual realities, events, figures, social structures, and so on? Do they, in other words, refer to their historical context (historical criticism; social science approach)? And what does that imply?[5]

We will deal with this below when we discuss J. L. Martyn's two-level reading of the FG. In light of the Gospel community debate it has become important to define the exact role the literary genre of the Gospels plays in determining the size of their intended audience. Thus we come to our first question: How does a first-century Gospel text reveal its audience?

Although literary questions were being asked of the NT in the ancient church, the literary-historical investigation is primarily a work of the nineteenth and twentieth centuries.[6] The Gospel texts themselves have a unique history. From the mid-second century through most of the nineteenth century the Gospels were viewed as some sort of biography.[7] But for nearly a century major discussion concerning the exact *Gattung* or literary genre[8] of the Gospels has occurred. There has been much confusion surrounding the Gospels from the standpoint of literary genre. "Not

---

[5] Klauck, "Community, History, and Text(s) – a Response" (paper presented at Life in Abundance: An International Conference on the Gospel of John: A Tribute to Raymond Brown, Baltimore, October 16–18, 2003), p. 1. Now published under the same title in John R. Donahue (ed.), *Life in Abundance*, pp. 82–90, quotation taken from p. 82.

[6] Georg Strecker, *History of New Testament Literature*, trans. Calvin Katter (Harrisburg, Pa.: Trinity Press International, 1997), p. 1.

[7] Craig S. Keener, *The Gospel of John: A Commentary*, 2 vols. (Peabody, Mass.: Hendrickson, 2003), vol. I, p. 4.

[8] This book will consider the French-English term *genre* to be synonymous with the German term *Gattung* and understands that they may be used interchangeably. For the most part, however, the former will be employed. Since we are only attempting to show how the genre of the Gospels affects our understanding of their intended audience, a detailed discussion of genre in literary theory will not be given here. For a discussion of the terms and their literary heritage see Philip L. Shuler, *A Genre for the Gospels: The Biographical Character of Matthew* (Philadelphia: Fortress Press, 1982), pp. 24–34.

only does one look in vain for a precise, universally acceptable definition of genre but the function of genre within literary criticism appears to be multiple."[9] In the classical and neo-classical periods, genre had a normative function within which an author wrote and by which a text was interpreted. In modern literary criticism genre has a more descriptive than regulative function.[10] According to literary theory genre is "a principle of order: it classifies literature and literature history . . . by specifically literary types of organization and structure."[11] Despite the many definitions of genre and seeking to avoid the pitfalls of the discussion, there are two features that are relevant to the discussion of the Gospels that seem to reflect a consensus within literary criticism.[12] First, instead of looking at the micro-level of the text, as in the form-critical approach, genre criticism looks at the macro-level of the text.[13] From the perspective of genre the text is seen as a whole with all the various parts (micro) functioning within the whole (macro) as a composite of specific traits or characteristics which are formal and material.[14] Second, genre is a comparative or derivative concept. "As a category or classification (both explicitly for the critic who seeks to identify and classify and implicitly for the interpreter who reads a text in terms of the 'sense of the whole') genre stems from one's conscious or unconscious observation of formally and materially similar or dissimilar texts."[15]

Since 1977, a growing consensus has been forming which views the Gospels as related to Greco-Roman biography.[16] The most recent and

---

[9] Robert Guelich, "The Gospel Genre," in Peter Stuhlmacher (ed.), *The Gospel and the Gospels* (Grand Rapids: Eerdmans, 1991), p. 173. See also William G. Doty, "The Concept of Genre in Literary Analysis," *SBLSP* (1972), pp. 413–48.

[10] Guelich, "The Gospel Genre," p. 173.

[11] René Wellek and Austin Warren, *Theory of Literature* (London: Jonathan Cape, 1949), p. 235.

[12] Guelich, "The Gospel Genre," p. 174.

[13] According to J. A. Baird, "Genre Analysis as a Method of Historical Criticism," *SBLSP* (1972), pp. 385–411, since Gunkel, "Form" refers to the smaller, individual units of which a "genre" (*Gattung*), the work as a whole, is composed (pp. 386–87). For an example of an earlier work that uses Form and *Gattung* interchangeably see Klaus Koch, *The Growth of the Biblical Tradition*, pp. 3–6.

[14] David Aune, *The New Testament in its Literary Environment*, LEC 8 (Philadelphia: Westminster Press, 1987), p. 13, states it well: "Literary genres and forms are not simply neutral containers used as convenient ways to package various types of written communication. They are social conventions that provide contextual meaning for the smaller units of language and text they enclose."

[15] Guelich, "The Gospel Genre," p. 174.

[16] Charles H. Talbert, *What is a Gospel? The Genre of the Canonical Gospels* (Philadelphia: Fortress Press, 1977) attempted to revive the comparison between the Gospels and Greco-Roman biography by attacking the form critics, most notably Bultmann, and their *sui generis* understanding of the Gospels. Although Talbert's classification of the Gospels

influential argument for defining the Gospels as Greco-Roman biography, building on the work done since 1977, has been by Richard Burridge, whose research in Gospel genre has become the standard defense for the *bios* genre of the Gospels.[17] The state of the research is best summarized in a recent monograph by Larry Hurtado which deals extensively with what he calls the "Jesus books." According to Hurtado, "the Gospels constitute a distinctive kind (or subgenre) of *bios* literature. But the flexibility of the *bios* genre was such that the authors apparently saw it as a literary form they could successfully adapt in their individual ways to serve the . . . concerns that led them to write."[18] Although we will not deal with the debate about the Gospels and their *bios*-like character, we will be dealing more substantially with Burridge, for he has been a participant in the Gospel community debate and has used Gospel genre as his starting point.

Even within Burridge's own work, confusion (or development) exists concerning the use of genre for establishing a Gospel's audience. In reference to John, Burridge claims: "the production and composition of the gospel is best understood within a corporate context, often called the Johannine Community, which developed its distinctive flavour . . ."[19] In *GAC* Burridge claims: "the context within which the Gospel was composed and the audience for whom it was written has arisen from a misunderstanding of the genre of the Gospels."[20] Burridge admits that genre does not answer all the questions concerning a text's audience:

> The main problem is that we have no evidence outside the Gospel texts themselves about their sociological setting, the contexts within which and for which they were written. A comparison with other Greco-Roman biographies may help us to reconstruct

and their genre types was heavily scrutinized by David Aune, "The Problem of the Genre of the Gospels: A Critique of C. H. Talbert's What is a Gospel?," in R. T. France and David Wenham (eds.), *Gospel Perspectives II: Studies of the History and Tradition of the Four Gospels* (Sheffield: JSOT Press, 1981), pp. 9–60, his research produced a renewed interest in the analogical comparison between the Gospels and Greco-Roman biographical literature. Another movement in the *bios* direction was made by Shuler, *A Genre for the Gospels*, in 1982. Unfortunately, Shuler, like Talbert, applied the Gospels to a specific type of function that was not well received (see the critique by Guelich, "The Gospel Genre," pp. 180–81). Finally, in 1987, Aune, *The New Testament in its Literary Environment*, argued comprehensively that the Gospels should belong within the Greco-Roman category of biography. According to Aune, "The features of Greco-Roman biography . . . offer many if not exact parallels to the major literary qualities and features of the Gospels" (p. 43).

[17] Burridge, *What are the Gospels?*

[18] Larry W. Hurtado, *Lord Jesus Christ: Devotion to Jesus in Earliest Christianity* (Grand Rapids: Eerdmans, 2003), p. 282.

[19] Burridge, *What are the Gospels?*, p. 214, see also pp. 228–31.

[20] Burridge, "About People, by People, for People," p. 144.

possible audiences or markets for the Gospels, as well as illuminate how and why these lives were written, published, or circulated.[21]

Thus, according to Burridge, since the biographical genre has a historical precedent, knowing the genre of the Gospels may help allude to the general character of the communicative form, and possibly allude to the expected audience. For Burridge, three general characteristics about the literary communication of the Gospels can be presumed from the *bios* genre of the Gospels.

First, the Gospels, like other biographies, have a person (Jesus) as their subject. This needs little proving; each of the Gospels reveals either in their initial sentence or in a purpose statement near the end that Jesus is their subject (Matthew 1:1, Βίβλος γενέσεως Ἰησοῦ Χριστοῦ; Mark 1:1, Ἀρχὴ τοῦ εὐαγγελίου Ἰησοῦ Χριστοῦ; John 20:31, ταῦτα δὲ γέγραπται ἵνα πιστεύ[σ]ητε ὅτι Ἰησοῦς ἐστιν ὁ χριστός).[22] This need not imply a monolithic presentation for their subject,[23] for certainly the Gospels were promulgating certain views about Jesus.[24] But as we will discuss below, it

---

[21] *Ibid.*, p. 131.

[22] Luke is different in that its preface should probably be seen as introducing the two-volume work, not just the Jesus biography.

[23] The fact that we have differences between the Gospels, especially the Synoptics and the FG, warrants explanation. According to Burridge's classification in *What are the Gospels?*, all four Gospels are certainly Greco-Roman *bioi*, even with their different characteristics. For Burridge, the *bios* genre should be seen as family resemblances; each child is of the same type, yet they each have their differences (pp. 236–39). Since the four canonical Gospels are so similar in type, Burridge classifies them as their own subgenre βίος Ἰησοῦ. In comparison with other Greco-Roman *bioi*, the four Gospels may be called their subgenre, and this subgenre is focused on the life of Jesus. It is this subgenre and its uniqueness that is often mistaken to be its own genre. The Gospels are unique in comparison to "other" *bioi*, not in and of themselves. The unique aspects of the Gospels do not imply that they are *sui generis*, even if they can be classified under their own subset in biographical literature.

[24] The idea of promulgation can often lead to a strong sociological reading of the Gospels: what were they trying to promote? Defend? What does this tell us of the social setting and social relations? This was Philip Esler's critique of *GAC* in "Community and Gospel in Early Christianity." According to Esler, "Bauckham pays insufficient attention to what flows from Matthew and Luke having significantly altered, radically amplified and even, in Luke's case, considerably abridged Mark. As far as they [the evangelists] were concerned, in many respects Mark had got it wrong . . . What they would have learned from the arrival of Mark in their congregations was not just the prospect that their Gospels might circulate as widely as Mark's, or that *their* Gospels would replace *Mark's*, but rather that *anything they wrote* was just as likely to be savaged in congregations it finally reached as Mark had been when it fell into their hands. In other words, what they had done to Mark would have alerted them to the *futility of attempting to reach a general audience*" (p. 241, emphasis original). In response, Bauckham, "Response to Philip Esler," claims that Esler's model of conflict and diversity, which goes back to F. C. Baur, is not connected to any anthropological theory but is a particular reconstruction of early Christian relations. In the face of Elser's picture of

makes it all the more difficult to move to the context of the promulgation when the text is a type of biography.

Second, the Gospels were not written by authoring committees and communities do not write books.[25] For Burridge, the community reconstructions, though they rarely implicate an authoring committee, place too much emphasis on the control the authoring setting (i.e. community) places on the writing of the Gospel:

> too much stress on events or issues in the evangelists' communities as determining the Gospel's special interests or theologies turns the writers back into the stenographer model, with the form-critical oral tunnel replaced by the redaction-critical community. There is also a circularity inherent in interpreting the texts in light of hypothetical communities, the nature of which has already been deduced solely from the texts![26]

Thus, the *bios* genre of the Gospels helps us to evaluate their ostensive reference with more sensitivity. Certainly the social setting of the evangelists affected what was written about Jesus; at the same time, what was written about Jesus certainly affected the social setting.[27]

Third, although one cannot simply assume a large intended audience for the Gospels, rarely were *bioi* around the time of the Gospels used specifically for a closed "group." The only comparison is the *bioi* from the philosophical schools, but even then the *bioi* were often used in a

diversity Bauckham argues for "group-identity and group-orientation within a new (Jewish) religious movement which rapidly spread through the Mediterranean world and (as we show from the evidence) maintained constant and close communications throughout its network of constituent communities . . . So far as I am aware, Mediterranean anthropology provides us with no analogy for this kind of social phenomenon" (pp. 250–51). As we argued in chapter 2, a relational model helps explain this new type of social context; a model which allows diversity and conflict to co-exist with group socialization and unity. As Bauckham claims, "The evidence for diversity (which itself clearly often existed without serious conflict) and conflict . . . only confirms this conclusion" (p. 251).

[25] Although this is certainly true, some "school" reconstructions behind the FG could nearly be described as an authoring committee. See Hengel, *The Johannine Question*, pp. 119–35.

[26] Burridge, "About People, by People, for People," p. 126. Although Burridge's statement is certainly rhetorically exaggerated, for external information does come into play with respect to the context of early Christians, what is important is his warning that contextual reconstructions have the ability to import a certain reading of the textual data; a reading that is not verifiable by our historical sources (e.g. there is no evidence for any "community" for any of the Gospels). Hence the task of this study is to critique the current "community" reconstruction of the FG, a reconstruction we are arguing that has forced the textual data to comply with an illegitimate context.

[27] It is pertinent here to recall the warning given by Johnson, "On Finding Lukan Community: A Cautious Cautionary Essay."

political fashion to promote one school's teacher over another school's.[28] This implies that a *bios* can be written for people outside the author's own group.[29] According to Burridge,

> Therefore this should cause us to hesitate about using "community-talk" for the Gospel audiences. This concept may be helpful in Pauline studies, where letters are clearly written to specific communities and include particular greetings or messages for named persons. Without such names or external evidence for the "Matthean" of "Johannine" communities, we cannot assume that reconstructions like those of Brown or Martyn are valid. If Greco-Roman *bioi* are not written solely for specific communities, then interpreting the Gospels as *bioi* provides a critique of much community-based sociological analysis of the Gospel audiences.[30]

For Burridge, it is better to think of *bioi* as having certain types of people (audiences) in mind when writing, which is more like our modern concept of "market," rather than just one narrow community.[31]

Although Burridge is correct to show that a *bios* is rarely used for one group's readership alone, certainly he cannot prove the point. The strength in Burridge's essay is not the conclusion that genre *cannot* be used by self-contained or closed groups, for certainly it may have been used by some fairly contained network of groups, but that it is a *rare or specialized use* of the biographical genre. If the role of genre is, by definition, to inform the reader of a narrative's content and to instruct the

---

[28] Unless, of course, one assumes that the Gospels were written to promulgate that "community's" views. But as we discussed above, the evidence is unconvincing that such promulgation was occurring between the Gospels, let alone between the "groups" behind the Gospels. But, using the *bioi* of the philosophical schools as an example, any apologetic and polemic would imply that a document was not intended for a single "community," but for a wider audience. See Burridge, "About People, by People, for People," p. 137.

[29] Burridge, "About People, by People, for People," p. 132. In fact, this implies a multiple use of the philosophical *bios*. It can be intended for readers from another philosophical school in the sense of propaganda, yet it can also be read by those from within the author's group as confirmatory of their teacher and philosophical system. Hence, it can be read by both "believers" and "unbelievers." The only criterion, one would assume, would be that the reader of the *bios* be related to the subject of the *bios*. For example, a "Life of Pythagoras" would presumably envisage at least all "Pythagoreans" as its audience. *Prima facie*, a *bios* of Jesus would be of interest to all followers of Jesus.

[30] *Ibid.*, p. 133.

[31] *Ibid.* Burridge is not assuming a conflict model here. Rather, as we discussed in chapter 2, Burridge is suggesting that instead of imagining hypothetical "communities" as intended by the Gospels, we should assume a wider readership that may have had different emphases for the various "types" of readers.

reader how to read it, then the *bios* genre does just that. Certainly there are rare cases of a narrative's use, or odd ways a certain group may have applied a reading to it. But that would be the exception and not the norm. Burridge has shown us that it was normal for a *bios* to be used in a "less limited" way. That is, a *bios*, though possibly reaching for one niche in the market of readers, is rarely intended for only one closed "group."[32] Thus, although the move from text to audience can only be at a general level, the use of genre allows the reader to establish what is being read and how one is to read.

John's two-level drama: a critique

We now turn to our second question: how would a first-century audience have appropriated a Gospel text? This question addresses an important issue concerning the use of the Gospels in the first century. Our focus on a first-century reading is no less a first-century reading than the type of reading form and redaction critics attempt when they read the Gospels. The very fact that the Gospel "community" behind each of the Gospels is placed in the first century implies a first-century reading. The concern that we present here is not whether the FG "can" be read as a two-level drama, which the development of form and redaction criticism has shown that it can, but "if" a first-century reader would have read it that way. But first it is important that we describe how the two-level drama is presented in the FG.

The primary hermeneutical impetus for the discovery of the JComm within the FG is the seeming impenetrability of the Johannine narrative.[33] As discussed above, it was the seminal work by J. Louis Martyn that popularized the two-level reading of the FG, or as Martyn calls it, the two-level drama. Martyn argues that in the FG there are two types of material: the traditional material and the reapplication of the traditional material, what we might call the redacted material.[34] The latter is what can be used to see the Johannine issues from a Johannine perspective. These two levels are playing out simultaneously in the narrative of the FG. While the traditional Jesus is being presented, the needs and issues of the community

---

[32] This is especially the case if the "group" that is the intended audience is also the "group" from which the document originated.

[33] In this way, talk of a "Johannine Problem" has been common over the last century. See Ernst Haenchen, "Aus der Literatur zum Johannesevangelium 1929–1956," *ThR* 23 (1955), pp. 295–33; Hartmut Thyen, "Aus der Literatur zum Johannesevangelium," *ThR* 39 (1974), pp. 1–69, 222–52, 289–330; 42 (1977), pp. 211–70; Robert Kysar, *The Fourth Evangelist and His Gospel*; Martin Hengel, *The Johannine Question.*

[34] Martyn, *History and Theology in the Fourth Gospel*, p. 30.

behind the Gospel are also being dealt with in a way that allows readers
to witness a second level in the narrative. According to Martyn, then,
if the narrative of the FG is read correctly, light may be shed on each
of the two levels occurring within the narrative.[35] Martyn is following
in the tradition of the redaction-critical principle that the Gospels bear
testimony not only to their subject matter, but also to the *Sitz im Leben* in
which they were produced.[36] In this way Martyn's hermeneutic has shed
light on John's history and theology: the history is the traditional Jesus
material used in the Gospel; the theology is the adaptation of that material
by the FE to speak to and about the JComm.[37] Then, by looking closely at
the theological discussion in the second level, glimpses of a history of the
JComm can be formed, hence, Martyn's later essay: "Glimpses into the
History of the Johannine Community."[38] Thus, by dissecting the literary
work of the FE Martyn believes he can see two levels simultaneously in
the FG: the traditional level and the redacted level that reveals glimpses
into the life and history of the JComm. But this entire hermeneutic is
resting on a literary decision concerning the genre of the FG. Concerning
John's genre Martyn remarks, "Someone created a literary genre quite
without counterpart in the body of the Gospels. We may indeed call it a
drama."[39]

---

[35] *Ibid.*, p. 29. Cf. D. Moody Smith, "The Contribution of J. Louis Martyn," in *History and Theology in the Fourth Gospel*, p. 6.

[36] As Martyn, *History and Theology in the Fourth Gospel*, p. 32, explains, "It is just possible . . . that careful attention to style and to accents characteristic of the discourses will enable us to distinguish – at least in the stories of the lame man and the blind beggar – between (a) traditional materials and (b) passages in which elements of John's own interests and experiences are more or less clearly reflected."

[37] As Smith, *The Theology of the Gospel of John* (Cambridge: Cambridge University Press, 1995), p. xi, explains, "To elucidate John's theology means not to destroy his narrative, but to show how its theological emphases arose from and relate to the emergence of that community . . ."

[38] Martyn, "Glimpses into the History of the Johannine Community," in Marinus de Jonge (ed.), *L'Evangile de Jean: Sources, redaction, théologie*, BETL 44 (Gembloux: Duculot, 1977); repr. in *History and Theology in the Fourth Gospel*, pp. 145–67. While Martyn calls his insights merely "glimpses," the control they have had on the interpretation of the FG speaks more than just glimpses. We will discuss this more in chapter 5.

[39] Martyn, *History and Theology in the Fourth Gospel*, p. 32. It would appear that Martyn is claiming that the FG's genre is different from the genre of the Synoptics. Although Martyn does not take that too far, for he claims that all four Gospels were "employing to some degree the same tradition" (p. 31), he does argue that there are striking differences, especially the way John constructed a sequence of scenes based on the miracle story. Martyn admits that he was not the first to see this, for he refers the reader to similar hints made by James M. Thompson, "An Experiment in Translation," in *The Expositor* (London: Hodder and Stoughton, 1875–1925), eighth series, vol. 16 (1918), pp. 117–25; and Hans Windisch, "Der johanneische Erzählungsstil," in Hans Schmidt (ed.), *EUCHARISTERION: Studien zur Religion und Literatur des Alten und Neuen Testaments: Hermann Gunkel zum 60,*

Martyn's two-level drama raises some interesting issues concerning the text of John. How are we to understand the narrative of John in relation to various *Sitze im Leben*? How does John speak of events that happened in the past? How do his own issues and circumstances direct how he speaks of the past? How does he give present meaning to the past? And in relation to these: In what way does John's literary form allow such a handling of past and present, history and theology? For Martyn the Gospel genre is a unique drama, a *sui generis* creation. In this regard Martyn is in agreement with the form critics.[40] But the FG is also a creative theological tract for a specific audience; a writing that reaches from Jesus to the reader in a creative way. In this regard Martyn is in agreement with the redaction critics of his time. According to Martyn, the only type of literature that could encompass what John did, one that was well known to John, was Jewish apocalyptic.[41]

In his final chapter in *History and Theology in the Fourth Gospel* Martyn describes the literary maneuver that John accomplished. Martyn argues that John did a "doubling of Jesus with the figures of the Christian witnesses in his own community."[42] Assuming that John was writing in order to narrate a history of Jesus from a post-resurrection viewpoint, yet realizing that John did not write a second volume that actually dealt with events after Christ's resurrection, John must have done so using only the received Jesus tradition. Martyn explains:

> Since we are acquainted with Luke's second volume in which a part of the post-resurrection history of the church is narrated, it strikes us that John could have narrated the history of his own church in a direct and straightforward manner. Instead, we find him presenting a two-level drama in which it is not an apostle but rather Jesus himself who ministers to Jews known to John . . .[43]

2 vols. (Göttingen: Vandenhoeck und Ruprecht, 1923), vol. II, pp. 174–213. It is here that we may already see how Martyn has abused the narrative of the FG. As we discussed above, it is generally assumed today that all four Gospels are of the same genre, and that this genre is Greco-Roman *bios*. Martyn's own discussion almost recognizes this, for Martyn, although claiming that John did not use the other Gospels *per se*, admits that "he did after all write a *Gospel*" (p. 31).

[40] Martyn, *History and Theology in the Fourth Gospel*, p. 35, n. 8, explains: "It is crucial to note that for the literary analysis pursued at this juncture, and at other key points in the present work, *the basic criteria are provided by the discipline of form criticism.*"

[41] Martyn is not claiming that John is an apocalypse and not a "Gospel," he is just claiming that both aspects were used by John in a unique and rare relationship. "John writes a gospel, not an apocalypse, but the relation of his Gospel to the Apocalypse should probably be reexamined in light of the way in which he presents his two levels" (p. 130, n. 198). We will discuss the problems with this below.

[42] *Ibid.*, p. 124.   [43] *Ibid.*

The Jesus of the FG is the real and present Lord not only to the original twelve and the immediate followers, but also to the JComm. A narrated history of this sort can only be accomplished by the common writing style of Jewish apocalyptic. "As the evangelist expands pieces of *einmalig* tradition into two-level dramas, he produces what we may call a dynamic Christological *movement* portrayed in a story about (a) Jesus of Nazareth who (b) in John's own day identifies himself with flesh-and-blood Christian witnesses and yet claims solemnly to be the Son of God."[44] Using the concept of the Son of Man within Jewish Apocalypticism, John tries to show that the present Jesus is Jesus the Son of Man.[45]

This entire literary process was not invented by John, Martyn argues. "John did not create the literary form of the two level drama. It was at home in the thought-world of Jewish apocalypticism."[46] For Martyn, the dicta most basic to the apocalyptic thinker are that God created both heaven and earth; these are dramas taking place both on the heavenly stage and the earthly stage. Hermeneutically, each actor is a corresponding pair (as in Revelation, a beast of a certain description in heaven represents a tyrannical king on earth).[47] The entire literary process forces the reader to have "stereo-optic vision," and it is this very stereo-optic vision that caused the FE to write this two-level story.[48] Admittedly, John does adjust some of the normal apocalyptic aspects in his Gospel. First, both of his stages are on earth; both the *einmalig* tradition and John's extension of it into the contemporary level of his drama portray events in the world.[49] Second, John changes the temporal distinction between the two stages in a different way. Instead of reaching from the future to the present as is normal in apocalyptic writings, John writes from the past to the present. Third, John does not give any overt indication to his readers that there is a

---

[44] *Ibid.*, p. 125.

[45] *Ibid.*, pp. 125–30. It is almost as if for Martyn the evangelist/author was not even aware of the two-level drama, for it was natural to his apocalyptic communication. But it is not as if the evangelist did not know there were two levels simultaneously presented, for as Martyn explains, the artistry with which the two-level drama was created required a detailed synthesis by the evangelist in both levels so that tradition and social context could function as one. Thus, according to Martyn, the evangelist placed various "clues" in the text (e.g. the anachronism in 9:22, which we will discuss below) so the reader would recognize when and where a two-level reading was to occur.

[46] *Ibid.*, p. 130.   [47] *Ibid.*

[48] *Ibid.* The stereo-optic vision that Martyn discusses was taken up further by Meeks, "The Man from Heaven in Johannine Sectarianism," pp. 54, 57. In some way, John experiences an epistemological crisis which John believes to be affected in the coming of Jesus. Cf. Martyn, "Source Criticism and *Religionsgeschichte* in the Fourth Gospel," *Perspective* 1 (1970), pp. 247–73, especially p. 257.

[49] Martyn, *History and Theology in the Fourth Gospel*, p. 130.

distinction between the two stages. The drama is so consistently wrapped-up in one another that it is like John is trying to emphasize that "This is *the* drama of life."[50] This, according to Martyn, is what makes the FG a "Gospel" and not an "apocalypse."[51]

The two-level drama, then, helps to make sense of many of the Johan-nine oddities when compared to the Synoptics. Why is John's eschatology often seen as more realized than future? Because "the contemporary level of the drama . . . makes clear that judgment by the Son of Man takes place essentially on earth and in the present, not in heaven and in the future."[52] Why is there such an emphasis on the Spirit-Paraclete, both in the farewell discourse and in Jesus' bestowal of the Spirit (20:22)? Why does the Par-aclete look so much like the first, Jesus? Because for John, the Paraclete functions in the two-level drama to meet the need of the disciples who have been left by the ascended Christ. Instead of simply having the departing Jesus speak of comforting dwelling places in heaven or speak of a mys-tical union between himself and his own, John allows the Lord to affirm both of these options. The dwelling place is not in heaven but on earth. "The paradox presented by Jesus' promise that his work on earth will be continued because he is going to the Father is 'solved' by his return in the person of the Paraclete. *It is, therefore, precisely the Paraclete who cre-ates the two-level drama.*"[53] In this way, when the prologue confirms that "we beheld his glory," it can do so not only because the Christian church possesses *einmalig* tradition about Jesus, but also because the Paraclete is even now showing Jesus in his glory.[54] The Jesus of the past and the Jesus of the present are both found in the text of John through a "Gospel" that utilizes a two-level drama found in apocalyptic literature.

Martyn's proposal is an ingenious attempt to understand the FG. Its influence over the last thirty-five years proves that it was more than just provocative. Unfortunately, Martyn's reading has distorted both the genre of the Gospel and how the first-century readers would have read the FG. First, initially one wonders which came first for Martyn: recognition of the gospel-mixed-with-apocalyptic genre and then a search for the two levels, or a discovery of "two levels" followed by a deduction that the

---

[50] *Ibid.*, p. 131. Martyn adds, "Only the reflective scholar intent on *analyzing* the Gospel will discover the seams which the evangelist sewed together so deftly. True exegesis demands, therefore, that we recognize a certain tension between our analysis and John's intentions."

[51] *Ibid.*, pp. 130–31.   [52] *Ibid.*, p. 134.   [53] *Ibid.*, p. 140.

[54] *Ibid.*, pp. 142–43. Contra Samuel Byrskog, *Story as History – History as Story: The Gospel Traditions in the Context of Ancient Oral History*, WUNT 123 (Tübingen: Mohr Siebeck, 2000) and Richard Bauckham, "The Eyewitnesses and the Gospel Traditions," *JSHJ* 1 (2003), pp. 28–60, for Martyn being a witness is a spiritual act not a physical one.

genre was more than purely "Gospel?" This is a misunderstanding of apocalyptic as a genre. The resemblances of apocalyptic literature cited by Martyn have nothing to do with apocalyptic genre.[55] Apocalyptic is not a way of "thought," it is a literary genre. The definition of apocalyptic that was used to describe and establish the influence and takeover of apocalyptic literary usage in the FG contradicts the working definition of apocalyptic writings.[56] The many differences between a Gospel and an apocalypse that Martyn admits make clear that his two-level reading is a distortion of the Gospel genre and cannot be maintained.

Second, although Martyn has found a referent in the text, observable through redaction criticism, it is not, we will argue, the referent that would have been read by first-century readers. And it is the readers' referent that even Martyn is attempting to find. For as he claims:

> We . . . hope to gain a clearer portrait of at least some of John's prospective [first-century] readers and, most important of all, a better understanding of his purpose in writing. Our first task, however, is to say something as specific as possible about the actual [first-century] circumstances in which John wrote his Gospel.[57]

[55] Martyn is not alone in his portrayal of John as apocalyptic. More recently two scholars have promoted Martyn's apocalyptic hypothesis. According to John Painter, *The Quest for the Messiah: The History, Literature, and Theology of the Johannine Community*, rev. and enl. edn (Edinburgh: T. & T. Clark, 1993), p. 133, "although the Gospels are not free from biographical concern . . . It is clear . . . that the Gospels as biographies have their own distinctive features having been formed under the impact of the oral preaching of the early believers." This distinctive perspective, Painter argues, is that they tell the story of Jesus (biography-like) but from "the perspective of faith in the risen Jesus" (pp. 133–34). Thus, for Painter, John is intentionally using apocalyptic motifs, even an apocalyptic *Weltanschauung*, to communicate between the two temporal periods. In a similar way, John Ashton, *Understanding the Fourth Gospel*, argues that early Christian theology was dominated by apocalyptic thinking. For Ashton, the key to understanding the FG is "revelation" (p. 381). Even before discussing the Gospel genre, he spends an entire chapter defining what he calls "intimations of apocalyptic" (pp. 383–406). Here Ashton quotes the controversial article of Ernst Käsemann, "The Beginnings of Christian Theology," in Ernst Käsemann (ed.), *New Testament Questions of Today* (London: SCM Press, 1969), pp. 82–107, where it is argued that apocalyptic thinking was the mother of all Christian theology. Ashton argues that although the FG "is decidedly not an apocalypse," it does have many similarities with apocalyptic writings, resemblances that reveal that the FG is "profoundly indebted to apocalyptic in all sorts of ways" (pp. 386–87). See also the earlier discussion by Joseph B. Tyson, *A Study of Early Christianity* (New York: Macmillan, 1973), p. 305.

[56] The most prominent work on the definition of the apocalyptic genre has been done by the SBL Genres Project (published in *Semeia* 1979), and later by John J. Collins, *The Apocalyptic Imagination: An Introduction to the Jewish Matrix of Christianity* (New York: Crossroad, 1984), who takes his start from the work of that group and develops further the genre implications of apocalyptic. Interestingly, Collins specifically warns that trying to find apocalyptic eschatology in the Gospels is more complex than simply noting similarities or resemblances (p. 9).

[57] Martyn, *History and Theology in the Fourth Gospel*, p. 29.

If the referent in the FG is not the same as what Martyn has claimed to find, then his "glimpses" into the audience of the FG may be much less discernible than previously assumed. Thus, it becomes important that we look more closely at the referent the first-century readers of the FG would have been predisposed to find. In order to do this we must look at the Gospel genre and its narrative referentiality.

Gospel genre and narrative referentiality

It must be made clear from the start that the question we are asking is not whether the Gospel narratives depict "real" or "historical" events, although certainly some believe the referentiality of the Gospels is "ideal" and not "ostensive." The debate that we enter upon has already admitted that there is referentiality in the Gospels, whether that be the particular Gospel "community" and its situational context or the evangelist's "version of Jesus."[58] The question we pose, then, is not "if" the Gospels have historical referents, but "which" referents would first-century readers have seen in the text. To answer this question we begin by turning to the work on narrative by Hans Frei.

Since 1974 Hans Frei's *The Eclipse of Biblical Narrative* has had a seminal influence on how interpreters approach biblical narratives. As Frei explains,

> Reading of the Bible in the days before the rise of historical criticism in the eighteenth century was usually strongly realistic, i.e. at once literal and historical, and not only doctrinal or edifying. The words and sentences meant what they said, and because they did so they accurately described real events and real truths that were rightly put only in those terms and no others.[59]

According to Frei, pre-critical interpretation of the biblical narrative was a "realistic" interpretation that involved three elements, each of which was assumed to be constant.[60] First, since the biblical story was assumed

---

[58] This is not to deny that other levels of referentiality have been suggested to exist in the Gospels. But since our purpose is focused against a "community" reference, we will use this over-simplistic dichotomy.

[59] Hans W. Frei, *The Eclipse of Biblical Narrative: A Study in Eighteenth- and Nineteenth-Century Hermeneutics* (New Haven: Yale University Press, 1974), p. 1.

[60] Another helpful work on pre-critical reading, primarily from a social-science perspective, is by Lucretia B. Yaghjian, "Ancient Reading," in Richard L. Rohrbaugh (ed.), *The Social Sciences and New Testament Interpretation* (Peabody, Mass.: Hendrickson, 1996), pp. 206–30, who provides a helpful guide to much of the recent research. See also the related but less helpful work by Malina, "Reading Theory Perspective: Reading Luke-Acts," in Jerome Neyrey (ed.), *The Social World of Luke-Acts: Models of Interpretation* (Peabody, Mass.: Hendrickson, 1991), pp. 3–23.

to be read literally, it automatically followed that this story referred to and described actual historical occurrences. The assumption of its true historical reference was directly responsible for the following assumption that the text made literal sense. As Frei points out, "This is a far cry from taking the fact that a passage or text makes best sense at a literal level as *evidence* that it is a reliable historical report."[61] It is worth quoting Frances Young at length here concerning this first element in pre-critical reading of the biblical narrative:

> the world of the text gives meaning to the world outside the text. Conversely, the world outside the text enables the meaning inside the text to be discerned . . . An authoritative text is understood to refer to the world in which people live, and so its meaning is bound to be received or contested in the light of the plausibility structures of the culture which receives the text. A culture which can conceive of the material universe as interpenetrated by another reality, which is transcendent and spiritual, will read the reference of scripture in those terms. This is far more significant for the differences between ancient and modern exegesis than any supposed 'method.'[62]

And again Young:

> No Antiochene could have imagined the kind of critical stance of the Biblical Theology movement, explicitly locating revelation not in the text of scripture but in the historicity of events behind the text, events to which we only have access by reconstructing them from the texts, treating the texts as documents providing historical data.[63]

The second element in pre-critical realistic reading was that if the real historical world described by the several biblical stories is a single world of one temporal sequence, there must then be one cumulative story to depict it.[64] Each of the biblical stories narrating sequential segments in time must fit together into one narrative. "The interpretive means for joining them was to make earlier biblical stories figures or types of later stories and of their events and patterns of meanings."[65] But according to Frei, a "literal" sense of biblical stories was not in conflict with a "figural" or "typological" reading of the same stories. For figuration "was literalism at the level of the whole biblical story and thus of the depiction of the

---

[61] Frei, *The Eclipse of Biblical Narrative*, p. 2.
[62] Young, *Biblical Exegesis and the Formation of Christian Culture*, p. 139. We will discuss this more fully below.
[63] *Ibid.*, p. 167.   [64] Frei, *The Eclipse of Biblical Narrative*, p. 2.   [65] *Ibid.*

whole historical reality."[66] This type of literal reading, a figural reading of the whole two-canon biblical narrative, is evidenced by the use of the OT in the NT.

The third element in pre-critical realistic reading is related to the first-century reader. Since the world truly rendered by combining biblical narratives into one was indeed the one and only real world, it must in principle embrace the experience of any present age (pre-critical) and reader.[67] Frei's comments are important here:

> Not only was it possible for him, it was also his duty to fit himself into that world in which he was in any case a member, and he too did so in part by figural interpretation and in part of course by his mode of life. *He was to see his disposition, his actions and passions, the shape of his own life as well as that of his era's events as figures of that storied world.*[68]

Thus, for Frei even when the story was adapted to new situations and ways of thinking, or underwent revision as redaction criticism helpfully points out, the revised form never became a different "story" or "world" but remained for the pre-critical reader the adequate depiction of the common and inclusive world until the coming of modernity.[69] It was only then that the literal reading of each narrative and the figural reading of the cumulative narratives were separated – and became two different readings. Realistic or literal reading of the biblical narratives found its closest successor in the historical-critical reconstruction of events and texts of the Bible. The question became: How reliable are the texts?[70]

---

[66] *Ibid.* Frei continues: "Figuration was at once a literary and a historical procedure, an interpretation of stories and their meanings by weaving them together into a common narrative referring to a single history and its patterns of meanings." It is important here to clarify what type of "figurative" interpretation (allegorical or typological) early Christians performed. The evidence points to figuration between the story of Jesus and the story of the Jewish faith; there is no evidence of a particular "community's" story being connected in a figurative way to the story of Jesus. For example, turning to Origen and claiming that such figuration was possibly in the mind of the early Christians is illegitimate. For Origen, the "story" in the "biblical" narrative was connected to God and his "story" and not to one particular Christian "community" and its "story." See R. P. C. Hanson, *Allegory and Event: A Study of the Sources and Significance of Origen's Interpretation of Scripture* (Louisville: Westminster John Knox Press, 2003), p. 364. The same can be witnessed in the exegesis of Paul, where no "biblical story" is ever connected to one Pauline "community." See Karlfried Froehlich (ed. and trans.), *Biblical Interpretation in the Early Church*, SECT (Philadelphia: Fortress, 1984), pp. 8–10.

[67] Frei, *The Eclipse of Biblical Narrative*, p. 3.

[68] *Ibid.* (emphasis added).   [69] *Ibid.*, pp. 3–4.

[70] The warrant for seeing the dichotomy that was created during the movement between pre-critical and modern biblical interpretation is not merely historical, but epistemological. See Neil B. MacDonald, "Illocutionary Stance in Hans Frei's *The Eclipse of Biblical*

Figural reading, concerned as it was with the unity of narratives, found its closest successor in the biblical theology movement.[71] This dichotomy so common in modern biblical interpretation was foreign to a pre-critical or first-century reading of biblical narratives.[72] As science advanced, so did the realization that the "world" of the Bible was not identical to the "world" of the modern interpreter. As Frei explains, it was realized that "There is now a logical distinction and a reflective distance between the stories and the 'reality' they depict."[73] The dichotomy so common

---

Narrative: An Exercise in Conceptual Redescription and Normative Analysis," in Craig Bartholomew, Colin Greene, and Karl Möller (eds.), *After Pentecost: Language and Biblical Interpretation*, SHS 2 (Carlisle: Paternoster Press/Grand Rapids: Zondervan, 2001), p. 322. In essence, MacDonald is critiquing Frei's conceptual framework as the grid by which the shift took place. For MacDonald, the movement from pre-critical to modern interpretation was also connected with the concept of belief. MacDonald uses the research of Nicholas Wolterstorff, "The Migration of the Theistic Arguments: From Natural Theology to Evidentialist Apologetics," in Robert Audi and William J. Wainwright (eds.), *Rationality, Religious Belief, and Moral Commitment* (Ithaca, N.Y.: Cornell University Press, 1986), pp. 38–81, to argue that a shift took place from a "faith seeking understanding" paradigm in pre-critical interpretation to what may be termed a "faith requiring justification" in modern interpretation. According to MacDonald, "the shift that Wolterstorff discerns in theistic belief occurred in close proximity to the one Frei identified in biblical hermeneutics. It would therefore not be surprising if they were in some way historically or even conceptually connected" (p. 325). A similar critique was presented against Frei by Meir Sternberg, *The Poetics of Biblical Narrative: Ideological Literature and the Drama of Reading*, ISBL (Bloomington: Indiana University Press, 1985), pp. 81ff.

[71] Frei, *The Eclipse of Biblical Narrative*, p. 8.

[72] This does not imply that Frei read the Gospel narratives, for example, with a pre-critical reading, for he insists that the literal sense of such texts is not equated with historical reference. For Frei, the Jesus of the Gospels is unsubstitutable; the Messiah is none other than Jesus of Nazareth *narratively rendered* especially in the accounts of his passion and resurrection. The Gospels do not describe some "everyman" character; the identity of Jesus is irreducible to something else. Thus, when Frei describes the Gospels as "history-like," he implies no particular historical claim. This is, of course, far different from what pre-critical readers assumed, as he himself shows. One year following *Eclipse*, Frei made more explicit his view concerning the history-like Gospels in *The Identity of Jesus: The Hermeneutical Bases of Dogmatic Theology* (Philadelphia: Fortress Press, 1975). Concerning Jesus and historical reference Frei states: "We must neither look for his identity in back of the story nor supply it from extraneous analytical schemes. It is evident that in the story Jesus' true being is not mysteriously hidden behind the action [ostensive reference] or within a supposedly distorted, 'objectified,' or 'mythological' self-manifestation [ideal reference]. No. He *is* what he appeared to be – the Savior Jesus from Nazareth, who underwent 'all these things' and who is truly manifest as Jesus, the risen Christ" (p. 138). As James Fodor, *Christian Hermeneutics: Paul Ricoeur and the Refiguring of Theology* (Oxford: Clarendon Press, 1995), explains concerning Frei's position, "biblical narrative features a sort of internal referent in so far as it creates its own world. Moreover, this textual world of the Bible is not only the necessary basis for our orientation within the real world, but is also sufficient for that purpose" (p. 268). See also Timothy Ward, *Word and Supplement: Speech Acts, Biblical Texts, and the Sufficiency of Scripture* (Oxford: Oxford University Press, 2002), pp. 150–61.

[73] Frei, *The Eclipse of Biblical Narrative*, p. 5.

in modern biblical interpretation[74] was foreign to pre-critical or first-century readings of biblical narratives. It is to this dichotomy in the work of Martyn that we now turn.

Martyn's reading of the Gospel text is problematic if he desires to show how the FG would have been understood in its first-century context. A task which we confirmed above was his primary goal: "We . . . hope to gain a clearer portrait of at least some of John's prospective [first-century] readers and, most important of all, a better understanding of his purpose in writing."[75] A task that must read the Gospel as it would have been read. Thus, for Martyn to read the FG "with the eyes . . . and ears of that community [or we might say audience],"[76] he must be dependent on how those very readers would have understood the Gospel narrative. For as Martyn admits, "Only in the midst of this endeavor will we be able to hear the Fourth Evangelist speak *in his own terms*, rather than in words which we moderns merely want to hear from his mouth."[77] Unfortunately, Martyn has imposed a modern (or critical) grid of understanding on the first-century readers of the FG.

Martyn admits that his research uses the "basic criteria provided by the discipline of form criticism."[78] But Martyn is himself a redaction critic. His technique is to listen to both the traditional material and to the Gospel's "new and unique interpretation of that tradition," thus being able to hear the presentation of the tradition in its own applied context.[79] Such a procedure is fully legitimate. Redaction criticism is helpful in locating the *Tendenzen* in the Gospels. But two issues arise that are important for our purpose.

First, the *Tendenzen* observable by redaction criticism are not easily transferable to a first-century setting of the Gospels. As we discussed in chapter 2, there have been many warnings against assuming a detailed correspondence between a redactional element and its origin or setting. Even Raymond Brown made this abundantly clear in the introduction to his own JComm reconstruction: "While I accept in principle the ability to

---

[74] Interestingly, it appears that others are moving in a direction similar to this study. In a recent article, Timothy Wiarda, "Scenes and Details in the Gospels: Concrete Reading and Three Alternatives," *NTS* 50 (2004), pp. 167–84, argues for what he calls "concrete reading," that is, "an approach to Gospel narratives that observes and emphasizes the way details function within the natural flow of the time-of-Jesus story that is being told" (p. 167). Although Wiarda says that a concrete reading treats Gospel narratives as "realistically depicted stories" or a "realistic scene," language that sounds like Frei, no mention of Frei is made. Although the term "realistic" is to be preferred over "concrete," Wiarda provides a helpful critique of the allegorical reading of Gospel narratives.

[75] Martyn, *History and Theology in the Fourth Gospel*, p. 29.
[76] *Ibid.* [77] *Ibid.* [78] *Ibid.*, p. 35, n. 8. [79] *Ibid.*, p. 30.

detect Christian community life beneath the surface of the Gospel story, I wish to be clear about the methodological difficulties of applying such a principle . . . we gain general knowledge about the life situation of the community, but it is difficult to move to specifics."[80] This was also part of Bauckham's critique of the community reconstruction process:

> It is difficult to avoid supposing that those who no longer think it possible to use the Gospels to reconstruct the historical Jesus compensate for his loss by using them to reconstruct the communities that produced the Gospels. All the historical specificity for which historical critics long is transferred from the historical Jesus to the evangelist's community.[81]

The tremendous amounts of varying reconstructions of the so-called Gospel communities make one wonder if the redactional criteria are in any way accurate or helpful. Maybe Robert Kysar states it best: "As I am grateful for the work of scholars like Brown and Martyn, I suppose I have simply tired of playing the game of abstract speculative constructions."[82]

Second, and more important for this study, the "world" depicted by the redaction is considered to be more "real" than the "world" depicted by the narrative. If our understanding of pre-critical reading is correct, then the narrative "world" was the real and important world, not the creative *Tendenzen* or the redactional elements. Certainly the first-century readers did not think the FG dropped from heaven, but they also did not read the FG as a modern-day redaction critic. Thus, the dichotomy that Martyn sees in the Gospel text and uses to "discover" the way the FG would have been "seen and heard" by its first-century reader is foreign to a pre-critical reading. The very fact that the so-called "two levels" were combined into one narrative implies that they were to be read as one narrative.[83] Martyn's claim of exegetical responsibility is telling: "Only the reflective scholar intent on *analyzing* the Gospel will discover the seams which the evangelist sewed together so deftly. True exegesis demands, therefore, that we recognize a certain tension between our analysis and

---

[80] Brown, *The Community of the Beloved Disciple*, p. 18.   [81] Bauckham, *GAC*, p. 20.

[82] Robert Kysar, "The Expulsion from the Synagogue: A Tale of a Theory" (paper presented at the annual meeting of the Society of Biblical Literature. Toronto, Canada, November 2005, 2002), p. 14.

[83] Helpful here is the critique of Martyn by Brevard Childs, *The New Testament as Canon: An Introduction* (London: SCM Press, 1984), p. 134: "in Martyn's concern to do justice to the various levels of this multi-layered text, he has separated elements whose coherent unity belongs to an essential witness of the text. Thus, the story is actualized for subsequent readers in a way different from that envisioned by Martyn . . . In sum, Martyn's thesis . . . is to be resisted when it interprets the chapter to conform to an historical reconstruction which actually runs in the face of the final form of the canonical story itself."

John's intentions."[84] Martyn's admission that "John does not *in any overt way* indicate to his readers a distinction between the two stages . . ." makes one wonder if the first-century reader would have ever supposed that one should read the Gospel narrative in such a way.[85]

Our goal has been to suggest that the Gospel was read as a narrative in the first century, and this narrative was read as reflecting "real" events that occurred in the same time-and-space "world" of the reader. Using Frei's analysis of narrative reading and the move from pre-critical to critical reading, we have discovered that the Gospels, as documents written in the first century, would have been read in a pre-critical way. This pre-critical reading only changed in the modern period when conceptual movements rooted in historical advances pressed the pre-critical reading of the Gospel narratives to be more critical. Thus, to read the Gospels in light of modern criticism, though helpful and legitimate, is not to read the Gospels as they were originally read. When we turn to Martyn's two-level reading of John, we find a critical (post-enlightenment) imposition on a pre-critical text. We found first that the information gleaned from Martyn's redactional technique, though insightful, is limited in specificity. But more importantly, it is also foreign to a pre-critical or first-century reading of the Gospel text. Our conclusion is that to read the FG the way Martyn proposes is most certainly not to read the FG "with the eyes . . . and ears of that community" or to "hear the Fourth Evangelist speak *in his own terms* . . ."[86]

John 9:22: the entry point into the two-level reading

Martyn did not create the two-level reading of the FG without warrant. The "seam" he has found in the healing of the blind man in John 9 has made the pericope famous, for it is the entry point from which Martyn sees the two-level drama. But as we have argued above, Martyn has made a dichotomy where one did not exist originally. That is, the "world" depicted by the redaction criticism of Martyn is not the "world" the first-century readers saw in the narrative of the FG. But in order to make this clearer it is necessary to look specifically at the intrusion Martyn finds in John 9:22 and the other "expulsion" passages so that a more appropriate reading can be presented.

As we have discussed above, Martyn proposes that one read the prominence of the Jews and their hostility to Jesus as representative of a real historical setting (as opposed to theological symbolism) in which the FG

---

[84] Martyn, *History and Theology in the Fourth Gospel*, p. 131.
[85] *Ibid.* (emphasis added).   [86] *Ibid.*, p. 29.

was composed.[87] With this in mind, Martyn reads the FG and finds two blatantly anachronistic verses concerning Jewish hostility (9:22; 12:42; cf. 16:2) that, though in the narrative they tell a story about the time of Jesus' earthly ministry, are most certainly dealing with an issue that could not have occurred until decades after Jesus' life, that is, the historical setting in which the FG was created. These three verses, then, are taken to be the primary key to the historical setting of the FG. Martyn's brilliant reconstruction of the historical setting behind John has linked the FG's Jewish-Christian conflict to a possible situation in the late first century and has provided, therefore, a way in which the Gospel is to be read. Using form- and redaction-critical assumptions to understand the text in light of its setting, Martyn has presented a coherent theory that attempts to make sense of the incomplete non-biblical evidence. But since the Gospel and the evidence of Jewish-Christian conflict are far from complementary, Martyn had to find a reading that "matched" the evidence. This is, of course, what historical work requires; our reconstruction will be no different. But this study is attempting to show that Martyn has misapplied the evidence, and in so doing has produced a reading of the FG that would have been foreign to first-century readers and skews the working picture of the Gospel's historical setting and function. According to Martyn it is in chapter 9, especially 9:22, where the "two-level drama" is best exhibited.

Martyn's development of the two-level reading in John 9 is based upon two aspects of John 9 and the other "expulsion from the synagogue" passages. The first is that the "perceptive" first-century reader would have seen each of the primary characters in the narrative as referring to a referent in their own present setting. The second is that this referent in their own setting is the specific removal from the synagogue that some or all of the JComm members are experiencing as a result of an official edict broadly decreed.[88] These two aspects are interrelated; the first allows the second to happen in the narrative, and the second allows the first to be realized. We will discuss each of these in turn.

The reader and an anachronism

In reference to the first aspect of Martyn's reading of John 9, that the perceptive first-century reader would have seen each of the primary

---

[87] *Ibid.*, pp. 46–47. Our reading of the FG will also read it historically.

[88] As we discuss below, although some JComm interpreters think Martyn's assumption of an "official edict" behind John is problematic, they still maintain that the text is referring to an "expulsion" of JComm Jewish-Christians from a local synagogue.

characters in the narrative as referring to a referent in their own present setting, based upon the anachronistic insertion of the "expulsion from the synagogue" statements, we must return to the reading strategy that we can assume first-century or pre-critical readers would have embraced. We have already argued above that a first-century reader, even a perceptive one, would have read this narrative as reflecting "real" events that occurred in the same time-and-space "world" in which they lived. This does not imply that authorial *Tendenzen* would not have been present, even *Tendenzen* from the perspective of a later time, but it does assume that the reader was a pre-critical reader, and not a critical reader like Martyn.

Of course, our assumption of the pre-critical reading of John is not merely based on pre-critical reading strategies, but on the narrative genre of the text itself. The *bios* genre of the Gospels does not communicate on two levels.[89] Recently Tobias Hägerland has argued, contra Martyn, that both the search for an ancient two-level genre and the supposed "hints of allegory" for the reader in the text of John are unsuccessful.[90] Hägerland explains his approach to this search as follows:

> I would like to emphasize at the outset that the "literal" or "historical" sense of John's Gospel that this study seeks to establish pertains solely to the author's aim. The question being asked of the text, as it were, is whether the author intended his Gospel to

[89] It is important here to clarify what is meant by claiming that the *bios* genre does not communicate on two levels. First, using a pre-critical understanding of reading a history-like or realistic narrative, especially in the *bios* and not apocalyptic genre, it was assumed that the story told *was* the story (Frei, *The Eclipse of Biblical Narrative*, p. 2). Certainly pre-critical readers knew the difference between different types (genres) of texts, and certainly they had seen apocalyptic texts in the Jewish or Platonic tradition, but they would not have supposed that history-like narratives would function like a non-history-like narrative. Second, the type of allegory that redaction and sociological criticism employ is of a different kind (not just degree) from the allegory (and typology) employed by pre-critical interpreters. The primary difference is as follows: while pre-critical interpreters employed allegory (and typology) *from the narrative itself*, redaction and sociological interpreters employ it *from behind the narrative*. That is, the allegorical readings never assumed that there existed a reading behind the "literal" reading that needed decoding; rather, they applied *theoria* which "recognizes a higher level of meaning which overlies the literal, without deleting or weakening it" (Simonetti, *Biblical Interpretation in the Early Church*, p. 67). Thus, the pre-critical readings were actually broadening rather than specific. Cf. Young, *Biblical Exegesis and the Formation of Christian Culture*, pp. 161–85. In this way, Martyn's allegorical reading of the FG, whereby a character or event in the time-of-Jesus narrative is claimed to be depicting an event in the history of the JComm, is foreign to first-century allegory. An allegorical reading in the first century would link the character or event to a universal theme or virtue, not another historical event!

[90] Tobias Hägerland, "John's Gospel: A Two-Level Drama?," *JSNT* 25 (2003), pp. 309–22.

be read "literally," as depicting the "historical" person of Jesus, or whether he fashioned it to be perceived as a kind of allegory. A different problem is to what extent, and in what sense, the Gospel may be regarded as "literally true" or "historically accurate" from our modern point of view . . .[91]

According to Hägerland, for a two-level reading of John to be possible, one would assume that there would be literary parallels to such a reading in non-apocalyptic literature, since Martyn himself admits that "Gospel" is like but different from apocalyptic,[92] and evidence or clues in the text itself that guide the reader to both levels of the drama.

Concerning the former, Hägerland focuses specifically on biographical literature since the Gospels are at least quasi-biographical.[93] Hägerland compares Philo's "Lives" of biblical characters, since they are relevant to the understanding of John's Gospel. Philo himself designates them as *bioi* (*Jos. 1*), but their content differs markedly from common ancient Lives by being completely allegorical. For example, already at the beginning of *De Josepho* Philo declares that his writing is intended to treat something else than Joseph as a historical person; and in *De Abrahamo* each narrative episode is followed by a piece of allegorical exegesis, the allegory being explicitly spiritualizing (e.g. *Abr.* 68). *De Abrahamo* and *De Josepho* focus not on the supposedly historical lives of Abraham and Joseph, but on the learning that can be extracted through allegorical reading of the biblical narrative.[94] But when one turns to Philo's *De vita Mosis*, one

[91] *Ibid.*, p. 310. Although we have been focusing on the reader up to this point, a concern with the author cannot be avoided as we turn to the text and genre.

[92] Martyn, *History and Theology in the Fourth Gospel*, pp. 130–31, gives changes that John makes to the Gospel genre that make it different from apocalyptic. By admitting these qualifications it would seem that Martyn has already admitted that they are not parallel at all.

[93] Hägerland does mention the ancient "novel" which has some affinity with the two-level drama. The comparison was initially made by Ulrich Luz, "Fiktivität und Traditionstreue im Matthäusevangelium im Lichte griechischer Literatur," *ZNW* 84 (1993), pp. 153–77. For Luz many novels are ambiguous (*doppelbödig*) and can tell two stories simultaneously in the sense that the superficial story was intended to be perceived as an allegorical description of human religious experience (pp. 168–71). Luz thinks this is what Matthew intended in order to tell the story of the Matthean community; but this is different from Martyn who links John's two-levels to the FE's apocalyptic thinking. Hägerland criticizes Luz's ancient novel comparison on two fronts. First, unlike ancient novels which were "fictional" from the start, the Gospels claim to be far more than fiction. John claims to have based his Gospel on the testimony of him "who saw" (19:35). Second, while the secondary story of the ancient novel was a spiritual, inward, or "superior" interpretation of an outward drama, the Gospels' second story is a second outward drama – one historical chain of events (community history) would be presented in the appearance of another equally historical chain of events (Jesus' history).

[94] Hägerland, "John's Gospel: A Two-Level Drama?," pp. 314–15.

finds major differences from the other Lives of Philo. The purpose of the Life of Moses is informative and probably also apologetic; Philo wants to depict the historical Moses, for "not many know who he really was" (*Vit. Mos.* 1.2; cf. 1.1).[95] According to Hägerland, the lack of explicit allegory[96] in *De vita Mosis* makes it comparable to the FG:

> On returning to the Gospel of John, one finds that its form and content are much closer to *De vita Mosis* than to the allegorical Lives. John's explicit purpose [20:31] is similar to Philo's opening words of the Life of Moses . . . And like Philo, the Gospel refers to its informant, who cannot be anything else than an eyewitness [John 19:35; 21:24; *Vit. Mos.* 1.4].[97]

By contrast, the FG does not display any resemblance to the allegorical Lives of *De Abrahamo* and *De Josepho*. Thus, for Hägerland, even where one might expect to find an ancient parallel to the two-level drama proposed by Martyn in the literature related to the Gospels, none is to be found.[98] Certainly it is common in early Christian exegesis to have two referents, one ostensive ("historical") and one ideal ("spiritual"), but never do we find in a narrative text two ostensive referents, both on the

---

[95] Peder Borgen, *Philo, John and Paul: New Perspectives on Judaism and Early Christianity*, BJS 131 (Atlanta: Scholars Press, 1987), p. 19, argues that the purpose of *De vita Mosis* is to show the divine calling of Moses and the Jewish people to worship God, keep the Sabbath and serve the whole world. Interestingly, Borgen argues that the book was "written for Gentile readers to tell them about the supreme law-giver whose laws they are to accept and honour. At the same time it was to strengthen the Jews for their universal role." Although Borgen claims that this dual purpose fits well with the Jewish community of Alexandria at the time, it also works well for the Jews who "were actively penetrating into the Greek community."

[96] But one might assume that Philo uses allegory implicitly? But Philo is hardly shy about his use of allegory, as explained by David Dawson, *Allegorical Readers and Cultural Revision in Ancient Alexandria* (Berkeley: University of California Press, 1992), p. 100, for it assists the reader in applying "the Scriptures" to "personifications of various types of souls or of faculties within the soul (see *Agr*.22)." In fact, as Dawson explains, Philo saw the importance of both the literal and allegorical (non-literal) to the point of revealing both to his audience as plausible interpretations of the same text that do not cancel one another (p. 101). "Allegorical composition and reading constantly play themselves off against a substratum of words that are not meant or read allegorically (*at least not at the same time* or according to the same allegory)" (p. 101, emphasis added). In contrast to Martyn, who argues that John's was meant to apply to the specific situation faced by the Johannine reader, Philo, according to Samuel Sandmel, *Philo of Alexandria: An Introduction* (Oxford: Oxford University Press, 1979), p. 18, uses "allegorical interpretation . . . to make [characters in the story] types of human beings who are to be found in every age and every place . . . he transforms biblical characters, or biblical place-names, into universal types of people or universal characteristics of mankind." See also Peder Borgen, *Philo of Alexandria: An Exegete for His Time*, NovTSup 86 (Leiden: Brill, 1997).

[97] Hägerland, "John's Gospel: A Two-Level Drama?," p. 316.   [98] *Ibid.*

same chronological plane (a mere generation or two apart).[99] Only by creating a *sui generis* category of "Gospel" can Martyn even attempt to succeed: *bios* narratives are functioning like apocalyptic literature.[100] Unfortunately, such a genre does not exist, nor has it existed.

Martyn's understanding of the FG's genre has allowed him to read the Gospel in an allegorical way.[101] Helpful here is a critique along the same lines by Stephen Motyer. As Motyer explains, "Quite apart from its rather arbitrary and subjective nature, the treatment of the stories (especially in John 5 and 9) as allegories needs to be justified on form-critical grounds."[102] Martyn must either call the FG's genre something other than apocalyptic, or he must offer some "form-critical support for John's radical translation of the dualism into a different genre."[103] It is here where

---

[99] One might argue that parables, or in John the reference to future trouble with "Jews" in 16:2, might be a second ostensive reference. But there is a difference. Martyn is actually arguing that two ostensive referents are being referred to simultaneously, but John 16:2 and the parables are certainly not ostensive in a specific sense, as if the reader should connect the various characters in the parables to specific individuals in their own setting, or that the future expectation of trouble with Jews was meant to only refer to the trouble to be expected by the "group" behind John. Nor is Martyn's reading comparable to the NT's typological reading of OT narratives (Gal. 4:21–31; Heb. 7). The NT's typological readings of OT narratives show both a distinction between the two ostensive referents and the specific connection between them. Martyn assumes the two ostensive referents are being referred to simultaneously, with no distinction or connection being made between them.

[100] Martyn, *History and Theology in the Fourth Gospel*, p. 32. Helpful here is Burridge, *What are the Gospels?* p. 41, who explains the difference between genre and mode.

[101] Of course, Martyn's "allegory" looks different than patristic allegory. Similar to Martyn's redaction-critical exegesis, patristic exegesis was also concerned primarily with the "reference." As Young, *Biblical Exegesis and the Formation of Biblical Culture*, p. 120, explains: "the fundamental question for understanding meaning was discerning reference. This did not mean a simplistic literalism; for the metaphorical nature of much language was something everyone was aware of . . ." The patristic interpreters produce both a "literal" or historical meaning and a "spiritual" meaning of the same text. Contra Martyn, there were not two "historical" meanings, but one. The spiritual meaning was a higher meaning. It still had a reference, but it was the reference of universal belief and divine concepts. See Henri de Lubac, "Spiritual Understanding," in Stephen E. Fowl (ed.), *The Theological Interpretation of Scripture: Classic and Contemporary Readings* (Cambridge, Mass.: Blackwell, 1997), pp. 3–25; David C. Steinmetz, "The Superiority of Pre-Critical Exegesis," in *The Theological Interpretation of Scripture*, pp. 26–38; Young, "Allēgoria *and* Theōria," in *Biblical Exegesis and the Formation of Christian Culture*, pp. 161–85; and Andrew Louth, "Return to Allegory," in *Discerning the Mystery: An Essay on the Nature of Theology* (Oxford: Clarendon Press, 1983), pp. 96–131.

[102] Motyer, *Your Father the Devil?* p. 28. The critique by Mark Stibbe, *John as Storyteller: Narrative Criticism and the Fourth Gospel*, SNTSMS 73 (Cambridge: Cambridge University Press, 1992), p. 148, is helpful here: "I recognize that the task of identifying the social function of narrative has sometimes been a rather arbitrary and subjective exercise. One of the problems with Johannine redaction criticism is that it tends to allegorize details of the gospel into incidents from the community's reconstructed history . . ."

[103] Motyer, *Your Father the Devil?* p. 28. See also the form-critical warnings by Ashton, *Understanding the Fourth Gospel*, p. 163.

the *bios* genre becomes important and where our argument, resting upon the growing consensus led by Burridge and others, becomes most pertinent.[104] For certainly if the FG is read on two levels, the Synoptic Gospels, which are as much *bios* as the FG, should also be read on two levels. The lack of consistency shows itself most at the level of form criticism.[105]

Returning to the second aspect of Hägerland's argument concerning the supposed "hints of allegory" for the reader in the text of John, that is, evidence or clues in the text itself that guide the reader to both levels of the drama, the conclusion is again in the negative. Martyn points to the anachronisms in the FG, especially the references to the expulsion from the synagogue, as providing the key to the reader that a two-level drama is taking place. Even without making use of Martyn's mistaken link to the *Birkat ha-minim* as the historical referent of the expulsion, Hägerland argues that such anachronistic imports into the Gospel hardly account for a supposed two-level reading.

> In a manner akin to that of the Synoptic Gospels, John's Gospel has certainly been coloured by the setting in which it was written, but its universal lack of historical reliability as compared to the Synoptics is nowadays questioned rather frequently.[106] An anachronism in the dialogue . . . is not a reason compelling enough to discredit the entire surrounding narrative.[107]

It is too much to assume that the first-century reader would find an anachronistic statement as an intrusion into the text and thus requiring a second reading of the whole text in light of that intrusion. As Francis Young explains, "The difference between ancient and modern exegesis

---

[104] Hägerland, "John's Gospel: A Two-Level Drama?," p. 316, n. 18.

[105] Surprisingly, Craig S. Keener, *The Gospel of John: A Commentary* (Peabody, Mass.: Hendrickson, 2003), p. 195, n. 208, gives a different conclusion: "Martyn's 'two-level' hypothesis fits ancient Hellenistic biographic and historiographic conventions; since it was normal procedure for educated readers to read a forensic speech in light of the context in which it was originally delivered (Quintilian 10.1.20–22) . . ." Although Keener is right to assume that ancient readers would read a text in its appropriate context, he is wrong to assume that the context would control the way the genre (form) of the text is handled. Would a history-like narrative no longer be history-like because it is written in the present context that differs from that history? How could history-like narratives ever be read of something other than being "completely" corrupted by their present authoring context?

[106] See the classic work by C. H. Dodd, *Historical Tradition in the Fourth Gospel* (London: Cambridge University Press, 1963); see also D. A. Carson, "Historical Tradition in the Fourth Gospel: After Dodd, What?," in R. T. France and David Wehnam (eds.), *Gospel Perspectives: Studies of History and Tradition in the Four Gospels*, 6 vols. (Sheffield: JSOT Press, 1981), vol. II, pp. 83–145; J. A. T. Robinson, *The Priority of John* (London: SCM Press, 1985), especially p. 35.

[107] Hägerland, "John's Gospel: A Two-Level Drama?," p. 318.

lies in the massive shift in what is found to be problematic."[108] Earlier Young even claims that "without the modern historical consciousness, none of this prevented anachronistic reading . . ."[109] Thus, it is impossible for us to assume that an anachronistic statement would have been taken by a first-century reader to refer to two different levels of historical consciousness.

Another phenomenon that has often brought evidence of the merger of two historical levels in the FG is the alleged inability of the narrative to distinguish between past and present. Martyn proceeds from 9:4a to 14:12 to arrive at the conclusion that the FE makes no distinction between what Jesus did once and what his followers are doing in the evangelist's time. Hägerland explains why such a position, especially in relation to John 2:19–22, is confusing:

> Only after his resurrection did the disciples realize the real sense of Jesus' words . . . The conviction that the disciples remembered (ἐμνήσθησαν; see 12.16) the past event was decisive to their faith. For the same reason, the eyewitness of 19.35 and 21.24 plays an important role. He is the guarantee for a continuity of remembering between those disciples who accompanied Jesus and those who came to believe later . . . Faith "now" is founded on what Jesus did (ἐποίησεν, 20.30; 21.25) "then." *The distinction between past and present in these passages is clear-cut enough to make its ever being doubted astonishing.*[110]

One wonders if the focus on the later *Sitze im Leben* of the Gospels in current Gospels scholarship has drawn the attention away from the "past" of the Gospels that is so prevalent. This is not to say that the Gospels are a history book of the earthly Jesus, or that the context in which the Gospels were written was the "only" grid from which they could see the past (Kant); but it does implicate that they were not divorced from the past. In fact, it was the past that defined their present reflection.

Helpful here are two fairly neglected works on this distinction between past and present in the Gospels. The first is a monograph by Eugene Lemcio entitled *The Past of Jesus in the Gospels*. According to Lemcio, all four Gospels show a recognizable distinction between past and present time. The past of Jesus, according to Lemcio, is important to the evangelists in the present.[111] If the Gospels at least portray some sense of

---

[108] Young, *Biblical Exegesis and the Formation of Christian Culture*, p. 207.   [109] *Ibid.*

[110] Hägerland, "John's Gospel: A Two-Level Drama?," p. 319 (emphasis added).

[111] Eugene E. Lemcio, *The Past of Jesus in the Gospels*, SNTSMS 68 (Cambridge: Cambridge University Press, 1991).

history, then this would seem to deny the two-level reading that Martyn claims to see in the FG; a reading that combines both past and present. The second is an article by Donald Carson entitled "Understanding Misunderstanding in the Fourth Gospel." Carson attempts to show how interpreters have misunderstood the various "misunderstandings" in the FG.[112] For example, Carson critiques Herbert Leroy's use of Johannine "riddles" to reconstruct the history of the JComm.[113] For Leroy the majority of the preaching of the JComm is because of the gift of the Paraclete. The "insiders" enjoy his presence and manifest his power primarily in the preached word; the "outsiders" do not enjoy his presence. But according to Carson, "what is remarkable about the teaching of John regarding the Spirit/Paraclete is that there are two dualities, not one."[114] Leroy only points to the first duality, where some have the Spirit and some do not, as is made clear in the antithesis of 14:17: the world cannot accept the Spirit of Truth but the disciples can. But the second duality is even more persuasive. "At the time Jesus is purported to speak, the Spirit has not yet been given; and his presence will be enjoyed only *after* Jesus returns to his Father by way of the cross and resurrection; and he bestows his Spirit, or asks his Father to do so, only in the wake of that triumph (7:37–39; 14:16, 23, 25–26; 15:26–27; 16:7, 12–15)."[115] Thus, at the time Jesus is speaking, *not even the disciples possess the Spirit* to the extent that Jesus envisages. The phrase "and he will be in you" (καὶ ἐν ὑμῖν ἔσται) seems to make clear that Jesus is referring to an event that is fully established in the future. Once again, past history is not amalgamated into the present in the FG.

In fact, according to Carson several passages require a solution that will only be given with the passage of time (post-resurrection). A prime example is 2:19–22 where the narrator (evangelist) explains that it was only after Jesus was raised from the dead that the disciples "remembered" the saying and believed the Scripture and the words Jesus had spoken. Although this passage is heavily debated, it is striking how the passage not only separates the past from the present, but uses the present perspective to explain the past. The same distinction can be made in 12:14–16, where the disciples fail to appreciate the scriptural significance of Jesus' triumphal entry into Jerusalem until after Jesus is glorified. Also, repeatedly

[112] Donald A. Carson, "Understanding Misunderstanding in the Fourth Gospel," *TB* 33 (1982), pp. 59–91.
[113] Herbert Leroy, *Rätsel und Missverständnis: Ein Beitrag zur Formgeschichte des Johannesevangelium*, BBB 30 (Bonn: Hanstein, 1966). For a summary see his "*Das johanneische Missverständnis als literarische Form*," *BL* 9 (1968), pp. 196–207.
[114] Carson, "Understanding Misunderstanding in the Fourth Gospel," p. 76.   [115] *Ibid.*

in the Farewell Discourse, the coming of the Spirit/Paraclete is not only made future to Jesus' speaking, but the understanding by the disciples of what Jesus means is made dependent on that future coming (e.g. 14:20, 26; 16:7, 12–15).[116] Thus, in line with Lemcio, Carson can state: "From this it is quite clear that the fourth evangelist is able and willing to maintain a distinction between *then* and *now*, the *then* of the situation during Jesus' ministry, and the *now* of the period following Jesus' glorification and the descent of the Spirit, and including the evangelist's day."[117] According to Carson, then, Martyn's proposal for a two-level reading of John, though recognizing the continuities between Jesus and the Paraclete, neglects the discontinuities. The death/resurrection/exaltation of Jesus "turns a corner" in the history of salvation that the FG presents. This turning of the corner does not simply introduce more of the same, albeit on a different historical level (the JComm's own level). From the perspective of the disciples' understanding and faith, nothing can ever be the same again.[118] The "purpose statement" (20:31) seems to allude to the continuing witness of the past in the present. This reading allows us to better understand Jesus' statement to Thomas in 20:29: "Because you have seen me you believe? Blessed are those who do not see and still believe."

The argument we have presented thus far critiques the method of reading the FG on two levels. We have argued that the reading proposed by Martyn would have been completely foreign to first-century readers and find no evidence for such a reading in the FG. There is no evidence of a biographical genre like the FG that was ever intended to be read on two levels. Martyn's creative amalgamation of both *bios* and apocalyptic genre can only be declared a mythical creation. The FG is biographical in its genre and must be read as a history-like or realistic narrative. The FG is not without a sense of history; a distinction is made between "then" and "now." Yet, the perspective of the present (of the evangelist) may be involved in the telling of the past. It is to that we now turn.

The expulsion from the synagogue

In reference to the second aspect of Martyn's reading of John 9, that this referent to their own setting is the specific removal from the synagogue that some or all of the JComm members are experiencing in relation to an official edict broadly decreed, recent evidence to the contrary, as we will discuss below, as well as the inappropriate form-critical assumptions

---

[116] *Ibid.*, p. 81.   [117] *Ibid.*, p. 82.   [118] *Ibid.*, p. 83.

discussed above, require that we more appropriately apply these "syno-gague" statements to their historical context. If the genre of the FG cannot be read in a dualistic or apocalyptic way without form-critical support, then the "expulsion from the synagogue" passages should not be read as a second level of the narrative. Certainly, if the text made no "literal" sense we could, as did the patristic exegetes, apply a more allegorical inter-pretation to the passage to make it mend. But that is not the case. The narrative of John 9:22 (and 12:42; 16:2) make complete sense without a "spiritual meaning," let alone another historical level.

In John 9:22 a man born blind from birth is healed by Jesus. The healing sparks debate between the blind man and the Pharisees, for not only was it a healing of a man that several knew to be blind (9:8–11), but it was also done on the Sabbath (9:14). The dialogue between the man who was healed and the Pharisees intensifies over the healer and his relation to God (9:16). The Pharisees turn to the man's parents. The parents admit that this man who can now see is their son, and he was born blind (9:20). But when asked how he can now see they reflect the question back to their son since he is "of age" and can speak for himself (9:21, 23). It is then that the narrator explains to the reader the motive behind the parents' response in 9:22: "His parents said this because they were afraid of the Jews; for the Jews had already agreed that anyone who confessed Jesus to be the Messiah would be put out of the synagogue."

For Martyn, 9:22 is an anachronistic intrusion in the text that signals to the readers, since they know that at the time of Jesus no expulsions were taking place, that the "story" is to be read as referring to their own day and time. Martyn explains how four elements in 9:22 command our attention.[119] The first and second are the expressions "the Jews" and "had already agreed." According to Martyn the first two elements show us clearly that the subject under discussion is a formal agreement or deci-sion reached by some authoritative group within Judaism prior to the writing of the FG. But is this necessarily so? Much has been written on the historical matching that Martyn has done with these expulsion passages. Martyn's assumption that this official decision was the *Birkat*

---

[119] What follows is taken from Martyn, *History and Theology in the Fourth Gospel*, pp. 46–49. Martyn was not the first to place these "expulsion" passages in the con-text of Jewish-Christian dialogue involving the FG. The earliest example can be found already in William Wrede, *Charakter und Tendenz des Johannes-evangeliums*, SVSGTR 37 (Tübingen: Mohr, 1933), who argued that the Jews in John reflected a Johannine conflict with contemporary Judaism. But it was Kenneth L. Carroll, "The Fourth Gospel and the Exclusion of Christians from the Synagogues," *BJRL* 40 (1957), pp. 19–32, who aligned the "expulsion" passages with the *Birkat ha-Minim*. At nearly the same time, T. C. Smith, *Jesus in the Gospel of John* (Nashville: Broadman, 1959), made a similar connection.

ha-Minim has been sufficiently criticized in subsequent scholarship.[120] It is no longer feasible to assume that the "expulsion" passages are referring to this specific event. Thus, the focus on Martyn's incorrect matching of the *Birkat ha-Minim* with 9:22 has caused Wayne Meeks to call it a "red herring" in Johannine research, that is, something that attracts attention away from the real issue.[121] But is it a "red herring"? Is it legitimate for Meeks to claim that this merely causes us to think of the Jewish-Christian split as a linear progression in which the promulgation of the *Birkat ha-Minim* was a culmination rather than the beginning of a development? Does this not force a JComm interpreter to have two intangibles rather than one: uncertainty concerning (1) what the "expulsion" passages really refer to and (2) the assumption of a "community" that stands behind the text? If we knew that the "expulsion" passages were referring to an event which we could specifically locate historically, and more so geographically, then we could be more assured that the audience for which the text was meant was in that historical period and/or geographical region. But we cannot. Unless it can be proven that the "expulsion" passages are anything more unusual or that the term is more officially descriptive than anything that would have occurred between Jews and Christians toward the end of the first century, then we are required to read the text

---

[120] As Smith, "The Contribution of J. Louis Martyn to the Understanding of the Gospel of John," explains, there are too many difficulties to establish Martyn's thesis with the Twelfth Benediction (p. 7). First, it is unclear that within the first century the Jamnian Academy had the kind of general authority that Martyn's thesis attributes to it. Second, the date of the Twelfth Benediction is uncertain, and since Martyn many have contested that it could have been composed as early as the 80s of the first century. Third, there is not direct or unambiguous evidence that the Benediction was formulated for the purpose of expelling Christians out of the synagogue or that it was ever actually used in that way. Yet, even amidst all these reservations, Martyn, *History and Theology in the Fourth Gospel*, pp. 60, n. 69; 61–62, n. 75, only claims to speak with more caution; and Wayne Meeks, "Breaking Away: Three New Testament Pictures of Christianity's Separation from the Jewish Communities," in Jacob Neusner and Ernest S. Frerichs (eds.), *"To See Ourselves as Others See Us:" Christians, Jews, and "Others" in Late Antiquity* (Chico, Calif.: Scholars Press, 1985), pp. 93–115, merely prefers to think of a linear development in which the promulgation of the *Birkat ha-Minim* was a culmination rather than the beginning of a development. For the critiques of Martyn's use of the *Birkat ha-Minim* and its general use in the first century see Peter Schäfer, "Die sogannante Synode von Jabne: Zur Trennung von Juden und Christen im ersten/zweiten Jh. n. Chr," in *Studien zur Geschichte und Theologie des Rabbinischen Judentums*, AGAJU 15 (Leiden: Brill, 1978), pp. 45–64; Reuven Kimelman, *"Birkat ha-Minim* and the Lack of Evidence for an Anti-Christian Jewish Prayer in Late Antiquity," in E. P. Sanders *et al.* (eds.), *Jewish and Christian Self-Definition*, 3 vols. (London: SCM Press, 1981), vol. II, pp. 226–44; William Horbury, "The Benediction of the *Minim* and Early Jewish-Christian Controversy," *JTS* 33 (1982), pp. 19–61; and Steven T. Katz, "Issues in the Separation of Judaism and Christianity After 70 C. E.: A Reconsideration," *JBL* 103 (1984), pp. 43–76.

[121] Meeks, "Breaking Away," p. 102.

as less situationally specific, and certainly less self-referential toward a specific group. Maybe by turning to Martyn's last two elements that are supposed to attract our attention in 9:22 we might find more conclusive evidence.

The third and fourth elements are the messianic confession of Jesus and the predicate nominative "an excommunicate from the synagogue." Concerning the third element, the messianic confession of Jesus, Martyn claims that "they," who he assumes is the group of Jewish-Christians in the JComm who are still attending the synagogue, "have evidently assumed that such a confession is compatible with continued membership in the synagogue."[122] This is, of course, what Martyn believes caused the fourth element to occur in 9:22: "after the [formal] agreement [has been made by Jews concerning Christians], the dual commitment is no longer possible," since the JComm members were still attending the synagogue.[123] For the term ἀποσυνάγωγος, which means "expulsion from the synagogue," is a "key term" which implies "the formal separation of the disciples of Jesus from the synagogue."[124] But again we have to ask if this is so! Only when Martyn begins with the assumption that the FG is a "community" document does the so-called "key" expulsion term concerning the so-called "formal" separation have any descriptive self-reference to the audience, which, of course, he assumes is not only a specific group, but one that is in an intimate (or at least co-worshipping) relationship with a specific synagogue.[125] Amidst all the assumptions that this requires, two further things need to be asked of 9:22 for the purpose of our argument: How anachronistic is the term? Does the term "signal" to the readers a two-level reading?

The key aspect that makes Martyn's exegesis of John 9 as a descriptive self-reference of the JComm is that the "expulsion" phrase is anachronistic. Martyn thinks 9:28 makes this more apparent: "You are a disciple of 'that one' but we are disciples of Moses." According to Martyn:

---

[122] Martyn, *History and Theology in the Fourth Gospel*, p. 47.   [123] *Ibid.*

[124] *Ibid.* Unfortunately, the term is unknown in non-biblical literature and the LXX. This is unfortunate because it allows Martyn to make a case on its "formal" meaning when such a use cannot be lexically verified or disproved.

[125] *Ibid.*, p. 146. Martyn claims that the Gospel "was written for a community of people who had a shared history . . . in the bosom of the [a] synagogue" (pp. 146, 150). In fact, for Martyn, what made the Johannine believers their own "community" was their conflict with the local synagogue: "Many members of the messianic group . . . paid the price for their convictions and suffered excommunication. From this point forward we may refer to those people . . . as *the Johannine community*, for it is obvious that the outworking of the *Birkath ha-Minim* in the city in question changed the Johannine circle – against their will – from a messianic *group* within the synagogue into a separate *community* outside that social and theological setting" (p. 155).

This statement is scarcely conceivable in Jesus' lifetime, since it recognizes discipleship to Jesus not only as antithetical, but also as somehow comparable, to discipleship to Moses. It is, on the other hand, *easily understood under circumstances* in which the synagogue has begun to view the Christian movement as an essential or more or less clearly distinguishable rival.[126]

But certainly these "easily understood circumstances" are not evidenced through the text; they are hypothetical with no external evidence.[127] Two aspects of 9:22 make it less anachronistic than Martyn would like us to think: one based upon a corrected reconstruction of the Jewish-Christian split in the first century; the other based upon the adverb "already."

First, without the historical or geographical reference behind the FG from which we can locate the "expulsion" reference, we cannot assume that the Jewish-Christian tension being described is anything more than a general reference to Jewish-Christian conflict, let alone to a specific conflict between the audience (whose specificity we cannot confirm) and a synagogue (whose issues, motives, and relation to the supposed JComm we cannot define). Far from being a "red herring," the lack of producible specificity in Martyn's thesis only makes his assumptions all the more presumptuous. Would not any messianic confession (Martyn's third element) be found in almost any "Christian" literature in early Christianity, and would that not be found disagreeable to any non-Christian Jew?

Second, the use of the adverb "already" (ἤδη) implies, based upon our discussion of John's sense of history, that whatever the "expulsion" is implying, it was already in process during Jesus' lifetime. That is, the conflict with the "Jews" that occurred in the earthly life of Jesus is no different in kind than what is being experienced by the Johannine readers, in fact, in retrospect, what "the readers" are experiencing was "already" in process in Jesus' day. For Martyn, the "already" emphasizes that the "agreement" or "decision" made by the Jews had been reached some time prior to John's writing. And since this "decision" was the *Birkat ha-Minim*, then such a suggestion is blatantly anachronistic. But if we do not begin with the assumption that the "agreement" is as formal as the *Birkat ha-Minim* then we are not forced to read the expression anachronistically. There is general confusion as to what type of "expulsion" the phrase might

---

[126] *Ibid.* (emphasis added).

[127] This is not to say that our reconstruction is not hypothetical, but that Martyn's reading is not evidenced in the text but based on his assumption of extra-textual realities.

be referring to, whether mild or excommunicatory.[128] But certainly the issue surrounds more than this. The key question is whether or not the phrase is meant to be descriptive of Jesus' time or of the evangelist's. C. K. Barrett chooses the latter: "That the synagogue had already at that time applied a test of Christian heresy is unthinkable . . ."[129] But in view of the lack of specificity we just discussed, Leon Morris' response to Barrett's comment is especially apt: "In view of our ignorance of much surrounding the subject this may be a little too confident."[130] It would appear that it is better to assume that the Jewish-Christian conflict was a general feature of the first century, even from the very beginning of the Jesus movement.[131] As Philip Alexander explains:

> It is abundantly clear from the New Testament itself that Christianity before 70 not only attracted support but also encountered strong and widespread opposition within the Jewish community. That opposition ranged from central authorities in Jerusalem (the High Priest and the Sanhedrin) to the leaders of the local synagogues. It extended from Palestine (both Galilee and Jerusalem) to the Diaspora (e.g. Asia Minor and Achaea). *It began in the time of Jesus himself and continued unabated in the period after the crucifixion.*[132]

More specifically, D. Neale has argued convincingly that during his lifetime Jesus was considered to be a *mesith*, one who leads people astray, based upon an examination of the Gospel accounts with reference to Deut. 13.[133] According to Neale,

> the examination of some New Testament texts that reflect a negative response to Jesus in light of literary traditions about the *mesith* and *meddiah* shows a reasonable possibility that the hatred reserved for the biblical *mesith* could have been directed

---

[128] Brown, *The Gospel According to John*, vol. I, p. 374. See also Emil Schürer, *The History of the Jewish People in the Age of Jesus Christ*, rev. and ed. Geza Vermes, Fergus Millar, and Matthew Black, 5 vols. (Edinburgh: T. & T. Clark, 1979), vol. II, p. ii.

[129] Barrett, *The Gospel According to St. John*, p. 361.

[130] Morris, *The Gospel According to John*, p. 488, n. 35.

[131] An early date is supported by the recent article by David Instone-Brewer, "The Eighteen Benedictions and the Minim before 70 CE," who argues that the curse of the *Minim* originated before 70 CE, probably in relation to debates between Jews and Samaritans.

[132] Philip S. Alexander, "'The Parting of the Ways' from the Perspective of Rabbinic Judaism," in James D. G. Dunn (ed.), *Jews and Christians: The Parting of the Ways A.D.70 to 135*, WUNT 66 (Tübingen: J. C. B. Mohr, 1992), p. 19.

[133] D. Neale, "Was Jesus a *Mesith*? Public Response to Jesus and his Ministry," *TB* 44 (1993), pp. 89–101.

toward Jesus. Furthermore, some enigmatic aspects of the public response to Jesus' ministry are made comprehensible in the light of this interpretation. Deuteronomy 13 and the subsequent *mesith* tradition provide a valuable addition to our basis for understanding the familial turmoil, civic unrest and personal struggle with loyalty at which the gospels hint.[134]

Even more, a recent article by David Instone-Brewer helps explain the common tensions that occurred between Jews and non-Jews before 70 CE.[135] According to Instone-Brewer, the curse in its earliest form is not directed to Christians, but to Jewish heretics, and maybe originally "to the Sadducees when they had the High Priesthood during the Second Temple Period."[136] Although in later rabbinic writings the general term *Minim* continued to be used, either as a general reference to "heretics," or as a reference to Christians, it was originally used by Pharisees as "a carefully crafted exegetical criticism of the Sadducees, reminding them of God's judgment on the wicked who prosper, and on those who offer incense wrongly."[137] Although Instone-Brewer never mentions Martyn's hypothesis, his evidence not only erases the link between a Johannine "group" and their "expulsion," but, by moving this type of conflict before 70 CE, adds further evidence to our proposal that the Johannine conflict had the potential of occurring in and around the time of Jesus.

Thus, rather than seeing John as being descriptive of one *point* of the linear progression that led to the *Birkat ha-Minim* (Meeks' position as a corrective to Martyn's), it is better to see John as being descriptive of the general Jewish-Christian conflict from the time of Jesus until the present day.[138] As we will discuss below, this fits best with the narrative's description, with John's sense of history, which we discussed above, and with the similar evidence found in the Synoptics. Beasley-Murray explains it well:

> On the one hand, we must remember that the followers of Jesus suffered much in the manner of the blind man from the time of Jesus on. And, contrary to Barrett, we must not forget that Jesus himself enunciated the crucial test of discipleship as confession

---

[134] *Ibid.*, p. 101. See also *b. Sanh.* 43a for evidence in Jewish tradition that Jesus was executed for "deceiving" Israel.

[135] David Instone-Brewer, "The Eighteen Benedictions and the *Minim* before 70 CE," *JTS* 54 (2003), pp. 25–44.

[136] *Ibid.*, p. 38.   [137] *Ibid.*, p. 42.

[138] This is not to assume that the term specifically covers the entire development, but that it assumes the Jewish-Christian conflict is an ongoing conflict, and 9:22 is reflective of that general linear conflict, not a specific point within it.

of him before men as Son of Man (Luke 12:8–9 = Matt 10:32–33; cf. John 9:35); the emphasis in Mark 8:37 on not being ashamed to confess Jesus doubtless expresses the concern in Mark's church [or audience] of the danger of denial in face of external pressures. Equally significant is the last beatitude in Matt 5:11–12, coming from the later period of Jesus' ministry, the parallel to which in Luke 6:22–23 is remarkably close to John 9: "Blessed are you when *they hate you, and when they exclude you and insult you and cast out your name as evil*, because of the Son of Man." Paul knew what it was to be thrown out of synagogues on mission (Acts 13:50), and he was not alone in that experience.[139]

Even C. H. Dodd, when remarking on 9:22, can state, "We must . . . conclude, it seems, that the prospect of such exclusion was before Christians of Jewish origin early enough, at least, to have entered into the *common tradition* behind both Luke and John."[140] Since Martyn himself, as a redaction critic, proceeds so that "by comparing John with the Synoptic Gospels we can identify many pieces which are obviously *traditional*,"[141] then it would seem as if 9:22 might actually meet his criterion of "traditional melodies."[142]

Thus, one wonders, as C. F. D. Moule expresses it, "whether there is any inherent reason for this ["expulsion" passage] to be declared unhistorical."[143] This is not to say that the "expulsion" term is not anachronistic in the sense of being a term that did not originate until after Jesus' time, but one that was used to describe an activity that, though certainly more

---

[139] George R. Beasley-Murray, *John*, 2nd edn, WBC 36 (Nashville: Thomas Nelson, 1999), p. 154.

[140] C. H. Dodd, *Historical Tradition in the Fourth Gospel* (Cambridge: Cambridge University Press, 1963), p. 410 (emphasis added).

[141] Martyn, *History and Theology in the Fourth Gospel*, p. 31.

[142] *Ibid.* Like Martyn, we are not assuming that John's perspective or circumstances did not circumvent the "telling" of this tradition, but certainly it has to be regarded as tradition-like enough to be of a firm historical nature.

[143] C. H. D. Moule, *The Birth of the New Testament*, 3rd edn (London: Continuum, 2002), pp. 155–56. Admittedly, one may disagree with the historical specificity with which JComm interpreters view the "expulsion" passages and not assume some level of traditional material. For example, Severino Pancaro, *The Law in the Fourth Gospel: The Torah and the Gospel, Moses and Jesus, Judaism and Christianity According to John*, NovTSup 42 (Leiden: Brill, 1975), pp. 247–53, argues that the "expulsion" passages are a literary fabrication. For similar views see also Douglas R. A. Hare, *The Theme of Jewish Persecution of Christians in the Gospel according to St. Matthew* (Cambridge: Cambridge University Press, 1967), p. 55; P. Winter, *On the Trial of Jesus*, 2nd edn (Berlin: Walter de Gruyter, 1974), p. 128; Norman Perrin, *The New Testament: An Introduction: Proclamation and Parenesis, Myth and History* (New York: Harcourt Brace Jovanovich, 1974), p. 222.

prevalent a generation or two removed, was already an issue in the time of Jesus and his disciples. As Moule explains concerning the narrative of John 9:

> In such ways as these, good traditions of the controversies of the Lord's life-time may have been re-set [in later terminology] in such a way as to continue topical in a later Palestinian community, or, later still, for the cosmopolitan populace of Ephesus where the mystic and the biblicist Jew, the dualist philosopher and the Ebionite might have jostled one another; and the story of the Word of God incarnate, with his creative words and his luminous deeds, had messages for them all.[144]

There is no doubt that the narrative is speaking of the cost of discipleship in terms of the conditions which are familiar to the readers; but this is nothing new, for since the beginnings of Jesus' ministry his followers have suffered much in the manner of the blind man. Thus, our conclusion is that the "expulsion" phrase in 9:22 is not to be read anachronistically as referring solely to the *Sitz im Leben* of the JComm, but to conflict occurring since the time of Jesus with specific applicative results for John's readers in whatever Jewish-Christian conflict they might be experiencing.[145]

But it is not simply 9:22 that convinces Martyn, for the same anachronistic term is used two other times in John. According to 12:42, even many of the authorities (Jewish) believed in him, but they did not confess (it) because they feared being "expelled" from the synagogue. This passage is similar to 9:22, for it speaks retrospectively of the ministry of Jesus.[146] Again, based upon our reading of 9:22, which gives less significance to ἀποσυνάγωγοι as a formal term signifying an official split between Judaism and Christianity in the late first century, 12:42 is referring to "traditional" events that occurred in Jesus ministry; events

---

[144] Moule, *The Birth of the New Testament*, p. 136.

[145] This is similar to what Bauckham, *GAC*, pp. 23–24, argues: "If John 9 addresses that situation, it addresses, not a circumstance peculiar to the Johannine community, but a circumstance that would have been common in the churches of the late first century. Only because Martyn starts with the presupposition that the Fourth Gospel was written for the Johannine community, and because he has no intention of trying to prove this point, can his argument function for him to characterize only the Johannine community's relationship to the synagogue." Of course, Bauckham does not discuss the specific problems with Martyn's readings, as this chapter has, but is helpful in showing how even Martyn's reading only works when he begins with the "community" assumption.

[146] Rudolf Schnackenburg, *The Gospel According to St. John*, 3 vols., trans. Cecil Hastings *et al.*, HTCNT (London: Burns and Oates, 1968–82), vol. II, p. 250. Unfortunately, Schnackenburg gives too much weight to formality of the "expulsion" term and is thus forced to deny that such a formal term could have been present in Jesus' day.

involving Jewish-Christian conflict. The comment in 12:43 also refers to the choice "men" were forced to make when confronted with the earthly Jesus, "for they loved human glory more than the glory that comes from God." As we described above, even if the term is anachronistic (has a post-Jesus origin) that still does not deny that it was being used by the FE to describe "real" events and conflicts beginning in Jesus' lifetime. If scholars agree, with obvious variance, that the conflict between Jesus and "the Jews" led to his eventual crucifixion, why could these three "expulsion" passages not be referring to that same conflict? This is especially so when the term used to describe this conflict, ἀποσυνάγωγος, has never been shown to be an official edict and was certainly not during the time when the official edict (*Birkat ha-Minim*) was given. The pressure by the "Pharisees" need not imply a post-70 authority, for if Jesus was already viewed as a *mesith*, certainly those who support him would receive similar treatment.

The third "expulsion" passage, unlike the previous two, is future instead of retrospective. According to 16:2, Jesus declares that a time is coming when you will be "expelled" from the synagogues. Again, based upon our reading of 9:22 and 12:42, 16:2 is referring to Jewish-Christian conflicts that have not yet occurred. If an official decree was known to the FE, or specific expulsions were already distinctly present, this phrase would be far from necessary. In a sense, 16:2 confirms the past and future distinction concerning the "expulsion" passages. The role of 16:2, like Matt 5:10–12 and Luke 6:22–23, is to tell of the future persecutions followers of Jesus will face. Thus, according to our reading, the FG tells of the conflict between "Jews" and followers of Jesus (past, present, and future) while giving practical implications for present readers. The Jewish-Christian conflict as presented in the FG is far from punctiliar, focused on the single experience of a local community. Since the days of Jesus there has been conflict with "the Jews." It happened in the past (9:22; 12:42) and it will happen in the future (16:2), even to the immediate disciples of Jesus. All three "expulsion passages" connect with any general first-century reader of the Gospel. For those who have faced persecution, they are not alone; for it has been ongoing since the days of Jesus, who himself was killed in such conflict. For those who have not, their time may well come.

In conclusion to the first question concerning the anachronistic nature of the "expulsion" passages, the Jewish-Christian conflict presented in these three passages, far from being imported into the text from purely present circumstances, resembles traditional material (Matt 5:10–12; Luke 6:22–23; Acts 13:50). This retrospective view of past events is far from rare in John. In several passages John describes events from a present position that would have been impossible to know or define at the original point of occurrence. Although we have already discussed a few examples above (12:14–16 and the "understanding through the Paraclete" passages, 14:20, 26; 16:7, 12–15), it is helpful here to discuss a few more. In 11:45–57, when the Jews plot to kill Jesus, Caiaphas the high priest tells the council that had gathered that it would be better for Jesus to die than for the entire (Jewish) nation to perish (vv. 49–50). The narrator explains that Jesus' death would not only "save" the Jewish nation, but also "the scattered children of God, to bring them together and make them one" (v. 52). Certainly this was not assumed by even the disciples prior to Jesus' death, let alone even immediately after (see Acts 10; and especially 11:18)![147] Another example is in 20:9 where, after the disciples saw that it was true that Jesus was not in his grave, the narrator explains "For as yet they did not understand the Scripture, that he must rise from the dead." Certainly if the apostles themselves did not understand at that time, then this retrospective description is anachronistic. But it is anachronistic in a sense of present explanation of the past, not a combining of the two. Finally, outside of the "expulsion" passages, the most famous example is 2:19–22. This passage instructs readers of the Gospel in "how to" look for the further meaning that Jesus' sayings have that were not perceived at first.[148]

The second question that needs to be asked of 9:22 for the purpose of our argument is as follows: Does the "expulsion" term "signal" to the readers a two-level reading? For Martyn the answer is simple: the anachronistic "expulsion" phrases alert the reader that the "literal" reading of the narrative is meant to be read "allegorically," or as a two-level drama. Ashton agrees and argues as much from 2:19–22; he even argues that the early placement of the temple incident in John, in contrast to the Synoptics, is to alert the reader to this reading strategy that is to be employed through the rest of the Gospel.[149] But if our reading is correct, that the anachronism is a retrospective description and not an out-of-place import into the text, then is it really a "clue" to a further or deeper reading? The statement from Young we quoted above is pertinent here: "Without the modern historical consciousness, none of this prevented anachronistic reading . . . The difference between ancient and modern exegesis lies in the massive shift in what is found to be problematic."[150] Thus, it is impossible for us to assume that an anachronistic statement

---

[147] We will discuss this concept further in chapter 5.

[148] Contra Ashton, *Understanding the Fourth Gospel*, pp. 416–17, the further meaning explained in 2:22 is an aspect of the pervasive Johannine irony, and not about the JComm.

[149] *Ibid.*, p. 414.

[150] Young, *Biblical Exegesis and the Formation of Christian Culture*, p. 207.

would have been taken by a first-reader to refer to two different levels of historical consciousness.[151] In fact, we must assume that the "world" of the text *was* descriptive of their world (Frei). No distortion was needed; no contemporary sociological insight was required. The "problem," as Martyn entitles his introduction, turns out to be no problem at all. Far from needing alerting, it should be assumed that the first-century readers of John would have needed no "insight" into the text. All the authorial *Tendenzen* and contemporary Jewish-Christian conflict surely colored the text's description of the past, but it was the past nonetheless. But to John's readers, the past was as formative of the present as the present was on any description of the past.

A "literal" reading of the Gospel narrative

This provocative sub-title is taken from Francis Watson's chapter in *GAC* entitled "Toward a Literal Reading of the Gospels." As Watson explains, the assumption that the Gospels were written to meet the needs of specific communities is, at one level, a straightforward hypothesis, and it is entirely appropriate that it should be criticized on this same level.[152] Clearly this is what historical-critical exegesis does. This study, then, is attempting to critique this "community" hypothesis by claiming, along with *GAC* and others in the Gospel community debate, that there is another, more viable hypothesis that must be considered. This is based first on historical assumptions that we dealt with in chapter 2 and second with the way the Gospel text was read by first-century readers.[153] Thus, our proposal is as follows: If we are no longer forced to assume that the FG (1) was written primarily for a local community (as chapter 2 has argued) and (2) was written in the midst of a specific conflict with a local synagogue, then we are allowed to read the Gospel narrative in what we have argued is a more pre-critical reading strategy. We will call this reading strategy, along with Watson, a "literal" reading of the Gospels.

For Watson, a "literal" reading is in opposition to an "allegorical" reading. In this way: a literal reading of the Gospel narratives, simply stated, reads them according to their "surface-level" subject matter. "The referential claim implied by the text is inseparable from its literal sense."[154] A "literal" reading does not try to understand the Gospel as primarily

---

[151] Even more simply, why should the readers know that the "expulsion from the synagogue" did not happen in Jesus' ministry?

[152] Watson, "Toward a Literal Reading of the Gospels," in *GAC*, pp. 195–96.

[153] Although as Watson, "Toward a Literal Reading of the Gospels," pp. 196–97, makes clear, no historical reading is without theological assumption.

[154] *Ibid.*, p. 211.

intended to fulfill a historical role – a role that complies with the needs of a local community – which is the key to explaining the "real" referent of the text's surface-level reading. This does not imply that in a "literal" reading the act of reference is successful. But it does imply that the Gospel text *intends* to refer to persons, events, and places in the world outside the text, and that the individual pericopae are not isolated entities but are embedded in a narrative continuum. Thus, this intentionality is integral to the text's "literal" meaning.[155] As Frei would describe it, a "literal" reading reads the text as a "realistic narrative." The identities of the narrative agents (Jesus; the disciples) are rendered in such a way as to be "unsubstitutable"; they do not serve as ciphers or symbols for other identities or realities.[156] Thus, the program of reconstructing an original *Sitz im Leben* as a grid for interpretation, whether for reasons of theological bias or from the sense that the verbal meaning alone is too obvious to be interesting, corrupts the way the text was read in the first century and has been read nearly ever since. This is in contrast to John Ashton, for example, who can almost claim that no one read John 9 correctly until J. L. Martyn came along, except for the original readers, of course.[157]

In this way the "literal" reading of the Gospel narratives should take precedence over the contextual reading. Watson gives a helpful example:

> It might be argued (although not very plausibly) that the original "significance" of the author's [Mark's] decision to begin his account of Jesus' ministry with this reference to his baptism lay in his intention of opposing an anti-sacramental group in his own community, who appealed to the Pauline claim that "Christ did not send me to baptize but to preach the gospel" (1 Cor. 1.17) to justify the discontinuing of the practice of baptism. On this hypothesis, the evangelist's argument would be that, if even Jesus submitted to baptism, how much more should we?[158]

First, the most obvious difficulty is that we cannot prove by the narrative itself that this passage of Mark was written in a baptism controversy. It is a circular enterprise to conclude Mark's created context from Mark's narrative alone. Second, and more importantly, the "literal" meaning of

---

[155] *Ibid.*

[156] See, for example, Hans Frei, *The Identity of Jesus Christ*; and George Hunsinger and William C. Placher (eds.), *Theology and Narrative: Selected Essays* (Oxford: Oxford University Press, 1993), pp. 45–93.

[157] Ashton, *Understanding the Fourth Gospel*, p. 413.

[158] Watson, *Text and Truth: Redefining Biblical Theology* (Grand Rapids: Eerdmans, 1997), p. 104.

the text stands at a certain distance from any particular contextual significance (its subject is Jesus, not the so-called Markan community).

> While it might be said . . . that Mark "intended" his words to
> be taken as an intervention in a current controversy, it can also
> be said that Mark "intended" the distance that he has in fact set
> between his statement and the current controversy by omitting
> any explicit reference to it, and that he therefore "intended" his
> statement to be capable of communicating its verbal meaning
> in contexts where the baptism controversy is no longer a live
> issue.[159]

The same may be said of John and the "expulsion" passages. We already
showed that the supposed anachronism, which is Martyn's entry point
into the two-level or community reading of the FG, is not anachronistic
as an import but as a retrospective description of the past. Yet, as with
this example in Mark, even if we were to grant that the "expulsion"
passages were in relation to local conflict between the JComm and the
synagogue, the very fact that there is *no explicit reference to this conflict*
implies that the "expulsion" passages are capable of communicating in
and to contexts far beyond their own – even to an "any and every" type of
audience, or at least an audience that can relate to these circumstances.
Thus, even if our explanation of the "expulsion" passages were not correct,
it would still not permit a two-level reading of the FG, for nothing in
the passages refers explicitly to an event like the *Birkat ha-Minim*, for
example. Thus, our reading allows that John may have been written in the
midst of conflict between his Jewish-Christian membership in his church
and a local audience, but this does not control the reading of the FG, for
the text does not require that it does. The text allows any Christian reader
who has conflict with Judaism in the late first century to connect with
the blind man and receive comfort from the words of the Gospel. The
narrative has hidden the contextual significance and made the "literal"
meaning its primary explication.

Of course, a "literal" reading need not imply a "literalistic" reading,
where the functional diversity of language is not allowed to function;
for John is certainly full of symbolic language and imagery. Craig
Koester, whose *Symbolism in the Fourth Gospel* is probably the best and
most recent work on Johannine symbolism, has found some interesting
results.[160] Koester argues that for the symbolism (symbols and metaphors)

---

[159] *Ibid.*, p. 105.
[160] Craig R. Koester, *Symbolism in the Fourth Gospel: Meaning, Mystery, Community*,
2nd edn (Minneapolis: Fortress Press, 2003).

to work, speakers and listeners must share certain kinds of information. This would seem to support a JComm interpretation of John where the symbolism is "closed" rather than "open." But Koester continues:

> Although some have argued that John's Gospel is a "closed system of metaphors" whose meaning is clear to insiders but opaque to the uninitiated,[161] we have tried to show the opposite. Those who read the Gospel for the first time often find its meaning to be rather obvious; the complexity and richness become increasingly apparent with rereading. . . Its message is accessible to less informed readers yet sophisticated enough to engage those who are better informed, incorporating both into the same community.[162]

Even though Koester accepts the "community" reconstruction presented by Brown,[163] his conclusions agree with our proposal: that a "literal" reading of John, not a two-level or cryptic reading, is the reading most appropriate to the narrative. In this way John 9 does not simply exchange one historical referent for another historical referent, but allows the characters to be symbolically "representative" of the reader who has been given spiritual sight and is now forced to make personal decisions concerning previous religious commitments and personal relationships.[164] But this is a far cry from assuming that the blind man is representative of a "historical" local group and that Jesus is representative of a "historical" leader or leadership in the JComm. Thus, a "literal" reading of John still takes into account the FG's symbolic and metaphorical language, as well as its spiritual application.[165]

Conclusion: early Christian Gospel

We asked two questions at the beginning of this chapter: How does a first-century Gospel text reveal its audience? And, how would a first-century audience have appropriated a Gospel text? Concerning the first question we turned to the growing consensus that the Gospels have a

---

[161] Probably referring to Meeks, "The Man from Heaven in Johannine Sectarianism," p. 68; Leroy, *Rätsel und Missverständnis*, pp. 21–25; Ashton, *Understanding the Fourth Gospel*, pp. 451, 530; and Tom Thatcher, *The Riddles of Jesus in John: A Study in Tradition and Folklore*, SBLMS 53 (Atlanta: Society of Biblical Literature, 2000), pp. 104–8.

[162] Koester, *Symbolism in the Fourth Gospel*, p. 259.   [163] *Ibid.*, p. 19, n. 34.

[164] We will develop this argument further in chapter 5.

[165] Our discussion of a "spiritual" referent is no different than the reading applications used by the patristic interpreters. This would explain why the Gospels never required a "broadening" for audiences outside their own "community."

family resemblance to Greco-Roman biography. Using the research of Richard Burridge, we concluded that although genre cannot define the type of audience that would have been expected, it can give focus or tendencies. The conclusion, then, was that the *bios* genre would be used by self-contained, sectarian-like groups or networks of groups in only a rare or specialized way. The normal use of a *bios* was broader dissemination, at least within a market niche. Certainly a Gospel could be used purely by a local "community," but that would be the exception and not the norm.

Concerning the second question we focused on two areas: the reading strategy and narrative referentiality of pre-critical readers and the two-level reading of John, especially 9:22. Using the research of Hans Frei, we concluded that the *Tendenzen* observable by redaction criticism are not easily transferable to the specific social setting of the first-century text, and more importantly, that the "world" depicted by the redaction is inappropriately considered to be more "real" than the "world" depicted by the narrative. Certainly the first-century readers did not think the FG dropped from heaven, but they also did not read the FG as a modern-day redaction critic. Thus, the dichotomy that Martyn sees in the Gospel text and uses to "discover" the way the FG would have been "seen and heard" by its first-century reader is foreign to a pre-critical reading. The very fact that the "two levels" were combined into one narrative implies that they were to be read as one narrative. Then, after establishing the pre-critical reading strategy, we looked at J. L. Martyn's primary entry point into the two-level drama in 9:22 and argued that his reading is neither confirmed by his historical reconstruction nor made explicit by the narrative. Since the Gospels would have been read as "literal" or "realistic" narratives, the Gospel must be taken as a narrative whole. The "expulsion" passages, far from being anachronistic import and thus a key to reading the narrative on two levels, are retrospective depictions of events beginning in Jesus' day. The FG is aware of the difference between past and present; so the implication that an anachronistic (post-resurrection) statement requires a two-level reading is critical, rather than pre-critical, and does not account for the narrative as a whole. Thus, the FG should be read with a "literal" reading; a strategy we will employ in chapter 5.

4

EARLY CHRISTIAN READER: AN EXPLICATION OF THE AUDIENCE OF THE FOURTH GOSPEL BY INQUIRING FOR THE IMPLIED READER

After looking at the Gospel as a text, we now turn to its reader.[1] We argued in chapter 2 that the language of the FG is not "insider" or antilanguage and that the Gospel "community" should be pictured as much broader than the sectarian-like groups normally supposed. We argued in chapter 3 that the very nature of an early Christian "Gospel" and its relation to the *bios* genre cannot define the audience of the text, but certainly make a local "community" reading rare or specialized. We also critiqued Martyn's two-level reading of John and presented a case for a "literal" reading of the Gospel text appropriate to the first century. But what type of audience does the narrative expect?

Narrative criticism has often been used by historical critics to define more clearly the audience a text would have expected. Of course, the recovery of the audience of a text is immediately faced with a dilemma: it is easier to determine if a text was written for a local, homogeneous group rather than a general audience, than it is to distinguish between a general (non-localized) audience and a local group that is heterogeneous.[2] Our focus, then, will be specifically on noting possible distinctions in the text between a local, heterogeneous audience and a general audience. Thus, since even "community" interpreters assume the JComm

---

[1] We admit that the term "reader" may appear anachronistic in a culture that was largely illiterate. But such does not change the fact that we have a written text, nor does it change the fact that the text itself was copied, preserved, and probably read aloud, maybe numerous times, in early Christian worship. The fact that the text remains, and is not just an oral tradition, seems to warrant the use of reading terminology. Theoretically, then, any time the term "reader" appears, we could transpose it for "hearer" or the more general term "audience." The fact that a large percentage of the society was illiterate is unimportant. We need to think of reading "groups" and not merely reading individuals. The issue in literacy is group literacy and not individual literacy. The fact that a group had a text and was informed by it is all that needs defending; whether each person could read it themselves is irrelevant.

[2] This does not include levels in the development of the text, which may have included later parts for later audiences. Although we will discuss textual layers toward the end of the chapter, our initial task is to determine the audience of the Gospel as we have it in this relatively final form.

152

was heterogeneous, we will also begin with that assumption; for a heterogeneous audience is congenial to our proposed audience. But in order to determine if the heterogeneity is located in a specific and necessarily limited audience or is inherent in a general audience, we will place the derivable "reader" of the text into the historical context of a hypothetical local "community" in order to verify if such a reading is viable. Our search for this derivable reader will be accomplished using the concept of the "implied reader" and the analysis of the implied reader provided by R. Alan Culpepper in his *Anatomy of the Fourth Gospel*.[3]

The quest of the implied reader: method and procedure in John

Symptomatic of the current reader-sensitive approach in biblical interpretation is a statement made by Culpepper: "Original readers are now more vital to the accuracy of the text than original manuscripts."[4] By "original" Culpepper is not referring to the original first-century audience, but to the mode of reading, namely, a reading that sees as much the story in the FG as the referent behind it. Traditionally, the reader was a detached observer of authorial intention or the verbal sense; but this is no longer the case.[5] Discussion of the reader and the biblical text, though an interesting and related topic, is well beyond the scope of this book. Although we will not be discussing the various theories of reading proposed by postmodern literary theory, we will certainly be using one aspect of that discussion in this chapter: the implied reader.[6] Narrative criticism has added a missing dimension in biblical studies research, especially in the Gospels.[7]

---

[3] R. Alan Culpepper, *Anatomy of the Fourth Gospel: A Study in Literary Design* (Philadelphia: Fortress Press, 1983).

[4] *Ibid.*, p. 237.   [5] Vanhoozer, *Is There a Meaning in this Text?* p. 149.

[6] Narrative discussions are often based on a certain concept of the text. As Culpepper, *Anatomy*, p. 5, explains: "The gospel as it stands rather than its sources, historical background, or themes is the subject of this study. 'Text' here means simply the words or signifiers of the story as recorded in the 26th edition of the Nestle-Aland *Novum Testamentum Graece*." See also Jeffrey Lloyd Staley, *The Print's First Kiss: A Rhetorical Investigation of the Implied Reader in the Fourth Gospel*, SBLDS 82 (Atlanta: Scholars Press, 1988), p. 22, n. 5.

[7] The history of the application of literary criticism to the study of the Gospels is well known. For a general survey of the method in application to the NT see William A. Beardslee, *Literary Criticism of the New Testament*, Guides to Biblical Scholarship (Philadelphia: Fortress Press, 1970) and Mark Allan Powell, *What is Narrative Criticism?* GBS (Minneapolis: Fortress Press, 1990). Some of the earliest works that apply literary criticism to the Gospels include David Rhoads and Donald Michie, *Mark as Story: An Introduction to the Narrative of a Gospel* (Philadelphia: Fortress Press, 1982); Charles Talbert, *Reading Luke: A Literary and Theological Commentary of the Third Gospel* (New York: Crossroad, 1982); Culpepper, *Anatomy*; and Jack Dean Kingsbury, *Matthew as Story* (Philadelphia: Fortress Press, 1986).

But the use of narrative criticism in biblical studies does not eliminate the historical aspect of its research. "While the approach of literary criticism is clearly distinct from that of historical-critical scholarship, there needs to be dialogue between the two so that each may be informed by the other."[8] Although a purely literary-centered or historical-centered project is appropriate and common, they are never completely isolated from one another. The historian uses literature as its only window into the history and the literary critic assumes a historical context in its evaluation of the literature. Although each criticizes the other for being short-sighted, neither can stand alone. While it would seem that historical and narrative criticism would be at an interpretive impasse, something of a relationship is beginning to form. Several Johannine scholars are attempting to integrate the two methods with each other.[9] The need for the integration of historical and literary methods is also pressing in this book. As W. Randolph Tate explains, "Texts reflect their culture, and to read them apart from that culture is to invite a basic level of misunderstanding."[10] Our goal is to find the intended reader in the text (implied reader) and place that reader in the two competing audience reconstructions for analysis. But who actually is the "implied reader?"[11]

Narrative critics generally speak of an implied reader who is presupposed by the narrative itself. "This implied reader is distinct from any real, historical reader in the same way that the implied author is distinct from any real, historical author. The actual responses of real readers are

---

[8] Culpepper, *Anatomy*, p. 5.

[9] See, for example, Mark Stibbe, *John as Storyteller*. Unfortunately, Stibbe falls into the very trap that he attempted to avoid. Even after critiquing the redaction-critical assumptions of J. Louis Martyn and Raymond Brown, especially the specific conclusion drawn by Martyn concerning the *Birkat ha-Minim*, Stibbe still uses their assumptions for his conclusion. No literary addition to his method was introduced. In fact, Stibbe's main addition to the discussion was a sociological one. Relying heavily on the work of Sternberg, *The Poetics of Biblical Narrative*, which attempts to decipher the social function of a narrative, Stibbe argues that the result of his method would try to define the social function of John's narrative. More recent are Motyer, "Method in Fourth Gospel Studies: A Way Out of the Impasse," *JSNT* 66 (1997), pp. 27–44, as well as his *Your Father the Devil?*; and Helen C. Orchard, *Courting Betrayal: Jesus as Victim in the Gospel of John*, JSNTSup 161, CGT 5 (Sheffield: Sheffield Academic Press, 1998). As we will discuss in chapter 5, Motyer's approach is congenial to our own. In contrast, Orchard assumes the social-historical context of the FG to be the JComm: an assumption this book is testing and cannot begin with.

[10] W. Randolph Tate, *Biblical Interpretation: An Integrated Approach* (Peabody, Mass.: Hendrickson, 1991), p. 4. By speaking of "culture" we do not intend to be vague (general Mediterranean world), but we do want to leave open the possible context in which the FG was intended and used. Thus, by not using "Jewish" or "Hellenistic," we avoid limiting the potential range of the first-century audience.

[11] Although some make a distinction between the implied reader and the narratee, we will use the term implied reader in a comprehensive manner. Cf. Staley, *The Print's First Kiss*, p. 47; and Kingsbury, *Matthew as Story*, p. 36.

unpredictable, but there may be clues within the narrative that indicate an anticipated response from the implied reader."[12] The term "implied reader" has gained wide currency in recognition of the fact that a text implies a role or persona for the reader.[13] In biblical studies, the term "reader" is an ambiguous term.[14] Often there is a dichotomy between the real (historical) reader and the implied (textually based) reader. Although in theory the textually presupposed reader is only ideal and not real, the implied reader can allude to the historical reader intended.

Thus, for our purposes, we will use the implied reader as a key to discovering the real reader presumed by the narrative. Our assumption is that the narrative story sheds light on the real world in which it was written; that is, the reader prescribed and assumed in the narrative reveals traits about the historical reader.[15] As Kingsbury describes it:

> Once one fully understands the "world of the story," one can then move to a reconstruction of the "world of the evangelist." Indeed, the "world of the story" may well prove itself to be an index of the "world of the evangelist," in the same way as the "implied reader," reconstructed from a study of the text, may prove to be an index of the "intended reader" who was at home in the evangelist's church.[16]

---

[12] Powell, *What is Narrative Criticism?*, p. 19.

[13] Robert M. Fowler, "Who is 'the Reader' in Reader Response Criticism," *Semeia* 31 (1985), pp. 5–23, especially p. 10. Cf. Seymour Chatman, *Story Discourse: Narrative Structure in Fiction and Film* (Ithaca: Cornell University Press, 1978), p. 151. See also Wayne Booth, *The Rhetoric of Fiction*, 2nd edn (Chicago: University of Chicago Press, 1983), p. 429, who uses the term "the postulated reader"; Peter Rabinowitz, "Truth in Fiction: A Reexamination of Audiences," *CI* 4 (1977), pp. 121–41, 126, who only speaks of the "authorial audience"; and Gerald Prince, *Narratology: The Form and Function of Narrative* (Berlin: Mouton, 1982), who uses the term "virtual reader."

[14] See Kevin J. Vanhoozer, "The Reader in New Testament Interpretation," in Joel B. Green (ed.), *Hearing the New Testament: Strategies for Interpretation* (Grand Rapids: Eerdmans, 1995), pp. 301–28. For a good discussion of the various proposed "readers" of the Gospels – historical-biographical, redaction-critical, and narrative-critical – see Jack Dean Kingsbury, "Reflections on 'The Reader' in Matthew's Gospel," *NTS* 34 (1988), pp. 442–60.

[15] Some attempt to make this distinction between implied and real reader by using the categories of narrative described by Chatman, *Story and Discourse*, pp. 19–27. See, for example, Mark Allan Powell, *Chasing the Eastern Star: Adventures in Biblical Reader-Response Criticism* (Louisville: Westminster John Knox Press, 2001), pp. 86–87. But even Powell admits that using Chatman is not without its problems, for the distinction between story and discourse is somewhat artificial. See a critique of the use of Chatman by David Lee, *Luke's Stories of Jesus: Theological Reading of Gospel Narrative and the Legacy of Hans Frei*, JSNTSup 185 (Sheffield: Sheffield Academic Press, 1999).

[16] Kingsbury, "Reflections on 'The Reader' in Matthew's Gospel," p. 459. As a corrective to Kingsbury's rhetorical emphasis, one can not "fully" understand the "world of the story." Interestingly, while Kingsbury uses the concept of the implied reader to reconstruct the reader in the evangelist's church, we are using the concept to see if the evangelist's reader was ever assumed to be in his church and no other.

Such an approach argues that implied readers are assumed to know certain things that original readers would have known (and to believe things that they would have believed). Thus, the concept of the implied reader may be informed by historical data concerning the actual, original readers, "but the concept retains a theoretical integrity of its own, grounded in what is actually presupposed for the narrative."[17]

Thus, using the language of Mark Allan Powell, we may begin to speak of the text's expected reading.[18] An expected reading makes sense based upon a consideration of historical concerns relevant to the text's created environment. A text taken in isolation from its communicative context could have many viable meanings; a pure reader-response method prefers this approach.[19] But this study assumes that the FG is to be read as a communicative act with intention for its own time and place.[20] Thus, by using the heuristic device of the implied reader we can begin to define the reader the text presupposes. That is, by understanding the implied reader as "an imaginary set of people who may be assumed to read a given text in the way that they are expected to read it, bringing to their reading experience the knowledge, competence, beliefs, and values that appear to be presupposed for the text . . ." we can establish the hypothetical reader in the text.[21] As a construct of the text the implied reader is accessible to scholarly discussion and reconstruction.[22]

Therefore, in this chapter we will be using the heuristic device of the implied reader discussed above in order to ask one question of the text of the FG: Would the various explanations or comments (or lack of) befit a

---

[17] Powell, *Chasing the Eastern Star*, p. 213, n. 136.   [18] *Ibid.*, pp. 57–130.

[19] This is because of the influence of deconstructionist readings. The text no longer has a historical context it can call home. Its new home, and interpretive meaning, is located solely in the reader and his or her present context. See Vanhoozer, *Is There a Meaning in this Text?*, pp. 148–95; and Anthony C. Thiselton, *New Horizons in Hermeneutics: The Theory and Practice of Transforming Biblical Reading* (Grand Rapids: Zondervan, 1992), pp. 471–555.

[20] The implication here is that the Gospels are communicative acts with a literary intention for their own historical context. What Paul Ricoeur, *Interpretation Theory: Discourse and the Surplus of Meaning* (Fort Worth: Texas Christian University Press, 1976), p. 93, calls "the omnitemporality of meaning" is more appropriate to significance than meaning. By our definition, meaning refers to its creative intention within its historical context, whereas significance can and does move beyond its created context. It is stated well by Norman R. Petersen, "The Reader in the Gospel," *Neotestamentica* 18 (1984), p. 40: "Because only authorial readers are actually participants in the communicative transaction, only they are actors in the text's interpretive context."

[21] Powell, *Chasing the Eastern Star*, p. 64. The two key works that deal with the implied reader in John are Culpepper, *Anatomy*, pp. 203–27, and Staley, *The Print's First Kiss*. We will be dealing with their discoveries, as well as critiquing their procedure, as we proceed through the text below.

[22] Kingsbury, "Reflections on 'the Reader' of Matthew's Gospel," p. 460.

text written for the author's specific, geographically local community? If our comparison is between "community" and non-"community" readings of the Gospels, then part of this chapter's assumption will be to evaluate the knowledge assumptions for a local, heterogeneous group in light of its hypothetical "community" context.[23] This is in contrast to the definition of community we presented in chapter 2. Thus, by using the implied reader as a heuristic device and placing the text setting in a potential "community," as normally reconstructed by JComm interpreters, we will now attempt to discover which audience the FG expects.

The search for the implied reader in the Gospel of John

The most thorough search through the text of John for the implied reader was done by Culpepper in *Anatomy of the Fourth Gospel*. Culpepper described his method as follows:

> We may begin by making the simple and perhaps overly wooden assumption that the character of the narratee can be drawn from the narration by observing what is explained and what is not. We will assume further that the narratee knows about things and characters that are alluded to without introduction or explanation but has no prior of things, persons, events, and locales which are introduced by the narrator.[24]

Culpepper then separated the various explanations into five areas: persons (or characters), places, languages, Judaism, and events. In order to make the results of this chapter more comparable, we will be using the same categories used by Culpepper. As was discussed above, since our task is more specific we will allow ourselves to be less "wooden" than Culpepper. Therefore, in each of the five areas we will introduce the problem in determining a general audience (hereafter, GA) from a local, heterogeneous audience (hereafter, LHA).

Persons (characters)

This section is one of the most difficult to evaluate. Although we cannot assume knowledge just because no explanation is provided, we may be

---

[23] Our definition of a Gospel "community" does not preclude a "network" of communities, as long as the entity is still in similar location and has frequent contact between members and leadership. Otherwise, one could hardly speak of a Gospel community at all, since the text would lose its ability to be self-referential of the community for which it was intended.

[24] Culpepper, *Anatomy*, p. 212.

able to assume a lack of knowledge if an explanation is given. But the difficulty lies in distinguishing between explanation and introduction. For certainly an introduction could be simply for rhetorical effect and not a true introduction. Since there is no reliable criterion to distinguish between them we must look at the various examples in the text with our definition of the context ("community") in mind. Another difficulty is the issue concerning the audience's knowledge of the Gospel story in general, whether through another Gospel (most likely Mark) or the oral tradition concerning Jesus events. Since many JComm interpreters see the characters in the narrative as representative of sub-groups within the JComm, our difficulty is magnified. Thus, with these ambiguities in mind, we now turn to our general question in this first area: With which characters in the narrative is the implied reader familiar?

The first question that needs to be asked is if the implied reader "knows"[25] the narrator. According to Culpepper, "Clearly it is assumed that they do, for the narrator uses 'we' with no explanation in 1:14, 16 and 21:24. He also addresses the readers using the first person singular, 'I,' in 21:25."[26] Again, it is difficult to know from what is left unexplained the exact level of knowledge, but certainly this would imply recognition in some capacity. Many theories have been listed as to the exact identification of the "we" in these passages. It could be referring to humanity in general,[27] the apostolic church,[28] or a group of eye-witnesses, whether or not the eye-witnesses are reporting from within a community.[29] Of course, many have assumed that the "we" the reader is expected to know is from within the reader's own community. According to D. Moody Smith:

> If the Johannine Community which produced the Gospel saw itself in traditional continuity with Jesus, we are in a position to perceive in the "we" of both prologues of both Gospel and

---

[25] This term is necessarily ambiguous. The implied reader need only know the title or oral introduction to the Gospel, and nothing else other than what the Gospel tells him, for an appropriate understanding.

[26] *Ibid.*, p. 213.

[27] For Rudolf Bultmann, *The Gospel of John: A Commentary*, trans. G. R. Beasley-Murray (Philadelphia: Westminster, 1971), pp. 68–69, the "seeing" is not an act of perception, as if an eye-witness could participate; the notion of the vision has been historicized. Anyone can "see" the glory of Jesus once the "vision of faith takes place in the process of the upturning of all man's natural aims in life . . ."

[28] According to Barrett, *The Gospel According to St. John*, p. 143, the "we" is referring to the church which is the bearer of the tradition of Jesus. It need not be referring to a literal eye-witness. "It is as if the church sets its seal on the veracity of its spokesman."

[29] Morris, *The Gospel According to John*, p. 104, n. 90 argues that the "we" must be restricted to those who actually saw the earthly Jesus.

> Epistle, not the apostolic witness *per se*, but a community which
> nevertheless understood itself as heir of a tradition based upon
> some historical witness to Jesus.[30]

But what does Smith mean by "Johannine Community?" Is Smith referring to the general church and its location behind the author, and their
being both the receiver and bearer of John's account of the Jesus tradition?
Or is Smith implying that the community is itself the tradition keeper and
its sole proprietor? It appears that the "community" paradigm is at play
here. The point need not be "we" the audience (i.e. community), but
"we" the authoritative and trustworthy tradition. Based on our discussion
in chapter 2 of the importance of the "apostolic witness" or, as Irenaeus
refers to it, "the tradition of the apostles"[31] in the patristic era, we are
less forced to deny the apostolic witness as if it can only be a *per se*
witness.[32] Certainly Christians in the late first century saw themselves as
participants in the tradition, as Smith suggests concerning the JComm,
but they also were recipients of the tradition. They knew a distinction
between past witness and present significance, as we argued in chapter 3.
Like Paul (1 Cor. 15:3) the author of John was "passing on" what he had
received, no matter how connected to the *per se* witness the authorial
"we" really is. If we exclude Bultmann's more universal understanding,
which denies any historical reading,[33] and accept some sort of tradition
of apostolic witness we are not forced to assume a communal audience.[34]
But a good law is not based on hard cases; thus we continue to examine
the evidence.

Second, we may also ask if the implied reader is assumed to know
Jesus prior to the Gospel account. Since Jesus is not formally introduced
until after his identity is already defined, it would seem that the implied

---

[30] D. Moody Smith, *Johannine Christianity: Essays on its Setting, Sources, and Theology*
(Edinburgh: T. & T. Clark, 1984), p. 20.

[31] *Adv. Haer.* 3.1.

[32] By "*per se* witness" we mean that which would have been part of the originating
witness.

[33] See the explanation by Bultmann, *The Gospel of John*, pp. 69–70.

[34] Interestingly, Culpepper, *Anatomy*, p. 213, admits that "The readers may or may not
be a part of the group for which the narrator speaks, but they at least know the narrator
(evangelist) and the group he represents." With such group language great confusion can
exist. What does he mean by "group?" We are not even sure what the group is, what it looks
like, the size or geographical distribution of it, or if it even existed as a coherent entity.
It seems as if the warnings by Cohen we discussed in chapter 2 would also be pertinent
here. Of course, if the "we" is taken to be apostolic witness, then it can be assumed that the
audience would be familiar with the "tradition of the apostles," but that could include most
early Christians, as the patristic writings make clear.

reader was already familiar with the person of Jesus.[35] The great majority of time spent on locating the *logos* in its cultural milieu may have been misleading, as if the term's cultural origin (Jewish or Hellenistic) would define the Gospel's audience. Once we allow the narrative to introduce Jesus in its own way, which it does after the *logos* explanation, then we can see how the prologue is more for definition than introduction. Based upon our methodological question, why would the evangelist write a document (which potentially many could not read in his church) in order to further explain the identity of Jesus to those who were confused? Community interpreters argue that it is to reinforce social identity of the group, especially one that has been recently fragmented, especially from a Jewish synagogue as in John's case. But this appears to be a case of Ockham's Razor. Our argument is not that social identity was absent from the Gospel, but that this identity was general rather than specific to a LHA. Far from assuming the basic answer, community interpreters are forced, once they assume a LHA, to make sense of explanatory or defining comments by positing a context in which it would have been probable, since no such situation is actually known outside of the document itself. Would not many if not most "Christian" churches in the late first century be wrestling with their identity with the Jews, just as conflict with the Jews was widespread, not specifically localized? It would seem more probable that the FE would write a document explaining Jesus' identity to those outside his local church(es); people who may have heard of Jesus, and maybe some of his "signs" and preaching, but did not really understand who he was; people who would not be sure how he related to them and their worlds.[36] When considering the narrative's delayed introduction and more immediate and powerful identifying presentation of Jesus, perhaps Culpepper is right, "The name will be recognized, but the identity may be mistaken."[37]

Third, we may ask if the implied reader is assumed to know John the Baptist. In reference to John the Baptist's introduction in 1:6–8, perhaps Culpepper is correct: the formality of the introduction "may owe more to the evangelist's desire to imitate the Old Testament than to the need to introduce John to readers who have never heard of him."[38] This is by

---

[35] As discussed above, this raises several issues, although none are more pertinent than John's use and knowledge of the Synoptics. For recent research on John's potential knowledge of Mark see Richard Bauckham, "John for Readers of Mark," in *GAC*, pp. 147–71. For a critique of this proposal see Wendy E. Sproston North, "John for Readers of Mark? A Response to Richard Bauckham's Proposal," *JSNT* 25 (2003), pp. 449–68.

[36] We will discuss the purpose of the FG in chapter 5.

[37] Culpepper, *Anatomy*, p. 213. As we have argued, "identity" need not imply a localized social identity.

[38] *Ibid.*

necessity an assumption of a rhetorical strategy in contrast to a proper introduction. But it is the parenthetical remark in 3:24 that offers the most basic evidence that the audience was already familiar with John the Baptist. In 3:23, John the Baptist is mentioned for the first time since 1:36. Nothing previous in the text would give any indication that the Baptist was doing anything other than baptizing. As Bauckham explains, "To understand the reason for the explanation, we are obliged to postulate implied readers/hearers who know more than the Gospel itself has told them."[39] In an article critiquing this essay by Bauckham, Wendy Sproston North admits "There is much to be said for his [Bauckham's] claim that the evangelist's remark on the timing of the Baptist's imprisonment was directed to readers who knew Mark's Gospel."[40] Or, for our purposes, the comment in 3:24 was directed to readers who were already familiar with John the Baptist. Therefore, the textual evidence presumes that the implied reader would be familiar with John the Baptist. It seems as if the evangelist is less interested in formally introducing him, than he is in defining who the Baptist is in comparison to Jesus (1:24–28).

Fourth, we may ask if the implied reader is assumed to know the disciples. The individual disciples are treated with varying degrees of familiarity. Although Simon Peter has not yet been introduced, Andrew is said to be his brother and a follower of John the Baptist (1:40).[41] Peter is certainly assumed to be known by the implied readers. Andrew is again introduced in 6:8. According to Culpepper, the repeated introduction with reference to Peter may simply be because of Peter's fame, not because he was completely unknown.[42] No special introduction is given to Philip or Nathaniel (1:43–51); their names were probably recognizable to the reader. Thomas is not individually introduced, but he is said to be "one of the disciples," which the readers would have surely recognized. Several times Thomas is designated as "the twin" (11:16; 20:24; 21:2). Culpepper argues that such a designation was not capable of introducing him, but meant to give him some individuality.[43] But it would seem that if Thomas had been known by some as "the twin" rather than Thomas, then the repeated designation would help clarify which Thomas the narrative was referring to. Therefore, although there is no consistency in the introductions or explanations of the disciples, the implied reader is certainly

---

[39] Bauckham, "John for Readers of Mark," p. 153.
[40] Sproston North, "John for Readers of Mark? A Response to Richard Bauckham's Proposal," p. 452. Although Sproston North questions Bauckham's implications of the parenthetical remark in 11:2, which we will discuss below, in reference to 3:24 she claims, "whether or not we are fully persuaded of Bauckham's argument on 3:24 in all its aspects, his overall point that John could and did presume a knowledge of Mark on the part of his readers is impossible to dismiss" (p. 453).
[41] Culpepper, *Anatomy*, p. 214.   [42] *Ibid.*   [43] *Ibid.*

assumed to know of the disciples and certain individual disciples in a more comprehensive way.

Fifth, we may ask if the implied reader is assumed to know the Beloved Disciple. With all the various proposals concerning the BD, especially in relation to his leadership role in the so-called JComm, it is surprising to find that he is introduced as a character unknown to the reader. In 13:23, he is referred to as "one of his disciples – the one whom Jesus loved," rather than "the disciple whom Jesus loved" as he is in 19:26, 20:2, and 21:7, 20. Culpepper admits that "the difference is slight but shows that the reader is not expected to recognize the Beloved Disciple."[44] In 21:24, the reader must be told that it was the BD who is testifying to these things and has written them (see also 19:35). This odd relationship between the unnamed BD and the Gospel he has supposedly written leads Culpepper to give the following reconstruction:

> Is this because the Beloved Disciple has no "roots" in the tradition and his role is fictionalized to a greater degree than that of the other disciples? Probably. In the concluding verses of the gospel, "the brethren," who may be the intended readers, misunderstand about the Beloved Disciple's death. The readers know this disciple, therefore, but must be told of his role in the story, and the "Beloved Disciple" must be identified as the witness and author of the gospel. The "we" and "I" of the final verses are also presumed to be known.[45]

But must this be the case? Could not the BD be a witness to the tradition? Since there is a vast amount of literature on the BD, with theories to match,[46] we will not digress into a potential identification. For our purposes, what is most revealing is that the narrative does not assume that the readers know the BD.[47]

Sixth, we may ask if the implied reader is assumed to know the "Jews" and other political leaders. For the Gospel of John the Jewish groups need no introduction or explanation. No information is given regarding

---

[44] *Ibid.*, p. 215. The readers could have heard of the disciple by his name, but the term "the disciple Jesus loved" was innovatory within the FG.

[45] *Ibid.*

[46] See especially Paul S. Minear, "The Beloved Disciple in the Gospel of John: Some Clues and Conjectures," *NovT* 19 (1977), pp. 105–23; Richard Bauckham, "The Beloved Disciple as Ideal Author," *JSNT* 49 (1993), pp. 21–44; Hengel, *The Johannine Question*; Andrew T. Lincoln, "The Beloved Disciple as Witness and the Fourth Gospel as Witness," *JSNT* 84 (2002), pp. 3–26. Each of these discussions of the BD assumes a "community" setting for the creation of the Gospel.

[47] We will discuss the role of representative figures like the BD in chapter 5.

the Jews, priests, Levites, Pharisees, or "rulers of the Jews."[48] Likewise, the chief priests (7:32) and high[49] priest (11:49) are given no further designation. The status of the βασιλικός as some type of official is known without explanation, but such individuals as Nicodemus (3:1), Caiaphas (11:49), Annas (18:13), and Joseph of Arimathea (19:38) must be introduced. Finally, Pilate and Caesar are well known.[50] Therefore, although some introductions are given, they are almost always brief so as to place particular individuals or smaller authoritative groups within the political system at the time. The Jewish leaders are all assumed to be recognized by the readers. For the community interpreters, recognition of the "Jews" implies recognition due to local conflict, but that is not necessary. Nothing in the text is overly descriptive so as to imply that the narrative is defining one specific group of Jews (known personally by the readers), rather than "Jews" and "Jewish leadership" in general.[51] An understanding of the Jews and Judaism would seem basic at some level to the average person in the first century, especially to Christians either through oral tradition or the prominence of the OT.

Finally, we may ask if the implied reader is assumed to know some of the more minor characters in the narrative. The three characters in the Lazarus narrative, Lazarus and the sisters Mary and Martha, represent an interesting case. Lazarus has to be introduced, but Mary and Martha are assumed to be known (11:1).[52] Mary and Martha are mentioned in Luke 10:38–42, but their brother Lazarus is only mentioned in John. The parenthetical quote in 11:2 implies that the reader should not only be aware of Mary, but of a previous event where she anointed Jesus and wiped his feet with her hair. Bauckham argues that 11:2 refers forward to that character's appearance later in the Gospel (12:1–8).[53] For Bauckham, the fact that the evangelist can refer forward to an event not yet told reveals

[48] For some community interpreters the phrase "of the Jews" is polemical and not explanatory.

[49] The distinction "chief" and "high" is only in English.

[50] Cf. Culpepper, *Anatomy*, p. 215.

[51] Although as Urban C. von Wahlde has argued in "The Terms for Religious Authorities in the Fourth Gospel: A Key to Literary Strata?," *JBL* 98 (1979), pp. 231–53, and "The Johannine Jews: A Critical Survey," *NTS* 28 (1982), pp. 33–60, the narrative does portray some "Jews" (high priests and a few Pharisees) as the Jewish leadership, those with political power. But this is a general depiction, not of a specific "group" in conflict with the readers.

[52] The fact that Lazarus is reintroduced in 12:9, "Lazarus, whom he [Jesus] had raised from the dead," reinforces the evangelist's assumption that the implied readers are unfamiliar with him. Although Bauckham, "John for Readers of Mark," p. 165, argues that this reference is not for identification so much as to explain the crowd's interest in Lazarus, the reminder still functions the same: to connect Lazarus to the event for which he is known, though not by the implied readers.

[53] Bauckham, "John for Readers of Mark," p. 163.

the assumption that the implied reader is already familiar with the event, most likely from the Gospel of Mark. The critique by Sproston North discussed above argues that the parenthetical statement in 11:2 does not point forward but back to something already known by the Johannine readers, probably within the JComm.[54] But even if we were to grant that the statement points back to something other than the Johannine narrative, the fact that an event dispersed among early Christianity in the Gospel of Mark, a Gospel most scholars assume was utilized by the Gospels of Matthew and Luke, would seem to imply that a non-Johannine tradition or narrative is being referred to. This tradition or narrative, whether it is Mark or simply oral, would almost certainly not be a tradition only found within a Johannine group's tradition, for it would be assumed that such a tradition would already be known within the so-called community. Yet this is not without problems. Thus, even if there is good reason to see this parenthetical remark in 11:2 to be referring to a tradition known in early Christianity, it does not specifically prove a general audience.

Turning to other examples of minor characters in the narrative, we can see that Jesus' brothers are referred to with no introduction. Culpepper thinks this may either be because they were already known, or because the realization of Jesus having brothers would not be surprising.[55] The servant whose ear was cut off when Jesus was arrested was identified as "Malchus" (18:10). The identification of such a minor character reminds us that the evangelist is aware of who would have been unfamiliar if not completely known to the audience to whom he writes.[56] The two women at the cross, Mary the wife of Clopas and Mary Magdalene, are identified with little explanation (19:25), but that need not imply that they were well known to the readers, for it would appear that their role in the narrative is to serve as witnesses to Jesus' death.

In conclusion, the evidence of persons does not clearly reveal the local or general nature of the audience, only that the reader's knowledge is varied. But two things were surprising, one specific and one general. First, in light of our primary methodological question, the need to introduce

---

[54] According to Sproston North, "John for Readers of Mark? A Response to Richard Bauckham's Proposal," p. 466, "the fact that he [the evangelist] expects his readers to know this information in advance of its retelling in the Gospel is the strongest possible indicator that John wrote for a people already in receipt of his teaching." But this assumes that John's readers could only have Johannine information; no non-Johannine information could possibly be known by John. The very fact that Matthew and Luke knew Mark, if not the hypothetical Q, reveals the misplaced logic in Sproston North's assumption.

[55] Culpepper, *Anatomy*, p. 216.

[56] Although Culpepper is right to say that the identification adds credibility to the narrator's account, it need not be a superfluous identification for the sake of posterity.

the BD is surprising. Unless one is able to argue that the BD is not real,[57] the common link of the BD with some form of leadership in the JComm contradicts the presentation of the BD in the narrative of John.[58] The implied reader needs an almost complete introduction to this "Beloved Disciple." How could the "leader of the JComm" (per Raymond Brown) need such an introduction, especially when it is admitted that he is the authoritative voice behind the written text (19:35; 21:24). Using Bauckham's argument, that the BD is portrayed in the FG not as the "ideal" disciple but as ideally qualified to be the author of the Gospel, there is no reason to suppose that this document was written specifically for a LHA.[59] In fact, the narrative role of the BD makes a communal audience extremely unlikely; at least one in which the BD plays a part. Second, and maybe most surprising, in light of the fact that most JComm interpreters suppose that the contents of the Gospel would have been the subject of preaching within the JComm for many years before the "publication" of the Gospels, it is surprising that any of the characters need an introduction. The need for introduction implies that the relationship of the Gospel to the JComm is different from what is normally presumed. Thus, although there is no other unexplainable evidence that would eliminate a LHA as being the assumed readership,[60] enough surprising elements have been raised to proceed further with the examination.

Places

Our examination of the discussion of persons (characters) reveals how complex it can be to define the implied reader in the text. It is no less complex when we turn to places in the FG. Similar to persons, the various places are assumed by "community" interpreters to be representative of groups of people (e.g. Samaritans in John 4) that come into contact

---

[57] Or both ideal and real, as is argued by Hengel, *The Johannine Question*, pp. 78, 125, 130–32. Although Bauckham, "The Beloved Disciple as Ideal Author," helps to reconcile this difficulty.

[58] The title of the book by Brown, *The Community of the Beloved Disciple*, alludes to the BD's leadership role in the proposed JComm. According to Brown, the BD is "the hero of the community" (p. 22).

[59] Bauckham, "The Beloved Disciple as Ideal Author."

[60] The FE seems more intent on explaining Jesus than defining him. But this is not surprising since it seems very probable that the readers were already familiar with Mark. Peter was also assumed to be known by the reader. But with Peter's leadership and large involvement in the early Christian movement, this is hardly surprising. For example, in reference to the primacy of Peter in recognized early Christianity, Clement of Rome conjoins Peter as one of the outstanding heroes of the faith (*1 Clem.* 5), and Ignatius uses words which suggest that Peter was an apostle of special authority (*Rom.*4.2).

or membership with the JComm.[61] We now turn to the evidence for places.

Culpepper summarizes it well: "The narrator assumes that the reader has a general knowledge of the geography of the gospel story."[62] As early as 1:28 the narrator locates the town of Bethany "beyond the Jordan." Of course, this may only assume the reader knows of the Jordan, a more famous river, and not its exact location. Interestingly, the narrator uses the Hellenized form of Ἱεροσόλυμα, and not the more Semitic Ἱερουσαλήμ, the form preferred by Luke-Acts. Although the choice may simply be idiomatic, it could also be to lend itself to a more Greek-speaking audience.[63]

It is difficult to tell how familiar the readers are with the region of Galilee. Although towns are named in the region (1:44; 1:45; 2:1; 2:12), they are never explained. This may assume that the region was familiar, but, as Culpepper posits, may simply be because they are to be taken as unimportant to the story.[64] In 6:1 the narrator reports that Jesus "crossed the sea of Galilee, which is the sea of Tiberias." Culpepper notes that some manuscripts, among them Codex Bezae, add that Jesus crossed the Sea of Galilee "to the region of" Tiberias.[65] The explanation might show that a general familiarity was expected of this location by the readers, especially since the feeding miracle took place there (6:23).

What is notable for our purposes is that the narrator calls the specific region Tiberias; something unique as compared with the other three accounts of this miracle in the Synoptics. The context of Mark's account of the feeding miracle implies that it occurred in the region of Galilee (6:1, 21), assuming the context of the previous pericope is the same as the feeding miracle, but the detail concerning the region of Tiberias is not mentioned. Only in 6:53 does Mark add "When they had crossed over [the Sea of Galilee], they came to land at Gennesaret and landed there." Matthew, like Mark, implies that the general region of the feeding miracle is in Galilee (13:53), and makes no mention of the location in the feeding miracle pericope (14:13–22). But in 14:34, following Jesus' walking on water (the Sea of Galilee is assumed), Matthew follows Mark 6:53 and states that "When they had crossed over [the Sea of Galilee], they came to land at Gennesaret." Luke also assumes a Galilean context for the feeding miracle, based on the context of the previous pericope which deals with

[61] Brown, *The Community of the Beloved Disciple*, pp. 35–40.

[62] Culpepper, *Anatomy*, p. 216.   [63] *Ibid.*   [64] *Ibid.*, pp. 216–17.

[65] *Ibid.*, p. 217. These variants may be a scribal addition attempting to explain the two genitives rather than a helpful clue to the implied reader's geographic knowledge. Cf. Schnackenburg, *The Gospel According to St. John*, vol. II, p. 13.

Herod the tetrarch and the mentioning of the Galilean town, Bethsaida (9:1). Luke's only mention of Gennesaret occurred in 5:1.[66] When compared with John's account of the feeding miracle, two things stand out. First, since none of the other three accounts is specific about the location of the feeding miracle (Mark has no specifics, Matthew only mentions it after the next pericope, and Luke's only mentioning of the location is four chapters earlier), John's detailed account, given almost emphatically at the beginning of the pericope, might suggest that John, if he was familiar with any of the Gospel accounts in some form (at least Mark who never mentions it), was giving detail to an account that was lacking it in the previous three accounts.[67] Second, even if we can make no conclusions concerning John's knowledge of the other Gospel accounts, his use of the Hellenistic term "Tiberias," rather than the more Jewish "Gennesaret," again lends itself to a more Greek-speaking audience.[68]

In summary, it is doubtful that the FG expected its readers to be well versed in Galilean geography. While some of the names and locations (Sea of Galilee) probably sound familiar, and may have been assumed to be common knowledge, there is no evidence that John expected intimate knowledge of their parts.[69]

Similar to Galilee, the readers of the FG were not expected to know many Samaritan or Transjordan regions. The only Samaritan city mentioned is Sychar (4:4), but it has to be introduced to the reader. Bethany is described as "beyond the Jordan" (1:28; 10:40). But the designation may only imply that the reader would be familiar with the location of the Jordan, thus placing the town of Bethany in a recognizable area. Or, as Culpepper mentions, it may also be to distinguish this Bethany from the

---

[66] The term "Gennesaret" is found only in the three Synoptic passages mentioned (Matt. 14:34; Mark 6:53; Luke 5:1). W. D. Davies and Dale C. Allison, Jr., *The Gospel According to Saint Matthew*, 3 vols., ICC (Edinburgh: T. & T. Clark, 1988–97), vol. II, p. 511, claim the term is "probably the name of the fruitful and well-forested valley on the northwest shore of the Sea of Galilee, south of Capernaum and north of Tiberias." But they add, "It might also be taken to have been a town which gave its name to the surrounding region as well as to the adjacent Sea of Galilee."

[67] See Bauckham , "John for Readers of Mark."

[68] This Greek-speaking bent needs to be explained in light of the context of Jewish conflict usually posited by JComm interpreters.

[69] The allegorical reading of John by some community interpreters has led some to suppose a group behind the geographic language. Kikuo Matsunaga, "The Galileans in the Fourth Gospel," *AJBI* 2 (1976), pp. 139–58, is a prime example: "In the Evangelist's congregation, which is primarily a Jewish Christian community, there are some Galilean converts . . . who accepted the Kerygma of John's church and believed in Jesus Christ. Or near the Evangelist's church, there is a certain Galilean Christian community . . ." (p. 158). See also Brown, *The Community of the Beloved Disciple*, pp. 39–40, who is in general agreement with Matsunaga.

one in Judea.[70] Of course, JComm interpreters have had great success in seeing in John 4 an entire group inclusion of, if not a mission to, Samaritans. As Rensberger explains, "Given the fact that . . . we are told the story of Jesus' far more successful dialogue with the Samaritan woman, many scholars would agree that the Johannine community included Samaritans among its numbers, and most likely we should therefore infer at least some ongoing Samaritan mission as well."[71] Why would JComm interpreters not also see a conversion of inhabitants from Bethany as well? This is a case of how the two-level reading is always highly inconsistent. After discussing in chapter 3 the immense form critical problems with such an allegorical reading, not to mention the lack of sensitivity to a pre-critical reading of the text, such a suggestion seems completely fictional.[72] Thus, at the narrative-critical level, the implied reader's knowledge of Samaria was assumed to be limited.

With it unexpected that the reader has much knowledge of Galilee or Samaria, we now turn to Judea to see if the FG assumed a basic knowledge of the region and its parts. The towns outside and around Jerusalem are certainly not assumed to be known by the reader. This can be seen in the narrator's explanation of Bethany. In 11:1 it is described as the village of Mary and her sister Martha and as "some two miles away" from Jerusalem (11:18), setting the scene for the death of Lazarus pericope. In the next chapter it is reintroduced as the place where Lazarus was raised from the dead (12:1), "implying that the reader would need such a reminder to remember where Bethany was."[73] Other towns in the Judean region are introduced for the reader: Ephraim is near the wilderness (11:54), and Aenon is described as "near Salim" (3:23).[74]

Details about Jerusalem are assumed to be generally unfamiliar to the reader. In 5:2, the narrator sets the scene of a healing miracle by explaining that in Jerusalem "by the Sheep Gate there is a pool, called in Hebrew Bethesda, which has five porticoes." In 9:7, the Pool of Siloam is not located but translated, most likely as a pun. The Kidron valley, the place where Jesus was arrested, seems have been a recognizable location to the readers. But the garden in which the arrest took place had to be introduced (18:1). The name "Gethsemane" given to the Garden in the Synoptics is not mentioned in John; it may be assuming Mark (Mark 14:32; Matt.

---

[70] Culpepper, *Anatomy*, p. 218.

[71] Rensberger, *Johannine Faith and Liberating Community*, p. 145.

[72] The representative function of John 4 will be discussed in more detail in chapter 5.

[73] Culpepper, *Anatomy*, p. 217.

[74] Aenon is almost certainly near Judea if not within it, but its exact location is uncertain. Cf. Brown, *The Gospel According to John*, vol. I, p. 151.

26:36). The sites at or around the location of the crucifixion are unknown to the readers. In 19:13, the narrator describes the site as "the judge's bench at a place called the Stone Pavement, or in Hebrew, Gabbatha." In 19:17, a location is called "The Place of the Skull, which is called in Hebrew, Golgotha." Finally, in 19:20, the narrator tells that Jesus was crucified "near the city." Culpepper explains these comments by the narrator as something provided "to authenticate the account rather than to identify the places for a reader who would know them by their Hebrew names."[75] We will deal with these translation issues in the language section below.

Locations in the temple in Jerusalem are mentioned twice, although neither is given explanation. In 8:20, the narrator says that he spoke "in the treasury." Since it is unlikely that Jesus was actually teaching in the temple's treasure chamber, it must refer to temple precincts where people came to cast their offerings (cf. Mark 12:41, 43; Luke 21:1).[76] Since almost every Jew understood what temple participation was like (even after 70 CE) and Gentiles often still participated in temple activities and gave some financial offering, this would be self-explanatory. In 10:23, the narrator describes how during the festival of the Dedication in Jerusalem Jesus "was walking in the temple, in the Portico of Solomon." The detail is of no importance to the story and cannot be assumed to have been an expectation for the reader, even if it was only a memory.[77] The only important aspect of the story is that Jesus was in the temple during a festival, thus setting the scene for Jesus' confrontation with the Jews.

Thus, Jerusalem and its temple, major landmarks in the Greco-Roman world, were given information that any reader would have been assumed to know or understand[78] without major explanation. Although the reader may have been assumed to have some knowledge of the major landmarks in Jerusalem, especially the temple precincts, nothing was expected that would have made the story incomprehensible to the uninformed reader.

In conclusion, no specific or highly technical (in-group) language or concepts were used in describing the places in John's narrative. Several geographic locations in the story needed to be introduced to the reader. Culpepper falls into the trap that we have tried to avoid in this section

---

[75] Culpepper, *Anatomy*, p. 218.   [76] Morris, *The Gospel According to John*, p. 444.

[77] It may have been remembered since it was the oldest portico and was commonly associated with Solomon, the builder of the first temple. See Josephus, *War* V.v.1, 184–85; *Ant.* XV.xi.3, 396–401; XX.ix.7, 221.

[78] "Understand" in a sense of being familiar with religious temples and their importance, their being the center of religious activity and teaching, and as a physical landmark for a religion.

of the comparison. For good reason, many have tried to find the locale of the Johannine Christians, and their assumed geographic knowledge has been the key to their placement. Culpepper states: "On the basis of . . . geographical references, it is difficult to conclude that the *reader* knows [any one] area better than the others."[79] This statement assumes that if we can calculate what the reader knows, we can discover where the reader is to be found. But this assumes that the FG was written for a local audience, hence a single location. But, as this book is attempting to test, that might not necessarily be the case. The fact that the reader has no general expertise in any of the major regions discussed may not be because they are not from that region, but because they *may not* be from that region. Yet, based upon our primary methodological question there is little place evidence to differentiate between a GA and a LHA. What was determined is that no single location is evident in the Johannine narrative; no one location was evidently familiar to the readers.[80]

Languages

As we turn to the evidence of languages in the FG we find a more fruitful conclusion. The assumption we hold here is that even in a LHA, various terms and expressions would not need to be explained, defined, or translated for a reading audience since they would have been repeatedly explained and understood in a worshipping and teaching context. This is especially the case when those words or terms have a significant Johannine meaning; a meaning which certainly an oral culture would have used and explained in previous preaching. We now turn to the evidence.

The immediate assumption is that the readers of the FG know Greek.[81] Where a different language is used, it is never used in isolation. We cannot claim that the readers only knew Greek or even primarily knew Greek. The fact that the narrative is in Greek, and to our knowledge always has been, requires that we assume that the communicative act was meant to

---

[79] Culpepper, *Anatomy*, p. 218.

[80] This makes Meeks', "Breaking Away," pp. 97ff., search for the location of the JComm based upon internal evidence seem extremely unfounded.

[81] The assumption is that unless the narrative gives indications to the contrary, the reader (narratee) only knows the language of the narrative. See Mary Ann Piwowarcyzk, "The Narratee and the Situation of Enunciation: A Reconsideration of Prince's Theory," *Genre* 9 (1976), pp. 161–77. The common sense, communicative assumption here is that the implied readers will at least be able to read the language of the text. Again, this need not imply that all the recipients were themselves able to read. Again, the issue is group literacy and not individual literacy.

transpire between Greek writer and reader. There are a few examples of language explanation that point to the implied audience.

The fact that certain words are translated implies that the readers may not be familiar with them or know that language. For example, common words such as "Rabbi" (1:38; 3:26; 4:31; 6:25; 9:2; 11:8), "Messiah" (1:41; 4:25) and "Rabboni" (20:16) need to be translated. The names of individuals are also translated to convey their meaning (Cephas, 1:42; Siloam, 9:7). Where Hebrew or Aramaic terms are introduced (Bethesda, 5:2; Gabbatha, 19:13; Golgotha, 19:17), they are referred to as foreign words ("in Hebrew") rather than as the names by which the reader would know these locations.[82] Such terminology has usually been taken to imply that at least some of the implied readers of the FG were "not" Jewish, since Jewish readers would have no need for translation. The combination of alleged strong Hellenistic influence on John and evidence of a "John" in Asia Minor have led many to take these Jewish translations as simply befitting a document written for a non-Jewish audience.[83] The literary evidence mentioned above, John's translation of basic Hebrew terminology, made the dominant view stand: John was written for a non-Jewish audience. But such a conclusion is not self-evident. While the translations certainly assume a non-Jewish readership, it in no way excludes a Jewish readership. In fact, as we shall see below, a strong Jewish understanding is assumed both theologically and culturally.[84] This is in agreement with what a LHA supports, but more can be implied. It would seem strange that a local congregation (or connected teaching network) would need explanation concerning these historically and theologically loaded terms. Why would a local "community" with both Jews and Gentiles need to be told that a term was "in Hebrew" (5:2; 19:13, 17)? But what is even more surprising is the translation provided for "Messiah." For Martyn,

---

[82] Culpepper, *Anatomy*, p. 219. Culpepper again takes Jewish translations as adding credibility to the account.

[83] Some of the forerunners of this view placed John and his community beside Paul. According to Rudolf Bultmann, *Theology of the New Testament*, 2 vols., trans. Kendrick Grobel (London: SCM Press, 1955), vol. II, p. 6, "It is true, however, that in regard to the current religious atmosphere Paul and John have certain things in common. Both come within the sphere of a Hellenism that is saturated with the Gnostic stream, so that a certain agreement between them in dualistic terminology is not surprising." Later, Reginald H. Fuller, *The Foundations of New Testament Christology* (London: Lutterworth Press, 1965), p. 203, placed the FG and the Johannine school within the Hellenistic Gentile mission in early Christianity and claimed that John's school carried on the work after Paul. Neither Bultmann nor Fuller based this on literary considerations, but on the Hellenistic concepts evident in the Gospel.

[84] See a similar argument by Motyer, *Your Father the Devil?*, pp. 110–14; Staley, *The Print's First Kiss*, pp. 34–36, 105–07.

the translations of the title "Messiah" is for non-Jewish readers.[85] But that is not a satisfactory answer, for Martyn himself admits that the title "'Messiah' occupies an important place in the whole of John's thought" for "It is clear that the issue of Jesus' messiahship stands at the center of the synagogue-church discussion."[86] It is contradictory for us to assume that a translation of a key religious term, maybe the most key term, would not be common knowledge to a "group" in which the very concept was at the center of severe persecution. Conclusive is 20:31 where Jesus is simply referred to as the "Christ," with no mention of the title "Messiah." This shows that the narrative assumes that after reading 1:41 and 4:25 the reader is assumed to already know what the title is referring to. Hence, it is the narrative and not the communal setting that is instructing the readers. This is why the term is translated, for some readers would not have had the opportunity to have explained to them the important Johannine titles. But this would not have been needed for a LHA.

In conclusion, the readers are certainly assumed to know Greek. What is striking and blatantly out-of-place is how a primary term for the so-called JComm needs translation, hence explanation. If the technical question of the JComm and its debates with a local synagogue was over the title "Messiah," how could the group not know what the term meant? This is especially so when John assumes so much Jewish knowledge in the rest of the Gospel, as our next section will reveal. It is "scarcely conceivable"[87] that a document with simple explanations concerning some supposed major Jewish-Christian issues for its readers would be intended for a communal setting!

Judaism

The evidence of Judaism is also difficult, primarily because there is so much knowledge that is assumed. The difficulty here is two-fold. First, when comments are given by the narrator, are they to be taken as explanatory or polemical? We have already argued in chapter 2 that John's language would have communicated to those outside the proposed JComm.[88] Thus, the narrative would need to make clear that the comments are polemical; simply deducing that the reconstructed context requires a

---

[85] Martyn, *History and Theology in the Fourth Gospel*, p. 91.   [86] *Ibid.*

[87] Martyn, *History and Theology in the Fourth Gospel*, p. 47, uses the phrase "scarcely conceivable" in reference to the blatantly anachronistic use of the "expulsion" term in John 9, which we argued in chapter 3 is far from blatant. The same phrase is applicable here in reference to the translation of "Messiah."

[88] See the related argument of Motyer, *Your Father the Devil?*, pp. 67–72.

linguistic response is hardly self-evident. Second, when comments are not given by the narrator, especially when an issue is less than obvious (e.g. "Son of Man"), how is one to relate the lack of comments with previous provided comments (e.g. "rabbi")? It is to these questions that we now turn. Culpepper distinguishes three sub-points under this heading: the Old Testament, Jewish institutions and festivals, and Jewish beliefs and practices. We will keep the same sub-points as we look at what the narrator assumed the implied reader would know about Judaism.

The narrator assumes that the implied reader has extensive knowledge of the OT. In some instances the OT writings are referred to directly. The formula "that the scripture might be fulfilled" is repeated in 13:18; 17:12; 19:24, 36, with variations in 12:38 and 15:25. In other instances OT imagery and symbols are in view. When John the Baptist is asked by the Jews whether he is Elijah or "the prophet" (1:21), no explanation is given. "Knowledge of the story of Moses' lifting up the serpent in the wilderness can be assumed (3:14), and when the Jews claim 'we are descendants of Abraham' (8:33) no explanation of Abraham's identity is required."[89] Various OT figures are discussed with no explanation. While John the Baptist is introduced in the prologue, Moses and the Law (1:17) are given no introduction. "What must be emphasized to the reader is that 'grace and truth came through Jesus Christ.'"[90] The assumption seems to be that the readers are familiar with the story and traditions of the OT and are able to see its connection to the Gospel narrative being presented. As Culpepper explains, "If it were simply that the fulfillment was important to the evangelist and he was attempting to persuade the reader of its importance also, he could not presuppose, as he apparently did, that the allusions to the Old Testament and its imagery and symbols would be understood by the intended reader."[91] The narrator assumes that the reader has a fairly broad knowledge of the OT. From Moses and the law (1:17) to the prophet Isaiah (1:23; 12:38), the OT is referred to and used as background for discussion. Based upon the narrator's comments, or lack of, and the general use of OT writings and images in the FG, the implied reader is assumed to have a rather extensive knowledge of the OT.

The implied reader's knowledge of Jewish institutions and festivals presents a unique case. Jesus' discourses at the Jewish festivals play an important role in the organization and thematic development of the Gospel. The narrator's explanations within these passages reveal a great deal about the assumed readership. In 2:13, the reader is told that the festival was the "Passover of the Jews" (cf. 6:4; 11:55). From a historical

[89] Culpepper, *Anatomy*, p. 220.   [90] *Ibid.*   [91] *Ibid.*

perspective, commentators are unsure of what to do with this phrase. According to Beasley-Murray, the phrase "indicates that the Church no longer observes the feast."[92] According to C. K. Barrett, "The feast is so defined partly because it is John's habit to set 'the Jews' as a body over against Jesus and the church, partly also, perhaps, because he knows of a Christian Passover."[93] Finally, Raymond Brown, in his usual way, finds tension in these three explanatory words. For Brown, "It may indicate a hostility to these feasts which are to be replaced by Jesus."[94] Brown's hypothesis is that such language would represent a deliberate distancing from the synagogue by "former" Jews. But this does not make sense when compared to the other similar phrases that are certainly explanatory and not polemical (e.g. 19:14).

We face the same issue with other additions by the narrator that explain Jewish institutions and festivals. Like Passover, the feast of Tabernacles is also identified as "of the Jews" (7:2). In 10:22, the narrator explains that the festival of the Dedication, Hanukkah, took place in winter. No Jewish reader would need to be told when the festival was celebrated, since it occurs at the same time every year. Finally, in 19:14, the reference to "the day of Preparation of the Passover"[95] does not require any special knowledge on the part of the reader. No explanations are offered regarding the synagogue or temple, but no great familiarity is assumed either. Thus a problem exists. As Culpepper explains:

> The main problem posed by these texts is that the significance of the discourses which occur in the context of the festivals can only be grasped fully by readers who know something about the festivals themselves. The discourses therefore seem to pre-suppose more familiarity with the Jewish festivals than do the narrator's comments. *Are the comments added for the sake of the non-Jewish readers while the heart of the narrative is intended for readers who would know a great deal about the festivals? Is the intended audience heterogeneous?* Is the implied reader (projected throughout the narrative by the implied author) more familiar with Judaism than the narratee (who is shaped exclusively by the narrator's voice)? Or must one resort to a theory of redaction during stages of a long composition history in which the material was fashioned for different audiences?[96]

[92] Beasley-Murray, *John*, p. 39.   [93] Barrett, *The Gospel According to St. John*, p. 197.
[94] Brown, *The Gospel According to John*, vol. I, p. 114.
[95] We will not deal here with the importance of this verse for distinguishing John from Synoptic chronology.
[96] Culpepper, *Anatomy*, p. 221 (emphasis added).

Culpepper's questions are revealing. Unless one resorts to a compositional theory for the FG that appeases the force of these questions, one discovers that the FG seems to bear witness to multiple implied readers. This, of course, works well with what we have found elsewhere. Furthermore, by using our primary methodological question we are able to test if such explanatory information would have been necessary to a "communal" LHA. Any explanation of the Passover, whether connecting to Judaism or describing the preparation of the Passover feast, would have been almost inconceivable in a context that was in constant conflict with the synagogue over these very issues. The communal context does not make sense of the evidence, unless one allows this "community" to have almost no formal control or contact; but then the "community" is far from "local" in the sense of being a functioning unit, especially one that is in the midst of a crisis together.

The implied reader's knowledge of Jewish belief and practices also reveals the possibility that more than one set of implied readers is expected. There are several beliefs and practices that are mentioned but not explained. No explanation is given for "the Son of man" (1:51), the expectation of "the prophet" (1:21, 25), or "the prophet who is to come into the world" (6:14). Reference is made to the devil (13:2) and Satan (13:27) without any explanation or definition. This is surprising in view of the translations that were provided for "Rabbi" and "Messiah" and the explanatory comments that told what language a term was ("in Hebrew") elsewhere in the Gospel.[97] The reader is assumed to have a basic knowledge of the Sabbath for the Jews (5:9), and when the disciples think that the blind man's birth defect is related to his or his parents' sin, no comment seems to be needed (9:2, 34). Even when the chief priests and Pharisees assemble in a council in 11:47, no explanation of their actions or the context and rules of such a meeting seem to be required.

But several Jewish beliefs and practices do require explanation or comment. "Matters pertaining to the practice of ritual purity are particularly obscure."[98] In 2:6, the stone water containers are said to be "for the Jewish rites of purification."[99] In 4:9, the reader must be told that "Jews do not share things in common with Samaritans." In 7:22, in a discussion between Jesus and the Jews, Jesus declares that Moses gave you (the Jews) circumcision. In a narrator's aside comment, it reads "it is, of course, not

---

[97] *Ibid.*   [98] *Ibid.*

[99] Although this phrase may not just be explanatory but to create a particular interpretation of the passage, it is impossible to establish with certainty that such is the case. Since this comment is similar if not identical to other explanatory comments, we will keep it as an example.

from Moses but from the patriarchs." For the Jewish reader the comment in 7:22 would need no specific explanation. But for the non-Jewish reader the explanation might resolve some confusion concerning Jesus' statement and further the FE's argument. In 18:28, the narrator explains that the Jews refused to enter the praetorium "so as to avoid ritual defilement, but might eat the Passover." Here it is assumed the reader will understand defilement, but not the specific type avoided by "the Jews," especially in relation to Passover. Even the burial of Jesus is said to be "according to the burial customs of the Jews" (19:40), but the materials used in the burial of Jesus, myrrh, aloes, and linen, are all left unexplained.

The narrator's general assumption of the reader's knowledge of Jewish beliefs and practices reveals that the reader has a fairly extensive knowledge of the OT and a general understanding of Jewish groups and beliefs, but not a complete understanding. At the same time, the reader is clearly assumed to be unfamiliar with the Jewish festivals and practices related to Jewish purity. For Culpepper, this implies that the reader is "not" Jewish. But such a conclusion seems almost ridiculous in light of the assumed knowledge of Judaism and, as we have seen elsewhere, assumes that a specific implied reader is in view. With a more general implied reader, that is, with the possibility of different (or multiple) implied readers, the assumption of a general knowledge base of Judaism but not the more specific practices related to purity becomes explainable.

In conclusion, the FG assumes that the implied reader has a general understanding of Judaism, but not some of its more specific aspects like purity and certain beliefs. For Culpepper, the only way to reconcile this dichotomy between the readers' fairly extensive knowledge of the OT and general Judaism but not the practices related to Jewish purity is to assume a Christian audience. According to Culpepper, "The combination of knowledge of the Old Testament . . . with indications that the reader is not Jewish and has little understanding of Jewish festivals and practices suggests that the reader is either a Christian or one familiar with Christianity."[100] Even Culpepper tries to not choose sides: Gentile or Jewish readership. But even claiming a "Christian" audience does not answer all of the Johannine peculiarities.[101] He tries to find middle ground and

---

[100] Culpepper, *Anatomy*, p. 222.

[101] See, for example, Motyer, *Your Father the Devil?*, p. 72, who, using the research of Gail R. O'Day, *Revelation in the Fourth Gospel: Narrative Mode and Theological Claim* (Philadelphia: Fortress, 1986), pp. 93–96, argues that John's irony is a literary device intended to draw the reader into the experience of revelation. This could even imply, as Motyer argues, that John was written to evangelize! We will discuss this possibility further in chapter 5.

assume an audience familiar with Christianity, that is, familiar enough with its Jewish background to not need certain explanations of Judaism. But Culpepper is still trying to find a single audience unit; a single and functioning audience that will somehow explain all the knowledge bases the narrator compensates for: Jewish, Gentile, and Christian. But as the evidence of Judaism has shown, that will not work. In the end, the evidence for Judaism has presented quite a conundrum. Some Jewish aspects are provided with an explanatory comment, but some more complex Jewish elements have no comment. It is not enough to claim that the audience is heterogeneous, for the context in which this audience existed must also be explained. It is here that our methodological question becomes important: would such explanations befit a local audience? It is in this perspective that a "communal" setting proves inadequate. As Motyer argues:

> One of the clearest indications of the overall rightness of the "Bauckham approach" (if we may call it that) is the way it can explain the long observed conundrum posed by the juxtaposition of explanations of the simplest Jewish terms and customs (e.g., 1:38, 41; 19:40) alongside unexplained references to quite abstruse or complex phenomena, such as the title "Son of man" and the allusions to details of the Tabernacle ceremonies. The inconsistency of treatment points to an awareness of great potential variety in the readership.[102]

Motyer correctly points to the fact that the comments cannot be explained as referring to one "group"; only a more general audience purview can encompass the variety of explanation. Culpepper assumes that the implied reader of John is a single entity or "group." This assumption, based upon several decades of "community" interpretations, is not supported by the evidence.

Events

This final area of comments which adds to the profile of the reader has to do with events in the story which have not yet been narrated. According to Culpepper, "Does the reader know a story of Jesus, or parts of it, before it is told? The Gospel suggests an affirmative answer."[103] The following comments by the narrator, comments that assume a previous knowledge of the story, need to be discussed in relation to the implied reader. This does not preclude a LHA; but it does show that a strong case can be made

---

[102] Motyer, *Your Father the Devil?*, p. 87, n.20.   [103] Culpepper, *Anatomy*, p. 222.

for the view that the FG was written, not for an isolated "community," but for general circulation among churches in which other Jesus stories were being told.

Certain key aspects of the story of Jesus are never explained. The meaning of baptism, whether John's or Jesus', is left unexplained. In 2:4, Jesus' "hour" is never explained, "either because the reader knows its meaning or because it is something the reader must infer from successive references later in the gospel."[104] The readers are assumed to be familiar enough not only with the theme of baptism or the "hour," but are able to relate these concepts with a general understanding of the entire early Christian story. It would seem, then, that the reader already knows *a* story of Jesus.

Probably the most striking example is in 2:22 where the narrator comments, "After he was raised from the dead, his disciples remembered that he had said this; and they believed the scripture and the word that Jesus had spoken." Culpepper summarizes the issue well: "Not only is there no effort to conceal the outcome of the events which are occurring, but the reader – in a radical departure from Prince's 'degree zero' narratee – is assumed to know about Jesus' resurrection already."[105] The lack of any explanation for 2:22 assumes, according to an implied reader, especially one reading the text for the first time, that the reader has some knowledge of the story before it is told. Nothing prior to 2:22 prepares the reader for what is found there. The narrator presumes the reader knows that Jesus was raised from the dead.[106]

According to Culpepper, the explanations that deal with the "fear of the Jews" (7:13) may imply that the reader is already acquainted with such fear, especially since the basis for the fear is not explained until 9:22. Many commentators believe that the specific situation behind the FG gave the readers their first-hand experience of fear of the Jews. This is especially the case, it is argued, when one turns to the events in John 9 where the blind man and his parents are confronted by the Jews. According to Culpepper:

---

[104] *Ibid*. This is not to make the term "hour" non-Johannine, but to imply that it must be understood as describing an event already known to the reader. Thus, John uses "hour" to define what is already known, not to use secretive or in-group language.

[105] *Ibid*.

[106] As we discussed in chapter 3, some understand this "prior knowledge" to refer to the type of Gospel *bios* that intentionally uses apocalyptic motifs; Jesus is seen from a pre- and post-resurrection position at the same time. According to Painter, *The Quest for the Messiah*, p. 133, the distinctive feature that the Gospels exhibit is that they tell the story of Jesus (biography-like) but from "the perspective of faith in the risen Jesus." From the perspective of narrative criticism, one still must reconcile the fact that the reader is assumed to be familiar with "both" the pre- and post-resurrected Jesus. Knowledge of the story must already be known for the narrative to be understood by the reader.

The explanation of the reason for the parents' fear of the Jews is that the Jews had already agreed to expel from the synagogue any who confessed that Jesus was the Christ (9:22). Are the readers unfamiliar with this decision or does the explanation provide the basis for them to see the similarity between their situation and that of their parents? From this comment alone it would be hard to tell, but the prominence of the word "already" suggests that the reader knows of the action but would not know that (in the narrative world at least) it has already been implemented during the ministry of Jesus.[107]

But the narrative only reveals that they knew of such conflict, not that they had been participators in it. Nor are the details evidently descriptive of real experiences, as we argued in chapter 3. While the reconstruction Culpepper follows may certainly be correct, it is not the only possibility. It seems as if Culpepper has again been influenced by "community" interpretations.

Several other unexplained facts allude to a readership that already knew a story of Jesus. The comments in 7:30 and 8:20 that the Jews could not seize Jesus because his "hour" had not yet come assume one of two possibilities: either the reader already knew what was meant by Jesus' "hour" or, if its meaning was unknown, the comments provide a clue to its meaning that was intended to heighten the reader's awareness of its importance.[108] The narrator's explanatory comment in 7:39, "for as yet there was no Spirit, because Jesus was not yet glorified," only makes sense if the reader understands that the Spirit had been given and what is meant by "glorified."[109]

Finally, in two passages we have already referred to, 11:2 and 3:24, the reader is assumed to be familiar with a version of the story before it is told. Bauckham argues that these parenthetical explanations assume not only that the reader already has knowledge of the Gospel story, but "are intended specifically for readers/hearers who also knew Mark's Gospel."[110] This can be seen clearly in 11:2. In 11:1, the narrator describes "Now a certain man was ill, Lazarus of Bethany, the village of Mary and her sister Martha." Then in 11:2 the narrator adds, "Mary was the one who anointed the Lord with perfume and wiped his feet with her hair; her brother Lazarus was ill." Bauckham argues that not only does the Gospel

---

[107] Culpepper, *Anatomy*, p. 223.   [108] *Ibid.*
[109] As was argued in chapter 3, this phrase indicates a distinction between past and present history.
[110] Bauckham, "John for Readers of Mark," p. 151.

explain what should have been common Johannine tradition material to his readers, he also writes with the assumption that his readers have already read the Gospel of Mark.

> the evidence outside 11:2 is consistent with the implication of that verse that at least many of the implied readers/hearers could be expected to know Mark's Gospel, and, like 11:1–2, it is entirely inconsistent with the view that the Gospel was addressed to the "Johannine community," which would already be familiar with specifically Johannine traditions.[111]

In response to Bauckham's proposal that the Johannine readers would be familiar with Mark, Sproston North argues that Bauckham's proposal is flawed.[112] Looking especially at 11:2, Sproston North admits that "all the indications are that this parenthesis refers *back*, that is, it repeats information that is already known to the reader."[113] But for Sproston North, 11:2 does not have to point back to Mark, but could still be implied for the JComm. "It appears that much of the story, at least, was already known to John's readers – either from oral tradition or, possibly, from an earlier edition of the Gospel – in advance of his later retelling of the event in the present text."[114] According to Sproston North, "Bauckham's argument that the Johannine community members should have known in advance of all three Bethany siblings relies on the assumption that *stories circulating orally will have been reproduced by John exactly as known when he included them in his Gospel*."[115] Thus, the issue at hand is this: since both confirm that 11:2 is pointing back to something, what is it pointing to? For our purposes it is worth noting that the narrator assumes that the reader is already familiar with the story told by the FG.

In conclusion, the reader is assumed to have prior knowledge of many of the key elements of the Gospel story: Jesus' death and resurrection, John the Baptist's imprisonment, the presence of the Spirit, the synagogue ban, the fear of the Jews, the anointing of Jesus by Mary, and probably the betrayal of Jesus (6:64; cf. 6:70–71). Even the meaning of Jesus' "glorification" and his "hour" can be seen as already understood by the reader.[116]

---

[111] *Ibid.*, pp. 168–69.

[112] Sproston North, "John for Readers of Mark? A Response to Richard Bauckham's Proposal."

[113] *Ibid.*, p. 455.   [114] *Ibid.*, p. 466.   [115] *Ibid.*, p. 460.

[116] Culpepper, *Anatomy*, p. 223. "Glorification" and "hour" are at least known in the sense of being given prominence in the narrative as referring to major events previously known to the reader. That is, John's readers know that Jesus dies, so the "hour" is seen as

For Culpepper, this again implies that either the reader is Christian or is at least very familiar with Christian beliefs and the Christian story. For our purposes, the primary importance of recognizing John's awareness, even use, of other Jesus traditions is to correct what James Dunn calls the "one document per community" fallacy.[117] It is this familiarity with other depictions of Jesus that leads us to our conclusion about the implied reader of the FG.

Conclusion: the implied, first-century reader of the Gospel of John

Using the concept of the implied reader, we discovered what the narrator *expects* the reader of the FG to know when encountering the text. The implied reader is assumed to recognize several of the characters in the story, but certainly not all of them. Jesus was certainly recognizable to the implied reader. The evangelist seems to be more intent on explaining Jesus than introducing him. Peter was well known to the reader, as well as John the Baptist and all of the general political characters. But, contrary to normal JComm interpretations, the BD was assumed to be unfamiliar to the reader and needed a complete introduction to the reader. The implied reader is assumed to know the major geographic regions but nothing more. The implied reader is assumed to know Greek. Several Jewish titles for Jesus are translated or explained for the reader. The implied reader is assumed to have a general understanding of Judaism, but not some of its more specific aspects like purity and certain beliefs. An audience with some connection to Christian beliefs and backgrounds is assumed. Finally, the implied reader is assumed to have prior knowledge of many of the key elements of the Gospel story. Again, the assumption is that the reader is at least familiar with Christian beliefs and the Christian story. It is this familiarity with Christianity that leads us to our conclusion concerning the implied reader of the FG.

The methodological question we asked at the beginning of this chapter was as follows: Would the various explanations or comments (or lack of) befit a text written for the author's specific, geographically local

---

in reference to that climactic event. At the same time, it is possible that the events were so partially known that the language could also have an enigmatic function which is intended to provoke the reader to think about what it could mean until eventually the story does make its meaning clear. In either case, a prior knowledge is assumed.

[117] James D. G. Dunn, *Jesus Remembered*, p. 150.

community? Since our comparison was between "community" and non-"community" readings of the FG's historical context, then the evidence had to be evaluated in light of those two proposed settings. After sifting through the evidence in the five areas of the narrative we found the following five arguments that support a general audience. First, the BD had to be introduced to the implied reader. Unless a special type of literary maneuver is occurring, it is surprising that the "leader of the community" would need an introduction. Second, since no one area of geographic description is assumed to be known to the implied reader, it would seem that no one geographic area can be correlated to the implied reader. This is surprising if the reader is in a geographic region which is known and shared by the author. Third, and maybe most surprising, the title "Messiah," a title which according to Martyn is central in the JComm's debate with their local synagogue, has to be translated for the reader. It is inconceivable to think that for a Christian "group" who is experiencing some form of persecution (at least expulsion) that they would not be aware of the most basic issue. Fourth, the combination of explanations for some basic aspects of Judaism with a complete lack of explanation for much more complex aspects make a single "group" audience, even a heterogeneous one, almost inconceivable. Since in a LHA an author would know well the level of his audience's knowledge base, and the LHA itself would provide its own boundaries for knowledge, the variety of assumed knowledge can best be pictured as providing information for more than one set of implied readers. Finally, the reader's familiarity with a version of the Jesus story implies a familiarity with Mark or at least some Jesus tradition. Such "distribution" forces us to see the Johannine audience as less separated or sectarian in its reception of early Christian tradition and, therefore, more participatory in early Christianity. It also frees us from assuming that John's audience is solely defined by his Gospel, and completely isolated from another "Gospel" or its tradition. It becomes difficult to define John's audience by John's Gospel, since other influences were surely in place. In light of the evidence from applying the heuristic device of the implied reader to the FG, this chapter has found that a reading of the Gospel against a context of a local audience, even a heterogeneous one, is untenable.

Culpepper's study of the implied reader reached a related conclusion, though he was unable to place it in the non-"community" paradigm. As we discussed above, such findings forced him to search the narrative data for a single, local readership. Where the evidence was most inexplicable was in reference to the implied reader's knowledge of Judaism. Culpepper's eventual admission is revealing:

The difficulty posed by the tension between presumption of familiarity with the Jewish festivals, especially in the discourses, and explanatory comments which make the gospel intelligible to readers unfamiliar with Judaism probably indicates that by the time the composition of the Fourth Gospel was completed *a broader readership was envisioned than was originally intended*. The later readership included gentile Christians who knew little about Judaism.[118]

Unless one resorts to a compositional theory for the FG that appeases the force of these questions, one discovers that the FG seems to bear witness to various implied readers. These various implied readers cannot be solved by simply supposing that the local "group" was heterogeneous, for as we have tried to show, the explanations that are given make no sense in a "communal" setting; unless, of course, one were to argue for an extremely complex "community." But even then, as we argued above, such a definition of a Gospel "community" would look more like a microcosm of the early Christian movement rather than a sectarian "community" whose document has a more self-referential purpose. Thus, the Gospel is written in such a way to allow the text to be accessible at different levels.

A similar argument was made over twenty years ago by R. T. France with reference to Matthew.[119] According to France there is a "'surface meaning,' which any reasonable intelligent reader might be expected to grasp, and what we may call a 'bonus' meaning accessible to those who are more 'sharp-eyed,' or better instructed in Old Testament Scripture . . ."[120] France's summary could be applied to our findings in the FG:

> For what any given reader will find . . . will vary with his exegetical background. What I want to suggest is that [the evangelist] would not necessarily have found this regrettable, that he was deliberately composing a chapter rich in potential exegetical bonuses, so that the more fully a reader shared the religious traditions and scriptural erudition of the author, the more he was likely to derive from his reading, while at the same time there was a surface meaning sufficiently uncomplicated for even the most naïve reader to follow . . . I am arguing, in other words, that [the evangelist] *was well aware of differing levels among his potential readership*.[121]

---

[118] Culpepper, *Anatomy*, p. 225 (emphasis added).
[119] R. T. France, "The Formula-Quotations of Matthew 2 and the Problem of Communication," *NTS* 27 (1981), pp. 233–51.
[120] *Ibid.*, p. 241.   [121] *Ibid.*, p. 250 (emphasis added).

This conclusion is contrary to Culpepper[122] who concludes that maybe C. H. Dodd was right when he suggested that John was written on two levels so that insiders (members of the JComm) can grasp the whole significance of the Gospel from each episode, while outsiders find it built up step by step.[123] Based upon our search for the implied reader, the only "insider" (or as France would say "advanced") knowledge that is required is knowledge of Judaism, which can hardly be claimed by one local "group."

In conclusion, by inquiring for the implied reader of the FG, and by placing that reader in a "communal setting," we have argued that the implied reader's knowledge is distributed unevenly so as to suggest that a "community" setting for the Gospel document is highly unlikely. The only setting of the text that is able to deal appropriately with the multiple implied readers is a general audience. The Gospel *expects* to be read by readers with different levels of knowledge (especially of Judaism) and Christian experience (even Jewish-Christian conflict). John is written to accommodate various levels, or more appropriately, various types of readers. Thus we may conclude that by using the heuristic device of the implied reader we have seen that the FG expects to be read by different types of readers. There is no need to force upon the text of John a local "community" audience when the text alludes in the opposite direction.

[122] Concerning the identity of the implied reader, Culpepper, *Anatomy*, p. 225, concludes: "Analysis of the gospel's indications of its intended audience confirms, or at least complements, much of the recent research which has concluded that John was written for a particular community of believers. We still do not know, however, how different the language of the Johannine community was from that of others outside the community, or how insular or rigidly defined its membership was." Culpepper's hesitancy concerning what this "community" was gives credence to our proposal. The search for a single "group" behind John is dominated by the current paradigm of "community" interpretations.

[123] C. H. Dodd, *The Interpretation of the Fourth Gospel* (Cambridge: Cambridge University Press, 1953), pp. 316–17.

5

READING THE FOURTH GOSPEL: THE FUNCTION OF THE GOSPEL OF JOHN IN LIGHT OF THE GOSPEL COMMUNITY DEBATE

Introduction

After spending four chapters setting the context of the Gospel community debate and challenging the current community readings of the Gospels, it is time to apply our proposal to the FG. It was Gail O'Day who pointed out that one of the weaknesses in Martyn's reconstruction of the JComm was that his reading strategy

> blocked out for a while all other ways both of reading the Gospel and of reading the historical data. Martyn's reading became totalizing, not because his claims or even his intentions and methods were totalizing, but because he read so well and so easily that we forgot it was a construction of the data. We . . . read Martyn instead of rereading the data . . .[1]

The question of reading the Gospels is the key issue in the Gospel community debate. But until now the debate has been entirely theoretical. The various conferences and article interchanges have only dealt with the exegetical principles and not exegetical practice. The newness of the debate has required more in-depth discussion and clarification, as this book has attempted to do in the first four chapters. But now we must turn to exegetical practice. Before we enter into exegesis, a brief summary of our proposed reading strategy is in order.

Our proposed reading strategy assumes, at the broadest level, that the Gospels were written for an indefinite audience, not an individual "church" or network of churches disconnected from the rest of the early Christian movement. This historical assumption does not posit a completely indefinite audience, but one that is appropriate to a first-century audience in the Greco-Roman world and allows for a general market

---

[1] Gail R. O'Day, "Response: 'The Expulsion from the Synagogue: A Tale of a Theory'" (paper presented at the annual meeting of the SBL, Toronto, Canada, November 25, 2002), p. 5.

niche. Using what we have argued is a more complex model of "community" (relational and not territorial) we have posited that the Gospels would have been appropriate reading material for a variety of geographic communities throughout early Christianity. Readers who were not even aware of the other's existence could participate together in the story told by the Gospels, based upon a symbolic construction which provided a specifically "Christian" identity for them and others (chapter 2). The Gospel text, which is a type of biography, would rarely be used by a self-contained group. The Gospel narrative would have been read by its pre-critical readers with a "realistic" reading strategy. Although the Gospel would have had various *Tendenzen* and interpretations included, it would not have been read on two levels in the redaction-critical way proposed by J. L. Martyn. In essence, a pre-critical (or post-enlightenment) reading of the Gospels is a "literal" reading, whereby the story the Gospels tell is the story meant to be heard (chapter 3). Finally, the reader the text expects, far from being a knowledgeable community reader, has only a general familiarity with the story in the narrative. The relative familiarity with the Christian story, yet at times a lack of specific knowledge concerning Judaism, reveals that the Gospel expected different types of readers. Such a maneuver on the part of the evangelist allows the text to be accessible at different levels, to a first-time reader and a more experienced reader;[2] the Gospel assumes a varied readership (chapter 4).

Therefore, this chapter will examine five related test cases in order to show that the FG was intended to be read by a general or indefinite audience. The five test cases involve the following areas of debate: representative figures, the lack of contextual importance of the "expulsion from the synagogue" passages, the purpose of the FG, the mission motif in the FG, and early Christian relations. Our discussion of these test cases will involve two aspects. First, we will argue that these test cases reveal how a non-community reading is more appropriate to the narrative of the FG and its exegesis. Second, we will analyze how current "community" interpretations of various pericopae are internally inconsistent and frequently tangential to the narrative. The work of several prominent community interpreters will be evaluated in the process of our exegesis. It is in this chapter that the methodological issues discussed in the previous four chapters will come to fruition.

---

[2] There are really two points here. First, after reading the Gospel several times, a reader will understand it better than on first reading. Second, a reader with certain types of knowledge extraneous to the Gospel will understand it better than a reader without that knowledge.

Representative figures in the fourth Gospel

We have already argued that the history-like narrative of the Gospel *bios* demands a "literal" reading of the Gospels. As James Dunn has recently argued, "If we take seriously the fact that the [Gospel] texts are historical texts, it follows that the old case for historical philology and the hermeneutical principle of plain meaning can still demand respect."[3] The idea of a "literal" reading is far from new.[4] From the outset both Jewish and Christian interpreters wrestled with the problem of the various senses of Scripture.[5] Brevard Childs notes an irony when a comparison is made between the pre-critical and post-enlightenment, historical-critical additions to the literal reading:

> The rise of the historical critical method brought a new understanding of the literal sense of the biblical text as the original sense. But what was intended as an attempt to free the text from the allegedly heavy hand of tradition and dogma proved to be a weapon that cut both ways. The effect was actually to destroy the significance, integrity, and confidence in the literal sense of the text. Whereas during the medieval period the crucial issue lay in the usage made of the multiple layers of meaning *above* the text, the issue now turns on the multiple layers *below* the text.[6]

The early church debates over the "literal" or "plain sense" have often occurred between a reading of the OT narrative and Paul's interpretation of it.[7] But there was not a debate concerning a "literal" reading of the OT narrative as it stands, or of the Gospel narratives. As Childs points out, debates certainly occurred over "above-the text" readings and the liberty the interpreter was given over the text's spiritual meaning, especially

---

[3] Dunn, *Jesus Remembered*, p. 115.

[4] The most recent discussion of a "literal" reading is by K. E. Greene-McCreight, *Ad Litteram: How Augustine, Calvin, and Barth Read the "Plain Sense" of Genesis 103*, IST 5 (New York: Peter Lang, 1999). See also the older but classic discussion of the problem by Brevard S. Childs, "The Sensus Literalis of Scripture: An Ancient and Modern Problem," in Herbert Donner, Robert Hanhart, and Rudolf Smend (eds.), *Beiträge zur Alttestamentlichen Theologie: Festschrift für Walther Zimmerli zum 70. Geburstag* (Göttingen: Vandenhoeck & Ruprecht, 1977), pp. 80–93. See the similar discussion of the *Sensus Literalis* and the reading of the biblical narrative by Hans Frei, "The 'Literal Reading' of Biblical Narrative in the Christian Tradition: Does it Stretch or Will it Break?," in Frank McConnell (ed.), *The Bible and the Narrative Tradition* (New York: Oxford University Press, 1986), pp. 36–77; and *The Identity of Jesus Christ*.

[5] See Childs, "The Sensus Literalis of Scripture," pp. 80–87.

[6] *Ibid.*, pp. 91–92.   [7] Greene-McCreight, *Ad Litteram*, p. 3.

between the Antiochene and Alexandrian exegetes,[8] but there was no debate over the "literal" reading as if one had to discover what it was. In a sense, the Gospels told a story that was rooted in the reality and identity of the early Christian faith; although spiritual, above-the-text applications from the story were certainly developed, it was important that the story at the level of the basic narrative stay constant.

The above-the-text aspect of the text, or its applicative sense, relates to the function of the Gospels. According to David Aune, the Gospels, like all Greco-Roman biography, had three generic aspects: content, form, and function.[9] Our discussion of the *bios* genre in chapter 3 dealt primarily with the first two aspects (content and form). But as we turn to the exegesis of the text, its function, or what we could describe as the applicative sense or *Tendenzen* of the author, becomes an important part of our discussion. This is especially the case when the Gospel texts are no longer seen as having a functional role in a specific "community," but having a more general and multi-faceted function in the early Christian movement.

Biography has both conscious and unconscious functions, although it can be difficult to separate them. Among the conscious or manifest functions, demonstrative (epideictic) is perhaps the most common, though biographies can mix deliberative and forensic elements with it.[10] The unconscious functions involve the historical legitimation of a social belief/value system personified in the subject of the biography.[11] Greco-Roman biographies often have a teaching or didactic function, presenting the subject and other characters as a paradigm of virtue. As Aune explains, "Author and audience were more interested in the subject [and characters] as a moral example and personification of professionally appropriate virtues than in his historical particularity."[12] Such an understanding fits well with our discussion of a pre-critical reader's understanding of the narrative as both "historical" and paradigmatic.[13] The function

---

[8] For a discussion of these debates see Simonetti, *Biblical Interpretation in the Early Church*, pp. 67–85. For good discussion and critique of the Alexandrian/Antiochene dichotomy see Young, *Biblical Exegesis and the Formation of Christian Culture*, pp. 161–213.

[9] Aune, *The New Testament in Its Literary Environment*, pp. 32–36.

[10] *Ibid.*, p. 35.   [11] *Ibid.*

[12] *Ibid.*, p. 36. At the same time, the precision in John seems to suggest a careful preserving of the historical particularity of Jesus.

[13] Unfortunately, Aune describes the paradigmatic function of the Gospels in relation to the "community" interpretations of redaction critics. According to Aune, not only does the redaction criticism approach assume that the Gospels each arose in a Christian "community," a hypothesis we have found to be unsuccessful, but it also "presupposes that the Gospels reveal more about their author's situations than about the historical situation of Jesus" (p. 60). Aune also misappropriates the "two-level" understanding of the Gospel narratives.

of the FG, therefore, would be no different from other *bioi* in the ancient world. Certainly informative and didactic aims are relevant to the purpose expressed in 20:31,[14] but the paradigmatic is also present. For example, the "belief" so encouraged in an *inclusio* from 1:12 to 20:31 is shown paradigmatically through the responses, both positive and negative, of the characters in the narrative who are themselves confronted by Jesus. It is here that advances in our understanding of patristic exegesis have been helpful.

But even more so, advances in narrative criticism used in combination with historical criticism, which we discussed in chapter 4, have become useful. In two somewhat neglected articles from nearly three decades ago, Raymond Collins shows how the characters in the FG are meant to be viewed as "representative figures."[15] According to Collins, "As . . . exegesis entered into the twentieth century and adopted the historico-critical method, it largely abandoned the allegorical method of interpretation and looked to the figures who appear in the Fourth Gospel in their historical individuality."[16] Although Collins uses "community language" (the Johannine Church), he does not imply by it that the representative figures are characters from the JComm's own history.[17] Rather, beginning with the assumption "that a process of oral tradition similar to that which lay behind the Synoptic Gospels also lies behind the Fourth Gospel,"[18] and the assumption that the stated purpose of the Gospel (20:30–31) is legitimate,[19] Collins explains how the characters in the FG serve as representative figures:

Certainly the Gospels use Jesus as a paradigm for the identity of subsequent Christians (as other NT documents do as well: 1 Pet. 2:21–23; Phil. 2:5–11), but there is a distinction between Jesus and his followers; while both are "servants" in some sense, Jesus is the servant *par excellence*. But even then, such narrative function is hardly depictive of a single "group," but fits any and all Christian readers.

[14] See Burridge, *What are the Gospels?*, pp. 229–31.

[15] Raymond F. Collins, "The Representative Figures of the Fourth Gospel – I," *DR* 94 (1976), pp. 26–46; "The Representative Figures of the Fourth Gospel – II," *DR* 94 (1976), pp. 118–32.

[16] Collins, "The Representative Figures of the Fourth Gospel – I," p. 26.

[17] This is an important distinction to make. A "community" assumes that the representative figure is rooted in the actual history or experience of the reading "community." But this is neither Collins' approach nor the approach commonly assumed by readers of *bios* literature. Like other ancient literature, the "representative figures" are paradigms that do not contain one historical-specific referent, but create a "type" that a reader is expected to emulate or not emulate. It is not descriptive of what is but what could be. This is the functional aspect of ancient literature and the Gospels especially.

[18] Collins, "The Representative Figures of the Fourth Gospel – I," p. 29.

[19] *Ibid.*, p. 30. For Collins, 20:30–31 "ought to receive prime emphasis in any consideration of the purpose of the Fourth Gospel."

we ought to envisage a series of homilies directed to enkindling faith in Jesus. In the development of these homilies, various persons were chosen from the common Gospel tradition or selected from his own tradition by the homilist in order to illustrate some point about the nature of faith, or lack of it, in Jesus Christ. Thus the various individuals of the Fourth Gospel do not stand as mere figments of the Evangelist's imagination . . . Rather they have been selected from the homiletic tradition . . . to teach the evangelist's readers something about that faith in Jesus Christ which is life-giving. In this way it is appropriate to look at the several individuals who appear in the Fourth Gospel as individuals who have been type-cast. In this individuality they represent a type of faith-response (or lack of faith-response) to Jesus who is the Christ and Son of God.[20]

For some Collins' approach was simply literary, but when applied with historical-criticism (not against it), and placed alongside the purview of pre-critical readers of a *bios*, a reading strategy is made more clear.[21]

The reading of the FG proposed by "community" interpreters has been largely dependent on the role of characters in the narrative. As Martyn explains, "Answers to these questions hinge . . . on an analysis of the way in which John portrays the characters in the drama."[22] We have already discussed the various issues of importance when determining the referent of a character in the narrative. What is needed is an examination of our reading proposal in light of these representative figures in the narrative itself. The important role of representative figures is nowhere more at stake than in the Nicodemus and Samaritan woman narratives in John 3–4.[23] But these roles are not merely for one "community," but for a

---

[20] *Ibid.*, p. 31.

[21] See the related but less developed "paradigmatic" approaches by C. F. D. Moule, "The Individualism of the Fourth Gospel," *NovT* 5 (1962), pp. 171–90, also cited by Collins; and Xavier Léon-Dufour, "Towards a Symbolic Reading of the Fourth Gospel," *NTS* 27 (1981), pp. 439–56. Also noteworthy are those that highlight the narrative characterization in the FG: William W. Watty, "The Significance of Anonymity in the Fourth Gospel," *ExpT* 90 (1979), pp. 209–12; Fred W. Burnett, "Characterization and Reader Construction of Characters in the Gospels," *Semeia* 63 (1993), pp. 1–28; David R. Beck, "The Narrative Function of Anonymity in Fourth Gospel Characterization," *Semeia* 63 (1993), pp. 143–58; and David Rhoads and Kari Syreeni, *Characterization in the Gospels: Reconceiving Narrative Criticism*, JSNTsup 176 (Sheffield: Sheffield Academic Press, 1999).

[22] Martyn, *History and Theology in the Fourth Gospel*, p. 85.

[23] Although John 3–4 reveal this paradigm most clearly, the entire Gospel reveals this paradigm throughout the narrative. For a related study see Johannes Beutler, "Faith and Confession: The Purpose of John," in J. Painter, R. A. Culpepper, and F. F. Segovia (eds.), *Word, Theology, and Community in John*, Festschrift for Robert Kysar (St. Louis: Chalice Press, 2002), pp. 19–31.

general reader; an indefinite reader who is rhetorically[24] invited to take part in the narrative.[25] Although this can be seen in each narrative individually, it is when they are read together that it becomes most clear.

Nicodemus and John 3:1–36

The Nicodemus narrative is frequently used by community interpreters in such a way that the main character, Nicodemus, is representative of a "group" related in some way to the JComm. According to David Rensberger, "All that we know about John's Nicodemus is what John tells us, and as usual he seems less concerned with the meaning of his character for Jesus' history than with his meaning for the history of the Johannine community."[26] Certainly Rensberger is correct to see the paradigmatic role that Nicodemus plays in the narrative, but a purely symbolic understanding of Nicodemus is hardly pre-critical. Calling the focus on the JComm "the new era in Johannine interpretation," Rensberger has situated himself deeply into the paradigm that this study is attempting to critique, and thus feels no need to defend his approach.[27]

For Rensberger the fact that Nicodemus is otherwise unknown in early Christian tradition and yet persistently appears in John suggests that he may have had some special significance for the FE and his "community."[28] Since Rensberger assumes a symbolic (paradigmatic) function for

---

[24] We will frequently speak of the FG's rhetoric or rhetorical invitation in this chapter. This assumes that the biographical genre would have had persuasion as an assumed goal of the writing. This is another difference between our method and Martyn's. While Martyn, *History and Theology in the Fourth Gospel*, pp. 5–16, sees the "dramatic" qualities of the narrative's style that led to the two-level drama, we will argue that FE had intentional pastoral and pedagogical techniques. This was initially introduced by Hans Windisch, "Der johanneische Erzählungsstil," but has since been supported by Brown, *The Gospel According to John*, vol. I, pp. cxxxv–cxxxvi; and Birger Olsson, *Structure and Meaning in the Fourth Gospel: A Text-Linguistic Analysis of 2:1–11 and 4:1–42*, trans. Jean Gray (Lund: Gleerup, 1974), pp. 249–50. See also Teresa Okure, *The Johannine Approach to Mission: A Contextual Study of John 4:1–42*, WUNT 2, Reihe 31 (Tübingen: J. C. B. Mohr, 1998), pp. 41–42, 257–61.

[25] As Margaret Davies, *Rhetoric and Reference in the Fourth Gospel*, JSNTSup 69 (Sheffield: Sheffield Academic Press, 1992), p. 367, explains it, "The implied reader of the Fourth Gospel is encouraged by its rhetoric to accept its view of Jesus' significance and to lead a life characterized by a love like Jesus'."

[26] Rensberger, *Johannine Faith and Liberating Community*, pp. 37–38. Rensberger argues that although there was at least one prominent man named Nicodemus living in Jerusalem prior to the First Revolt known from Jewish sources, their information sheds no light on the figure in John 3 (p. 37). Cf. Barrett, *The Gospel According to St. John*, p. 204; Brown, *The Gospel According to John*, vol. I, pp. 129–30.

[27] Rensberger, *Johannine Faith and Liberating Community*, pp. 15–36.

[28] *Ibid.*, p. 37. For a convincing argument about the historical Nicodemus see Richard Bauckham, "Nicodemus and the Gurion Family," *JTS* 47 (1996), pp. 1–37.

Nicodemus, the question becomes: what does Nicodemus symbolize?[29] "He is usually seen as a man who was genuinely interested in Jesus but failed to understand him, and only later came to something like faith in him." This "type of man," then, is viewed by Rensberger as a "communal symbolic figure."[30] The "type of man" that Nicodemus represents is identical to John 2:23–25, where Jesus did not trust himself to certain people in Jerusalem who had believed in him when they saw the signs that he did because "he knew what was in a man."[31] Thus, Nicodemus is portrayed as one of the untrustworthy believers. This is made emphatic by Nicodemus' "we" language (3:2; and Jesus' "we" response in 3:7, 11–12). "Nicodemus evidently does not stand for himself alone but for some specific group, which is rather negatively portrayed. In the same manner Jesus undoubtedly speaks for the Johannine Christians and stands for them over against the group represented by Nicodemus."[32] Nicodemus' other two appearances reveal a similar "type." Rensberger argues that in 7:45–52 Nicodemus defends Jesus in a way hardly satisfactory to the FE. And again in 19:38–42 his actions are less than satisfactory and should be viewed as unbelief.[33] "Throughout the Gospel, then, Nicodemus appears as a man of inadequate faith and inadequate courage, and as such he represents a *group* that the author wishes to characterize in this way."[34] Brown and Martyn also assume a "group" standing behind Nicodemus as secret Christian Jews or "crypto-Christians," although Brown does not regard Nicodemus as a representative of this specific "group."[35]

But several problems exist with the paradigmatic interpretation given to the Nicodemus character. As we discussed above, the ancient narrative could and did function in a paradigmatic way, with characters representative of various virtues, and especially for Christian narratives, as models of appropriate (or inappropriate) Christian faith and action. But we cannot assume that these virtues were to be read by (pre-critical) readers as descriptive of another historical referent. To test this hypothesis we

---

[29] See a similar method of symbolic representation of characters by Kevin Quast, *Peter and the Beloved Disciple: Figures for a Community in Crisis*, JSNTSup 32 (Sheffield: JSOT Press, 1989), pp. 21–25.

[30] Rensberger, *Johannine Faith and Liberating Community*, p. 38.

[31] *Ibid*. Also in agreement is Brown, *The Gospel According to John*, vol. I, p. 135; but in disagreement are Bultmann, *The Gospel of John*, p. 133, and Schnackenburg, *The Gospel According to St. John*, vol. I, p. 365.

[32] Rensberger, *Johannine Faith and Liberating Community*, p. 38.

[33] *Ibid*., p. 40.   [34] *Ibid*.

[35] See Martyn, "Glimpses," pp. 159–63, and Brown, *The Community of the Beloved Disciple*, pp. 71–73. See also the significant article by Marinus de Jonge, "Nicodemus and Jesus: Some Observations on Misunderstanding and Understanding in the Fourth Gospel," *BJRL* 53 (1971), pp. 337–59.

must determine if the Nicodemus character is portrayed negatively or positively. If he is portrayed negatively, as Rensberger and Martyn suggest, it would support the community interpretation that assumes that the FG was written for a "community" in direct relation with other conflicting "groups." If he is portrayed positively, then it can be argued that the Nicodemus character has a more general function. Of course, a general function does not rule out a community interpretation, as Brown's interpretation of Nicodemus shows, but it would require a more complex social context in order to explain the rhetorical function of the pericope. Since Rensberger has provided the most thorough community interpretation of the Nicodemus narrative, it is with his position that we will interact.

Rensberger is correct to see the Nicodemus character as having a "symbolic" role, but he posits incorrectly both the narrative's depiction of the role, as well as a specific ostensive referent implied behind it. Concerning the narrative's depiction of Nicodemus, Rensberger's conclusion is that Nicodemus appears as a man of inadequate faith and inadequate courage in all three appearances in the FG.[36] But such a conclusion is far from evident. Several points make this clear. First, the connection between "man" in 2:25 and 3:1, which implies that Nicodemus is to be viewed negatively, is hardly evident. What Rensberger calls "clearly evident" is not even agreed upon by commentators.[37] As we shall see, several aspects of the narrative place him as one who is extending himself to Jesus. Also, if we were to suppose that the key to this connection is the use of "man," further problems would persist. For example, ἄνθρωπος is hardly given over to negativity in a Johannine sense by its depiction in 2:25, for as early as 1:6 it is used positively and in a similar syntactical fashion for John the Baptist. Even earlier, it would appear that it was to "men" whom Jesus was sent to "enlighten" (1:4), which fits well with the "seeking" attitude exemplified by Nicodemus. Thus, it is too presumptuous for Rensberger to conclude that Nicodemus is "negatively portrayed" in John 3, for certainly the narrative itself gives little indication of such a conclusion, especially once the link with 2:23–25 has been shown to be inadequate.

Second, Rensberger's push for a continuation of negativity with Nicodemus is stretched even further with his interpretation of 7:45–52. Nicodemus' protest before all the "negatively" depicted Pharisees that Jesus should be given a fair trial (v. 51) is simply brushed off by Rensberger: "it is hardly likely that this timid legal quibble would constitute a confession of faith satisfactory to the FE."[38] Interestingly,

---

[36] Rensberger, *Johannine Faith and Liberating Community*, p. 40.   [37] *Ibid.*, p. 38.
[38] *Ibid.*, p. 39.

Rensberger's only support for a negative portrayal in John 3 disagrees with him here.[39] What Rensberger describes as a "timid legal quibble" is portrayed in the narrative as positive in two ways. First, in the previous verse (v. 50) the narrator reminds the reader that Nicodemus was "one who had gone to Jesus before." This connection is hardly without intention, for it shows a contrast between the Pharisees who accuse Jesus intensely and Nicodemus as one who would defend him; for he too was like one who could claim like the guards in v. 46: "Never has anyone spoken like this!" Second, and most clearly, the following verse (v. 52) reveals that the Pharisees understood Nicodemus' comments to be in defense of Jesus and against them. It is surprising that Rensberger would take such blatant disagreement between the Pharisees and Nicodemus in v. 52, where the Pharisees actually ridicule this "teacher of the Jews" by rhetorically asking if he is also "Galilean," a most offensive attack, and simply refer to it as discussion "confined to the realm of Pharisaic legal debate."[40] Contra Rensberger, then, although in John 3 Nicodemus was pictured as Jesus' interlocutor, though not fully in a negative sense, in 7:45–52 he is actually the interlocutor on behalf of Jesus against the Pharisees, who are most certainly portrayed negatively in John.

Third, Rensberger's negative interpretation of Nicodemus in 19:38–42 is again unsustainable. Without the support of several commentators[41] Rensberger argues that Nicodemus' role in the burial of Jesus and the contribution of the burial spices is not a gesture of true devotion but an "act of unbelief."[42] According to Rensberger: Nicodemus shows himself capable only of burying Jesus, ponderously and with a kind of absurd finality, so loading him down with burial as to make it clear that Nicodemus does not expect a resurrection any more than he expects a second birth."[43] But such a reading is hardly tenable. Far from criticizing Nicodemus, the narrative shows him as exemplifying belief through his presence at his death and his care for his body following; a kind of belief that was

---

[39] See Brown, *The Gospel According to John*, vol. I, p. 330.

[40] Rensberger, *Johannine Faith and Liberating Community*, p. 39.

[41] Rensberger's continual disagreement with other JComm interpreters (see p. 50, nn. 14–16) makes it difficult to believe that his goal is "to offer at this point a generic or consensus portrait, one that could be regarded as generally agreed upon by most scholars in the field" (p. 25).

[42] *Ibid.*, p. 40.

[43] *Ibid.*, p. 40. Rensberger seeks support from Alfred Loisy, *Le quatrième évangile* (Paris: Picard, 1903), pp. 895–96, who claimed that Nicodemus and Joseph of Arimathea confess nothing and have nothing to do with Jesus except with his corpse. But even here, Loisy is claiming that the narrative depicts a lack of evidence for full belief, not complete unbelief.

appropriate to a pre-Easter setting. Even Brown sees this reading in the narrative:

> Nicodemus' role is . . . to show how some who were attracted to Jesus did not immediately understand him. Presumably some never came to understand him (the Jerusalemites of 2:23–25), but some like Nicodemus did. When he first came by night (3:2), he was afraid; and it was soon shown that he did not understand Jesus at all (3:10). But we see him later speaking up indirectly for Jesus to the Pharisees (7:50). His final appearance illustrates the word of Jesus in 12:32–33: "And when I am lifted up from the earth, I shall draw all men to myself". . . Nicodemus comes forward publicly after the crucifixion of Jesus to bury Jesus (19:39). He . . . in asking for the body of Jesus is now making his faith public (19:38).[44]

For Brown, himself a community interpreter, "Nicodemus' role is not to illustrate or personify the attitudes of a contemporary group in the Johannine experience . . ."[45] Besides the problems that this raises with Brown's use of the narrative to depict a JComm,[46] it verifies that Rensberger's reading of the narrative is dominated by his need to place the Nicodemus "type" within the experience of the JComm, which he argues must be in conflict with the JComm in a sense of never coming to full belief, even when such a reading does not fit the textual evidence.

Based upon our correction of Rensberger's view that the narrative depicts Nicodemus paradigmatically as one of unbelief, there is no evidence to support his further claim that the Nicodemus paradigm symbolically represents another ostensive referent: an unbelieving "group" contemporary with the JComm. The evidence we have mounted against a purely negative portrayal of the Nicodemus character shows how Rensberger inappropriately assumed a negative portrayal. If the portrayal is progressively positive, as the evidence would suggest, then Rensberger's use of Nicodemus as symbolic of a "group" of inadequate faith and

---

[44] Brown, *The Community of the Beloved Disciple*, p. 72, n. 128. Brown disagrees with those who treat Nicodemus as a "crypto-Christian," for he confines himself methodologically "to clear references to those who believe in Jesus but refuse to confess him publicly." For Brown, the narrative shows the gradual acceptance of Jesus by Nicodemus.

[45] *Ibid.*

[46] Related to what we will discuss below, if Brown can see the narrative function in a paradigmatic way that does not need a "community" setting, it becomes less probable that other uses would be specifically for a "community." Interestingly, Brown never places Nicodemus in his community reconstruction.

courage is not feasible.[47] It seems as if Rensberger worked the evidence to the conclusion he already decided upon, based upon the Gospel community paradigm. Even more, because Rensberger is looking for a kind of faith that could be expected for post-Easter Christians, he evaluated Nicodemus' faith as inadequate. He fails to see how the FG places Nicodemus *before* the resurrection, when no one in John's narrative has a fully adequate faith. Thus, in light of the facet of ancient narratives that provide paradigmatic examples to the reader, the Nicodemus character would be more appropriately viewed as encouraging those who are slow to find "faith and courage" in the example of Nicodemus, who, in the midst of conflict (7:38–42) and his own personal wrestling with "God" (3:1–21), was willing to take a risk for one who has "come from God" (3:2) about which it had been said: Never has anyone spoken like this! (7:46). Using Burridge's language of a market niche, we might say with John McHugh that "These verses outline the central conviction of those who had been converted from mainstream Judaism to Christianity, and their message, though ostensibly addressed to Nicodemus in private, is manifestly directed to all adherents of Pharisaic Judaism."[48] But even then, almost any reader who was reading/hearing the "witness" of the Gospel would be able to relate, both past and present, to the experiences of Nicodemus and feel the encouragement from his example to meet Jesus where Nicodemus did: at the cross. The Nicodemus narrative, with its dialogue with Jesus, allowed the FE to both define the faith needed of those "interested," and eventually, through the rest of the Gospel (7:45–52; 19:38–42), to encourage the interested to "believe" in full.

The Samaritan woman and John 4:4–42

Our detailed look at the paradigmatic function of the Nicodemus character in John 3 will allow us to be briefer here. The pericope of the Samaritan woman is another example of the community interpretation's misuse of the paradigmatic function of ancient narratives. According to Raymond Brown, "the appearance of such a story in John may well reflect the post-resurrectional history of the Christian movement."[49] John 4 provides

---

[47] As Johannes Beutler, "Faith and Confession," explains, "if we take faith and public confession of one's adherence to Christ together, there should be no doubt that Nicodemus is seen very positively in this text" (p. 24).

[48] John McHugh, "In Him was Life," in James D. G. Dunn (ed.), *Jews and Christians: The Parting of the Ways, A.D. 70 to 135: The Second Durham-Tübingen Research Symposium on Earliest Christianity and Judaism* (Tübingen: J. C. B. Mohr, 1992), p. 127.

[49] Brown, *The Community of the Beloved Disciple*, p. 36.

evidence of a Samaritan "group's" entrance into the JComm.[50] For Brown, the acceptance of the Samaritans by the JComm caused further separation between the JComm and the Jewish synagogue with whom they were in conflict.[51] Malina and Rohrbaugh go even further and describe the entrance of Samaritans into the JComm as a "social transformation" as two competing ideologies were fused together.[52] According to Ashton, the entire scene reveals what he calls the "Samaritan connection" whereby the JComm was joined by a number of Samaritan converts that assisted in the Christological ideology of the entire "community."[53] But again we see that community interpretations place the Samaritan character as depicting a "group" in the experience of the JComm.

A more preferable reading of the Samaritan woman pericope would see that the narrative provides the reader with paradigmatic examples and didactic *Tendenzen* to follow.[54] The market niche for this pericope would probably have been Samaritan if not all non-Jews.[55] The narrator makes this clear in v. 9, where the Samaritan woman says to Jesus: "'How is it that you, a Jew, ask a drink of me, a woman of Samaria?' (Jews do not share things in common with Samaritans.)" Two aspects reveal themselves to the reader here. First, the relationship between Jews and Samaritans is obviously problematic, and yet Jesus is not acting to code, as the woman's question makes clear. Second, and even more striking, the roles of male and female are being challenged. Notice how she describes herself as a Samaritan "woman" (ἡ γυνὴ ἡ Σαμαρῖτις), but Jesus simply as a Jew (Ἰουδαῖος). Why did she not just call herself a Samaritan? Because being a woman and a Samaritan were both problematic.[56] The Samaritan

---

[50] Martyn, "Glimpses," p. 163, is wary of positing how many Samaritans were in the JComm, but is convinced that John 4 implies that at least "a few" were present.

[51] Brown, *The Community of the Beloved Disciple*, p. 37.

[52] Malina and Rohrbaugh, *Social-Science Commentary on the Gospel of John*, p. 102.

[53] Ashton, *Understanding the Fourth Gospel*, pp. 294–99. On the Samaritans in John and the JComm see also John Bowman, "Samaritan Studies 1: The Fourth Gospel and the Samaritans," *BJRL* 40 (1957/8), pp. 298–327; George Wesley Buchanan, "The Samaritan Origin of the Gospel of John," in Jacob Neusner (ed.), *Religions in Antiquity: Essays in Memory of Erwin Ramsdell Goodenough*, ed. Jacob Neusner, SHR 14 (Leiden: Brill, 1968), pp. 149–75; J. D. Purvis, "The Fourth Gospel and the Samaritans," *NovT* 17 (1975), pp. 161–98; Oscar Cullmann, *The Johannine Circle*, pp. 50–51.

[54] As before, this is accomplished by applying both literary and historical methods to the narrative.

[55] As Dodd, *The Interpretation of the Fourth Gospel*, p. 239, explains, in this Gospel the Samaritans represent the Gentile world over against the Jews.

[56] Although the Samaritan issue is probably the more prevalent, as the narrator's comment in v. 9 makes clear, it is interesting to note that JComm interpreters never claim that the "group" represented here was really a "female group," or even that the group was more accurately an "all-female Samaritan group," rather than simply a "Samaritan group." Yet the disciples' reaction to the dialogue in v. 27 focuses on her as a woman, not as a Samaritan.

or non-Jewish market niche is made clear by the narrator's comments, which would be unneeded by a Jew.

Jesus' response to the woman's question completely avoids the issue of race or gender and turns immediately to the issue at hand: that a "gift of God" is available for you, a Samaritan woman (v. 10). The term "gift" (δωρεάν) occurs elsewhere as an adverb with the meaning "freely," but this is the only place in any of the Gospels where the noun is found in the sense of "free gift."[57] The dialogue continues at a higher plane; Jesus' offer of this free gift is at a place where all can get it, they need not worship on their own sacred mountain (v. 21), for true worship will soon be performed in spirit and truth (v. 23). And this type of worship and worshiper, Jesus claims, is what God seeks (v. 23). Such a statement must have rung in the ears of all, even the Jewish-Christians, but especially the non-Jews, who are admitted not to an ethnic holy ground but in the very spirit and truth of God himself. As the narrative goes on to explain in the dialogue, the "Messiah" who will come and explain everything is now here, it is Jesus (v. 25). In v. 27 the issue of her as a woman is brought up by the disciples who enter the scene, providing a nice counter-balance to the focus on Jewish-Samaritan worship and salvation. The narrative has now extended beyond Jewish males to Samaritans (non-Jews) and females.[58]

Finally, the dialogue turns from the woman and Jesus to the disciples and Jesus. After broadening the "gift of God" beyond the Jews, this new dialogue focuses more broadly on harvesting this "gift." Jesus proclaims: "open your eyes and look at the fields! They are ripe for harvest" (v. 35). But it is v. 38 that makes clear that this pericope is not focusing merely on the JComm and its own Christian history. For Jesus the disciples are in the midst of salvation-history, for which they need be both grateful and responsible. The narrative then immediately turns to an example of harvest (vv. 39–42), and the benefits to both the sower and reaper (vv. 36–37), for the Samaritan woman became a "witness" to Jesus and many believed. The pericope ends with a focus on Jesus as "the savior of the world" (v. 42).[59]

---

[57] Morris, *The Gospel According to John*, p. 260, n. 27.

[58] For further discussion on the Samaritan woman see J. Eugene Botha, *Jesus and the Samaritan Woman: A Speech Act Reading of John 4:1–42*, NovTSup 65 (Leiden: Brill, 1991); and Martinus C. de Boer, "John 4:27 – Women (and Men) in the Gospel and Community of John," in George J. Brooks (ed.), *Women in the Biblical Tradition* (New York: Edwin Mellen, 1992), pp. 208–30.

[59] We will return to Jesus as "the savior of the world" below when we examine the mission motif.

The larger narrative function of representative figures

We have argued that the Nicodemus and Samaritan woman characters are meant to be read as representative figures in their own right. The (pre-critical) readers would have read the text as telling a "real" (traditional) story with paradigmatic virtues or responses for the reader. The characters are not representative for one "community," but for the general reader. This was argued for each narrative individually. But the argument is made more potent when the two narratives are read together at the macro-level as part of the larger narrative. The placement of the Nicodemus narrative alongside the Samaritan woman narrative was no accident; the two narratives have a united function.[60] The characters in both narratives provide representative significance for the readers. The characters do not provide "glimpses" into the initial readers' communal make-up, but act as mirrors for the readers themselves. A closer look will make this clear.

The characters in the larger narrative represent different "types" of readers that the FG would encounter. A similar conclusion was made by Francis Moloney over twenty-five years ago.[61] Moloney argues that the entire section from 2:1 to 4:54 is a single literary unit that provides several examples for the readers of correct (and incorrect) faith.[62] Although Moloney only draws the immediate literary conclusions and the concept of faith they project, he admits that various other conclusions could be drawn from this analysis.[63] Our own analysis of the first-century reader of the FG is complemented by Moloney's analysis. Nicodemus represents for the reader the proper Jew, one whose ethnic practices or position ("a leader of the Jews") would seem to disqualify them from interaction with Jesus. The Samaritan woman represents for the reader the ethnic and religious outcast, the Samaritan or even non-Jew, who is beyond any Jewish hope and who would be excluded from Jesus because he is the king of Israel (1:49). Both narratives redefine where such hope lies. For the Nicodemus type one's birth (ethnic identity) is changed.[64] For the Samaritan woman type one's place of worship is changed. Both of these

---

[60] Even Painter, *The Quest for the Messiah*, p. 199, argues that "John 4 is closely connected with the preceding material."

[61] Francis J. Moloney, "From Cana to Cana (John 2:1–4:54) and the Fourth Evangelist's Concept of Correct (and Incorrect) Faith," in E. A. Livingston (ed.), *Studia Biblica 1978: II: Papers on the Gospels*, JSNTSup 2 (Sheffield: JSOT, 1980), pp. 185–213.

[62] *Ibid.*, pp. 185–87, 201–02.   [63] *Ibid.*, p. 199.

[64] See the helpful discussion of this by Malina and Rohrbaugh, *Social-Science Commentary on the Gospel of John*, pp. 81–82. Although they define this concept for a geographic "community," it just as easily functions for the relational community we argued for in chapter 2.

redefinitions would have been well understood by the types of readers.[65] Both fit a specific type of reader. Both narratives provide the character type with a problem to be solved; a problem that involves their relation to Jesus. The positive depiction of Nicodemus that we argued for above provides for that "type" of reader the exact type of belief involved. The positive response of the Samaritan woman provides hope of belief for the Samaritan (non-Jew) type.

But even more can be argued. Nicodemus and the Samaritan woman are not merely ethnic types, but also "believing types." The slow and cautious belief of Nicodemus proclaims to the reader the steps that might, if not must, be taken in "belief." The Samaritan woman is more representative of one who is quick to believe, even emphatic in her response. These different "believing types" are meant to encourage the reader not just to believe, which is the starting point, but to believe to the full and have "life" (20:31). We will discuss this more when we examine the purpose of the FG. To examine a pericope in isolation from what comes before or after it is unfair to the FE, whose artistry is not just within one pericope, but exists at the macro-level of the narrative.

This is further supported by a brief examination of John 9 and its surrounding context. Following the textually problematic pericope of the woman caught in adultery, 8:12 begins with a direct statement by Jesus that leads to a trial of Jesus by the Jews: "I am the light of the world. Whoever follows me will never walk in darkness but will have the light of life." The Pharisees immediately challenge his own "witness" and the trial dialogue begins. The reader is given a clear picture into the Gospel's "testimony" about Jesus.[66] If the dialogue in 8:12–20 defined who Jesus was, the dialogue in 8:21–59 explains his mission and what he will do. The trial ends climactically with Jesus' powerful claim: "Very truly, I tell you, before Abraham was, I am" (v. 58).

It is within the context of this trial of Jesus in John 8 that we come to John 9. But here it is a "disciple," not Jesus, who is on trial. Lincoln explains it well:

> Jesus had been on trial for claims about his identity, particu-
> larly the claim (repeated here immediately before the miracle in
> 9:5) to be the light of the world. Part of the earlier claim was,
> "Whoever follows me will never walk in darkness but will have

---

[65] It is also important to note, as Beutler, "Faith and Confession," makes clear, that these confession "types" are made in a social context (p. 24). In this way, it is not merely an example of various types of belief in Jesus, but various forms of public confession.

[66] See Lincoln, *Truth on Trial*, pp. 37–38.

the light of life" (8:12). Now Jesus' verification of the claim through the giving of sight to the blind man leads to this man's interrogation . . . the force of the narrative is clear. If the one who is the light is subjected to opposition, trial, and rejection by the forces of darkness, it will be no different for his followers who have experienced the light of life.[67]

Like 8:13–20 did for Jesus, 9:1–7 define the "disciple" who is to face trial. The dialogue between Jesus and his disciples in vv. 1–3 after first seeing the blind man sets the tone for the divine use of the "disciple." This is followed by two key statements by Jesus. The first key statement is in v. 4 where Jesus claims that "We must work the works of him who sent me while it is still day for night is coming when no one can work." The "we" causes confusion here, especially since in the second clause Jesus uses "me."[68] What is significant is the collocation of plural and singular pronouns. The "we" seems to allude to conjoined forces, while the "me" acknowledges that the primary worker, by the nature of him being sent by the Father, is Jesus.

The trial of the disciple, similar to the trial of Jesus in 8:21–59 and the pericopae discussed above, allows the reader to connect paradigmatically with "the disciple." Contra Martyn, the trial dialogue is not descriptive of one specific conflict with "Jews," for the readers, at least the Jewish-Christian ones, would have all faced conflict of this sort. If the FE's inspiration was a specific conflict in his own experience, the narrative gives no such indication. A lengthy comment by C. H. Dodd, though in reference to the trial between Jesus and the Pharisees, is perfectly relevant here:

> Indeed, if it seems probable that the dialogue has its roots in the "Judaistic" controversy,[69] it is far from being a mere broadsheet in the interests of one party to an ecclesiastical dispute. The genius of the Fourth Evangelist has lifted the whole argument . . . to a level where its local and temporary aspects recede, and the issues are universal and radical: truth and reality, the death-desires that spring from the lie and bring incapacity to hear the

---

[67] *Ibid.*, pp. 96–97.

[68] The textual evidence supports this reading. The several alterations and assimilations of these pronouns that exist in various manuscript traditions verify this reading as original. Cf. Bruce M. Metzger, *A Textual Commentary on the Greek New Testament*, 2nd edn (New York: American Bible Society, 1994), p. 194.

[69] By the term "Judaistic controversy" Dodd is referring to the entire conflict that early Christianity had with Judaism.

Word, and, finally, a man's ultimate relation to God. By this time
we do not care greatly who the . . . "Jews" may have been . . .
John would have his readers consider such possibilities and face
the consequences.[70]

The blind man becomes for the reader "the disciple" who must choose
Jesus and be faithful. The narrative closes emphatically with "the disciple"
reconfirming his commitment to Jesus (vv. 35–41), a confirmation to the
witness the Gospel already claimed to depict (1:51). A warning is given
to those who are unwilling to commit (v. 39). The true "disciple," who
"sees" correctly, will recognize who Jesus is and do his works.[71]

It is here that we find Lincoln's *Truth on Trial* to be an inadequate depiction of the need for a "witness" or "testimony" document for the use of
a closed, already-believing "community." Lincoln is in basic agreement
with the "community" *Sitz im Leben* presented by Martyn and Brown and
sees no need to avoid "community" language.[72] But it appears that Lincoln's evidence leads him in the opposite direction, for Lincoln admits
that the narrative's depictions of a "community's" "experiences in the
recent past were deemed to be of wider appeal to an audience that now
included Gentiles and other Jews."[73] For example, in his discussion of
John 9, Lincoln argues that "The blind man begins as a representative
of all humanity because there is a sense in which all are born blind and
in darkness."[74] This is in contrast to his later comment, in the middle of
a discussion of the community paradigm concerning expulsion from the
synagogue, where Lincoln claims that "the experience of the man born
blind in John 9 would have resonated with their own."[75] Unfortunately, if
the narrative can resonate with numerous readers, not just those in a specific Jewish-Christian conflict, then the value and evidence for John 9 as a
"community" reading is significantly reduced. That is, John 9 either must
be shown to resonate in a special and unique way with a specific audience and that audience alone, or it must, like all narratives, be allowed to
function for a much broader audience. Lincoln provides superb narrative

---

[70] C. H. Dodd, *More New Testament Studies* (Manchester: Manchester University Press,
1968), p. 52. Interestingly, Dodd goes on to connect the Jew-Christian dialogue with all
such dialogue in the other NT documents. Such a move, it would seem, correctly envisions
a widespread phenomenon, not a problem simply faced by a sectarian-like "group."

[71] Maybe even more can be stated about the public nature of this confession. Johannes
Beutler, "Faith and Confession," has pointed out that John uses "confessing" four times,
half of them involve two of the "expulsion" passages (9:22; 12:42). As Beutler argues, "the
narrative strategy of John is used to present characters who show increasing courage in
confessing Christ even with the danger of losing their lives" (p. 20).

[72] Lincoln, *Truth on Trial*, pp. 264–65; see also pp. 19–21.

[73] *Ibid.*, p. 265.   [74] *Ibid.*, p. 98.   [75] *Ibid.*, p. 278.

analysis but remains bound to Martyn and other "community" interpretations when he moves from the text to its social-historical location.

Interestingly, the "worker" motif does not stop in John 9. The trial of Jesus continues into John 10. That the blind man narrative is still connected is made clear by 10:21. It is in this context that 10:16 must be heard: "I have other sheep that do not belong to this fold. I must bring them also, and they will listen to my voice. So there will be one flock, one shepherd." Jesus' words remind the "disciple" that he is not alone; there are others who also hear the same voice and do the same work. This reading is confirmed in Jesus' prayer for his "disciples" in 17:20: "I ask not only on behalf of these, but also on behalf of those who will believe in me through their word . . ." We will return to this when we discuss the mission motif.

Thus, by looking at the macro-level of the narrative we are able to see how John 3–4, and then briefly John 9, has a more unified function. In this light the ending of the Samaritan woman pericope, where Jesus is described as "the savior of the world" (4:42), is no accident. The previous pericopae intend to draw the various "types" of readers into their own "meeting with Jesus." The community interpretations that have focused on individual pericopae and have tried to place them into a so-called history of the JComm have distorted the paradigmatic function of the larger narrative and its genre. The FE is not describing to his own "community" who its members are,[76] but is inviting potential readers, who constitute different ethnic backgrounds and levels of belief, to participate in something that is not limited by ethnicity and gender, and expects nothing but full commitment.

The contextual significance of the "expulsion from the synagogue" passages

In chapter 3 we examined Martyn's two-level reading of John and the importance he placed on the "expulsion form the synagogue" passages for interpreting the FG. We argued that such a procedure does not match the narrative evidence. After dealing at the micro-level of the narrative we now turn to the macro-level issues, specifically the contextual significance of the "expulsion from the synagogue" passages. If Martyn is correct in placing so much importance on these passages, then other passages should also be clearly dependent on the "expulsion" motif for their own

---

[76] Just because the modern scholar asks this question does not mean it was asked by the original readers.

understanding. Our test for this will be as follows: if Martyn is correct to assume that the "expulsion from the synagogue" is the key to reading the text in its historical context, then the passages where it is manifest would necessarily be of more hermeneutical importance and clearly be set apart from other, more supportive, passages. That is, if Martyn is correct then one would assume that at the macro-level of the narrative the character of the blind man in John 9, the clue to the two-level reading of the narrative, would necessarily be established as more important to the FG than other characters in other pericopae. Since Martyn's argument requires several stages of progression, we shall examine their coordinated claims in their own contexts before looking at their importance for the Gospel as a whole.[77]

We have already examined the problems with Martyn's two-level reading at the micro-level of John 9:22 and the other "expulsion" passages (12:42; 16:2), but we have yet to provide an analysis of Martyn's macro-level reading of the Gospel and its depiction of the JComm. Martyn's "putting the pieces together" from the "expulsion" passages involves the following stages.[78] First, 9:22 refers to the action taken under Jewish leadership to reword the *Birkat ha-Minim* so as to make it an effective means for detecting Christian heresy. Thus, "the Jews" in 9:22 is John's way of referring to the Jamnia Academy. Second, in 12:42 the "Pharisees" refer either to the messengers who delivered the newly formulated Benediction to the Jewish community in John's city, or to members of the local Gerousia who enforce this formulation, much to the discomfort of believing "rulers." These believing rulers escape detection, perhaps by seeing to it that others are appointed to lead in prayer. Third, 16:2a merely tells us, as has already been indicated, that certain members of the JComm have been detected as Christian heretics and have been excommunicated from the synagogue. Martyn's reconstruction of the "expulsion" events does not stop with these three passages; more can be "seen" in the narrative. Fourth, 16:2b shows that the authorities could not view the matter as closed. Even in the face of excommunication, synagogue members continued to make the forbidden confession. Therefore, a step beyond

---

[77] Our focus is on Martyn's reconstruction of the JComm because his was the first that provided a complete methodological analysis and thorough reconstructive analysis of the narrative. Those that followed began with his assumptions, even if details of their reconstructions were different.

[78] The following is taken from Martyn, *History and Theology in the Fourth Gospel*, pp. 65–72. We are less concerned with the smaller referential decisions that have since been criticized, than we are with the entire "community" reconstruction. Our goal is not to present a different "community" reconstruction, but to critique the entire enterprise.

excommunication was called for, the imposition of the death penalty on at least some Jews who espoused the messianic faith.

This fourth stage is the latest to be found in the FG. Martyn argues that similar to the "expulsion" passages this extreme fourth stage "so impressed John that he allowed it to be clearly reflected in dramatic form elsewhere in the Gospel."[79] The question becomes: where in the Gospel is there the threat of someone coming to believe in Jesus and is subsequently arrested, tried, and executed for their faith? The answer is Jesus himself. For Martyn, then, at the *einmalig* level murderous steps are taken against Jesus, but the two-level drama reflects that these murderous steps were taken against Jewish-Christian preachers (leaders) in the JComm. Since threats were made against "Jesus" long before the passion story in John 5 and 7, we should look there for clues to the fourth stage of the JComm.

Martyn argues that an element in John 5 is given by the FE a "double role."[80] Although Martyn sees in v. 16 the *einmalig* level similar to the tradition found in the Synoptics (Mark 3:6), vv. 17–18 function on two levels. The Jews sought to kill "Jesus" not only because he broke the Sabbath, but because "he" was "making himself equal to God" (v. 18). Thus, for Martyn, "There are reasons for seeking to kill Jesus during his earthly lifetime, and there are reasons for seeking to kill *him* now, in John's own day!"[81] The "him," of course, is not the earthly Jesus but his worker who is involved in the leadership of the JComm. This much is similar to the blind man narrative in John 9. The difference is the response by the person healed to the Jewish authorities. In 5:12 the lame man is confronted by the Jewish authorities and when asked to identify his healer he complies. For Martyn, the two-level reading reveals that the "lame man" is a contemporary of the JComm, so that his response is a passive participation in the hostile steps taken against the healer, "Jesus." According to Martyn, "In John 5, the evangelist intends from the outset to focus his reader's attention not on measures taken against the healed man, but rather on hostile steps taken against the Jewish Christian himself."[82] The Jewish authorities are now after "Jesus," the Jewish-Christian healer. And they do so because Jewish-Christians are worshipping a second God (5:18b). This reconstruction immediately follows the "expulsion" passages and has intensified to the point of the threat of death for Jewish-Christians, especially their leaders.

But even more can be "seen" in the narrative. For Martyn the legal reasons for this intensified action against Jewish-Christians can be found in

---

[79] Martyn, *History and Theology in the Fourth Gospel*, p. 71.
[80] *Ibid.*, p. 73.   [81] *Ibid.*, p. 74 (emphasis added).   [82] *Ibid.*, p. 75.

John 7. Two things make it "obvious" to Martyn that John 7 reflects events contemporary with John. First, 7:1 is identical to 5:18 in the claim that the Jews were seeking to kill "Jesus." Second, and what Martyn considers to be the most obvious, is 7:12 where it is said that "Jesus" is leading people astray.[83] This "leading people astray" is rooted in the same crime found in John 5, the leading of people into the worship of a second God. We must remember that for Martyn this is blatantly anachronistic only when one assumes that the *Birkat ha-Minim* is already fully functioning. For Martyn, since the Jewish authorities find this "leading astray" to be illegal, and since "the Synoptic Gospels do not know of it as a legal procedure employed against Jesus or anyone else,"[84] the action must reflect events contemporary with the JComm. Thus, Martyn concludes:

> In portraying action taken against Jesus on the basis of this charge, John is not dependent on "Jesus-tradition," but rather primarily on his own experience. In his [the leader of the JComm] city the second and awesome step taken by the Jewish authorities (16:2b) was designed not to frighten synagogue members with the threat of excommunication, but rather to stop Jewish-Christians once for all from missioning among their own people . . . In spite of their having been excommunicated, they are therefore, *in the technical and legal sense*, persons who lead the people astray.[85]

Martyn has provided an ingenious reconstruction. But there are several problems with both the reconstruction he has created and his reading of the narrative. We will begin by critiquing some of the "clues" Martyn finds in John 5. First, Martyn too easily bifurcates 5:17–18 from 5:16. How are vv. 17–18 not also "wholly understandable in the *einmalig*, Palestinian frame of Jesus' life?"[86] Unlike his argument for the anachronism of 9:22, nothing in vv. 17–18 is anachronistic. Martyn even hurts his case by linking v. 16 to Mark 3:6 where the Pharisees are trying to "destroy" Jesus. Certainly "destroy" in Mark 3:6 is more closely related to the "kill" in 5:18 than to the "persecute" in 5:16. Thus, if Mark 3:6 is traditional Jesus material, as well as 5:16, the form-critical evidence Martyn provides for taking 5:17–18 as reflective of the JComm's experiences is not credible.

Second, not only is Martyn's "doubling" of the lame man as a contemporary of the JComm suspect, as we discussed earlier, but his analysis of the narrative's depiction of him is incorrect. The narrative does not depict the lame man as remaining loyal to the synagogue by his response to their

---

[83] *Ibid.*, p. 77.   [84] *Ibid.*, p. 78.   [85] *Ibid.*, p. 83.   [86] *Ibid.*, p. 74.

inquiry.[87] That the lame man was a Jew, made clear by the authorities accusing him of working on the Sabbath (5:10), makes the scene hardly a criminal investigation of "Jesus" alone, but of both the lame man and his healer. The lame man is also being threatened here. But even more, the very fact that the lame man *did not know who his healer was* makes a deliberate loyalty to the synagogue highly unlikely. Unless Martyn is willing to reconstruct the "lame man's" intentions and claim he was lying to protect himself, the narrative gives no indication that the inquisition of the lame man by the Jewish authorities was affected by anything other than his own behavior on the Sabbath. There is simply no evidence in the narrative that the interaction between the lame man and the Jewish authorities reflects a wholly other conflict between two warring "groups" over issues completely unrelated to the scene at hand. Although most interaction is between the Jewish authorities and Jesus, John 5 is not the only example of the authorities inquiring of others concerning Jesus. For example, all three Synoptics have the Pharisees questioning the disciples about Jesus in a similar fashion (Matt. 9:11; Mark 2:16; Luke 5:30). Thus, Martyn has provided no credible evidence that John 5 depicts a "wholly other" conflict between the JComm and contemporary Jewish authorities.

Martyn's "clues" in John 7 are also problematic. Martyn's legal iden-tification, one that he must connect to his *Birkat ha-Minim* proposal, is exaggerated. We have already shown how Martyn's link with the *Birkat ha-Minim* is extremely problematic; a fact that would seem to devastate his hope of finding "a recoverable historical reference . . . in John's own setting" with which to place the narrative's context.[88] Therefore, when Martyn claims that the depiction of Jesus as one who "is leading the peo-ple astray" in John 7 "reflects the contemporary drama" in John's day, he is forced to link this accusation of deception to official legal actions current in John's day but not in Jesus'.[89] This again shows how incorrect Meeks was when he called Martyn's link of the *Birkat ha-Minim* to John a "red herring."[90] For if Martyn cannot establish an official legal action from which to place the authority of the Jewish authorities in John's own day, then it must be conceded that it is plausible that similar conflict was possible even in Jesus' own day. Martyn tries to argue against this by claiming that the rest of the NT knows of no such legal procedure. Martyn dismisses an almost identical concept in Matt. 27:62–66, claiming that it "is plainly a late piece of tradition in which elements of Jewish-Christian

---

[87] *Ibid.*, p. 75.   [88] *Ibid.*, p. 78.   [89] *Ibid.*, p. 77.
[90] Meeks, "Breaking Away," p. 102.

debate are reflected."[91] But this is too flippant a rejection, for it is certainly possible that the Jewish authorities in Jesus' day believed that his followers had been deceived. Martyn even admits that Paul himself had been called a deceiver (2 Cor. 6:8; 1 Thess. 2:3). But what hurts Martyn's argument the most is his use of Justin's *Dialogue*. Martyn provides the following facilitated quote from Justin:

> The fountain of living water [cf. John 7:38; 4:10] which gushed forth from God upon a land devoid of the knowledge of God, the land of the Gentiles, that fountain is Christ, who appeared in the midst of your people [cf. John 1:11] and healed those who from birth were blind, deaf, and lame [cf. John 9 and 5]. He cured them by his word, causing them to walk, to hear and to see. By restoring the dead to life, he compelled the men of that day to recognize him [cf. John 12:11, 17–19]. Yet though they saw these miraculous deeds, they attributed them to magical art [cf. John 8:48]. Indeed they dared to call him a magician and a deceiver of the people. But he performed these deeds to convince his future followers, that if anyone . . . should be faithful to his teaching, he would raise him up at his second coming [cf. John 5:25] . . .[92]

Martyn then explains that the similar motifs describing Jesus as a deceiver by Justin cannot be trusted for he may have depended on the FG:

> Not all of the motifs for which I have provided Johannine parallels are peculiar to John; Justin certainly drew on several sources for these two paragraphs. I am only suggesting that among these sources may have been the Fourth Gospel; and . . . we must exercise extreme caution in suggesting that Justin offers independent *historical data* which illumine John 7.[93]

By suggesting that Justin may have depended on the FG,[94] Martyn weakens his own reading of the narrative. If Justin used the FG as a source for historical data, which "data" was he seeing in the narrative? Martyn assumes that the data Justin would have found in the FG were data

---

[91] Martyn, *History and Theology in the Fourth Gospel*, p. 79. As we discussed in chapter 3, for evidence in the Gospels that such a Jewish legal procedure was active in Jesus' day see Neale, "Was Jesus a *Mesith*?"

[92] *Dialogue*, p. 69. See also Martyn, *History and Theology in the Fourth Gospel*, p. 79.

[93] Martyn, *History and Theology in the Fourth Gospel*, p. 79 (emphasis added).

[94] Martyn also suggests that Matt. 27 might also have been a source for Justin.

concerning the *einmalig* Jesus, not the "Jesus" of the JComm.[95] If this is the case, then Justin's reading of the FG contradicts Martyn's. If Justin read and used the FG so that its narrative description was "literal" in the sense of without the allegory portrayed by Martyn, then Martyn's reading is foreign to Justin. Justin makes no mention of a second-level narrative concerning the "groups" represented by Jesus or the people he healed. Thus, Martyn has again provided no credible evidence that John 7 depicts a "wholly other" conflict between the JComm and contemporary Jewish authorities. In fact, the very evidence he used to support his own argument has worked against him.

Thus, we are now able to make an evaluation of the contextual significance of the "expulsion from the synagogue" passages in the narrative of the FG. There are also several problems concerning Martyn's handling of the macro-level of the narrative. Three aspects are important here. First, Martyn's analysis of the narrative parts creates a completely different narrative whole. It is interesting that several times Martyn has to claim that he is not doing decoding work.[96] Martyn's reconstruction would construct the narratives (by chapter) we have already discussed in this order: 9, 12, 16, 5, and 7.[97] Chapters 5 and 7 are actually later stages in the JComm's experience than chapter 9, yet they come before it. This would be problematic if the narrative at the *einmalig* level, using Martyn's terminology, shows a progression of narrative development. And we will argue that it does. For example, we already discussed how the narrative's depiction of Nicodemus develops as the narrative progresses. John 3 is the primary and most detailed Nicodemus pericope, but Nicodemus is also discussed in a progressive manner in chapters 7 and 19. In 7:50 the narrative refers back to chapter 3 at the first mention of Nicodemus: "who had gone to Jesus before." The narrative assumes that the reader has already read chapter 3 before coming to chapter 7. Chapter 19 is no different. At the first mention

---

[95] Whether Justin actually used the FG as a source is unimportant for our argument, for Martyn admits the type of reading he expects Justin would have used; a reading contradictory to his own.

[96] Martyn, *History and Theology in the Fourth Gospel*, p. 85, admits concerning his own reading of the narrative: "At this point caution is necessary. Have we not overstepped the bounds of probability? The drama may indeed reflect two levels *in general*. But do we not press the case too far if we take *these* developments as reflections of actual events in John's milieu?" Later Martyn admits, "I do not suggest that the dramatis personae can be explained in no other way . . . John was neither playing a kind of code-game, nor trying to instruct members of his church about points of correspondence between the Jewish hierarchy of Jesus' day and that of their own" (p. 89).

[97] It is 16:2b that links the three "expulsion" passages (9:22; 12:42; 16:2a) with chapters 5 and 7. Thus, the progression necessarily moves against the flow of the narrative at the *einmalig* level.

of Nicodemus the narrative reminds the reader that he is the one "who had at first come to Jesus by night." Again, the narrative assumes that the reader has followed its own progression. Helpful here is the discussion of the narrative's progression or plot development by R. Alan Culpepper.[98] Culpepper argues that John has a narrative development that is vital to its individual parts. Although the Gospel has a wide variety of individual narratives that each have an individual function, "John allows each episode to have a meaning place in the story" as a whole.[99] Martyn disrupts the FG's own plot development for his own plot, a plot not found in the narrative of the FG.

The second problem concerning Martyn's macro-level handling of the narrative is his allegorical reading of the narrative's plot. To accommodate his reading Martyn is required not only to "double" characters of Jesus' day with characters in the time of the JComm, but he is also required to "double" the plot as well. That is, since Martyn can only create his "wholly other" reading of the narrative by "doubling" the characters he must do the same with the plot; for there is no second plot for him to utilize. Thus, in reference to Jews seeking to kill Jesus, Martyn explains: "There are reasons for seeking to kill Jesus during his earthly lifetime, and there are reasons for seeking to kill *him now*, in John's own day!"[100] By "now" Martyn assumes that the plot is "doubling" so as to report events contemporary with the JComm. It would be one thing for Martyn to notice a sub-plot to the narrative or an emphasis in the telling of the *einmalig* level that reveals a current contextual crisis. But Martyn never argues for that. His assumption is that the narrative is telling of two distinct events in the one narrative. Such a proposal is either a most amazing coincidence or a brilliant fiction. The latter is to be preferred. For Martyn is forced to divorce the ending of the FG, the passion story, from the earlier narrative for his reading to be successful. He even admits as much. For example, while Martyn admits that 5:16 "looks toward the passion story," he makes a similar concession concerning 5:17–18, verses he simply calls editorial additions.[101] He is also forced to divorce the Synoptics from the FG. He admits that all three Synoptics "show only one dramatically developed attempt to arrest Jesus, the successful one," yet he assumes John shows two![102] Such an outrageous assumption can only be controlled by factors external to the narrative, for the narrative is unified in its progression to the passion.

---

[98] Culpepper, *Anatomy*, pp. 89–97.   [99] *Ibid.*, p. 97.
[100] Martyn, *History and Theology in the Fourth Gospel*, p. 74 (emphasis added).
[101] *Ibid.*   [102] *Ibid.*, p. 78.

The third problem concerning Martyn's macro-level handling of the narrative is the complex historical reconstruction required to make sense of his reading. Our detailed examination of Martyn's argument has shown it to be based upon multiple assumptions about not only the narrative and its function (the allegorical use of characters and plot), but also the "type" of audience and the specific circumstances involved. There is no external evidence that even alludes to a specific "group" behind the FG, let alone the events that he describes. It is simply too convenient to claim that the JComm experienced a nearly identical conflict with the Jewish authorities that the earthly Jesus did; that the JComm leaders were wanted for doing miraculous acts nearly identical to those of Jesus; and that the members of the JComm were forced to choose "sides" in the same way that the readers of the Gospel are. This appears to be another case for Ockham's Razor.

After examining the problems with Martyn's macro-level reading of the "expulsion from the synagogue" narratives, a brief examination of some non-"expulsion" narratives is in order to test further his reading strategy. Again, our test hypothesis is that if Martyn's historical reconstruction were correct, then the "expulsion" passages should have a dominating influence on the rest of the Johannine narrative, even where the expulsion is not explicitly mentioned, because the narrative is intimately tied to the *Sitz im Leben* proposed by Martyn.

Helpful here is an essay by Adele Reinhartz, who attempts to read two other passages with Martyn's two-level reading: 11:1–44 and 12:11.[103] The first passage tells of the sisters, Mary and Martha, who are in mourning for their recently deceased brother Lazarus. Though apparently known to be related to Jesus, even called his "beloved," these women have clearly not been excluded from the Jewish community, as evidenced by the fact that they are comforted in their grief by "many of the Jews" (11:19). As Reinhartz explains,

> In a two-level reading of the Gospel, these sisters would represent Johannine Christians. If, as the consensus view asserts, such Christians had already been excluded from the synagogue and hence from the Jewish community as a whole, how is it that they are surrounded by Jewish mourners?[104]

---

[103] Adele Reinhartz, "The Johannine Community and Its Jewish Neighbor: A Reappraisal," in Fernando F. Segovia (ed.), *"What is John?" Volume II. Literary and Social Readings of the Fourth Gospel.* SBLSymS 7 (Atlanta: Scholars Press, 1998), pp. 111–38.

[104] *Ibid.*, p. 121.

The second passage Reinhartz examines is John 12:11, where it states that on account of Jesus "many of the Jews were going over to Jesus and putting their faith in him." They believed in Jesus because they witnessed him raise Lazarus from the dead. As Reinhartz explains, "A second-level reading of this verse implies an incompatibility between believing Jesus to be the Christ and maintaining membership in the Jewish community, yet it does not attribute this separation to an official Jewish policy of expulsion."[105] According to Reinhartz, the combination of these two passages with the "expulsion" passages creates three different models of relationship between the JComm and the Jews.

Neither of these two passages is able to function with Martyn's two-level reading. In fact, if we are consistent with Martyn's reading strategy, we get two different "glimpses" of the Johannine *Sitz im Leben*, a third if we include Martyn's own examination of the specific expulsion from the synagogue passages. Thus, it appears that we have either a very complex set of relationships between the Jews and Johannine Christians portrayed in the Johannine narrative, or the historical reconstruction proposed by Martyn is impossible to harmonize with Gospel of John at the macro-level of the narrative. As Reinhartz explains, in combination with the two-level reading strategy proposed by Martyn, "these readings . . . are difficult to defend exegetically. They also constitute a substantial revision of the expulsion theory by downplaying its impact on the historical experience of the community, quite contrary to the view of scholars who see the expulsion as a, perhaps even the, formative event of Johannine Christianity."[106]

Thus, by overemphasizing the use of "the expulsion of the synagogue" passages in the FG, Martyn has distorted their contextual significance and has misread the macro-level of the narrative. Martyn has created a "wholly other story" than the one told by the narrative. In his attempt "to hear the Fourth Evangelist speak *in his own terms*," Martyn's own "terms" have taken priority. This is problematic because of what Gail O'Day admitted above: Martyn has "blocked out for a while all other ways both of reading the Gospel and of reading the historical data. Martyn's reading became totalizing . . . because he read so well and so easily that we forgot it was a construction of the data. We . . . read Martyn instead of rereading

---

[105] *Ibid.*

[106] *Ibid.*, p. 130. See also Adele Reinhartz, "Women in the Johannine Community: An Exercise in Historical Imagination," in Amy-Jill Levine (ed.), *A Feminist Companion to John*, FCNT 5 (London: Sheffield Academic Press, 2003), vol. II, pp. 14–33, for a further testing of the problems with a two-level reading of the FG.

the data . . ."[107] We have argued that Martyn's reading of the text is without warrant, and his reconstruction of the historical context in which the Gospel was created is not credible.[108] Our proposed reading of the Gospel's audience helps alleviate the control Martyn's reading has had over Johannine scholarship over the last several decades.

The purpose of the fourth Gospel

The community interpretations of the FG have assumed that the purpose of the Gospel was to reinforce the ideology of the JComm, since the setting in which the FG was written is assumed to be "communal."[109] The conflict in which the "community" was engaged necessitated the type of "belief" the Gospel exhorts. But the stated purpose statement of the FG in 20:31 is not decisive in this direction due to a controversial textual variant. Too often the seemingly indecipherable variant has deterred the use of this statement of purpose in providing assistance to the meaning and function of the FG. But our proposal challenges its lack of use. If the characters in the narrative provide an invitation to the reader to believe, maybe there is more to 20:31 than has normally been assumed.

The textual issue traditionally involves two areas of debate. First, what type of "belief" is expected? Is πιστεύ[σ]ητε meant to imply continuation in belief (present subjective) or a coming to belief (aorist subjunctive)? Second, what is the reader meant to believe? Is Jesus the subject or the predicate? We will discuss these two textual issues and then look at a third issue more recently introduced: the relation of the 31a to 31b.

The first issue concerning 20:31 is textual. The term πιστεύ[σ]ητε in 20:31a is such an indecipherable textual variant that the *Textual Commentary* keeps the variant letter in brackets [σ].[110] The use of the variant letter in brackets was because both variants "have notable early support."[111] According to the *Textual Commentary*, "the aorist, strictly interpreted, suggests that the Fourth Gospel was addressed to non-Christians so that they might come to believe that Jesus is the Messiah; the present tense suggests that the aim of the writer was to strengthen the faith of

---

[107] O'Day, "Response: 'The Expulsion from the Synagogue: A Tale of a Theory,'" p. 5.

[108] It should also be noted that Martyn's two-level reading cannot be applied to the whole of the Gospel narrative. It is unfortunate that Martyn's reading, which only involves a few pericopae, has come to dominant the entire Gospel narrative.

[109] For the most recent summary of various "community" proposals see Raymond E. Brown, *An Introduction to the Gospel of John*, ed. Francis J. Moloney, ABRL (New York: Doubleday, 2003), pp. 151–88.

[110] Metzger, *A Textual Commentary on the Greek New Testament*, p. 219.

[111] *Ibid.*

those who already believe."[112] The lack of extrinsic support for either reading is what may have caused the general neglect of 20:31 in defining the purpose of the FG, since only intrinsic evidence could be used.

In 1987 D. A. Carson challenged the neglect of 20:31 and attempted a "reconsideration" of its relation to the purpose of John.[113] Carson argues that the emphasis on the JComm has taken the focus away from this explicit statement of purpose and that interpreters have simply assumed by their reconstructions that the present subjunctive is the original variant.[114] For Carson the complex textual evidence actually points in favor of an evangelistic purpose. Whatever one concludes the outcome of the text-critical question to be, an outcome Carson views as indeterminable,[115] the meaning of the verse is not determined solely by the tense of this one verb.[116] Both the present and the aorist can be used in reference to the process of coming to faith.[117] "In short, the text-critical evidence is not determinative, not only because it is evenly balanced but also because both the present subjunctive and the aorist subjunctive can occur in the context of coming to faith and in the context of continuing in faith."[118]

Carson's hesitancy to take a text-critical stance was soon criticized by Gordon Fee.[119] According to Fee the textual question of 20:31 can be resolved with a much greater degree of certainty than is often allowed or attempted.[120] By examining 20:31 with 19:35, the other place where the FE speaks directly to his readers, in this case in language very much like

---

[112] *Ibid.*

[113] D. A. Carson, "The Purpose of the Fourth Gospel: John 20:31 Reconsidered," *JBL* 106 (1987), pp. 639–51.

[114] *Ibid.*, p. 639.   [115] As does Cullmann, *The Johannine Circle*, p. 15.

[116] Carson, "The Purpose of the Fourth Gospel: John 20:31 Reconsidered," p. 640.

[117] In fact, in a more recent article, a response to Fee's response, Carson, "Syntactical and Text-Critical Observations on John 20:30–31: One More Round on the Purpose of the Fourth Gospel," *JBL* 124 (2005), pp. 693–714, is willing to concede, for the sake of argument, that the verb is a present subjunctive, although the issue for Carson now centers on the significance of the present subjunctive based upon verbal aspect theory (pp. 703–08). In the end, Carson's position remains unchanged; it is merely more nuanced to interact with Fee. As Carson explains, "without wanting for a moment to deny that there is a semantic distinction between the aorist and the present . . . the evidence emphatically shows that it is not exegetically possible to tie one tense to unbelievers who are coming to faith, and the other to believers who are going on in their faith in some durative sense. Both tenses can be applied by John to both unbelievers and believers. Fee's discussion does not in any way threaten the 'minor' point made by my original essay" (p. 708).

[118] *Ibid.* A similar comment is made by Schnackenburg, *The Gospel According to St. John*, vol. III, p. 338.

[119] Gordon D. Fee, "On the Text and Meaning of John 20,30–31," in F. van Segbroek *et al.* (eds.), *The Four Gospels, 1992*, 3 vols. (Leuven: Leuven University Press, 1992), vol. III, pp. 2193–205.

[120] *Ibid.*, pp. 2193–94. Fee criticizes Metzger, *A Textual Commentary on the Greek New Testament*, for not even giving the committee's choice on the matter.

that of 20:31, Fee argues that the early and trustworthy nature of P[66] and the other clues in the manuscript tradition give preference to the present subjunctive and, therefore, a more "community" reading.[121] But there are several problems with Fee's text-critical hypothesis. First, Fee relies too heavily on P[66]. His earlier work on the myth of textual recension in P[66] seems to dominate his evaluation of the textual evidence in this case.[122] Second, Fee's implicit conclusions are far from evident. For example, Fee claims that even though the verb in 19:35 is on two separate scraps in P[66vid], when put beside one another the amount of space between them would only be enough for five letters, not six.[123] This is hardly a case of conclusive evidence, especially when one is dealing with two separate, ancient, and fading manuscripts. Thus, Fee's conclusion that "it is certain that P[66] supports the present subjunctive in 20:31" is hardly conclusive.[124] Such a conclusion gives Carson's less assertive analysis all the more warrant.

But Fee not only asserted a text-critical decision with meager evidence in favor of the present tense, he also argues for the present based upon the use of the ἵνα-clause in the FG and general observations about scribal proclivities. Regarding the former, the basis of Fee's argument is that "since final ἵνα-clauses are one of the certain stylistic features of this Gospel, one can measure the author's own proclivities regarding *Aktionsart* in such clauses, and have a broad enough sampling so as to insure relatively reliable conclusions."[125] Using data from the FG,[126] Fee argues that since there is a ratio of 3:1 of aorist to present in the FG, which is a much higher incidence level than one would expect in normal prose, then there is a greater likelihood that the variant in 20:31 is present and not aorist. But certainly Fee is relying too strongly on "possibility," for the very same data, that two-thirds of the final clauses are aorist, could easily be used against him. Such a sampling is hardly a "reliable conclusion."[127] Regarding the latter, the basis of Fee's argument is that "one can

---

[121] *Ibid.*, pp. 2194–95.
[122] See Fee, "P[75], P[66] and Origen: The Myth of Early Textual Recension in Alexandria," in Richard Longenecker and Merrill C. Tenney (eds.), *New Dimensions in New Testament Study* (Grand Rapids: Zondervan, 1974), pp. 19–45.
[123] Fee, "On the Text and Meaning of John 20,30–31," p. 2195.
[124] *Ibid.*   [125] *Ibid.*, p. 2196.
[126] Fee obtains his statistical data from William Hendriksen, *Exposition of the Gospel According to John* (Grand Rapids: Baker, 1953), pp. 45–53; and Edwin A. Abbott, *Johannine Grammar* (London: Adam and Charles Black, 1906), pp. 369–89. See also H. Riesenfeld, "Zu den johanneischen ἵνα –Satzen," *ST* 19 (1965), pp. 213–20, who argues that John commonly uses the present tense after i{na. Riesenfeld is criticized by Fee, and especially Carson, for resorting to usage in 1 John for his analysis.
[127] Fee, "On the Text and Meaning of John 20,30–31," p. 2196.

check the manuscript tradition against the subjunctives in these clauses to see if there are clear tendencies in one direction or the other when scribal errors are made with these subjunctives."[128] Unfortunately, Fee's intrinsic assumptions of these scribal errors require too much guessing and assumption to provide any conclusive evidence. Thus, Fee's conclusion that the present subjunctive is to be preferred in 20:31 based upon text-critical and grammatical evidenced is unfounded.

The second issue concerning John 20:31 is grammatical. Is Jesus the subject or the predicate? Strictly interpreted, if "Jesus" is the subject then the Gospel was answering the question: who is Jesus? If "Messiah" is the subject then the Gospel is answering the question: who is the Messiah? The latter is potentially evangelistic, the former is more didactic. Since the textual issue was inconclusive, we now turn to this grammatical issue.

Unlike Fee, Carson admitted that the problem of 20:31 was not to be resolved textually. According to Carson the best evidence that 20:31 is evangelistic, and supportive of the aorist sense since either could function evangelistically, is the subject of 31a. Using the published dissertation of Lane McGaughy, which claims that "the word or word cluster determined by an article is the subject,"[129] Carson argues that "Messiah" is the subject of 31a since it has the definite article.[130] But as Carson admits, this disagrees with McGaughy who considers 20:31 to be one of five exceptions and takes "Jesus" to be the subject.[131] Carson disagrees with McGaughy on the basis of the review by E. V. N. Goetchius, who points out that there are other examples of these "Christological" terms separated by a "to be" verb and argues that there are no syntactical or contextual reasons to understand these examples as exceptions, as originally argued by McGaughy.[132] This three-page review by Goetchius gives Carson all the evidence he needs. For from this evidence Carson concludes that there is now "every syntactical reason for thinking that the crucial clause should be rendered 'that you may believe that the Christ, the Son of God, is Jesus'" and that 20:31 is evangelistic.[133]

But such a grammatical conclusion is not without its problems. First, Carson's denial that 20:31 is an exceptional case, as defined by

---

[128] *Ibid.*

[129] Lane C. McGaughy, *Toward a Descriptive Analysis of EINAI as a Linking Verb in New Testament Greek*, SBLDS 6 (Missoula, Mont.: SBL, 1972).

[130] Carson, "The Purpose of the Fourth Gospel: John 20:31 Reconsidered," p. 643.

[131] *Ibid.*

[132] E. V. N. Goetchius, review of Lane C. McGaughy, *Toward a Descriptive Analysis of EINAI as a Linking Verb in New Testament Greek*, *JBL* 95 (1976), pp. 147–49.

[133] Carson, "The Purpose of the Fourth Gospel: John 20:31 Reconsidered," p. 643.

McGaughy, cannot be overturned by Goetchius' three examples with the infinitive of "to be" from Acts (5:42; 18:5, 28). Adding three examples to the original five and defining their content as "Christological" hardly eliminates their abnormal tendencies. Second, Carson's application of McGaughy's findings to John is also problematic. As Fee notes, McGaughy's observations are made on the basis of the verb εἶναι without adequate attention to John's usage of the article with proper names.[134] According to Fee when Johannine uses are examined in particular, a case can be made that favors an anarthrous personal name as the subject when the name precedes the verb.[135] Thus, the denotation of the subject with a "to be" verb is notoriously difficult to demonstrate.[136] Third, Carson's conclusion requires him to force the available evidence to fit his proposal. We discussed above how Carson was less rigid concerning the text-critical evidence and the meaning of the different verb tenses, admitting that the "evidence is not determinative."[137] So instead of providing an answer to the old text-critical debate, Carson is forced to use grammar to find the identity of the enigmatic subject; a task no less elusive. Thus, although Carson has helpfully shown that a non-community reading is more than possible, he has been unable to demonstrate this with any confidence.

Finally, the third and more recent issue concerning John 20:31 is the relation of 31a to 31b. The focus on the textual and grammatical issues in 20:31a, though necessary, has been too narrow. The clause in 31a has been isolated as if it alone could provide the answer. Recently it has been argued that by comparing 31a to 31b we may be able to see more clearly the general thrust of John's purpose; a thrust that is missed when 31a is examined on its own. It is to this that we now turn.

We have already discussed above that 20:31 is very similar to 19:35. In fact, both verses have the identical textual variant. It is generally assumed that 20:31 adds nothing to 19:35 beyond the mention of the result of faith – life. Recently Stephen Motyer has argued convincingly that the addition of "life" to 20:31 defines the type of belief expected.[138] Motyer, relying

---

[134] Fee, "On the Text and Meaning of John 20,30–31," p. 2205, n. 29.

[135] *Ibid.* See also Fee, "The Use of the Definite Article with Personal names in the Gospel of John," *NTS* 17 (1970–71), pp. 168–83.

[136] See also Daniel B. Wallace, *Greek Grammar Beyond the Basics: An Exegetical Syntax of the New Testament* (Grand Rapids: Zondervan, 1996), pp. 46–47, who argues, contra Carson, that no grammatical argument can be made since the evidence is ambiguous.

[137] Carson, "The Purpose of the Fourth Gospel: John 20:31 Reconsidered," p. 640.

[138] Motyer, *Your Father the Devil?*, pp. 57–62.

on the work of Martin Warner[139] and several commentators,[140] argues that the Gospel is aware of several "sorts" or "stages" of faith. As Warner explains, "Not all who 'believe' in his name have 'life' in his name, but there is an internal relation between a certain sort of belief and a certain form of 'life.'"[141] This is not to say that John is describing "stages of faith."[142] Rather, as Motyer explains, "it is that faith is consistently associated with other things by which it must be supplemented if it is to lead to life. Faith on its own carries no automatic promise of life at all."[143] Interestingly, several recent commentators have hinted at this concept. As Craig Keener explains, "John's goal is not simply initial faith but persevering faith . . ."[144] Or as Carson adds, "By not preserving, this faith proves to itself to be false. That is one why . . . John's Gospel can demand faith conceived by the author as process (i.e. cast in the present tense), even when . . . dealing with unbelievers."[145] Thus, using the terminology we have used earlier in this study, John depicts different "types" of faith and different faith responses. These "types" of faith are meant to reflect different "types" of readers that might encounter the Gospel.

Returning to the Nicodemus narrative in John 3, we see in this initial encounter with Jesus that although Nicodemus came to Jesus, he had not fully understood, or fully "believed." Jesus initially tells him that he must be born again (v. 3); a concept that Nicodemus does not even understand (vv. 4, 9). Jesus rebukes Nicodemus, whom he calls "a teacher of Israel," for not understanding these things (v. 10); and accuses him of not accepting his testimony (v. 11) or "believing" (v. 12). Thus, as Motyer explains: "Against this background, 3:14–16 functions as a warning, as much as a promise."[146] Jesus must not be acknowledged as a "teacher from God" (v. 2), but as the exalted Son of Man (vv. 13–14) and the "one

---

[139] Martin Warner, "The Fourth Gospel's Art of Rational Persuasion," in Martin Warner (ed.), *The Bible as Rhetoric: Studies in Biblical Persuasion and Credibility* (London: Routledge, 1990), pp. 153–77.

[140] Brown, *The Gospel According to John*, vol. I, pp. 530–31; Schnackenburg, *The Gospel According to St. John*, vol. I, pp. 570–71; and R. Alan Culpepper, "The Theology of the Gospel of John," *RevExp* 85 (1988), pp. 417–32.

[141] Warner, "The Fourth Gospel's Art of Rational Persuasion," p. 154.

[142] Yu Ibuki, "'Viele glaubten an ihn' – Auseinandersetzung mit dem Glauben im Johannesevangelium," *AJBI* 9 (1983), pp. 128–83, is correct to reject the idea of "stages of faith," but goes too far when he claims that "there are fundamentally no different kinds of faith, but either faith or unbelief" in John (pp. 142–43). Motyer, *Your Father the Devil?*, pp. 58–59, has a helpful critique of Ibuki's commitment to a Bultmannian rejection of all legitimation for faith.

[143] Motyer, *Your Father the Devil?*, p. 59,

[144] Keener, *The Gospel of John*, p. 1216.

[145] Carson, "Syntactical and Text-Critical Observations on John 20:30–31," p. 713.

[146] *Ibid.*

and only Son" (v. 16) if one is to have eternal "life" (vv. 15, 16). As we argued earlier this portrayal of Nicodemus is not negative; for "the one who believes in him is not condemned" (v. 18). It is this that connects what many assume are the narrator's comments immediately following Jesus' interaction with Nicodemus (3:16–21). These verses make clear that Jesus' "rebuke" of Nicodemus is not one of condemnation, but a call to complete faith in him, to "life" eternal. Motyer explains it well:

> The faith that means eternal life is faith that takes the step that Nicodemus has not yet taken – it "hears my word and believes him who sent me" (5:24). Implicit in the faith of 5:24 is a *discipleship* which is prepared to run the gauntlet of the opposition which Jesus' word has just provoked (5:17f). So, in its narrative context, it is more than just intellectual assent . . . Faith *even of the fullest kind* is immediately put to the test. Peter's confession in 6:69 means a commitment to discipleship in contrast to those who leave Jesus at that point, and is immediately challenged with the prediction that one of the twelve will betray Jesus (6:70). Martha's confession in 11:27 is immediately tested before Lazarus' tomb . . . Her hesitation in 11:39 is countered by Jesus' "Did I not say to you that *if you believe* you will see the glory of God?" (11:40). She has already believed, as her confession shows; but the confession alone is not enough.[147]

It is with this in mind that we return to 20:31. The addition of 31b to the similar purpose statement of 19:35 and 20:31a is not insignificant. As 20:31 explains, belief is expected to lead to life. Unfortunately, not all who believe receive life; faith on its own carries no automatic promise of life – life is what God gives (6:63; 10:28; 17:2). Thus, if faith is just a starting point, then the view that 20:31 reveals an evangelistic purpose for the FG is strengthened.[148] As Motyer points out, "If the Gospel were aimed simply at reinforcing the faith of a Christian community, we would expect the substance just of the second purpose-clause [31b] to be expressed here – which is what we find in the parallel statement of purpose in 1 John 5:13": "I write these things *to you who believe* in the name of the Son of God, *so that you may know that you have eternal life.*"[149] Therefore, it is highly likely that the Gospel is aimed not just at different "types of readers," but also at different "types of faith." As Andrew Lincoln suggests, "If the disciples are characters with whom the implied readers are most likely to identify, then the phenomenon of their struggle to come to full belief

---

[147] *Ibid.*, p. 60.   [148] *Ibid.*, p. 61.   [149] *Ibid.*

and understanding may also shed light on the statement of purpose in 20:31…"[150] For example, Nicodemus is not just representative of a Jewish reader, but of one who has assented to the idea of Jesus as a teacher but has yet to worship him as the Son of Man. Or the Samaritan woman, taking another example, is not just representative of a Samaritan (or non-Jewish) reader, but of one who comes with a different concept of "faith." In this sense, the Gospel "seeks to move all believers, whatever their conviction, to the kind of discipleship [belief] which will give life."[151]

Mission in the fourth Gospel

If our analysis of 20:31 and the purpose of the FG are correct then we might expect to find a more general invitation within the narrative's rhetorical address. That is, if the FE assumed a more indefinite audience, one which we have argued for in the previous four chapters, then we might expect to find a mission-like rhetoric in the FG. Recent research has argued that mission is a leitmotif or foundational theme in the FG. Thus, by examining the mission in the FG and attempting to discover its potential function in the social setting of the FG, we hope to highlight further the indefinite audience that the narrative both expects and invites.

Discussion of a mission leitmotif is not new to Johannine scholarship. In fact, although the precise meaning, nature and scope of mission in the FG are subjects of perennial debate, the existence of a mission leitmotif is "hardly a matter for dispute."[152] "Sending" terminology dominates the

---

[150] Lincoln, *Truth on Trial*, pp. 249–50. For Lincoln 20:31 shows that "The narrative itself has been written as the testimony through which 'you' – the readers – may have appropriate belief in Jesus and thereby enjoy the life made available on the basis of his death and resurrection" (p. 244).

[151] Motyer, *Your Father the Devil?*, p. 61. This is in contrast to the view of Ashton, *Understanding the Fourth Gospel*, p. 520, concerning 20:31: "it is hard not to see in this conclusion one last spark of the familiar Johannine irony, as the reader reflects how much more the fourth evangelist offers than a plain account of Jesus' deeds and how little such an account would do to elicit the kind of faith that interests him." The irony is that Ashton, with a sectarian-like "community" interpretation, has misunderstood what the FE specifically tried to make explicit.

[152] Okure, *Mission*, p. 1. See also Rudolf Bultmann, "Die Bedeutung der neuerschlossenen mandäischen und manichäischen Quellen für das Verständnis des Johannesevangeliums," *ZNW* 24 (1925), pp. 100–46, especially p. 102; Ernst Haenchen, "'Der Vater der mich gesandt hat,'" *NTS* 9 (1963), pp. 208–16; Werner Bieder, *Gottes Sendung und der missionarische Auftrag nach Matthäus, Lukas, Paulus und Johannes*, *ThStud* 82 (Zurich: EVZ-Verlag, 1965); James McPolin, "Mission in the Fourth Gospel," *ITQ* 36 (1969), pp. 113–22, especially p. 114; and more recently, Andreas J. Köstenberger, *The Missions of Jesus and The Disciples According to the Fourth Gospel: With Implications for the Fourth Gospel's Purpose and the Mission of the Contemporary Church* (Grand Rapids: Eerdmans, 1998).

Gospel,[153] as do concepts related to the motif of mission: "seeing" and "believing."[154] Even those who do not specifically emphasize the predominance of the mission motif in the FG do still recognize the centrality in the Gospel of Jesus' self-revelation and salvific work.[155] As Teresa Okure explains, "The absence of the word 'mission' perhaps explains the general reluctance of scholars to embrace the term when discussing the life and work of Jesus. Thus, the idea of 'sending' rather than of 'mission' dominates . . . important studies."[156] Yet if these various ideas of "sending" in John, and the rest of the NT, can be freely regarded as "mission," "there seems to be little justification for begrudging the same term to the idea of sending which permeates the Gospel and which applies to Jesus' sending by the Father."[157] For this reason, the mission leitmotif has become well accepted in Johannine scholarship.[158]

Even JComm interpreters have been forced to deal with the theme of mission in the FG. Generally "community" interpreters tend to gravitate toward one of three major options in their efforts to explain the "mission" material in the FG.[159] The first interpretive handling assumes that the JComm pursued a direct evangelistic purpose by addressing the FG to a Jewish synagogue with which the "community" was in conflict. W. C. van Unnik, for example, argued that the FG was written to missionize visitors to a Jewish-Hellenistic synagogue in the Diaspora, including both Jews and proselytes.[160] "In this way he pioneered the idea that the missionary life-setting for the Fourth Gospel was the controversy of the 'Johannine Community' with the synagogue."[161] This depiction of a missionizing JComm is rare. Although several have postulated that the FG is in some way a *Missionsschrift*,[162] rarely do modern JComm interpreters assume that the missionary effort would have included the entire "community."

---

[153] See Calvin Mercer, "APOSTELLEIN and PEMPEIN in John," *NTS* 36 (1990), pp. 619–24.

[154] Brown, *The Gospel According to John*, vol. I, pp. 497–518.

[155] See Raymond Brown, "The Kerygma of the Gospel According to John: The Johannine View of Jesus in Modern Studies," *Interpretation* 21 (1967), pp. 387–400.

[156] Okure, *Mission*, p. 1, n. 3.

[157] *Ibid.*, p. 2, n. 3. Cf. Martin Hengel, "Die Ursprunge der christliche Mission," *NTS* 18 (1971), pp. 15–38, especially pp. 35–37, who claims that if anyone deserves the term "*Urmissionar*" it is Jesus himself.

[158] For detailed surveys of the developing acceptance of the mission leitmotif in the FG see Okure, *Mission*, pp. 7–35; and Köstenberger, *Missions*, pp. 5–16.

[159] The following is taken from Köstenberger, *Missions*, pp. 205–06.

[160] W. C. van Unnik, "The Purpose of St. John's Gospel," in Kurt Aland *et al.* (eds.), *Studia Evangelica I*, TU 73 (Berlin: Akademie, 1959), pp. 382–411.

[161] Köstenberger, *Missions*, p. 202.

[162] See, for example, Karl Bornhäuser, *Das Johannesevangelium: Eine Missionsschrift für Israel*, BFCT 2/15 (Gütersloh: Bertelsmann, 1928); Wilhelm Oehler, *Das Johannesevangelium, eine Missionsschrift für die Welt, der Gemeinde ausgelegt* (Gütersloh: Bertelsmann, 1936); Oehler, *Zum Missionscharakter des Johannesevangeliums* (Gütersloh:

The second interpretive handling that deals with the JComm and the mission motif assumes that the FG may have been written by a group within the JComm that sought to stir up their fellow group members to greater faith and missionary zeal. Thus, while the FG's intent was not primarily evangelistic, "there is nevertheless a strong '*Missionsgedanke*' which reveals a dynamic within" the JComm, i.e. its inner discussion and struggle concerning its relationship to the surrounding world.[163] The unavoidable motif of mission in the FG has caused many to reconstruct the type and function of this *Missionsgedanke*. For these JComm interpreters the issue usually surrounds a later stage in the JComm's history and its eventual growth. As we discussed earlier, the JComm interpreters begin with the assumption that the narrative is to be read referentially as an allegory depicting the "community's" own history. Thus, the mission motif is taken as depicting a stage in the (diachronic) experience of the JComm. For example, Raymond Brown and Martin Hengel argue that the JComm eventually included those outside of Judaism. For Brown the Samaritan woman pericope in John 4 reveals a time in the JComm's history when numerous Samaritans joined the "community." A lengthy comment by Brown is helpful here:

> An opening [mission?] toward the Gentiles (with or without a geographic move) and the need to interpret Johannine thought to them involved much more than the occasional parenthetical note explaining Hebrew or Greek terms. It would have been necessary to adapt Johannine language so that it could appeal more widely . . . It need not have been a case of John's borrowing from the other literature (or vice versa); rather, *there may have been a Johannine attempt to make Jesus intelligible to another culture.*[164]

Brown relies on various source-critical proposals to make sense of the various stages of the JComm's experience.[165] A similar approach is made by

Bertelsmann, 1941); Oehler, *Das Johannesevangelium, eine Missionsschrift für die Welt,* 3 vols. (Württemberg: Buchhandlung der Evangelischen Missionsschule Unterweissach, 1957); Albrecht Oepke, "Das missionarische Christuszeugnis des Johannesevangeliums," *EMZ* 2 (1941), pp. 4–26.

[163] Köstenberger, *Missions,* p. 206.

[164] Brown, *The Community of the Beloved Disciple,* p. 57 (emphasis added). Brown refers to George W. MacRae, "The Fourth Gospel and Religionsgeschichte," *CBQ* 32 (1970), pp. 13–24, who argues that John may have been uniquely universalist in presenting Jesus in a multitude of symbolic garbs, appealing to men and women of all backgrounds, so that they understood that Jesus transcends all ideologies.

[165] Brown cites approvingly of a comment by Stephen Smalley, *John: Evangelist and Interpreter* (Exeter: Paternoster, 1978), p. 67: "The Hellenistic features of the Fourth Gospel tell us more about its final audience than about the background of its author or its tradition."

Martin Hengel. For Hengel the predominantly Gentile-Christian character of the Johannine "school" implies that the FE "had long since departed
company with the synagogue. The 'expulsion' lies quite far in the past
and was not dependent on one historical act of excommunication or upon
the specific decision of an alleged Jewish 'synod' in Palestinian Jamnia."[166] In fact, Hengel argues that the Gospel was not even meant for
Jewish-Christians at all; the Gospel, i.e. the "school," has the mission to
the Gentiles in view.[167] Yet Hengel is quick to mention that the FG is not
a missionary writing. "It was hardly suitable as an 'advertising brochure'
for unbelievers or a *protreptikos* for catechumens . . . Matthew was more
useful for this purpose and was therefore also more successful in the
church from the start. By contrast John sought to give 'solid food'. . ."[168]
Thus, Brown and Hengel are representatives of many who take the FG's
mission motif as depicting a later stage in its development.[169]

   Another example of a JComm interpreter attempting to reconstruct the
type and function of this *Missionsgedanke* within the "community's" history is J. L. Martyn. In contrast to Brown and Hengel, Martyn argues that a
Gentile mission did not replace an earlier Jewish one.[170] Martyn criticizes
both Brown and Hengel for too easily placing the JComm alongside "the
emerging Great Church" rather than more appropriately viewing it as of
a different "stream."[171] The Gospel certainly does have a mission motif,
but its function was not for Gentiles but for "Jewish Christians belonging
to conventicles known but separate from the Johannine community."[172]
For Martyn the "other sheep" are other Jewish-Christians who have also
been expelled from the synagogue but have not been fully joined to the
JComm. The FG's mission motif is wholly devoted to them, not to some
external entity beyond the "group," and certainly not to the entire "world"
(4:42).

   Two final examples of JComm interpreters attempting to reconstruct
the type and function of this *Missionsgedanke* within the "community's"
history are Takashi Onuki and David Rensberger. In contrast to Brown and
Hengel's Gentile, more universal hypothesis, and Martyn's Jewish, more
sectarian hypothesis, Onuki takes a more mediating position and argues

---

[166] Hengel, *The Johannine Question*, p. 119.
[167] *Ibid.*, p. 121.   [168] *Ibid.*
[169] John Bowman, "The Fourth Gospel and the Samaritans," *BJRL* 40 (1958), pp. 298–
308; Edwin D. Freed, "Samaritan Influence in the Gospel of John," *CBQ* 30 (1968), pp. 580–
87; Freed, "Did John Write His Gospel Partly to Win Samaritan Converts?," *NovT* 12 (1970),
pp. 241–56.
[170] J. Louis Martyn, "A Gentile Mission That Replaced an Earlier Jewish Mission?," in
R. Alan Culpepper and C. Clifton Black (eds.), *Exploring the Gospel of John: In Honor of
D. Moody Smith* (Louisville: Westminster John Knox Press, 1996), pp. 124–44.
[171] *Ibid.*, p. 135.   [172] Martyn, "Glimpses," p. 164.

that the FG's mission motif serves a more internal purpose rather than external emphasis.[173] This is different from Meeks, an interpreter who belongs in the third category of interpretive handling, who argues that the FG's mission motif provides "a reinforcement for the community's social identity."[174] For Meeks such a concern is completely internal; but for Onuki the concern is also external. While Onuki argues that the FG is not a missionary tractate, it is not a sectarian tractate either. The community is not closed to the world surrounding it. Recovering from its initial trauma with "the Jews," it prepares to reach out to its neighbors once again.[175] Rensberger agrees with Onuki and argues that "Johannine Christianity is not a pure example of introversionism."[176] Acknowledging that there is a mission motif in John, Rensberger argues that "the function of the Fourth Gospel, then, is to enable the community to step back from its situation of rejection, reflect upon it in the light of the fate of Jesus, and to be sent out again with its faith renewed."[177] Thus, the "community" is not only distanced from the world, but is also confirmed in its identity and in the possibility of salvation for the people in the world. This second interpretive handling of the mission motif in John is rooted in various reconstructions of the "community" and its history.

The third interpretive handling that deals with the JComm and the mission motif assumes that since the FG was written by and for a "community" the mission is insignificant or absent from the book. Some of these JComm interpreters view the "community" as sectarian and thus completely uninterested in any external entity. This is represented best by Wayne Meeks. For Meeks, the FG "could hardly be regarded as a missionary tractate, for we may imagine that only a very rare outsider would get past the barrier of its closed metaphorical system. It is a book for insiders . . ."[178] A book for insiders has no need for a mission motif, nor could a mission motif exist. As K. G. Kuhn explains, "Johannesevangelium und – briefe zeigen uns eine Gemeinde, die im Grunde gar nicht missionarisch denkt. Diese Gemeinde weiß sich streng geschieden von der Welt, ausgegrenzt aus ihr, im Gegensatz zu ihr stehend . . . darum gibt es hier auch keine eigentliche Mission im Sinn des werbenden Gewinnens

---

[173] Tanashi Onuki, *Gemeinde und Welt im Johannesevangelium: "Ein Beitrag zur Frage nach der theologischen und pragmatischen Funktion des johanneischen "Dualismus,"* WMANT 56 (Neukirchen-Vluyn: Neukirchener, 1984).

[174] Meeks, "The Man From Heaven in Johannine Sectarianism," p. 70.

[175] Onuki, *Gemeinde und Welt im Johannesevangelium*, pp. 85–93.

[176] Rensberger, *Johannine Faith and Liberating Community*, p. 140.

[177] *Ibid.*, p. 144.

[178] Meeks, "The Man From Heaven in Johannine Sectarianism," p. 70.

neuer Gläubiger."[179] In this third interpretive handling the sectarian reconstruction of the JComm removes any possibility that a mission motif could be at work in the Gospel.

Although there are other slight variations concerning the Gospel document and the mission motif,[180] in general most JComm interpretations of the mission motif are located in one of these three interpretive handlings. Unfortunately, as this book has already argued, the "community" paradigm has become totalizing and has corrupted a fresh reading of the narrative data. As interpreters we have been reading for the "community" instead of rereading the narrative data. If the mission motif is a dominant characteristic in the FG, one that controls its theological and Christological emphases as well as its rhetorical invitation to the reader, then it becomes an excellent test case for determining the implied audience. If any of the three "community" interpretations are correct, one would expect to find evidence of an internal function for the mission motif; one which was controlled by the "community." But if the audience does not control the *Missionsgedanke* but is invited toward it, one would be forced to assume a more external function. Therefore, using the mission motif as a test case we will examine various pericopae in the FG where the mission motif is present, connect them to the Gospel's overall mission leitmotif, and attempt to show how such a theme reveals an indefinite audience and a general rhetorical invitation.

"Those who are sent": a Christology of mission

Many approach the mission theme without reference to the JComm, usually in theologies of the NT. We may call this the theological-Christological approach. Discussion here centers upon two major issues

---

[179] Karl Gustav Kuhn, "Das Problem der Mission in der Urchristenheit," *EMZ* 11 (1954), pp. 167–68. Quoted in Werner Bieder, *"Gottes Sendung und der missionarische Auftrag der Kirche nach Matthäus, Lukas, Paulus, und Johannes,"* ThStud 82 (Zurich: EVZ, 1965), p. 41.

[180] For example, Johannine source critics argue that a signs-source was initially used as a missionary document, designed to win variously assumed target audiences, but that the FG in its final form was intended to serve the needs of the JComm. Cf. Wilhelm Wilkins, *Zeichen und Werke. Ein Beitrag zur Theologie des 4. Evangeliums in Erzählungs- und Redestoff,* ATANT 55 (Zurich: Zwingli, 1969); Robert T. Fortna, *The Gospel of Signs: A Reconstruction of the Narrative Source Underlying the Fourth Gospel* (Cambridge; Cambridge University Press, 1970); and Willem Nicol, *The Semeia in the Fourth Gospel: Tradition and Redaction,* NovTSup 32 (Leiden: Brill, 1972). Another example is the theological-Christological approach, which we will discuss below, that looks at the important "sending" motifs in the Gospel but does not place it in the Gospel's rhetorical context. Cf. Okure, *Mission,* pp. 23–28.

within the Johannine narrative: the role of the Father in the missionary enterprise (theological) and the different aspects and meaning of the mission of the Son (Christological).[181] Our discussion of this approach is not to develop it within the Johannine narrative, but to show how "community" interpretations have skewed this aspect of the narrative's plot in the reconstruction of the FG's social-historical context.

As Okure explains, "The discussion on the role of the Father in the missionary enterprise takes its point of departure from 3:16."[182] The Father's sending of the Son shows his supreme love for humanity. In brief, the Father is the origin and goal of the missionary enterprise, the unsent sender of the Son.[183] As McPolin explains, the Father is "the mission center, the source from which all missions derive."[184] It is in this sense that we may speak of the Father as the "sender" and the Son as the "sent one."[185] The "sent one" is to bring glory to the one who sent him (7:18). He is not to do his own will but the will of the sender, to do his works and to speak his words, and to be accountable to the sender (4:34; 5:19–20, 36; 9:4). The "sent one" has the responsibility of representing his sender (5:19–23; 12:44–45; 13:20; 14:9b). This unique relationship between the Father and the Son, the "sender" and the "sent one," is duplicated later between Jesus and his disciples. But before we turn to that relationship it is important to focus specifically on the "sent one" *par excellence*. The mission of the Son is not separate from the Father, but is incorporated into this broader relational context. But the Gospel focuses on the mission of the Son over all others. As Okure explains, "In relation to the other missions mentioned in the Gospel, Jesus' mission is seen as central and normative. All the other missions derive from and are in function of his . . ."[186] In brief, Köstenberger argues that "Jesus is shown in the Fourth Gospel to possess divine as well as human . . . characteristics that qualify him for a unique mission."[187] According to Köstenberger, the FG provides three portraits of Jesus not only to present Jesus as the Messiah, but to define what kind of Messiah he is. First, Jesus is presented as the "sent son." Within the framework of Johannine teaching on mission, the sending of the Son seems to represent the element focusing on the "human" side of Jesus' mission, i.e. the aspects of obedience and dependence of the

---

[181] Okure, *Mission*, p. 23.   [182] *Ibid.*

[183] *Ibid.* See also Paul Feine, *Theologie des Neuen Testaments*, 21st edn (Berlin: Evangelische Verlagsanstalt, 1953), pp. 312–16.

[184] McPolin, "Mission in the Fourth Gospel," pp. 114, 121.

[185] The following is taken from Köstenberger, *Missions*, pp. 107–11.

[186] Okure, *Mission*, p. 24.

[187] Köstenberger, *Missions*, p. 46. Köstenberger offers the most comprehensive summary of the FG's depiction of the mission of Jesus (pp. 45–140).

sent one on his sender.[188] Second, Jesus is presented as the coming and returning one (descending-ascending one). In cooperating contrast with the first portrait of Jesus, the idea of the coming and returning one seems to represent the element focusing on the "divine" side of Jesus' mission. "He is not just a human figure but is heaven-sent."[189] Third, Jesus is presented as the eschatological shepherd-teacher. The emphasis here is not so much on Jesus' teaching as such, but on his "launching of the reaping of the eschatological Messianic harvest."[190] Therefore, "The function of the mission theme in the Fourth Gospel with reference to Jesus thus appears to be that of providing a multifaceted comprehensive portrayal of the person and mission of the Messiah for the purpose of leading others to believe."[191] Yet the portrayal is not completely evangelistic in the sense of being useful for non-believers only. For, as Köstenberger points out, one may view the FG as consisting of two different but related parts: chapters 1–12 present the mission of the earthly Jesus, whereas chapters 13–21 portray the mission of the exalted Jesus.[192] It is this latter part which so helpfully engages those who already believe.

What is most interesting concerning the theological-Christological approach is how the mission it presents includes the disciples of the "sent one." The Gospel makes certain that Jesus' mission is central. Every other mission is derivative of his. Nevertheless, "John makes clear that Jesus' mission, while pre-eminent, was not to stand alone; it was to be

---

[188] *Ibid.*, p. 121.

[189] *Ibid.*, p. 139. The question of appropriate theological or sociological categories is important here. According to Meeks, "The Man From Heaven in Johannine Sectarianism," pp. 46–47, John's "mythological" language tends to be reduced by interpreters to theological categories, upon which various historical judgments are then made "on the basis of the presumed logical priority of one or the other of these categories." But Meeks must first assume that John's language is mythological. The mythological language assumption is based on the earlier and influential work of Bultmann, "Die Bedeutung der neuerschlossenen mandäischen und manichäischen Quellen für das Verständnis des Johannesevangeliums," *ZNW* 24 (1925), pp. 100–44, and Leroy, *Rätsel und Missverständnis*, who argued that John's language was a "special language, one that was expressed in several "riddles." This has been argued more recently by Malina, "John's: The Maverick Christian Group: The Evidence of Sociolinguistics." But as we argued in chapter 2, there are several problems with the assumption that John is speaking a "special language." As Motyer, *Your Father the Devil?*, p. 71, argues, "Our growth in knowledge of Judaism in this period seriously undermines the view that John employs a private language comprehensible only within closed Christian circles." We showed a similar conclusion in our search for the implied reader in chapter 4. As Köstenberger, *Missions*, p. 123, explains, Meeks mistakenly treats the descending-ascending of Jesus in a reductionistic manner. Not only has Meeks failed to provide sufficient integration between the various elements within this aspect of the FG's teaching on mission, but he has drawn an inappropriate inference from the concept to a putative social-historical background. Cf. Okure, *Mission*, p. 206.

[190] Köstenberger, *Missions*, p. 130.   [191] *Ibid.*, p. 139.   [192] *Ibid.*, p. 140.

continued in the mission of his followers."[193] As we have already discussed, recent Johannine scholarship has increasingly viewed the FG's disciples as representing the JComm. Within this framework the disciples in the FG become vehicles of the history of the JComm. John's representation of the disciples is viewed as an expression of the JComm's self-understanding in the light of its faith in Jesus. Such a reading of the Gospel is mistaken. In the Gospel narrative the "disciples" are broadened to include a wider readership, as the mission motif makes clear. But before we examine this readership, a brief discussion of the disciples' role in the Johannine mission motif is in order.

The mission of the disciples is an extension of the mission of Jesus. "The Fourth Gospel describes the mission of the disciples in terms of 'harvesting' (4:38), 'fruitbearing' (15:8, 16), and 'witnessing' (15:27). All of these terms place the disciples in the humble position of extending the mission of Jesus."[194] The task of the disciples is clearly different from the task of Jesus. Jesus did signs, the disciples do not. Schnackenburg explains it well:

> Thus the later heralds of the faith can only recount, attest and recall the revelation given by Jesus in "signs" (and words), which becomes thereby "present" in their own day. It is presupposed implicitly that he who once wrought these "signs" on earth . . . still effects the salvation of believers. But his revelation, as a historical and eschatological event, is closed, and it only remains to explain it further, disclose its riches and explicate its full truth.[195]

Not only does the FG never assign "signs" to the disciples, it "takes pains not to rival Jesus' role. . ."[196] This supports our critique of Martyn above where he claims the FG "doubles" Jesus and a later "disciple" in the JComm. Interestingly, the disciples of Jesus are not merely "sent" to participate in his mission, but are encouraged to continue to "follow" him. The FG continually employs a dialectic concerning the disciples: those who follow are sent, those who are sent follow.[197] Just as Jesus

---

[193] *Ibid.*, p. 141.

[194] *Ibid.* Köstenberger offers the most comprehensive summary of the FG's depiction of the mission of the disciples (pp. 141–98).

[195] Schnackenburg, *The Gospel According to St. John*, vol. I, p. 524.

[196] Köstenberger, *Missions*, p. 170. The "greater works" in 14:16 are no exception to the difference in role.

[197] *Ibid.*, p. 177. As Köstenberger explains: "The Fourth Gospel does not dichotomize between 'discipleship' on the one hand and . . . 'missions' on the other. Those who follow Jesus closely are at the end commissioned to be sent into the world. . . a person's 'discipleship' *includes* and *entails* that person's mission to the world" (p. 177).

was sent by the Father, so also are the disciples sent by Jesus, as 20:21 makes clear. Brown's explanation of the force of καθώς in 20:21 is helpful here:

> The special Johannine contribution to the theology of this mission is that the Father's sending of the Son serves as the model and the ground for the Son's sending of the disciples. Their mission is to continue the Son's mission; and this requires that the Son must be present to them during this mission, just as the Father had to be present to the Son during his mission.[198]

Brown's explanation implies that the disciples are not just to represent Jesus, but to re-present him.[199] Never is their work solely their work, nor are they ever the subject of their work; the focus of those who are sent remains on the "sent one" *par excellence*. Thus, the FG explicates an important role of both discipleship and mission to the disciples.

But who are these "disciples?" Are they representative of the JComm? We have already discussed how John is aware of a difference in time between his era and that of Jesus. This, of course, relates to our discussion above of representative figures. Our goal here is not to discuss referentiality again but to see if the Gospel widens its portrayal of "disciples" within the mission motif. The evidence suggests that it does. A lengthy quote from Brown is relevant:

> The characteristically Johannine outlook does not demote the Twelve, but rather turns these chosen disciples into *representatives of all the Christians* who would believe in Jesus on their word. And so, sometimes it is difficult to know when John is speaking of the disciples in their historical role as the intimate companions of Jesus and when he is speaking of them in their symbolic role . . . Seemingly in the Last Supper scene the disciples who are addressed are chiefly the Twelve; yet through most of the Last Discourse Jesus is not speaking only to those envisaged as present but also *to the much wider audience whom they represent*.[200]

Here Brown is noticing the rhetorical invitation the narrative presents. Such a maneuver by the FE allows him to transition from the disciples

---

[198] Brown, *The Gospel According to John*, vol. II, p. 1036.
[199] Köstenberger, *Missions*, p. 191.
[200] Brown, *The Gospel According to John*, vol. II, p. 1034 (emphasis added). But Brown significantly exaggerates the historical significance of the disciples. Cf. 15:27.

of the earthly Jesus to later believers, whoever they might be – for one function of the Gospel is the creation of new believers. Such a literary tactic is evidenced by the FG's frequent use of corporate metaphors like flock and branches.[201] Therefore, the FE appears to show a concern with both the disciples' historical role and their representative or paradigmatic function for later believers. According to the FG, "discipleship is at least potentially extended . . . to include anyone who believes in Jesus, regardless of that person's race, ethnic origin, or gender. Samaritans, Jews, and Greeks, women and men alike are to be disciples of the Messiah."[202]

The social-historical context of the mission motif

If Jesus' mission was to be continued in the mission of his followers and if these "followers" were broadened by the narrative to include a wider readership of "disciples" within the FG's mission motif, then we can begin to reconstruct the social-historical context for John's audience; a context not dominated with "community" concerns. Since we cannot be comprehensive we will examine the mission motif in three areas: the "other sheep" (10:16), the "world," and "those who believe in me through their word" (17:20). Our task will be to locate them in the readership context that the first four chapters of this book have already defined. Our goal is to provide a needed social-historical context in which to place the FG's mission motif; something which the "community" interpretations have been unable to accomplish. By listening to the voice of invitation from within the confines of a "community" and its history, these interpretations have silenced the Gospel's rhetorical strategy; a strategy intimately linked to the mission motif.

"Other sheep"

Most pertinent here is the question: who are the "other sheep?" For Martyn, the answer is simple: "The sheep stand in the first instance for the Johannine community."[203] As we discussed above concerning representative figures, Martyn's conclusion is rooted in his assumption of the referential nature of the Johannine characters. Martyn argues against most

---

[201] Köstenberger, *Missions*, pp. 161–67.
[202] *Ibid.*, p. 169.   [203] Martyn, "Glimpses," p. 163.

commentators[204] by claiming that the "other sheep" are not Gentiles.[205] Rather, "the other sheep are Jewish Christians belonging to conventicles known but separate from the Johannine community."[206] Martyn finds clues to such meaning in the latter part of 10:16: "I must bring [gather] them also, and they will listen to my voice. So there will be one flock, one shepherd." For Martyn, this emphasis on unification and gathering implies that some members *known* to the FE have been scattered. Martyn links 10:16 with 11:52, where Caiaphas' ironic prophecy is told: "to gather into one the dispersed children of God," in order to show that the elements are thoroughly Jewish and not Gentile. In this way Martyn is able to maintain the importance of the *Birkat ha-Minim* for his interpretation of John. Thus, 10:16 helps Martyn explain how the "expulsions" were "in fact introduced over a wide geographic area."[207] Thus, Martyn's answer to the meaning of 10:16 is the following: "It is, then, a vision of the Johannine community that the day will come when all of the conventicles of scattered [Johannine] Jewish Christians will be gathered into one flock under the one Good Shepherd."[208]

But there are several problems with Martyn's proposal that lead us to our proposed reading of 10:16.[209] First, Martyn forces too strong a dichotomy between the "Jewish elements" and universality. Martyn would be hard pressed to find a reading of the OT that does not incorporate the world beyond Israel or the Jews. Was it not the prophet Jeremiah who proclaimed that "all the nations shall gather" to Jerusalem, to the presence of the Lord that resides there (3:17)?[210] Second, the entire debate between Martyn and the other commentators over the Jewish or Gentile nature of 10:16 is misleading from the beginning; the combination of Jewish and Gentile mission motifs in the FG is not accidental. This returns us to

---

[204] See, for example, Raymond E. Brown, "'Other Sheep Not of This Fold': The Johannine Perspective on Christian Diversity in the Late First Century," *JBL* 97 (1978), pp. 5–22; Brown, *The Community of the Beloved Disciple*, p. 90; Brown, *The Gospel According to John*, vol. I, pp. 396–98; Barrett, *The Gospel According to St. John*, p. 376; Bultmann, *The Gospel of John*, pp. 383–84; Carson, *The Gospel According to John*, p. 388.

[205] Of course, even these other commentators often link it to a later Gentile mission of the JComm, not mission in the sense we are investigating. For a more detailed argument against a Gentile mission see Martyn, "A Gentile Mission That Replaced an Earlier Jewish Mission?" for a more detailed discussion of the debate between JComm interpreters.

[206] Martyn, "Glimpses," 164.   [207] *Ibid.*, p. 166.   [208] *Ibid.*

[209] It is not just Martyn's proposal that is problematic, but Martyn represents the most extreme case.

[210] On "the nations" in OT prophecy and Jewish literature see Keith Nigel Grüneberg, *Abraham, Blessing, and the Nations: A Philological and Exegetical Study of Genesis 12:3 in its Narrative Context*, BZATW 332 (Berlin: Walter de Gruyter, 2003).

the difficulty "community" interpreters have in dealing with the mission motif apparent in all parts of the FG. Martyn is forced to conclude that the FG is a history book of not only the JComm, but even "a chapter in the history of *Jewish* Christianity."[211] By focusing entirely on the JComm, Martyn and other "community" interpreters have mistakenly turned the Gospel on its head. As we discussed in chapter 4, far from being a diachronic presentation of one audience's history, the Gospel is more synchronic; it portrays several different types of expected audience members simultaneously. The FE was well aware that different types and levels of readers would be the readership of his Gospel. Third, by assuming that 10:16 is a "vision" of what will come, Martyn has nearly aligned himself the relational definition of "community" we presented in chapter 2. For Martyn 10:16 is a symbolically constructed "group," not a real one. If the FE and his readers can conceptualize that such a group will exist in the future, then certainly they can conceptualize themselves as part of something bigger than their own geographic "church" in the present. Unknowingly, Martyn has argued against the definition of "community" required for his reading of the FG.

When the FG is read as a "community" document the mission motif is confusing, often seen to be contradictory, and completely misunderstood. Martyn's reconstruction, for example, requires a highly complex and detailed referential component that requires more imagination than external data. Nothing in the narrative locates the "other sheep" in 10:16 to a specific "group" known to the reading audience. No narrative direction or clues are given to its referent. The reason is clear: the referent, those who were to become the "sheep," were still unknown. It was yet to be seen who would hear the voice of the Good Shepherd. The FG is a witness to the voice of the Shepherd.

The "world" in the fourth Gospel

If John depicts a mission that is broad enough to incorporate "others" who are yet to be known, how wide is the mission field? Okure explains it best:

> Though historically Jesus exercised his mission in Palestine, the scope of this mission is the whole world (1:9, 10a; 3:16–17; 16:28), and its destined audience, "all flesh" (17:2; cf. 12:32) . . . As Jesus' immediate audience in Galilee (1:29–2:12; 4:44–54;

---

[211] Martyn, "Glimpses," p. 167.

6:1–7:9; 21), Jerusalem (2:13–3:21; 5; 7:10–10:39; 11:55–57; 12:12–20:31), Judea (3:22–36; 11:1–54; 12:1–11) and Samaria (4:4–42) were challenged to respond to him, so are all peoples of the world challenged to make the same faith response to the same mission of Jesus . . . Whether personally proclaimed by him or reported later by his disciples . . .[212]

Yet it is here that "community" interpreters have gone awry. Older descriptions of Johannine dualism[213] combined with more recent sociological assumptions of a sectarian-like "community" have led to the reconstruction of an introspective "group" which views itself in isolation from this "world." We discussed this in relation to Malina's theory of Johannine antilanguage in chapter 2.[214]

More recent Johannine research, especially but not only those not dominated by the "community" approach, has advocated the more complex relational nature of "world." Rather than being a specific referent for the readers or their "group," it is argued that according to the FG the "world" is the place or realm where God is at work; the place that is the main focus of God's attention.[215] Rensberger alludes to it as a "dimension of encounter" between God and man.[216] Köstenberger describes it as "a dark place that is alienated from God but nevertheless remains an object of his love."[217] But maybe the best description is given by Keener: "The world is thus the arena of the light's salvific invasion of darkness . . . 'the lost' that Jesus came to seek and to save."[218] The language of evil that pervades the FG's depiction of the "world" does not classify it in a completely negative sense, although those who remain in the darkness remain negative, for out of this same "dark world" are those who Jesus came to save.[219] Thus, our proposed reading of the "world" in John is moved away from those that see the building of sociological walls between the readers and those outside, but rather a reading that invites those who are outside to come in. To not do so is the decision (to not "believe") of the potential reader and, if chosen wrongly, their own condemnation. A few examples of this reading will make this clear.

---

[212] Okure, *Mission*, p. 198.

[213] Due in no small part to the influence of Bultmann, *Theology of the New Testament*, vol. II, p. 21.

[214] See, for example, Ashton, *Understanding the Fourth Gospel*, pp. 206–08, who reads the term as dualistic opposition.

[215] Davies, *Rhetoric and Reference in the Fourth Gospel*, p. 155. Lincoln, *Truth on Trial*, p. 260, similarly describes this realm as "cosmic."

[216] Rensberger, *Johannine Faith and Liberating Community*, p. 137.

[217] Köstenberger, *Missions*, p. 187.   [218] Keener, *The Gospel of John*, p. 329.

[219] See Brown, *The Gospel According to John*, vol. I, p. 509.

Beginning with the prologue we find the Gospel's invitation to those in the "world." In fact, the beginning of the prologue sets the whole Gospel in an emphatically cosmic context. In 1:9–14 the FE describes how the light came into the world, but the world "did not know" or "receive" this light, even though its own origin is connected to the light. But 1:9–11 is immediately followed by an invitation to the reader – an invitation to belief (vv. 12–13). Brown argues that vv. 12–13 describe the "community's share" in the light that came into the world; but such a reading is mistaken.[220] 1:12–13 are a testimony to belief in this light, the Word; a belief that becomes the goal of the entire Gospel (20:31).[221] Here the prologue surveys the function of the Gospel: a witness to the "world" about Jesus for the purpose of belief.

Jesus' conversation with the Samaritan woman provides another interesting case of the use of "world" in the FG. After many of the Samaritan people believed in Jesus, they came to the Samaritan woman and said: "It is no longer because of what you said that we believe, for we have heard for ourselves, and we know that this is truly the Savior of the world" (4:42). The tendency of commentators has been either to locate the Samaritan meaning of the phrase "savior of the world" or to locate this "Samaritan influence" brought into the JComm.[222] For Brown, the influx of some Samaritan converts brought with it a higher Christology that had a more universal outlook, of which the phrase "savior of the world" in 4:42 is primary evidence. But the more relationally complex understanding of "world" that we have already discussed allows 4:42 to fit well with the rest of the FG. That is, only when the FG is given a "community" interpretation does 4:42 seem out of place. For example, is 1:9, which speaks of the true light which enlightens "every man," any less universal than 4:42? If the "light" in 1:9 is similar or identical to the "light of the world" in 8:12, is it then any different for Jesus to also be the "Savior of the world?" In both cases the phrases take on a cosmic scope. It expresses, in the words of Josef Blank, "the universal saving significance of the person of Jesus."[223] Certainly the tone of the term "savior" is different from "light" (8:12; 9:5), "lamb" (1:29), or "bread" (6:33), but they are all related in their rhetorical invitation, even if a different market niche is in view. In reference to the Samaritan "savior of the world" Dodd explains:

[220] *Ibid.*, p. 30.   [221] See Lincoln, *Truth on Trial*, pp. 47, 198–99.

[222] See especially Brown, *The Community of the Beloved Disciple*, pp. 34–58.

[223] Josef Blank, *Krisis: Untersuchungen zur johanneischen Christologie und Eschatologie* (Freiburg: Lambertus, 1964), p. 184.

in the Hellenistic world it [savior] was a very common attribute of pagan gods (and of emperors),[224] and it seems likely that it was in Hellenistic Christian circles that it gained currency. The evangelist may even have been conscious of a certain dramatic propriety in putting it in the mouth of Samaritans, who in this gospel represent in some sort the Gentile world over against the Jews.[225]

The phrase looses its awkwardness when it is allowed to serve as a witness to the reader who may be Gentile (or specifically Samaritan); a reader who is told of the one "who is truly the savior of the world" (4:42).[226]

Finally, a good pericope that defines the relational aspect of the "world," one that broadens its referent, is in Jesus' discussion of the world's hatred in 15:18–27. Our reading sees this discussion as referring to the cosmic realm in which the relations between God and man exist; a realm in which Jesus and his followers alone take part. In vv. 18–19 the term "world" is used six times: "If the *world* hates you, be aware that it hated me before it hated you. If you belonged to the *world*, the *world* would love you as its own. Because you do not belong to the *world*, but I have chosen you out of the *world* – therefore the *world* hates you." 15:18 makes clear that the central issue of conflict is Jesus; he faced it and his followers will experience it also. But it is in v. 19 that we are given a helpful description of the referent of those "in the world" and those "out of the world." If Jesus' followers (i.e. the readers of the FG) were of the world, the world would love them (v. 19a). But the world does not love them because they are not of the world (v. 19b). Why? Because Jesus chose them out of the world! Interestingly, this implies that they were at one time part of the world. There is no fortified dualism between "us" and "them"; just a description of the cosmic realm, the revelation and judgment that has come to it, and decision to be made in that realm by the reader. The rest of the pericope (vv. 20–27) focuses on the revelation and judgment motif so common in the Gospel.[227]

---

[224] Cf. Sjef van Tilborg, *Reading John in Ephesus*, NovTSup 83 (Leiden: Brill, 1996), pp. 56–57.

[225] Dodd, *The Interpretation of the Fourth Gospel*, p. 239.

[226] As Okure, *Mission*, p. 176, explains, "John 4:22 and the Gospel as a whole provide sufficient grounds for the use of the title."

[227] See the similar description by Beasley-Murray, *John*, p. 161, and Bultmann, *The Gospel of John*, p. 549. Interesting here is v. 22 which is thematically identical to 9:39–41 where this same revelation/judgment motif is introduced to the Pharisees after the healing of the man born blind. This same motif is emphasized following the Nicodemus narrative (3:16–21). See Okure, *Mission*, p. 125, n. 98.

For John the "world" is not a value system that the sectarian-like JComm needed to reject, for they are still connected to the world and come from it (15:19). At the same time, the "world" is not a specific and localized "group," like the Jews (Malina/Rohrbaugh) or, in a progressive way, Gentiles (Brown), for the term is more relationally complex than such referents allows. Rather, the FG's personification of the "world" creates a *class of people*. Johannine usage of the "world" is too broad to be classified as belonging to one specific "group," let alone one localized "group." The "world" to which the Son has come, and to which his disciples have been sent, is the realm of decision; a realm of decision that has cosmic results. The FG appeals to its readers, those who are participants in this "world," to make a correct alliance.

In this sense, the FG creates and divides its readers into two classes of people. But this dualism of belief is not between one "group" and those outside. Rather, it involves potentially all who enter into the belief outlined by the FG. As we discussed in chapter 2, this concept has potential for assisting our understanding of the identity formation of early Christians. According to Judith Lieu, the identity of Christians as a "third race" was confirmed by the use of the term "the world." As Lieu explains:

> Although it has its roots in the Jewish eschatological contrast between "this world" and "the world to come," this opposition to "the world" is characteristically, although not exclusively, Christian. Within the NT it is most developed in the Johannine literature where it has often been dubbed "sectarian," yet in principle it may become a fundamental organizing point for Christian self-identity, capable of multiple expressions. This is the language of internal identity-formation, not of external visible perception.[228]

In this way our reading proposal facilitates an understanding of the internal perception of the "us" and the "them"; an understanding that depicts an invitation for the "them," or those in the "world," to become one of "us." For as the Johannine Jesus declares: "And I, When I am lifted up from the earth, will draw all people to myself" (12:32).

---

[228] Lieu, *Neither Jew Nor Greek?*, p. 188. Cf. Vincent L. Wimbush, "'... Not of this World...' Early Christianities as Rhetorical and Social Formation," in Elizabeth A. Castelli and Hal Taussig (eds.), *Reimagining Christian Origins: A Colloquium Honoring Burton Mack* (Valley Forge, Pa.: Trinity Press International, 1996), pp. 23–36.

"Those who believe in me through their word"

The prayer of Jesus in John 17 provides an interesting few verses concerning the mission motif. After praying for their protection and sanctity in the truth as he sends his disciples into the world (vv. 18–19), the cosmic realm where the decision of belief is to be made, Jesus continues, "I ask not only on behalf of these, but also on behalf of those who will believe in me through their word" (v. 20). The Gospel connects Jesus' prayer with its own goal: that its readers may believe. No limit is placed on those who are to believe, no "group" distinction; in fact, there is a smooth transition between the disciples who believed and those who would believe after them. As Jesus continues in v. 21, the goal is for unity, for them all to be one. A unity wrapped into the unity of the Father and Son, for whom the world, both present and future believers, are in gratitude.

A similar view to future believers within the mission motif is vocalized in Jesus' conversation with Thomas in 20:24–29. Jesus uses Thomas' "belief by sight" as an example for those who believe but will not see. Those who believe without seeing are blessed (v. 29). As Brown comments, "The blessing is probably *intended for all Christians* other than eye-witnesses, not for those only who were able to believe without signs and wonders."[229] 20:24–29 is a fitting final "Jesus conversation" before the stated purpose of the Gospel. This confession is the climactic Christological confession in the Gospel. Readers who have reached this point in the narrative are now able to join with Thomas. The FG, then, is a witness to those who have not seen with their own eyes; they are blessed if they trust in its witness and believe.

Finally, the directive from Jesus to Peter to "feed my sheep" is certainly meant to locate future Christians in the trajectory of the divine mission. As we will discuss below, the FG's depiction of Peter is not polemical. In the case of future Christians, the FG depicts Peter as central in the experience of those who will believe. Such a move not only assumes a connection between Peter and the readers of the FG, at least those who come to believe, but it also transitions the readers from the leadership of Jesus to the leadership in the early Christian movement. Too much attention has been on this passage's depiction of Peter and his pastoral rehabilitation; future believers are also in view.

For example, the 153 fish in the first pericope of John's epilogue, though viewed by many as enigmatic in its exact detail, most certainly reflects

---

[229] Brown, *The Gospel According to John*, vol. II, p. 574 (emphasis added).

the FG's desire "to symbolize the breadth or even the universality of the Christian mission."[230] Schnackenburg explains the symbolism well:

> the quantity of fish is justification for the supposition that the [FE] saw in it a symbol of universality. That lies within the "ecclesiastical" perspective of the whole chapter, but also finds support in Jn 1–20. The picture of the flock in 21:15–17 directs our attention back to 10:16, where, likewise, mission and church unity are thought of together . . . The net in which the fish are *gathered* can even illustrate well the idea of 11:52 (gathering of God's scattered children).[231]

These various verses make clear that the Gospel envisioned an indefinite incorporation of future believers.

Conclusion

The mission motif in the FG has for too long been dominated by "community" interpretations. From the depiction of the Father, to the task of the Son, to the work of the disciples, "mission" is a leitmotif in the FG. Contrary to the three major "community" interpretations, no evidence was found of an internal function for the mission motif. No mission of a "community" was found; nor was there a segment of a "community" more mission-minded than another. Rather, the entire Gospel, from start to finish, tells a story centered on the mission of the Son, a mission that the readers are invited to join. Such an understanding alludes to the multivalent function and use of the Gospel in the early Christian movement.[232] One of those primary functions was its rhetorical witness to the reader; a fact that the Gospel's *Missionsgedanke* makes clear. Therefore, the mission motif in the FG reveals that the Gospel functioned with a rhetorical invitation for an indefinite audience.

Early "Christian" relations in the fourth Gospel

If the FG were a sectarian or a quasi-sectarian "community," we would expect to find in the Gospel text some distinct separation between their "group" and the rest of the early Christian movement. Entire volumes

---

[230] *Ibid.*, p. 1075.

[231] Schnackenburg, *The Gospel According to St. John*, vol. III, p. 358.

[232] See Charles E. Hill, *The Johannine Corpus in the Early Church* (Oxford: Oxford University Press, 2004). According to Hill, the FG had "wide and authoritative use . . . and habitual attribution to a common apostolic origin" in the early church (pp. 474–75).

have been written defining the so-called "Johannine Christianity."[233] The proposal of this book is not that the FG represents no unique contribution to the early Christian movement; for we know that it eventually became a major contributor. Rather, this book proposes that the FG does not depict itself and its audience as standing *against* or *outside of* the rest of the Christian movement. In the midst of all the diversity and tensions, there was a unity and commonality that is reflected in the narrative of the FG.

In a 1978 article Raymond Brown attempted to define the Johannine perspective on Christian diversity in the late first century.[234] Brown's interest is the applicability of the religious term "sect" to the JComm in its relationship to other Christian "communities" in the early Christian movement. "Was this community an accepted church among churches or an alienated and exclusive conventicle?"[235] Brown's criterion was as follows: "the Johannine community would *de facto* be a sect ... if explicitly or implicitly it had broken *koinōnia* with most other Christians, or if because of its theological or ecclesiological tendencies, most other Christians had broken *koinonia* with the Johannine community."[236] Brown attempts to approach the issue of the relations between the JComm and other "Christian" communities by examining the various "groups" portrayed in the narrative of the FG. Using Brown's criteria and evaluation as a starting point, this section will examine two possible areas of dissent between the FG and the early Christian movement.

The first possible area of dissent is between the FG and the Jewish-Christians of inadequate faith. Brown argues that the FG displays a hostile attitude to certain Jewish-Christians who, like the JComm, had left the synagogue but did not "believe" as they should. He uses 2:23–25 as a primary example of this hostility. As is normal for "community" interpreters, for Brown these three verses are representative of some "group" current with the JComm in whom John has no trust.[237] Another passage linked to this "group" by Brown is 7:3–5, where Jesus' brothers "did not really believe in him." For Brown, the hostile portrait of the brothers of Jesus, without any hint of their conversion, is striking when we reflect that the FG was written after James had led the Jerusalem church for nearly thirty years and had died a martyr. Brown concludes:

> Since his [James] name was revered as a teaching authority by Jewish Christians (James 1:1; Jude 1:1), are we having reflected in John a polemic against Jewish Christians, particularly in

---

[233] Smith, *Johannine Christianity.*
[234] Brown, "Other Sheep Not of This Fold."
[235] *Ibid.*, p. 6.   [236] *Ibid.*   [237] *Ibid.*, p. 12.

Palestine, who regarded themselves as the heirs of the Jerusalem church of James? Are their church leaders the hirelings of 10:12 who do not protect the sheep against the wolves, perhaps because they have not sufficiently distanced their flocks from "the Jews"?[238]

Besides Brown's problem of reference when he assumes 2:23–25 and 7:3–5 are representative of "groups" contemporary to the JComm, an issue we discussed above concerning representative figures, Brown has mistaken John's rhetoric for polemic. Beginning with the Jewish-Christians to whom Jesus refuses to entrust himself in 2:23–25, it is no wonder that Brown finds it "difficult to interpret."[239] By taking these verses in isolation and applying them to the history of the JComm, Brown has lost the literary context in which they function. Earlier we argued that the placement of the Nicodemus narrative alongside the Samaritan woman narrative was no accident; the two narratives have a united function. The characters in both narratives provide representative significance for the readers. The characters do not provide "glimpses" into the initial readers' communal make-up, but act as mirrors for the readers themselves. 2:23–25 is also connected to this united function; it links the earlier signs ministry to the Nicodemus and Samaritan woman narratives.[240] For the narratives that follow it functions like a prologue that introduces its rhetorical witness: an encouragement to various "types of believers" to come to full faith in Jesus. As Beasley-Murray explains: "Just as 2:1 harks back to the events of chap. 1 yet commences a new division of the Gospel, so 2:23–25 is linked with the setting of the previous episode yet belongs essentially with chap. 3, since it provides a context for the Nicodemus narrative and an important clue to its understanding."[241] By removing 2:23–25 from its literary context Brown has mistakenly assumed as polemical what was intended to be rhetorical.[242]

A similar mistake was made by Brown in reference to 7:3–5. Brown's reconstruction of James and the Jerusalem Christians through these few

---

[238] *Ibid.*, p. 13.   [239] *Ibid.*

[240] Interestingly, Beasley-Murray, *John*, p. 47, also links 2:23–25 to the Nicodemus narrative in his account of the literary structure of the Gospel. Cf. Moloney, "From Cana to Cana (John 2:1–4:54) and the Fourth Evangelist's Concept of Correct (and Incorrect) Faith."

[241] Beasley-Murray, *John*, pp. 45–46.

[242] According to Richard Bauckham, *Gospel Women: Studies of the Named Women in the Gospels* (Edinburgh: T. & T. Clark, 2002), pp. 203–23, a significant historical point against Brown's hypothesis is the presence of Mary of Clopas at the cross. She was the mother of Simeon son of Clopas, successor to James and the Jewish-Christian leader in Palestine when the Gospel was written.

verses, though ingenious, is more fanciful than credible. Since Mark 6:3 portrays a similar tradition it is difficult to so easily apply this tradition to the contemporary situation of the FE.[243] Rather, John's rhetoric of "belief" is again being deployed, not a polemic. The "brothers" of 7:3–5 are not being replaced by current disciples, but are used as examples of the "type of belief" required. The fact that Jesus' own brothers did not believe in him stands as a stark warning to others. No human relation guarantees the type of "life" that Jesus requires. Thus, by assuming that the reference behind John's discussion of Jesus' brothers in 7:3–5 was "disciples" in leadership in Jerusalem, Brown has mistaken rhetoric for polemic. Brown's narrative decoding has misplaced the FE's rhetorical strategy.

The second possible area of dissent according to Brown is between the FG and the Christians of Apostolic churches. According to Brown, "If we call upon Peter and the other named disciples as clues to John's attitude toward these Apostolic Christians, his attitude is fundamentally favorable . . . Nevertheless, these named disciples do not seem to embody the fullness of Christian perception."[244] For Brown, this is revealed when a comparison is made between the disciples in general and Simon Peter in particular, and the BD, which for Brown is the symbolic representation of the JComm:

> The others are scattered at the time of Jesus' passion leaving him alone (16:32), while the beloved disciple remains with Jesus even at the foot of the cross (19:26–27). Simon Peter denies that he is a disciple of Jesus (18:17, 25), a particularly serious denial granted the Johannine emphasis on discipleship as the primary Christian category; and so he needs to be rehabilitated by Jesus who three times asks whether Peter loves him (21:15–17). Closer to Jesus both in life (13:23) and in death (19:26–27), the beloved disciple sees the significance of the garments left behind in the empty tomb when Peter does not (20:8–10); he also recognizes the risen Jesus when Peter does not (21:7). The Johannine Christians, represented by the beloved disciple, clearly regard themselves as closer to Jesus and more perceptive than the Christians of the Apostolic Churches.[245]

But again Brown has mistaken rhetoric for polemic. Two points will make this clear. First, besides all the complexities of the reference behind the

---

[243] We have argued in chapter 3 that John is aware of a time distinction between Jesus' ministry and his own.

[244] Brown, "Other Sheep Not of This Fold," p. 15.   [245] *Ibid.*, pp. 15–16.

BD,[246] Brown has mistakenly viewed the BD as the *ideal disciple* rather than as the *ideal witness*. The BD's presence at the cross is not only an example of faithfulness, but of witness to the event. His "closeness" to Jesus is evidence of appropriate testimony, not spirituality for a "group" contemporary with the FE. Helpful here is the article by Bauckham entitled "The Beloved Disciple as Ideal Author."[247] Bauckham shows that all the focus on a historical referent for the BD has missed his role in the narrative as an ideal "witness" to the proclamation of the FG. By mistaking the reference of the BD and by narrowing the narrative's function to a "community," Brown has again confused rhetoric for polemic.

Second, the narrative's portrayal of certain negative aspects of Peter the disciple is paradigmatic for the *reader* not representative of the Apostolic churches. Again, beside the problem of reference, Brown has misunderstood the paradigmatic function of the disciples in the narrative. As we discussed earlier, characters in the narrative, among whom Peter and the disciples are included, are depicted as paradigmatic (representative figures) for the readers. John's Gospel is not alone in this presentation; the Gospel of Mark is more "critical" of the disciples for the purpose of representing appropriate discipleship to his readers than John.[248] Mark portrays the disciples as hard of heart (6:52), spiritually weak (14:32–42), and very dim-witted (8:14–21). But this narrative depiction is hardly depictive of an underlying polemic, but is a rhetorical demonstration for the readers. It is for the sake of response not merely contemporary historical depiction – for this is a function of ancient literature like the Gospels. Thus, when Brown writes concerning the comparison between Peter and the BD that "No such rehabilitation is necessary and no such questioning is even conceivable in the case of the disciple *par excellence*, the disciple whom Jesus loved,"[249] he commits what Luke Timothy Johnson warned us about concerning "community" interpretations: the fallacy of description over prescription.[250] Brown's mirror reading by textual reflection mistakenly reads the text as a *history* of the "community" and not as a *message* for the reader.

---

[246] We have no intention of proposing a solution to the debate over the identity or function of the BD. For a comprehensive discussion of the BD see James H. Charlesworth, *The Beloved Disciple: Whose Witness Validates the Gospel of John?* (Valley Forge, Pa.: Trinity Press International, 1995).

[247] Richard Bauckham, "The Beloved Disciple as Ideal Author," *JSNT* 49 (1993), pp. 21–44.

[248] See Ernest Best, *Following Jesus: Discipleship in the Gospel of Mark*, JSNTSup 4 (Sheffield: JSOT Press, 1981).

[249] Brown, "Other Sheep Not of This Fold," p. 15.

[250] Johnson, "On Finding Lukan Community: A Cautious Cautionary Essay."

Thus, even beyond the difficulty of defending the referentiality of the characters in the narrative Brown has proposed, his hypothesis still requires an extremely complex historical reconstruction of events. To assume that 1:50, where the disciples are told that they are yet to see greater things, implies that the Johannine Christians have a one-upmanship Christology in comparison to the disciples mistakes the rhetoric of the narrative for polemic. Taken at the level of narrative, 1:50 is a literary signal not a historical debate. Neither can an argument from silence concerning "church" structure and practice imply a polemic against Apostolic church institutionalization.[251] It is here that our focus on the narrative's sequence is helpful. The disciples see these "greater things" later in the Gospel; no external "disciples" are required to make sense of the narrative.

Even 21:15–25,[252] where Peter and the BD are purposefully linked, has a rhetorical not a polemical strategy. Though the individual leaders are central to the pericope, we still can not link certain "groups" or early "Christian" sub-movements to them. This would have been the opportune time for the so-called JComm to use one-upmanship against their rival "group" represented by Peter. But nothing of the sort takes place. A lengthy comment by Lincoln is helpful here:

> Significantly, Peter's question about the fate of the beloved disciple . . . links these two witnesses and leaders. One is the shepherd who becomes a martyr, the other a witness who does not meet martyrdom but dies a natural death (v. 23). To prevent odious comparisons and to underline the validity of both types of witnesses, the narrative stresses that what counts is not the actual outcome of the witness but the will of Jesus, which determines the outcome (v. 22). In this light, the following reference, at the end of the narrative, to the role of the witness of the beloved disciple in the writing of the Gospel can be more clearly seen as a specific task within the more general assignment of witnessing that *he shares with all the disciples* as they continue the mission of Jesus.[253]

Rather than having a polemical purpose, the Johannine epilogue functions to bring unity between various Christian "witnesses."

---

[251] Brown, "Other Sheep Not of This Fold," pp. 17–18.
[252] Our proposal is unaffected by the possible late addition of John 21. For a good summary see Paul S. Minear, "The Original Functions of John 21," *JBL* 102 (1983), pp. 85–98.
[253] Lincoln, *Truth on Trial*, p. 155 (emphasis added).

In contrast to the older polemical model,[254] Kevin Quast has argued that the narrative attempts to unite sections of the second-generation "church" and not promote one section (the Johannine Christians) over and against another (the Petrine Christians). Quast assumes that John 21 was written to correct the JComm's incorrect view of other Christian groups.[255] In this way the FE is trying to unite them to share in the one Gospel heritage.[256] Besides Quast's "community" assumption, which he never defines or defends, our rhetorical proposal matches well with his. The contextual reconstruction is far from polemical. In contradistinction from the "community" in which he lives and ministers the FE is writing to *correct* their view. This again confirms Luke Timothy Johnson's warning about trying to read the "community's" reflection from a text.

Independent of *GAC*, Richard Bauckham has come to a similar conclusion. Bauckham argues that the second half of chapter 21 functions as a deliberate *inclusio* with 13:23–25, indicating that the double story of Peter and the BD which began there ends here. "After ch. 20 no more needs to be said about Jesus himself: the central Christological purpose of the Gospel has been fulfilled. But more does need to be said about the disciples: the loose ends which the story of Peter and the beloved disciple up till this point has left must be taken up before the Gospel is complete."[257] Linking 21:24 with 19:35, Bauckham argues that BD is portrayed as the ideal witness. In 21:20–22 the BD is given superiority to Peter only in respects which qualify him for his own role as a "perceptive witness to Jesus." The BD is also present at key points in the Gospel story.[258] Thus, the relation between Peter and the BD is more understandable. As Bauckham explains:

> The beloved disciple is better qualified to be the author of a Gospel, but he is not better qualified to be the chief undershepherd of Jesus' sheep, which is Peter's mode of discipleship . . . The different complementary roles of the two disciples shows that it is not a rivalry between two different branches

---

[254] A model still in use, though. See, for example, Ismo Dunderberg, "The Beloved Disciple in John: An Ideal Figure in an Early Christian Controversy," in Ismo Dunderberg, Christopher Tuckett, and Kari Syreeni (eds.), *Fair Play: Diversity and Conflicts in Early Christianity: Essays in Honour of Heikki Räisänen*, NovTSup 53 (Leiden: Brill, 2002), pp. 243–69; Rodney A. Whitacre, *Johannine Polemic: The Role of Tradition and Theology*, SBLDS 67 (Chico, Calif.: Scholars Press, 1982); D. Bruce Woll, *Johannine Christianity in Conflict: Authority, Rank, and Succession in the First Farewell Discourse*, SBLDS 60 (Chico, Calif.: Scholars Press, 1981).

[255] Quast, *Peter and the Beloved Disciple*, pp. 164–65.   [256] *Ibid.*, p. 166.

[257] Bauckham, "The Beloved Disciple as Ideal Author," p. 28.   [258] *Ibid.*, pp. 36–37.

of early Christianity (the so-called great church and the Johannine churches) that is at stake in their relationship. The Gospel acknowledges Peter's leading role in the whole church . . . while claiming for the beloved disciple a role of witnessing to the truth of Jesus which is equally significant for the whole church.[259]

The narrative has concluded its portrayal of Peter and the BD in order to connect the reader to their complementary leadership functions in the present Christian movement.

The polemical reading of the FG that we have been critiquing requires an elaborate historical reconstruction, a decoding of the narrative referents, one that requires linking different words or concepts across several unrelated chapters in the Gospel, and a misunderstanding of rhetorical strategy. It has been the argument of this book that part of the problem is an incorrect starting assumption of a "community" standing behind the FG and an overemphasis of distinct "groups" in early Christianity. The narrative placed the witnesses of both Peter and the BD, leaders in the early "Christian" movement, in appropriate relation. The FG has claimed to be a true witness by one connected to the very story of the Gospel. The FG is not in a deep-rooted polemic with other Jesus traditions, but cooperates with the general witness of early Christian mission.

Conclusion: reading the fourth Gospel

Our proposed reading strategy of the FG in light of the Gospel community debate has attempted to establish a "literal" reading that is intended for a general or indefinite reading audience. The text was seen to have various authorial *Tendenzen* for a more diverse audience; *Tendenzen* that may assume different types and levels of readers. Key to the Gospel community debate and our reading of the FG was the role of representative figures in the narrative. We have shown that far from representing specific "groups," the figures become representative for the reader. This was most visible when the narrative was viewed from the macro-level. For example, JComm interpretations are necessarily inconsistent. One would expect that if Nicodemus, Peter, and the BD represent various groups, so should Thomas, Mary Magdalene, Martha and Mary, and Lazarus. All these have distinguishing features. But the number of different groups needed if one were to push the view consistently becomes absurd. The varied representative figures' interpretation we have argued for can cope

---

[259] *Ibid.*, p. 38.

with this proliferation.[260] In this way the FG was shown to have a rhetorical witness that included a specific purpose of invitation, a mission rooted in the very subject of the biography, and a goal of being included in the wider early Christian movement.

Our goal in this book has not only been to critique the previous paradigm, but to build a more appropriate model for reading the FG and establishing its functional potential. We have not erased the *Sitz im Leben* of the FG, but allowed it to be understood within a more complex model of "community"; a model that functions broadly in the early Christian movement and tradition. We have seen how a non-community reading of various pericopae is more appropriate to the narrative of the FG and its exegesis. Some "community" interpretations distorted the text in order to "fit" their assumed historically reconstructed contexts; others were simply not needed. Since we have only been able to introduce the function of the Gospel and various nuances of its more indefinite social-historical location, we will discuss several avenues of further research in chapter 6. Our reading strategy has opened the text to be read afresh in light of the rhetorical "witness" it proclaims.

---

[260] In fact, it is possible that for the male figures in the FG who go through the whole story, there is a progression from their confessions of faith in chapter 1 to Thomas' climactic confession in chapter 20.

6

THE SHEEP OF THE FOLD: SUMMARY AND CONCLUSION

Nearly thirty years ago Robert Kysar did a complete survey of scholarship on the Gospel of John.[1] When summarizing the results of the investigation Kysar noted that one of Johannine scholarship's recent accomplishments was that "Contemporary Johannine criticism has confirmed that the gospel is a community's document."[2] Kysar claimed that the inclinations long found in scholarly literature have confirmed in a substantial manner that the FG must be interpreted as the document of a community:

> The works associated with source-tradition and composition criticism, the quest of the concrete situation of the evangelist, and theological analysis have all merged upon a common tenet: The contents of the gospel are the result in large part of the conditions of a community of persons . . . The theology of every stratum of the gospel relates to the community of faith; it addresses the needs of that community at that moment . . . *The gospel cannot be read meaningfully apart from some understanding of the community out of which and to which it was written* . . . its thought is sustained in the atmosphere of that occasion and nowhere else.[3]

Such a statement describes well the paradigm that this study has attempted to correct. It is notable that nearly thirty years later Kysar has moved in the opposite direction. Concerning the importance of knowing "as much about the [historical] occasion as possible," Kysar now concludes:

> An investigation of the past usually tells us more about the investigator than the past . . . Maybe we are just learning that the testing of any hypothesis is an ongoing necessity and that working hypotheses do not always "work" without flaw . . . As

[1] Kysar, *The Fourth Evangelist and his Gospel.*
[2] *Ibid.*, p. 269.   [3] *Ibid.*, pp. 269–70 (emphasis added).

I am grateful for the work of scholars like Brown and Martyn, I suppose I have simply tired of playing the game of abstract speculative constructions.[4]

In another setting Kysar claims:

My own view is that there is now sufficient evidence in these early years of the twenty-first century that the whither of the Johannine community is likely to include its demise. Gather the evidence that points toward what is to come about in biblical studies in this century, and the sum points clearly away from historical reconstructions such as those we call the Johannine community.[5]

Kysar's tiredness "of playing the game of abstract speculative constructions" is not reason enough to deny the assumption of "community" in Gospels exegesis.[6] Nor has it been the primary motivation of this book. Rather than finding such a hermeneutical approach tiring, we have argued that the entire approach is unfounded. By attempting to provide further definition to various aspects of the Gospel community debate, and by using the Gospel of John as a test case, we have argued that the Gospel of John was never intended for a local, geographic "community" or "network of communities." This is itself a reconstruction of the evidence, since we have no external evidence of the early audience – hence, the need for such a study. This book, then, has entered within the Gospel audience debate and challenged the current "community" reconstructions assumed in the interpretation of the FG. Such paradigm debates are not new within the scholarly guild, for it was Albert Schweitzer who once explained that "A deeper understanding of a subject is only brought to a pass when a theory is carried out to its utmost limit and finally proves its own inadequacy."[7] It is our conclusion that the theory of Gospel "community" reconstructions has been carried to its outer limit and has been proven inadequate.

---

[4] Robert Kysar, "The Expulsion from the Synagogue: A Tale of a Theory," pp. 12–15.

[5] Kysar, "The Whence and Whither of the Johannine Community," p. 1. For a more thorough discussion of Kysar's move away from JComm reconstructions see Klink, "The Gospel Community Debate."

[6] For as John Dominic Crossan, *The Historical Jesus: The Life of A Mediterranean Peasant* (New York: Harper Collins, 1992), p. 426, explains, "If you cannot believe in something produced by reconstruction, you may have nothing left to believe in."

[7] Albert Schweitzer, *The Quest of the Historical Jesus: A Critical Study of Its Progress from Reimarus to Wrede*, trans. W. Montgomery (London: Adam & Charles Black, 1910), p. 221. Cf. the comment by Michael Stanford, *An Introduction to the Philosophy of History* (Oxford: Blackwell, 1998), p. 113: "The progress of science, notoriously, is made over the corpses of dead theories."

Summary of results

As we outlined in chapter 1, the Gospel community debate is centered around four primary areas of definition. In order to test the audience and origin of the FG, and in response to the four areas in need of definition within the Gospel community debate, we centered our discussion on four areas of inquiry: the term "community" (chapter 2), Gospel audience and patristic exegesis (chapter 2), the nature and function of the Gospel genre (chapter 3), and the Gospel narrative's implied reader (chapter 4).

We concluded, at the broadest level, that the Gospels were written for an indefinite audience, not an individual "church" or network of churches disconnected from the rest of the early Christian movement. This historical assumption does not posit a completely indefinite audience, but one that is appropriate to a first-century audience in the Greco-Roman world and allows for a general market niche. Using what we have argued is a more complex model of "community" (relational and not territorial) we have posited that the Gospels would have been appropriate reading material for a variety of geographic communities throughout early Christianity. Readers who were not even aware of the other's existence could participate together in the story told by the Gospels, based upon a symbolic construction which provided a specifically "Christian" identity for them and others (chapter 2). The Gospel text, which is a type of biography, would rarely be used by a self-contained group. The Gospel narrative would have been read by its pre-critical readers with a "realistic" reading strategy. Although the Gospel would have had various *Tendenzen* and interpretations included, it would not have been read on two levels in the redaction-critical way proposed by J. L. Martyn. In essence, a pre-critical reading of the Gospels is a "literal" reading, whereby the story the Gospels tell is the story meant to be heard (chapter 3). Finally, the reader the text expects, far from being a knowledgeable community reader, has only a general familiarity with the story in the narrative. The relative familiarity with the Christian story, yet at times a lack of specific knowledge concerning Judaism, reveals that the Gospel expected different types of readers. Such a maneuver on the part of the evangelist allows the text to be accessible at different levels, to a first-time reader and a more experienced reader; the Gospel assumes a varied readership (chapter 4).

The application of this reading strategy to the FG revealed that the FG was intended to be read by a general or indefinite audience; a reading that deals more appropriately with the textual evidence and is less internally inconsistent. Using five test cases we argued, first, that "community" interpretations have misunderstood the function of characters in the narrative, especially their paradigmatic function. This is most apparent at the macro-level of the narrative where the figures, rather than representing unique stages in a "community's" history, function together by inviting potential readers to participate in the message of the Gospel. Second, arguing specifically against the influential work of J. L. Martyn, we argued that the contextual significance of the "expulsion from the synagogue" passages has been overemphasized by "community" interpretations and has been misread at the macro-level of the narrative. There are neither clues in the narrative nor evidence outside of it for the reading proposed by Martyn. Third, with a non-community audience in view, we were drawn to the strong contextual evidence for an "evangelistic" reading of the FG. In light of 20:31b we argued that it is highly likely that the Gospel is aimed not just at different "types of readers," but also at different "types of faith." This correlates well with the paradigmatic function of the representative figures in the narrative. Fourth, and related to John's purpose, we argued that our proposed audience and reading strategy makes more coherent the mission *leitmotif* and the general rhetorical address in the FG. The entire Gospel, from start to finish, tells a story centered on the mission of the Son, a mission that the readers are invited to join. Such an understanding alludes to the multivalent function and use of the Gospel in the early Christian movement. Finally, we argued that contrary to the sectarian understanding of the FG and its audience, the FG does not depict itself and its audience as standing *against* or *outside of* the rest of the Christian movement. In the midst of all the diversity and tensions in early Christianity there was a unity and commonality that is reflected in the narrative of the FG. The Gospel of John is not in a deep-rooted polemic with other Jesus traditions, but cooperates with the general witness of the early "Christian" mission.

Conclusion: the Gospel community debate and the fourth Gospel

Thus, by pressing forward the Gospel community debate, and by using the FG as a test case, we have three general conclusions. First, the hypothesis that the audience of the FG was a single "group" or "network of groups" frequently called a "community" does not match well to external data. After examining internally the assumed audience of the Gospel, the patristic exegetical assumptions and origin legends of the original audience, the normal audience of the biographical genre, and the audience depicted by the heuristic device of the implied reader, a single, geographic "community" was not reconcilable with the evidence. At the same time, there was no historical evidence that the FG at any time ever belonged to one geographic "church" or "community." The common portrait of an actual JComm, a single and coherent "group" behind the document, is historical fiction.

Second, the use of a Gospel "community" reconstruction in the interpretation of the FG is internally inconsistent. By starting with a "community" as the audience and situational context of the Gospel interpreters have misaligned the textual evidence in the FG, especially at the macro-level of the narrative. Martyn and Brown are prime examples of this mistake. Martyn's two-level reading strategy forces him to change the actual plot given by the FG in order to match it with the so-called plot of the JComm. In a similar manner, Brown is required to read the narrative diachronically, in complete opposition to the narrative's own synchronic depiction, in order to align the story with the "history" of the JComm. The end result creates a mismatch between the narrative's story and the story of the JComm. Although JComm interpreters have attempted to alleviate this problem with highly complex reconstructions of the social-historical situation, the internal inconsistencies remain.

Third, the data derived from our proposed general audience of the FG are similar to what we know of the early Christian movement as a whole. The various types and levels of readers depicted by the narrative of the FG matches well the types and levels of readers understood to have been part of early Christianity. Even more, from what we know of the use of the Gospels in the early Christian movement, the Gospels were used and read in a similar, more general fashion, at least by the mid-second century, if not before. Such a conclusion makes the assumption that the Gospels began as isolated, sectarian-like documents for one "group" but very soon became almost universal reading material highly untenable. The "Church" faced the issue of the multiplicity of the Gospels, not their particularity.

The conclusion of this book, then, is that both the use and concept of "community" in the historical depiction of the Gospel audiences and as the beginning assumption in the interpretation of the Gospel narrative be abandoned. Not only is the term very ambiguous, but it carries a conceptual meaning that has been found to be inaccurate. The current concept of a Gospel "community" is an inappropriate model of the Gospel audience. In light of this conclusion several fresh avenues of research are now made clearer. This conclusion has furthered the Gospel community debate in several ways. First, we have applied the current debate specifically to the FG. Although *GAC* helpfully stated the theoretical problem in general Gospel scholarship, it was unable to examine any of the individual

Gospels. Second, we have brought clarification and definition to the concept of "community" so common in Gospel exegesis. Third, we have linked our modern discussion with the patristic evidence related to both the origin of the Gospels, as well as the pre-critical reading strategy assumed. Fourth, we have provided more clarification to the use of the *bios* genre in the Gospel community debate. Fifth, we have helpfully integrated both historical and literary criticisms in our methodology. Finally, we have advanced further the discussion of the function of the Gospels, and more specifically, the purpose of the FG.

Implications of this study for future research

This study has attempted to assist in taking the shackles off the reading of the Gospels that has for so long dominated Gospel scholarship. The realization of the more general audience of the Gospels has implications for three areas of future research. The first is the function and use of the Gospels in early Christianity. We are aware that at a fairly early date the Gospels had authority in Christian circles and that they were used to some degree in the worship services of the early churches.[8] Recently D. Moody Smith has argued that the Gospels may have been intended to function as Scripture, or at least the continuation of the Jewish Scripture.[9] According to Smith:

> The early Christian claim that the narrative and prophecies of old are fulfilled and continued in Jesus and the church prefigures, perhaps even demands, the production of more scripture, which will explain how this happened. Such scripture is required to explain this not first of all to outsiders but rather to Christians themselves. It becomes an essential part of their identity and self-understanding.[10]

For Smith, "The earliest development of Christian scripture occurred in a Jewish milieu that was becoming Christian."[11] And the Gospels were probably at the center of this development:

---

[8] From Justin Martyr (*First Apology* 67) we learn that at least by the mid-second century the Gospels ("the memoirs of the apostles") were read along with the prophets at Sunday services.

[9] D. Moody Smith, "When Did the Gospels Become Scripture?," *JBL* 119 (2000), pp. 3–20.

[10] *Ibid.*, p. 12.   [11] *Ibid.*, p. 17.

> In the case of the earliest Christian Gospels . . . the initial and fundamental impulse for their composition came with the proclamation of Jesus as the fulfillment of scripture. The use of the Gospels alongside the older, Jewish scriptures in worship, certainly as early as the mid-second century, probably much earlier, was a likely continuation of the use to which the earlier Gospels traditions had already been put.[12]

Certainly Smith is correct when he posits that the Gospels would have served in a Scripture-like fashion from an early date.[13]

But Smith's hypothesis is not new. Although they have been silenced for several decades due to the dominance of the "community" paradigm, scholars from a generation ago were noticing a similar potential function of the Gospels. According to C. F. D. Moule, "at the time the Gospels were being written and first used . . . they filled a place broadly comparable to the narrative parts of the Hebrew Scriptures in the Synagogues, as the historical background against which the interpretive writings might be read."[14] For Moule the Gospels were written to make a "narrative statement."[15] Viewed in this way, the Gospels (or equivalent material now no longer extant) "are first and foremost addressed '*from* faith,' indeed, but not '*to* faith' so much as to unbelief."[16] In this way Moule concludes that

> all four Gospels alike are to be interpreted as more than anything else evangelistic and apologetic in purpose; and . . . represent primarily the recognition that a vital element in evangelism is

[12] *Ibid.*, p. 19.

[13] As Bruce Metzger, *The Canon of the New Testament: Its Origin, Development, and Significance* (Oxford: Clarendon Press, 1987), p. 6, explains, after quoting Justin Martyr's mid-second-century reference to the Christian documents being used in public worship: "Thus it came about that Christian congregations grew accustomed to regard the apostolic writings as, in some sense, on a par with the older Jewish Scriptures, and such liturgical custom, though doubtless varying in different congregations, set its seal on certain Gospels and Epistles as worthy of special reverence and obedience." See also Oscar Cullmann, *Early Christian Worship*; Paul Glaue, *Die Vorlesung heiliger Schriften im Gottesdiente*, BEAK (Berlin: University of Berlin, 1907); C. R. Gregory, "The Reading of Scripture in the Church in the Second Century," *AJT* 13 (1908), pp. 86–91; and Adolf von Harnack, *Bible Reading in the Early Church*, trans. J. R. Wilkinson (London: Williams & Norgate, 1912).

[14] C. F. D. Moule, "The Intention of the Evangelists," in his *The Phenomenon of the New Testament: An Inquiry into the Implications of Certain Features of the New Testament*, SBT Second Series 1 (London: SCM Press, 1967), p. 100. Originally published in A. J. B. Higgins (ed.), *New Testament Essays: Studies in Memory of T. W. Manson* (Manchester: Manchester University Press, 1959), pp. 165–79.

[15] *Ibid.*, p. 101.   [16] *Ibid.*, p. 103.

the *plain* story of what happened in the ministry of Jesus. Thus, all four are to be regarded as having been written primarily with a view to the outsider, although . . . Luke and John are more likely to have been intended to be read by the outsider, whereas Matthew and Mark may well represent instruction for Christians, with a view to equipping them in turn for spoken evangelism.[17]

Moule's hypothesis needs testing in its specifics, but fits well with our proposal of a wider audience and the different market niche of each of the Gospels. A similar view was presented over fifty years ago by C. H. Dodd, who argued that the FE was

"thinking," in the first place, not so much of Christians who need a deeper theology, as of non-Christians who are concerned about eternal life and the way to it, and may be ready to follow the Christian way if this is presented to them in terms that are intelligibly related to their previous religious interests and experience.[18]

These older proposals saw correctly the more indefinite context of the Gospels, allowing each Gospel to function differently in different contexts. It is the hope of this study that new research will begin that examines the potential function of the Gospels within the audience model this book has proposed. A study of this type, though not directly related to the Gospel community debate, has recently been presented by Stephen Motyer, who argues that the harsh response to the Jews in chapter 8 is to be interpreted as a passionate appeal to change direction, to not reject and murder Jesus as a blasphemer, but to confess him as the Christ.[19] Such a conclusion fits well with the mission *leitmotif* of the FG. Our study allows other scholarly hypotheses to be made concerning the more indefinite social-historical context and other viable proposals taken from textual data.

The second implication for future research is the identity of early Christianity. D. Moody Smith argued above that the Gospels become an essential part of Christian "identity and self-understanding."[20] Our proposed model for the audience of the Gospels is better able to analyze the complexities of identity in early Christianity. As we argued in chapter 2, John Barclay's research on Jews in the Mediterranean Diaspora and Judith

---

[17] *Ibid.*, p. 113 (emphasis added).
[18] Dodd, *The Interpretation of the Fourth Gospel*, p. 9.
[19] Motyer, *Your Father the Devil?*, p. 212.
[20] Smith, "When Did the Gospels Become Scripture?," p. 12.

Lieu's research on early Christians relate well to our proposed model for the Gospels' audience.[21] A similar argument has been made by Averil Cameron who argues that "if ever there was a case of the construction of reality through text, such a case is provided by early Christianity . . . Christians built themselves a new world."[22] Using our audience model and proposed reading we may begin to see conceptual connections between all four Gospels,[23] as well as other connections within the early Christian movement.[24]

The third implication for future research is the reading of the Gospels for today. The Gospels have always been and will continue to be important reading for the contemporary Christian church. The reconstruction provided by "community" interpreters, at least in regard to the FG, has misplaced rhetoric for polemic. The narrative of the FG is inviting potential readers, even those who constitute different ethnic backgrounds and levels of belief, to participate in its witness to Jesus. The Gospels invite all readers into their message.[25] Historical studies involving the reception of the Gospels in the Christian church may provide interesting comparisons with their early use and function. Our study also facilitates the Church's current belief that the Gospels belong to Christians in the present, not just to a "community" in the past.[26]

Conclusion

This book has provided a critique of the common template in Gospel scholarship that places the key hermeneutical principle for interpretation as the quest for the delineation and explication of the community that each Gospel represents. In light of the Gospel community debate this study has argued that such a hermeneutical approach is unfounded. By using the Gospel of John as a test case, we discovered that Gospel reveals a large early Christian audience, in contrast to the current "community"

---

[21] Judith Lieu, *Neither Jew Nor Greek?*; and John Barclay, *Jews in the Mediterranean Diaspora*.

[22] Cameron, *Christianity and the Rhetoric of Empire*, p. 21.

[23] As Bauckham, "John for Readers of Mark," has already attempted.

[24] Some connections worth pursuing include the relationship of the FG to the rest of the Johannine literature.

[25] For example, see Stanley E. Porter (ed.), *Reading the Gospels Today*, MNTS (Grand Rapids: Eerdmans, 2004).

[26] A comment by Rowan Williams, the Archbishop of Canterbury, is helpful here: "The Fourth Gospel is a narrative located unmistakably in the past of the world as we have it, yet active on us always as the present word of God" (paper delivered at the St. Andrews Conference on the Gospel of John and Christian Theology, St. Andrews, Scotland, July 3, 2003).

reconstructions which assume that the Gospel was written by and for a specific Gospel "community" – the Johannine community. This "community" paradigm has created inappropriate reconstructions of the FG's audience and origin, leading to mistaken assumptions in the reading of the narrative of John. In an attempt to further the Gospel community debate, this book has presented a new audience and social-historical context for reading the FG and by implication all four Gospels.

BIBLIOGRAPHY

Abbott, Edwin A. *Johannine Grammar*. London: Adam and Charles Black, 1906.

Aberle, David. "A Note on Relative Deprivation Theory as Applied to Millenarian and Other Cult Movements," in *Millennial Dreams in Action: Studies in Revolutionary Religious Movements*. Edited by Sylvia L. Thrupp. CSSHSup 2. The Hague: Mouton, 1962, pp. 209–14.

Achtemeier, Paul. "Towards the Isolation of Pre-Markan Miracle Catenae." *JBL* 89 (1970), pp. 265–91.

Adams, Edward. *Constructing the World: A Study in Paul's Cosmological Language*. SNTW. Edinburgh: T. & T. Clark, 2000.

Aitken, Ellen B. "At the Well of Living Water: Jacob Traditions in John 4," in *The Interpretation of Scripture in Early Judaism and Christianity*. Edited by Craig A. Evans. JSPSSup 33. SSEJC 7. Sheffield: Sheffield Academic Press, 2000, pp. 342–62.

Aland, Kurt. *Synopsis Quattuor Euangeliorum: Locis parallelis evangeliorum apocryphorum et patrum adhibitis*. 13th edn. Stuttgart: Württembergische Bibelanstalt, 1985.

Alexander, Loveday. "Luke's Preface in the Context of Greek Preface-Writing." *NovT* 28 (1986), pp. 48–74.

"Fact, Fiction, and the Genre of Acts." *NTS* 44 (1988), pp. 380–99.

"Ancient Book Production and the Circulation of the Gospels," in *The Gospels for All Christians: Rethinking the Gospel Audiences*. Edited by Richard Bauckham. Grand Rapids: Eerdmans, 1998, pp. 71–111.

Alexander, Philip S. "Midrash and the Gospels," in *Synoptic Studies: The Ampleforth Conferences of 1982 and 1983*. Edited by C. M. Tuckett. JSNTSup 7. Sheffield: JSOT Press, 1983, pp. 1–18.

"Rabbinic Biography and the Biography of Jesus: A Survey of the Evidence," in *Synoptic Studies: The Ampleforth Conferences of 1982 and 1983*. Edited by C. M. Tuckett. JSNTSup 7. Sheffield: JSOT Press, 1983, pp. 19–50.

"Rabbinic Judaism and the New Testament." *ZNW* 74 (1983), pp. 237–46.

"'The Parting of the Ways' from the Perspective of Rabbinic Judaism," in *Jews and Christians: The Parting of the Ways A.D. 70 to 135*. Edited by James D. G. Dunn. WUNT 66. Tübingen: J. C. B. Mohr, 1992, pp. 1–25.

Allison, Dale C., Jr. "Was there a 'Lukan Community?'" *IBS* 10 (1988), pp. 62–70.

The New Moses: A Matthean Typology. Edinburgh: T. & T. Clark, 1993.

Alon, Gedaliah. *The Jews in Their Land in the Talmudic Age (70–640 C.E.)*. Translated and edited by Gershon Levi. 2 vols. Jerusalem: The Magnes Press, the Hebrew University, 1980–84.

Alter, Robert. *The Art of Biblical Narrative*. London: George Allen & Unwin, 1981.

"How Conventions Help Us Read: The Case of the Bible's Annunciation Type-Scene." *Proof* 3 (1983), pp. 115–30.

Anderson, Benedict. *Imagined Communities: Reflections on the Origin and Spread of Nationalism*. Rev. edn. London: Verso, 1991.

Anderson, Hugh. *Jesus and Christian Origins*. New York: Oxford University Press, 1964.

Anderson, Paul N. "John and Mark: The Bi-Optic Gospels," in *Jesus in Johannine Tradition*. Edited by Robert T. Fortna and Tom Thatcher. Louisville: Westminster John Knox, 2001, pp. 175–88.

Anthony, Dick and Thomas Robbins. "From Symbolic Realism to Structuralism." *JSSR* 14 (1975), pp. 403–14.

Antoni, Carlo. *From History to Sociology: The Transition in German Historical Thinking*. Translated by Hayden V. White. London: Merlin Press, 1959.

Applebaum, Shim'on. "The Organization of the Jewish Communities of the Diaspora," in *The Jewish People in the First Century*. Edited by Samuel Safrai and Menahem Stern. Philadelphia: Fortress, 1974, vol. I, pp. 464–503.

"The Social and Economic Status of the Jews in the Diaspora," in *The Jewish People in the First Century*. Edited by Samuel Safrai and Menahem Stern. Philadelphia: Fortress, 1976, vol. II, pp. 701–27.

Arend, Walter. *Die typischen Szenen bei Homer*. Berlin: Weidmann, 1933.

Ascough, Richard S. "Matthew and Community Formation," in *The Gospel of Matthew in Current Study*. Edited by David E. Aune. Grand Rapids: Eerdmans, 2001, pp. 96–126.

Ashton, John, ed. *The Interpretation of John*. London: SPCK, 1986.

Understanding the Fourth Gospel. Oxford: Clarendon Press, 1991.

"Riddles and Mysteries: The Way, the Truth, and the Life," in *Jesus in Johannine Tradition*. Edited by Robert T. Fortna and Tom Thatcher. Louisville: Westminster John Knox, 2001, pp. 333–42.

Attridge, Harold W. "Genre Bending in the Fourth Gospel." *JBL* 121 (2002), pp. 3–21.

Aune, David Edward. *The Cultic Setting of Realized Eschatology in Early Christianity*. NovTSup 28. Leiden: Brill, 1972.

"The Problem of the Genre of the Gospels: A Critique of C. H. Talbert's What is a Gospel?" in *Gospel Perspectives: Studies of History and Tradition in the Four Gospels*. Edited by R. T. France and David Wenham. Sheffield: JSOT Press, 1981, vol. II, pp. 9–60.

Review of Wayne A. Meeks, *The First Urban Christians: The Social World of the Apostle Paul*. *Interpretation* 39 (1985), pp. 80–82.

The New Testament in its Literary Environment. LEC 8. Philadelphia: Westminster, 1987.

"Greco-Roman Biography," in *Greco-Roman Literature and the New Testament: Selected Forms and Genres*. Edited by David E. Aune. SBLSBS 21. Atlanta: Scholars Press, 1988, pp. 107–26.

Baasland, Ernst. "Urkristendommen I sosiologiens lys." *Tidskrift for Teologi og Kirke* 54 (1984), pp. 45–57.

Bacon, B. W. *Is Mark a Roman Gospel?* HTStud 7. Cambridge, Mass.: Harvard University Press, 1919.

Baird, J. A. "Genre Analysis as a Method of Historical Criticism," in *SBLSP*. Chico, Calif.: Scholars Press, 1972, pp. 385–411.

Baker, Derek, ed. *The Church in Town and Countryside*. SCH 16. Oxford: Blackwell, 1979.

Baker, Dom Aelred. "Form and the Gospels." *DR* 88 (1970), pp. 14–26.

Balch, David L., ed. *Social History of the Matthean Community: Cross-Disciplinary Approaches*. Minneapolis: Fortress, 1991.

Baltzer, Klaus. *Die Biographie der Propheten*. Neukirchen-Vluyn: Neukirchener Verlag, 1975.

Banks, Robert. *Paul's Idea of Community: The Early House Churches in their Historical Setting*. Exeter: Paternoster, 1980.

Banton, Michael, ed. *Anthropological Approaches to the Study of Religion*. ASAM 3. London: Tavistock, 1966.

Bar-Efrat, Shimon. *The Art of Narration in the Bible*. Tel Aviv: Sifriat Hapoalim, 1979.

Narrative Art in the Bible. Translated by Dorothea Shefer-Vanson. JSOTSup 70. Sheffield: Sheffield Academic Press, 1989.

Barclay, John M. G. "Mirror-Reading a Polemical Letter: Galatians as a Test Case." *JSNT* 31 (1987), pp. 73–93.

"Deviance and Apostasy: Some Applications of Deviance Theory to First-Century Judaism and Christianity," in *Modeling Early Christianity: Social-Scientific Studies of the New Testament in its Context*. Edited by Philip F. Esler. London: Routledge, 1995, pp. 114–27.

Jews in the Mediterranean Diaspora from Alexander to Trajan (323 BCE – 117 CE). Edinburgh: T. & T. Clark, 1996.

"The Family as Bearer of Religion in Judaism and Early Christianity," in *Constructing Early Christian Families*. Edited by Halvor Moxnes. London: Routledge, 1997, pp. 66–80.

Barr, David L. *"Towards a Definition of the Gospel Genre: A Generic Analysis and Comparison of the Synoptic Gospels and the Socratic Dialogues by Means of Aristotle's Theory of Tragedy."* Ph.D. diss., Florida State University, 1974.

Barr, James. *Holy Scripture: Canon, Authority, Criticism*. Oxford: Clarendon Press, 1983.

Barrett, Charles Kingsley. "The Old Testament in the Fourth Gospel." *JTS* 48 (1947), pp. 155–69.

The Gospel of John and Judaism. Translated by D. M. Smith. London: SPCK, 1975.

The Gospel According to St. John. 2nd edn. London: SPCK, 1978.

"Johannine Christianity," in *Christian Beginnings: Word and Community from Jesus to Post-Apostolic Times*. Edited by Jürgen Becker. Louisville: Westminster John Knox, 1993, pp. 330–58.

"John and Judaism," in *Anti-Judaism and the Fourth Gospel*. Edited by Reimund Bieringer, Didier Pollefeyt, and Frederique Vandecasteele-Vanneuville. Louisville: Westminster John Knox Press, 2001, pp. 231–46.

Barthes, Roland. *S/Z*. Translated by Richard Miller. New York: Hill and Wang, 1974.

Barton, John. *Holy Writings, Sacred Text: The Canon in Early Christianity*. Louisville: Westminster John Knox, 1997.

Barton, Stephen C. "The Communal Dimensions of Earliest Christianity." *JTS* 43 (1992), pp. 399–427.

"Early Christianity and the Sociology of the Sect," in *The Open Text: New Directions for Biblical Studies?* Edited by Francis Watson. London: SCM Press, 1993, pp. 140–62.

"Living as Families in the Light of the New Testament." *Interpretation* 52 (1998), pp. 130–44.

"Can We Identify the Gospel Audiences?" in *The Gospels for All Christians: Rethinking the Gospel Audiences*. Edited by Richard Bauckham. Grand Rapids: Eerdmans, 1998, pp. 173–94.

"Christian Community in the Light of the Gospel of John," in *Christology, Controversy, and Community: New Testament Essays in Honour of David R. Catchpole*. Edited by David G. Horrell and Christopher M. Tuckett. NovT-Sup 99. Leiden: Brill, 2000, pp. 279–301.

Bassler, Jouette M. "The Galileans: A Neglected Factor in Johannine Community Research." *CBQ* 43 (1981), pp. 243–57.

Bauckham, Richard J. *Jude and the Relatives of Jesus in the Early Church.* Edinburgh: T. & T. Clark, 1990.

"The Parting of the Ways: What Happened and Why?" *ST* 47 (1993), pp. 135–41.

"Papias and Polycrates on the Origin of the Fourth Gospel." *JTS* 44 (1993), pp. 24–69.

"The Beloved Disciple as Ideal Author." *JSNT* 49 (1993), pp. 21–44.

"The Apocalypse of Peter: A Jewish Christian Apocalypse from the Time of the Bar Kokhba." *Apocrypha* 5 (1994), pp. 87–90.

"Nicodemus and the Gurion Family." *JTS* 47 (1996), pp. 1–37.

"Introduction," in *The Gospels for All Christians: Rethinking the Gospel Audiences*. Edited by Richard Bauckham. Grand Rapids: Eerdmans, 1998, pp. 1–7.

"For Whom Were the Gospels Written?," in *The Gospels for All Christians: Rethinking the Gospel Audiences*. Edited by Richard Bauckham. Grand Rapids: Eerdmans, 1998, pp. 9–48.

"John for Readers of Mark," in *The Gospels for All Christians: Rethinking the Gospel Audiences*. Edited by Richard Bauckham. Grand Rapids: Eerdmans, 1998, pp. 147–71.

"Response to Philip Esler." *SJT* 51 (1998), pp. 248–53.

"The Audience of the Fourth Gospel," in *Jesus in Johannine Tradition*. Edited by Robert T. Fortna and Tom Thatcher. Louisville: Westminster John Knox, 2001, pp. 101–11.

Gospel Women: Studies of the Named Women in the Gospels. Edinburgh: T. & T. Clark, 2002.

"The Eyewitnesses and the Gospel Traditions." *JSHJ* 1 (2003), pp. 28–60.

Bauckham, Richard J., ed. *The Gospels for All Christians: Rethinking the Gospel Audiences*. Grand Rapids: Eerdmans, 1998.

Baumbach, Günther. "Die Anfänge der Kirchwerdung im Urchristentum." *Kairos* 24 (1982), pp. 17–30.

Baumgarten-Crusius, Ludwig. *Theologische Auslegung der johanneischen Schriften*. Thüringen: Jena, 1843–45, vols. I–II.

Baxter, Tony. Review of Richard Bauckham, ed., *The Gospels for All Christians*. *Evangel* 19 (2001), p. 55.

Beardslee, William A. *Literary Criticism of the New Testament.* GBS. Philadelphia: Fortress, 1970.

Beasley-Murray, George R. *John.* 2nd edn. WBC 36. Nashville: Thomas Nelson, 1999.

Beaton, Richard. Review of David C. Sim, *The Gospel of Matthew and Christian Judaism: The History and Social Setting of the Matthean Community. JTS* 51 (2000), pp. 242–46.

Beavis, May Ann. *Mark's Audience: The Literary and Social Setting of Mark: 4.11–12.* JSNTSup 33. Sheffield: Sheffield Academic Press, 1989.

Beck, David R. "The Narrative Function of Anonymity in Fourth Gospel Characterization." *Semeia* 63 (1993), pp. 143–58.

Becker, Howard S. *Outsiders: Studies in the Sociology of Deviance.* New York: Free Press, 1963.

Becker, Howard S., ed. *The Other Side: Perspectives on Deviance.* New York: Free Press, 1964.

Beckford, James A. "Religious Organization." *CS* 21 (1973), pp. 1–170.

Bellah, Robert N. "Christianity and Symbolic Realism," in *Beyond Belief: Essays on Religion in a Post-Traditional World.* Edited by Robert Bellah. New York: Harper & Row, 1970, pp. 236–59.

"Comment on 'The Limits of Symbolic Realism.'" *JSSR* 13 (1974), pp. 487–89.

Benson, J. Kenneth and James H. Dorsett. "Toward a Theory of Religious Organizations." *JSSR* 10 (1971), pp. 138–51.

Berger, Klaus. *Exegese des Neuen Testaments: neue Wege vom Text zur Auslegung.* Uni-Taschenbücher 658. Heidelberg: Quelle & Meyer, 1977.

Berger, Peter L. "The Sociological Study of Sectarianism." *SR* 21 (1954), pp. 467–85.

The Sacred Canopy: Elements of a Sociological Theory of Religion. Garden City: Doubleday, 1967.

Berger, Peter L. and Thomas Luckmann. *The Social Construction of Reality: A Treatise in the Sociology of Knowledge.* Garden City: Doubleday, 1966.

Best, Ernest. *Following Jesus: Discipleship in the Gospel of Mark.* JSNTSup 4. Sheffield: JSOT Press, 1981.

Mark: The Gospel as Story. SNTW. Edinburgh: T. & T. Clark, 1983.

Best, Thomas. "Sociological Study of the New Testament: Promise and Peril of A New Discipline." *SJT* 36 (1983), pp. 181–94.

Betz, Otto. "The Concept of the So-Called 'Divine Man' in Mark's Christology," in *Studies in New Testament and Early Christian Literature: Essays in Honor of Allen P. Wikgren.* Edited by David E. Aune. NovTSup 33. Leiden: Brill, 1972, pp. 229–40.

Beutler, Johannes. *Die Johannesbriefe: Übersetz und erklärt.* 3rd edn. RNT. Regensburg: Friedrich Pustet, 2000.

"Faith and Confession: The Purpose of John," in *Word, Theology, and Community in John.* Edited by J. Painter, R. A. Culpepper, and F. F. Segovia. Festschrift for Robert Kysar. St. Louis: Chalice Press, 2002, pp. 19–31.

Bieder, Werner. *Gottes Sendung und der missionarische Auftrag der Kirche nach Matthäus, Lukas, Paulus und Johannes.* ThStud 82. Zurich: EVZ-Verlag, 1965.

Bieringer, Reimund, Didier Pollefeyt, and Frederique Vandecasteele-Vanneuville. "Wrestling with Johannine Anti-Judaism: A Hermeneutical Framework for the Analysis of the Current Debate," in *Anti-Judaism and the Fourth*

Gospel. Edited by Reimund Bieringer, Didier Pollefeyt, and Frederique Vandecasteele-Vanneuville. Louisville: Westminster John Knox, 2001, pp. 3–37.

Bilezikian, Gilbert G. *The Liberated Gospel: A Comparison of the Gospel of Mark and Greek Tragedy.* Grand Rapids: Baker, 1977.

Blank, Josef. *Krisis: Untersuchungen zur johanneischen Christologie und Eschatologie.* Freiburg: Lambertus, 1964.

Blenkinsopp, Joseph. "Interpretation and Tendency to Sectarianism: An Aspect of Second Temple Judaism," in *Jewish and Christian Self-Definition: Aspects of Judaism in the Graeco-Roman Period.* Edited by E. P. Sanders with A. I. Baumgarten and A. Mendelson. Philadelphia: Fortress, 1981, vol. II, pp. 1–26.

Bloch, Marc. *The Historian's Craft.* Translated by Peter Putnam. Manchester: Manchester University Press, 1954.

Blomberg, Craig. L. "Form Criticism," in *Dictionary of Jesus and the Gospels.* Edited by Joel B. Green, Scot McKnight, and I. Howard Marshall. Downers Grove, Ill.: Intervarsity, 1992.

Review of Richard Bauckham, ed., *The Gospels for All Christians. Themelios* 25 (2000), pp. 78–80.

The Historical Reliability of John's Gospel: Issues and Commentary. Downers Grove, Ill.: Intervarsity, 2001.

"The Historical Reliability of John: Rushing in Where Angels Fear to Tread?," in *Jesus in Johannine Tradition.* Edited by Robert T. Fortna and Tom Thatcher. Louisville: Westminster John Knox, 2001, pp. 71–82.

"Interpreting Old Testament Prophetic Literature in Matthew: Double Fulfillment." *TJ* 23 (2002), pp. 17–33.

Böcher, Otto. "Johanneisches in der Apokalypse des Johannes." *NTS* 27 (1981), pp. 310–21.

Boer, Martinus C. de. "John 4:27 – Women (and Men) in the Gospel and Community of John," in *Women in the Biblical Tradition.* Edited by George J. Brooks. New York: Edwin Mellen, 1992, pp. 208–30.

"The Depiction of 'the Jews' in John's Gospel: Matters of Behavior and Identity," in *Anti-Judaism and the Fourth Gospel.* Edited by Reimund Bieringer, Didier Pollefeyt, and Frederique Vandecasteele-Vanneuville. Louisville: Westminster John Knox, 2001, pp. 141–57.

Bogart, John. *Orthodox and Heretical Perfectionism in the Johannine Community as Evident in the First Epistle of John.* SBLDS 33. Missoula, Mont.: Scholars Press, 1977.

Boismard, Marie-Émile. *Moses or Jesus: An Essay in Johannine Christology.* BETL 84-A. Translated by B. T. Viviano. Leuven: University Press, 1993.

Boismard, Marie-Emile and Arnaud Lamouille. *L'Evangile de Jean: Synopse des quatre évangiles.* Paris: du Cerf, 1977, vol. III.

Boon, James A. *Other Tribes, Other Scribes: Symbolic Anthropology in the Comparative Study of Cultures, Histories, Religions, and Texts.* Cambridge: Cambridge University Press, 1980.

Booth, Wayne. *The Rhetoric of Fiction.* 2nd edn. Chicago: University of Chicago Press, 1983.

Borgen, Peder. *Bread from Heaven: An Exegetical Study of the Concept of Manna in the Gospel of John and the Writings of Philo*. NovTSup 10. Leiden: Brill, 1965.

Philo, John and Paul: New Perspectives on Judaism and Early Christianity. BJS 131. Atlanta: Scholars Press, 1987.

Philo of Alexandria: An Exegete for His Time. NovTSup 86. Leiden: Brill, 1997.

Bornhäuser, Karl. *Das Johannesevangelium: Eine Missionsschrift für Israel*. BFCT 2/15. Gütersloh: Bertelsmann, 1928.

Bornkamm, Günther, Gerhard Barth, and Heinz Joachim Held. *Tradition and Interpretation in Matthew*. Translated by Percy Scott. London: SCM Press, 1963.

Botha, J. Eugene. *Jesus and the Samaritan Woman: A Speech Act Reading of John 4:1–42*. NovTSup 65. Leiden: Brill, 1991.

Bottomore, Tom and Robert Nisbet, eds. *A History of Sociological Analysis*. London: Heinemann, 1978.

Bourdieu, Pierre. *Language and Symbolic Power*. Edited by John B. Thompson. Translated by Gino Raymond and Matthew Adamson. Cambridge: Polity Press, 1991.

Bowe, Barbara E. Review of Richard Bauckham, ed., *The Gospels for All Christians*. *CTM* 27 (2000), p. 295.

Bowersock, G. W. *Fiction as History: Nero to Julian*. SCL 1991. Berkeley: University of California Press, 1994.

Bowman, John W. "Samaritan Studies 1: The Fourth Gospel and the Samaritans," *BJRL* 40 (1957–58), pp. 298–327.

The Gospel of Mark: The New Christian Jewish Passover Haggadah. Studia Post-Biblica 8. Leiden: Brill, 1965.

Box, G. H. "The Jewish Environment of Early Christianity." *The Expositor* 12 (1916), pp. 1–25.

Boyarin, Daniel. *Dying for God: Martyrdom and the Making of Christianity and Judaism*. Stanford: Stanford University Press, 1999.

Brawley, Robert L. "An Absent Complement and Intertextuality in John 19:28–29." *JBL* 112 (1993), pp. 427–43.

Brenk, Frederick E. Review of Richard Burridge, *What are the Gospels? A Comparison with Graeco-Roman Biography*. *Gnomon* 66 (1994), pp. 492–96.

Bretschneider, Karl G. *Probabilia de evangelii et epistolarum Joannis Apostoli, indole et origine*. Leipzig: University Press, 1820.

Brodie, Thomas L. *The Quest for the Origin of John's Gospel: A Source-Oriented Approach*. New York: Oxford University Press, 1993.

The Gospel According to John: A Literary and Theological Commentary. New York: Oxford University Press, 1993.

The Crucial Bridge: The Elijah-Elisha Narrative as an Interpretive Synthesis of Genesis-Kings and A Literary Model for the Gospels. Collegeville, Minn.: Liturgical Press, 2000.

Brown, Raymond E. *The Gospel According to John*. AB 29. Garden City: Doubleday, 1966, vol. I.

"The Kerygma of the Gospel According to John: The Johannine View of Jesus in Modern Studies." *Interpretation* 21 (1967), pp. 387–400.

The Gospel According to John. AB 29a. Garden City: Doubleday, 1970, vol. II.

"Jesus and Elisha." *Perspective* 12 (1971), pp. 85–104.

"Johannine Ecclesiology – The Community's Origins." *Interpretation* 31 (1977), pp. 379–93.

"'Other Sheep Not of This Fold': The Johannine Perspective on Christian Diversity in the Late First Century." *JBL* 97 (1978), pp. 5–22.

The Community of the Beloved Disciple: The Life, Loves, and Hates of an Individual Church in New Testament Times. New York: Paulist Press, 1979.

"New Testament Background for the Concept of Local Church." *PCTSA* 36 (1981), pp. 1–14.

The Epistles of John. AB 30. London: Geoffrey Chapman, 1982.

The Churches the Apostles Left Behind. London: Geoffrey Chapman, 1984.

An Introduction to the Gospel of John. ABRL. Edited by Francis J. Moloney. New York: Doubleday, 2003.

Bruce, F. F. *Men and Movements in the Primitive Church: Studies in Non-Pauline Christianity.* Exeter: Paternoster, 1979.

Bryant, J. M. "The Sect-church Dynamic and Christian Expansion in the Roman Empire: Persecution, Penitential Discipline, and Schism in Sociological Perspective." *BJSoc* 44 (1993), pp. 303–39.

Buchanan, George Wesley. "The Samaritan Origin of the Gospel of John," in *Religions in Antiquity: Essays in Memory of Erwin Ramsdell Goodenough.* Edited by Jacob Neusner. SHR 14. Leiden: Brill, 1968, pp. 149–75.

Introduction to Intertextuality. Lewiston: Mellen Biblical Press, 1994.

Bühner, Jan Adolph. *Der Gesandte und sein Weg im vierten Evangelium: Die Kultur- und religionsgeschichtlichen Grundlagen der johanneischen Sendungschristologie sowie ihre traditionsgeschichtliche Entwicklung.* WUNT 2/2. Tübingen: J. C. B. Mohr, 1977.

Bultmann, Rudolf. "Die Bedeutung der neuerschlossenen mandäischen und manichäischen Quellen für das Verständnis des Johannesevangeliums." *ZNW* 24 (1925), pp. 100–46.

Theology of the New Testament. Translated by Kendrick Grobel. London: SCM Press, 1952, vol. I.

Theology of the New Testament. Translated by Kendrick Grobel. London: SCM Press, 1955, vol. II.

Primitive Christianity in its Contemporary Setting. Translated by Reginald H. Fuller. Philadelphia: Fortress, 1956.

The History of the Synoptic Tradition. Translated by John Marsh. Oxford: Basil Blackwell, 1963.

The Gospel of John: A Commentary. Translated by G. R. Beasley-Murray. Philadelphia: Westminster, 1971.

The Johannine Epistles: A Commentary on the Johannine Epistles. Translated by R. Philip O'Hara, Lane C. McGaughy, and Robert W. Funk. Hermeneia. Philadelphia: Fortress, 1973.

Burge, Gary M. *The Anointed Community: The Holy Spirit in the Johannine Tradition.* Grand Rapids: Eerdmans, 1987.

"Situating John's Gospel in History," in *Jesus in Johannine Tradition.* Edited by Robert T. Fortna and Tom Thatcher. Louisville: Westminster John Knox, 2001, pp. 35–46.

Burke, Peter. *History and Social Theory*. Cambridge: Blackwell, 1992.

Burnett, Fred W. "Characterization and Reader Construction of Characters in the Gospels." *Semeia* 63 (1993), pp. 1–28.

Burridge, Kenelm. *New Heaven, New Earth: A Study of Millenarian Activities*. Oxford: Basil Blackwell, 1969.

Burridge, Richard A. "Gospel," in *A Dictionary of Biblical Interpretation*. Edited by Richard J. Coggin and James L. Houlden. London: SCM Press, 1990, pp. 266–68.

—— *What are the Gospels? A Comparison with Graeco-Roman Biography*. SNTSMS 70. Cambridge: Cambridge University Press, 1992.

—— "About People, by People, for People: Gospel Genre and Audiences," in *The Gospels for All Christians: Rethinking the Gospel Audiences*. Edited by Richard Bauckham. Grand Rapids: Eerdmans, 1998, pp. 113–45.

—— "Gospel Genre, Christological Controversy and the Absence of Rabbinic Biography: Some Implications of the Biographical Hypothesis," in *Christology, Controversy, and Community: New Testament Essays in Honour of David R. Catchpole*. Edited by David G. Horrell and Christopher M. Tuckett. NovTSup 99. Leiden: Brill, 2000, pp. 137–56.

—— *What are the Gospels? A Comparison with Graeco-Roman Biography*. 2nd edn. Grand Rapids: Eerdmans, 2004.

Busch, E. W. "Tragic Action in the Second Gospel." *JR* 11 (1931), pp. 346–58.

Busse, Ulrich. "Die Tempelmetaphorik als ein Beispiel von implizitem Rekurs auf die biblische Tradition im Johannesevangelium," in *The Scriptures in the Gospels*. Edited by Christopher M. Tuckett. BETL 131. Leuven: Leuven University Press, 1997, pp. 395–428.

Byrskog, Samuel. *Story as History-History as Story: The Gospel Traditions in the Context of Ancient Oral History*. WUNT 123. Tübingen: Mohr Siebeck, 2000.

Caird, G. B. *New Testament Theology*. Edited and completed by L. D. Hurst. Oxford: Clarendon Press, 1994.

Cairns, David. "The Thought of Peter Berger." *SJT* 27 (1974), pp. 181–97.

Cameron, Averil. *Christianity and the Rhetoric of Empire: The Development of Christian Discourse*. SCL 55. Berkeley: University of California Press, 1991.

Campenhausen, Hans von. *The Formation of the Christian Bible*. Translated by John Austin Baker. London: Adam and Charles Black, 1974.

Carlson, Stephen C. "Clement of Alexandria on the 'Order' of the Gospels." *NTS* 47 (2001), pp. 118–25.

Carney, T. F. *The Shape of the Past: Models and Antiquity*. Lawrence, Kans.: Coronado Press, 1975.

Carrington, Philip. *The Primitive Christian Calendar: A Study in the Making of the Markan Gospel*. Cambridge: Cambridge University Press, 1952.

Carroll, Kenneth L. "The Fourth Gospel and the Exclusion of Christians from the Synagogues." *BJRL* 40 (1957), pp. 19–32.

Carson, Donald A. "Historical Tradition in the Fourth Gospel: After Dodd, What?," in *Gospel Perspectives: Studies of History and Tradition in the Four Gospels*. Edited by R. T. France and David Wenham. Sheffield: JSOT Press, 1981, vol. II, pp. 83–145.

"Understanding Misunderstanding in the Fourth Gospel" *TB* 33 (1982), pp. 59–91.

"The Purpose of the Fourth Gospel: John 20:31 Reconsidered." *JBL* 106 (1987), pp. 639–51.

"John and the Johannine Epistles," in *It is Written: Scripture Citing Scripture: Essays in Honor of Barnabas Lindars*. Edited by D. A. Carson and H. G. M. Willaimson. Cambridge: Cambridge University Press, 1988, pp. 245–64.

The Gospel According to John. PNTC. Grand Rapids: Eerdmans, 1991.

"Redaction Criticism: On the Legitimacy and Illegitimacy of a Literary Tool," in *Scripture and Truth*. Rev. and enl. edn. Edited by D. A. Carson and John D. Woodbridge. Grand Rapids: Baker, 1992, pp. 115–42.

"Syntactical and Text-Critical Observations on John 20:30–31: One More Round on the Purpose of the Fourth Gospel." *JBL* 124 (2005), pp. 693–714.

Carter, Warren. "Community Definition and Matthew's Gospel," in *SBLSP*. Chico, Calif.: Scholars Press, 1997, pp. 637–63.

Casson, L. *Travel in the Ancient World*. London: Allen & Unwin, 1974.

Charlesworth, James H. *The Beloved Disciple: Whose Witness Validates the Gospel of John?* Valley Forge, Pa.: Trinity Press International, 1995.

"The Gospel of John: Exclusivism Caused by a Social Setting Different from That of Jesus (John 11:54 and 14:6)," in *Anti-Judaism and the Fourth Gospel*. Edited by Reimund Bieringer, Didier Pollefeyt, and Frederique Vandecasteele-Vanneuville. Louisville: Westminster John Knox, 2001, pp. 247–78.

Charlesworth, M. P. *Trade Routes and Commerce in the Roman Empire*. 2nd edn. Cambridge: Cambridge University Press, 1926.

Chatman, Seymour. *Story and Discourse: Narrative Structure in Fiction and Film*. Ithaca: Cornell University Press, 1978.

Childs, Brevard S. "The Sensus Literalis of Scripture: An Ancient and Modern Problem," in *Beiträge zur Alttestamentlichen Theologie: Festschrift für Walther Zimmerli zum 70. Geburtstag*. Edited by Herbert Donner, Robert Hanhart, and Rudolf Smend. Göttingen: Vandenhoeck & Ruprecht, 1977, pp. 80–93.

"The Canonical Shape of the Prophetic Literature." *Interpretation* 32 (1978), pp. 46–55.

The New Testament as Canon: An Introduction. London: SCM Press, 1984.

Biblical Theology of the Old and New Testaments: Theological Reflection on the Christian Bible. Minneapolis: Fortress, 1992.

"Retrospective Reading of the Old Testament Prophets." *ZAW* 108 (1996), pp. 362–77.

Clayton, Jay and Eric Rothstein, eds. *Influence and Intertextuality in Literary History*. Madison: The University of Wisconsin Press, 1991.

Coenen, L. "ἐκκλησία," in NIDNTT. Edited by Colin Brown. Grand Rapids: Zondervan, 1975–86, vol. I, pp. 291–307.

Cohen, Anthony P. *The Symbolic Construction of Community*. KI 1. London: Routledge, 1985.

Cohen, S. J. D., ed. *The Jewish Family in Antiquity*. BJS 289. Atlanta: Scholars Press, 1993.

Collins, Adela Yarbro. "Narrative, History, and Gospel." *Semeia* 43 (1988), pp. 145–53.

Review of Richard Burridge, *What are the Gospels? A Comparison with Graeco-Roman Biography. JR* 75 (1995), pp. 239–46.

Collins, John J. *The Apocalyptic Imagination: An Introduction to the Jewish Matrix of Christianity.* New York: Crossroad, 1984.

Collins, Raymond F. "The Representative Figures of the Fourth Gospel – I." *DR* 94 (1976), pp. 26–46,

"The Representative Figures of the Fourth Gospel – II." *DR* 94 (1976), pp. 118–32.

"Speaking of the Jews: 'Jews' in the Discourse Material of the Fourth Gospel," in *Anti-Judaism and the Fourth Gospel.* Edited by Reimund Bieringer, Didier Pollefeyt, and Frederique Vandecasteele-Vanneuville. Louisville: Westminster John Knox, 2001, pp. 158–75.

Colpe, Carsten. "The Oldest Jewish-Christian Community," in *Christian Beginnings: Word and Community from Jesus to Post-Apostolic Times.* Edited by Jürgen Becker. Louisville: Westminster John Knox, 1993, pp. 75–102.

Conway, Colleen M. "The Production of the Johannine Community: A New Historicist Perspective." *JBL* 121 (2002), pp. 479–95.

"Speaking through Ambiguity: Minor Characters in the Fourth Gospel." *BI* 10 (2002), pp. 324–41.

Conzelmann, Hans. *The Theology of St. Luke.* Translated by Geoffrey Buswell. New York: Harper & Brothers, 1960.

"Luke's Place in the Development of Early Christianity," in *Studies in Luke-Acts: Essays Presented in Honor of Paul Schubert.* Edited by Leander Keck and J. Louis Martyn. Nashville: Abingdon, 1966, pp. 298–316.

Coser, Lewis. *The Functions of Social Conflict.* New York: Free Press, 1956.

Creed, J. M. *The Gospel According to St. Luke.* London: Macmillan, 1930.

Crosman, Robert. "Do Readers Make Meaning?," in *The Reader in the Text: Essays on Audience and Interpretation.* Edited by Susan R. Suleiman and Inge Crosman. Princeton: Princeton University Press, 1980, pp. 3–45.

Crossan, John Dominic. *The Historical Jesus: The Life of A Mediterranean Peasant.* New York: Harper Collins, 1992.

The Birth of Christianity: Discovering What Happened in the Years immediately after the Execution of Jesus. San Francisco: Harper & Collins, 1998.

Culler, Jonathan. "Prolegomena to a Theory of Reading," in *The Reader in the Text: Essays on Audience and Interpretation.* Edited by Susan R. Suleiman and Inge Crosman. Princeton: Princeton University Press, 1980, pp. 46–66.

The Pursuit of Signs: Semiotics, Literature, Deconstruction. Ithaca: Cornell University Press, 1981.

Cullmann, Oscar. "Les récentes études sur la formation de la tradition évangélique." *RHPR* 5 (1925), pp. 564–79.

Early Christian Worship. Translated by A. Stewart Todd and James B. Torrance. SBT 10. London: SCM Press, 1953.

"The Plurality of the Gospels as a Theological Problem in Antiquity: A Study in the History of Dogma," in *The Early Church: Oscar Cullmann.* Edited by A. J. B. Higgins. Translated by A. J. B. Higgins and S. Godman. London: SCM Press, 1956, pp. 39–54.

The Johannine Circle: Its Place in Judaism, Among the Disciples of Jesus and in Early Christianity: A Study in the Origin of the Gospel of John. Translated by John Bowden. London: SCM Press, 1976.

Culpepper, R. Alan. *The Johannine School: An Evaluation of the Johannine-School Hypothesis Based on an Investigation of the Nature of Ancient Schools.* SBLDS 26. Missoula, Mont.: Scholars Press, 1975.

"The Narrator in the Fourth Gospel: Intratextual Relationships," in *SBLSP.* Chico, Calif.: Scholars Press, 1982, pp. 81–96.

Anatomy of the Fourth Gospel: A Study in Literary Design. FFNT. Philadelphia: Fortress, 1983.

"The Theology of the Gospel of John," *RE* 85 (1988), pp. 417–32.

"Anti-Judaism in the Fourth Gospel as a Theological Problem for Christian Interpreters," in *Anti-Judaism and the Fourth Gospel.* Edited by Reimund Bieringer, Didier Pollefeyt, and Frederique Vandecasteele-Vanneuville. Louisville: Westminster John Knox, 2001, pp. 61–82.

Cweikowski, Frederick J. *The Beginnings of the Church.* Dublin: Gill and Macmillan, 1988.

Dahl, Nils Alstrup. "The Plurality of the Pauline Epistles as a Problem in the Ancient Church," in *Neotestamentica et patristica, eine Freundesgabe, Oscar Cullmann zu seinem 60 Geburtstag.* Edited by A. N. Wilder, *et al.* NovTSup 6. Leiden: Brill, 1962, pp. 161–71.

Jesus in the Memory of the Early Church. Minneapolis: Augsburg, 1976.

Damrosch, David. *The Narrative Covenant: Transformations of Genre in the Growth of Biblical Literature.* San Francisco: Harper & Row, 1987.

Daniélou, Jean. "Christianity as a Jewish Sect," in *The Crucible of Christianity: Judaism, Hellenism and the Historical Background of the Christian Faith.* Edited by Arnold Toynbee. London: Thames & Hudson, 1969, pp. 275–82.

Davies, Margaret. *Rhetoric and Reference in the Fourth Gospel.* JSNTSup 69. Sheffield: JSOT Press, 1992.

Davies, William D. *The Gospel and the Land: Early Christianity and Jewish Territorial Doctrine.* Berkeley: University of California Press, 1974.

Davies, William D. and Dale C. Allison. *A Critical and Exegetical Commentary on the Gospel According to Saint Matthew.* ICC. 3 vols. Edinburgh: T. & T. Clark, 1988–97.

Dawson, David. *Allegorical Readers and Cultural Revision in Ancient Alexandria.* Berkeley: University of California Press, 1992.

DeConick, April D. "John Rivals Thomas: From Community Conflict to Gospel Narrative," in *Jesus in Johannine Tradition.* Edited by Robert T. Fortna and Tom Thatcher. Louisville: Westminster John Knox, 2001, pp. 303–11.

Deeley, Mary Katharine. "Ezekiel's Shepherd and John's Jesus: A Case Study in the Appropriation of Biblical Texts," in *Studies in Scripture in Early Judaism and Christianity: Investigations and Proposals.* Edited by Craig A. Evans and James A. Sanders. JSNTSup 148. SSEJC 5. Sheffield: Sheffield Academic Press, 1997, pp. 252–64.

Deissmann, Adolf. *Light from the Ancient Near East: The New Testament Illustrated from Recently Discovered Texts of the Graeco-Roman World.* 2nd edn. Translated by Lionel R. M. Strachan. London: Hodder & Stoughton, 1910.

Demerath, Nicholas J., III. "In a Sow's Ear: A Reply to Goode." *JSSR* 6 (1967), pp. 77–84.

"Son of a Sow's Ear." *JSSR* 6 (1967), pp. 257–77.

Derrida, Jacques. *Of Grammatology*. Translated by Gayatri Chakravorty Spivak. Baltimore: Johns Hopkins University Press, 1976.

Detweiler, Robert. "How to Read a Jaguar: A Response to Mary Gerhart." *Semeia* 43 (1988), pp. 45–51.

Dettwiler, Andreas. *Die Gegenwart des Erhöhten: Eine exegetische Studie Zu den johanneischen Abschiedsreden (Joh. 13,31–16,33) unter besonderer Berücksichtigung ihres Relectere-Charakters*. FRLANT 169. Göttingen: Vandenhoeck & Ruprecht, 1995.

Dewey, Arthur J. "The Eyewitness of History: Visionary Consciousness in the Fourth Gospel," in *Jesus in Johannine Tradition*. Edited by Robert T. Fortna and Tom Thatcher. Louisville: Westminster John Knox, 2001, pp. 59–70.

Dewey, Joanna. "The Gospel of John in Its Oral-Written Media World," in *Jesus in Johannine Tradition*. Edited by Robert T. Fortna and Tom Thatcher. Louisville: Westminster John Knox, 2001, pp. 239–52.

Dibelius, Martin. *From Tradition to Gospel*. Translated by Bertram Lee Woolf. London: Ivor Nicholson and Watson, 1934.

Dieffenbach, Ludwig A. "Über einege wahrscheinliche Interpolationen im Evangelium Johannis," *KJNTL* 5 (1816), pp. 1–16.

Dihle, Albrecht. "The Gospels and Greek Biography," in *The Gospel and The Gospels*. Edited by Peter Stuhlmacher. Translated by John Bowden. Grand Rapids: Eerdmans, 1991, pp. 361–86.

Dittes, James E. "Typing the Typologies: Some Parallels in the Career of Church-Sect and Extrinsic-Intrinsic." *JSSR* 10 (1971), pp. 375–83.

Dodd, Charles H. "The Framework of the Gospel Narrative." *ExpT* 43 (1931–32), pp. 396–400.

The Apostolic Preaching and its Developments: Three Lectures with an Appendix on Eschatology and History. London: Hodder & Stoughton, 1936.

The Interpretation of the Fourth Gospel. Cambridge: Cambridge University Press, 1953.

Historical Tradition in the Fourth Gospel. Cambridge: Cambridge University Press, 1963.

More New Testament Studies. Manchester: Manchester University Press, 1968.

Dods, Marcus. *The Gospel of St. John*. 10th edn. London: Hodder & Stoughton, 1906.

Donahue, John R. "The Quest for the Community of Mark's Gospel," in *The Four Gospels 1992*. Edited by F. Van Segbroeck *et al.* BETL 100. Leuven: Leuven University Press, 1992, vol. II, pp. 817–38.

Donahue, John R., ed. *Life in Abundance: Studies of John's Gospel in Tribute to Raymond E. Brown*. Collegeville, Minn.: Liturgical Press, 2005.

Doty, William G. "The Concept of Genre in Literary Analysis," in *The Genre of the Gospels: Studies in Methodology, Comparative Research and Compositional Analysis*. Missoula: Society of Biblical Literature, 1972, pp. 29–64.

Douglas, Mary. *Purity and Danger*. London: Routledge & Kegan Paul, 1996.

Essays in the Sociology of Perception. London: Routledge & Kegan Paul, 1982.

Natural Symbols: Explorations in Cosmology. New York: Pantheon Books, 1982.

Downing, F. Gerald. *The Church and Jesus: A Study in History, Philosophy, and Theology*. SBT, Second Series 10. London: SCM Press, 1968.

"Contemporary Analogies to the Gospel and Acts: 'Genres' or 'Motifs'?," in *Synoptic Studies: The Ampleforth Conferences of 1982 and 1983*. Edited by C. M. Tuckett. JSNTSup 7. Sheffield: JSOT Press, 1983, pp. 51–65.

Duff, David. "Intertextuality versus Genre Theory: Bakhtin, Kristeva and the Question of Genre." *Paragraph* 25 (2002), pp. 54–73.

Duff, Jeremy. Review of Richard Bauckham, ed., *The Gospels for All Christians*. *Anvil* 16 (1999), pp. 134–35.

Duke, Paul D. *Irony in the Fourth Gospel*. Atlanta; John Knox, 1985.

Dunderberg, Ismo. "The Beloved Disciple in John: Ideal Figure in an Early Christian Controversy," in *Fair Play: Diversity and Conflicts in Early Christianity: Essays in Honor of Heikki Räisänen*. Edited by Ismo Dunderberg, Christopher Tuckett, and Kari Syreeni. NovTSup 103. Leiden: Brill, 2002, pp. 243–69.

Duling, Dennis C. "Millennialism," in *The Social Sciences and New Testament Interpretation*. Edited by Richard L. Rohrbaugh. Peabody: Hendrickson, 1996, pp. 183–205.

Dunn, James D. G. *Unity and Diversity in the New Testament: An Inquiry into the Character of Earliest Christianity*. 2nd edn. London: SCM Press, 1990.

The Parting of the Ways between Christianity and Judaism and their Significance for the Character of Christianity. London: SCM Press, 1991.

"Let John be John: A Gospel for its Time," in *The Gospel and The Gospels*. Edited by Peter Stuhlmacher. Grand Rapids: Eerdmans, 1991, pp. 293–322.

"The Embarrassment of History: Reflections on the Problem of 'Anti-Judaism' in the Fourth Gospel," in *Anti-Judaism and the Fourth Gospel*. Edited by Reimund Bieringer, Didier Pollefeyt, and Frederique Vandecasteele-Vanneuville. Louisville: Westminster John Knox, 2001, pp. 41–60.

Christianity in the Making: Volume 1: Jesus Remembered. Grand Rapids: Eerdmans, 2003.

Dunn, James D. G., ed. *Jews and Christians: The Parting of the Ways A.D. 70 to 135*. WUNT 66. Tübingen: J. C. B. Mohr, 1993.

Durkheim, Emile. *The Rules of Sociological Method*. Translated by Sarah A. Solovay and John H. Mueller. New York: Free Press, 1965.

Drummond, James. *An Inquiry into the Character and Authorship of the Fourth Gospel*. London: Williams and Norgate, 1903.

Dyson, S. "The Relevance for Roman Archeologists of Recent Approaches to Archeology in Greece." *JRA* 2 (1989), pp. 143–46.

Eckermann, Jacob C. R. "Uber die eigentlich sicheren Gründe des Glaubens an die Hauptthatsachen der Geschichte Jesu, und über die wahrscheinliche Entstehung der Evangelien und der Apostelgeschichte," *ThB* 2 (1976), pp. 106–256.

Eco, Umberto. *The Role of the Reader: Explorations in the Semiotics of Texts*. London: Hutchinson, 1981.

Edwards, Mark J. "Biography and Biographic," in *Portraits: Biographical Representation in the Greek and Latin Literature of the Roman Empire*. Edited by Mark J. Edwards and Simon Swain. Oxford: Clarendon Press, 1997, pp. 227–34.

Eister, Alan W. "Toward a Radical Critique of Church-Sect Typologizing: Comment on 'Some Critical Observations on the Church-Sect Dimension.'" *JSSR* 6 (1967), pp. 85–99.

"H. Richard Neibuhr and the Paradox of Religious Organization: A Radical Critique," in *Beyond the Classics?* ESSR. Edited by Charles Y. Clock and Phillip E. Hammond. New York: Harper & Row, 1973, pp. 355–408.

Ellingworth, Paul. Review of Richard Bauckham, ed., *The Gospels for All Christians. EvQ* 71 (1999), pp. 273–75.

Elliott, John H. *A Home for the Homeless: A Sociological Exegesis of 1 Peter, Its Situation and Strategy.* Philadelphia: Fortress, 1981.

Review of Wayne A. Meeks, *The First Urban Christians: The Social World of the Apostle Paul. RSR* 11 (1985), pp. 329–35.

"Social-Scientific Criticism of the New Testament: More on Methods and Models." *Semeia* 35 (1986), 1–33.

What is Social-Scientific Criticism. GBSNTS. Minneapolis: Fortress, 1993.

Ellis, E. Earle. "Gospels Criticism: A Perspective on the State of the Art," in *The Gospel and The Gospels.* Edited by Peter Stuhlmacher. Grand Rapids: Eerdmans, 1991, pp. 26–52.

The Old Testament in Early Christianity: Canon and Interpretation in the Light of Modern Research. WUNT 54. Tübingen: J. C. B. Mohr, 1991.

Enz, Jacob J. "The Book of Exodus as a Literary Type for the Gospel of John." *JBL* 76 (1957), pp. 208–15.

Esler, Philip F. *Community and Gospel in Luke-Acts: The Social and Political Motivations of Lucan Theology.* SNTSMS 57. Cambridge: Cambridge University Press, 1987.

The First Christians in Their Social Worlds: Social-Scientific Approaches to New Testament Interpretation. London: Routledge, 1994.

"Community and Gospel in Early Christianity: A Response to Richard Bauckham's *Gospels for All Christians.*" *SJT* 51 (1998), pp. 235–48.

Esler, Philip F., ed. *Modelling Early Christianity: Social-Scientific studies of the New Testament in its Context.* London: Routledge, 1995.

Eslinger, Lyle. "The Wooing of the Woman at the Well: Jesus, the Reader and Reader-Response Criticism." *JLT* 1 (1987), pp. 167–83.

"Inner-Biblical Exegesis and Inner-Biblical Allusion: The Question of Category." *VT* 49 (1992), pp. 47–58.

Evans, Craig A. and James A. Sanders, eds. *The Function of Scripture in Early Jewish and Christian Tradition.* JSNTSup 154. SSEJC 6. Sheffield: Sheffield Academic Press, 1998.

Evans, Christopher Francis. *Saint Luke.* TPINTC. Philadelphia: Trinity Press International, 1990.

Evans, C. Stephen. *The Historical Christ and the Jesus of Faith: The Incarnational Narrative as History.* Oxford: Clarendon Press, 1996.

Ewald, Heinrich. *History of Israel.* 2 vols. Translated by Russell Martineau. London: Longmans and Green, 1869–86.

Fackre, Gabriel. "Narrative Theology: An Overview." *Interpretation* 37 (1983), pp. 340–52.

Farley, Edward and Peter C. Hodgson. "Scripture and Tradition," in *Christian Theology: An Introduction to its Traditions and Tasks.* Edited by Peter C. Hodgson and Robert H. King. Philadelphia: Fortress, 1982, pp. 35–61.

Farmer, William R. "The Problem of Christian Origins: A Programmatic Essay," in *Studies in the History and Text of the New Testament in Honor of Kenneth*

Willis Clark. Edited by Daniel T. Suggs. Salt Lake City: University of Utah Press, 1967, pp. 81–88.

Jesus and the Gospel: Tradition, Scripture, and Canon. Philadelphia: Fortress, 1982.

Farrell, Thomas J. "Kelber's Breakthrough." *Semeia* 39 (1987), pp. 27–45.

Fascher, Erich. *Die formgeschichtliche Methode: Eine Darstellung und Kritik, Zugleich ein Beitrag zur Geschichte des Synoptischen Problems*. BZNTW 2. Berlin: Alfred Töpelmann, 1924.

Fawcett, Thomas. *Hebrew Myth and Christian Gospel*. London: SCM Press, 1973.

Fee, Gordon D. "The Use of the Definite Article with Personal Names in the Gospel of John." *NTS* 17 (1970–71), pp. 168–83.

"P[75], P[66] and Origen: The Myth of Early Textual Recension in Alexandria," in *New Dimensions in New Testament Study*. Edited by Richard Longenecker and Merrill C. Tenney. Grand Rapids: Zondervan, 1974, pp. 19–45.

"On the Text and Meaning of John 20, 30–31," in *The Four Gospels, 1992*. 3 vols. Edited by F. van Segbroek *et al.* Leuven: Leuven University Press, 1992, vol. III, pp. 2193–205.

Feine, Paul. *Theologie des Neuen Testaments*. 21st edn. Berlin: Evangelische Verlagsanstalt, 1953.

Ferguson, Everett. "Factors Leading to the Selection and Closure of the New Testament Canon: A Survey of Some Recent Studies," in *The Canon Debate*. Edited by Lee Martin McDonald and James A. Sanders. Peabody: Hendrickson, 2002, pp. 295–320.

Festinger, Leon. *A Theory of Cognitive Dissonance*. Stanford : Stanford University Press, 1957.

Festinger, Leon, Henry W. Riecken, and Stanley Schachter. *When Prophecy Fails: A Social and Psychological Study of a Modern Group That Predicted the Destruction of the World*. New York: Harper & Row, 1956. Repr. Minneapolis: Minnesota University Press, 1964.

Fewell, Danna Nolan, ed. *Reading between Texts: Intertextuality and the Hebrew Bible*. LCBI. Louisville: Westminster John Knox, 1992.

Filson, Floyd V. "The Significance of Early House Churches." *JBL* 58 (1939), pp. 105–12.

Finn, T. M. "Social Mobility, Imperial Civil Service and the Spread of Early Christianity." *SP* 17 (1982), pp. 31–37.

Fiorenza, Elizabeth Schüssler, ed. *Aspects of Religious Propaganda in Judaism and Early Christianity*. Notre Dame: University of Notre Dame Press, 1976.

In Memory of Her: A Feminist Theological Reconstruction of Christian Origins. London: SCM Press, 1983.

The Book of Revelation: Justice and Judgment. 2nd edn. Minneapolis: Fortress, 1998.

Fischel, Harry. "Studies in Cynicism and the Ancient Near East: The Transformation of a Chria," in *Religions in Antiquity: Essays in Memory of Erwin Ramsdell Goodenough*. Edited by Jacob Neusner. Leiden: Brill, 1968, pp. 372–411.

Fitzmyer, Joseph A. *The Gospel According to Luke I–IX*. AB 28. New York: Doubleday, 1981.

Flusser, David. *Judaism and the Origins of Christianity*. Jerusalem: The Magnes Press, the Hebrew University, 1988.

Fodor, James. *Christian Hermeneutics: Paul Ricoeur and the Refiguring of Theology.* Oxford: Clarendon Press, 1995.

Forkman, Göran. *The Limits of the Religious Community: Expulsion from the Religious Community within the Qumran Sect, within Rabbinic Judaism, and within Primitive Christianity.* CBNTS 5. Lund: Gleerup, 1972.

Fortna, Robert Tomson. *The Gospel of Signs: A Reconstruction of the Narrative Source Underlying the Fourth Gospel.* SNTSMS 11. Cambridge: Cambridge University Press, 1970.

The Fourth Gospel and its Predecessor: From Narrative Source to Present Gospel. Edinburgh: T. & T. Clark, 1988.

Fortna, R. T. and B. R. Gaventa, eds. *The Conversation Continues: Studies in Paul and John.* Nashville: Abingdon, 1990.

Fowl, Stephen E. *Engaging Scripture: A Model for Theological Interpretation.* CCT. Oxford: Blackwell, 1998.

Fowler, Alastair. *Kinds of Literature: An Introduction to the Theory of Genres and Modes.* Oxford: Clarendon Press, 1981.

Fowler, Robert M. "Who is 'the Reader' of Mark's Gospel?" in *SBLSP.* Chico, Calif.: Scholars Press, 1983, pp. 31–53.

"Who is 'the Reader' in Reader Response Criticism?" *Semeia* 31 (1985), pp. 5–23.

Let the Reader Understand: Reader-Response Criticism and the Gospel of Mark. Minneapolis: Fortress, 1991.

France, R. T. "The Formula-Quotations of Matthew 2 and the Problem of Communication." *NTS* 27 (1981), pp. 233–51.

"Jewish Historiography, Midrash, and the Gospels," in *Gospel Perspectives III: Studies in Midrash and Historiography.* Edited by R. T. France and David Wenham. Sheffield: JSOT Press, 1983, pp. 99–127.

Matthew: Evangelist and Teacher. Exeter: Paternoster, 1989.

Freed, Edwin D. *Old Testament Quotations in the Gospel of John.* NovTSup 11. Leiden: Brill, 1965.

"Samaritan Influence in the Gospel of John" *CBQ* 30 (1968), pp. 580–87.

"Did John Write His Gospel Partly to Win Samaritan Converts?" *NovT* 12 (1970), pp. 241–56.

Freedman, Aviva and Peter Medway. *Genre and the New Rhetoric.* CPLE. London: Taylor & Francis, 1994.

Frei, Hans W. *The Eclipse of Biblical Narrative: A Study in Eighteenth- and Nineteenth-Century Hermeneutics.* New Haven: Yale University Press, 1974.

The Identity of Jesus Christ: The Hermeneutical Basis of Dogmatic Theology. Philadelphia: Fortress, 1975.

"The 'Literal Reading' of Biblical Narrative in the Christian Tradition: Does it Stretch or Will it Break?," in *The Bible and the Narrative Tradition.* Edited by Frank McConnell. New York: Oxford University Press, 1986, pp. 36–77.

Frend, William H. C. *Martyrdom and Persecution in the Early Church: A Study of a Conflict from the Maccabees to Donatus.* New York: New York University Press, 1965.

The Rise of Christianity. London: Darton, Longman, & Todd, 1984.

Froehlich, Karlfried, ed. *Biblical Interpretation in the Early Church.* SECT. Philadelphia: Fortress, 1984.

Frye, Northrop. *Anatomy of Criticism: Four Essays.* Princeton: Princeton University Press, 1957.

Fuglseth, Kre Sigvald. *Johannine Sectarianism in Perspective: A Sociological, Historical, and Comparative Analysis of Temple and Social Relationships in the Gospel of John, Philo, and Qumran.* NovTSup 119. Leiden: Brill, 2005.

Fuller, Reginald H. *The Foundations of New Testament Christology.* London: Lutterworth Press, 1965.

Gagé, Jean. *Les Classes socials dans l'empire romain.* BH. Paris: Payot, 1964.

Gager, John G. *Kingdom and Community: The Social World of Early Christianity.* Englewood Cliffs: Prentice-Hall, 1975.

"Social Description and Sociological Explanation." *RSR* 5 (1979), pp. 174–80.

"Shall We Marry our Enemies? Sociology and the New Testament." *Interpretation* 36 (1982), pp. 256–65.

Review of Robert M. Grant, *Early Christianity and Society: Seven Studies*; Abraham J. Malherbe, *Social Aspects of Early Christianity*; and Gerd Theissen, *Sociology of Early Palestinian Christianity. RSR* 5 (1979), pp. 174–80.

Gallagher, Eugene V. *Divine Man or Magician?* SBLDS 64. Chico, Calif.: Scholars Press, 1982.

Gamble, Harry Y. *Books and Readers in the Early Church: A History of Early Christian Texts.* New Haven: Yale University Press, 1995.

Garfinkel, Alan. *Forms of Explanation: Rethinking the Questions of Social Theory.* New Haven: Yale University Press, 1981.

Geertz, Clifford. *The Interpretation of Cultures: Selected Essays.* New York: Basic Books, 1973.

Gerhart, Mary. "Generic Studies: Their Renewed Importance in Religious and Literary Interpretation." *JAAR* 45 (1977), pp. 309–25.

"Generic Competence in Biblical Hermeneutics." *Semeia* 43 (1988), pp. 29–44.

Gese, Hartmut. *Essays on Biblical Theology.* Translated by Keith Crim. Minneapolis: Augsburg Publishing House, 1981.

Gill, D. W. J. and C. Gempf, eds. *The Book of Acts in Its Graeco-Roman Setting.* Grand Rapids: Eerdmans, 1994.

Gill, Robin. "Berger's Plausibility Structures: A Response to Professor Cairns." *SJT* 27 (1974), pp. 198–207.

Theology and Social Structure. London: Mowbrays, 1977.

Glasson, T. Francis. *Moses in the Fourth Gospel.* SBT 40. London: SCM Press, 1963.

Glasswell, M. E. "St. Matthew's Gospel – History or Book." *CV* 24 (1981), pp. 41–45.

Glaue, Paul. *Die Vorlesung heiliger Schriften im Gottesdiente.* 1 Teil. BEAK. Berlin: University of Berlin, 1907.

Gloag, Paton J. *Introduction to the Johannine Writings.* London: James Nisbet, 1891.

Goetchius, E. V. N. Review of Lane C. McGaughy, *Toward a Descriptive Analysis of EINAI as a Linking Verb in New Testament Greek. JBL* 95 (1976), pp. 147–49.

Goguel, Maurice. *The Birth of Christianity.* Translated by H. P. Snape. London: Allen & Unwin, 1953.

Goldingay, John. *Models for Scripture.* Grand Rapids: Eerdmans, 1994.

Models for Interpretation of Scripture. Grand Rapids: Eerdmans, 1995.

Goode, Erich. "Some Critical Observations on the Church-Sect Dimension." *JSSR* 6 (1967), pp. 69–77.

Goppelt, Leonhard. *Typos: The Typological Interpretation of the Old Testament in the New*. Translated by Donald H. Madvig. Grand Rapids: Eerdmans, 1982.

Goulder, Michael D. *Midrash and Lection in Matthew*. London: SPCK, 1974.

  The Evangelist's Calendar: A Lectionary Explanation of the Development of Scripture. London: SPCK, 1978.

  Luke: A New Paradigm. Sheffield: Sheffield Academic Press, 1989.

  "The Pre-Markan Gospel." *SJT* 47 (1994), pp. 453–71.

Graham, Willaim A. "Scripture," in *The Encyclopedia of Religion*. Edited by Mircea Eliade. 16 vols. New York: Macmillan, 1987, vol. IV, pp. 133–45.

Grant, Robert M. *Early Christianity and Society: Seven Studies*. New York: Harper & Row, 1977.

Green, Joel B. "Scripture and Theology: Failed Experiments, Fresh Perspectives." *Interpretation* 56 (2002), pp. 4–20.

Green, Joel B., ed. *Hearing the New Testament: Strategies for Interpretation*. Grand Rapids: Eerdmans, 1995.

Green, Joel B., Scot McKnight, and I. Howard Marshall, eds. *Dictionary of Jesus and the Gospels*. Downers Grove, Ill.: Intervarsity Press, 1992.

Greene, Kevin. *The Archaeology of the Roman Economy*. Berkeley: University of California Press, 1989.

Greene-McCreight, Kathryn E. *"Ad Litteram" How Augustine, Calvin, and Barth Read the "Plain Sense" of Genesis 1–3*. IST 5. New York: Peter Lang, 1999.

Gregory, C. R. "The Reading of Scripture in the Church in the Second Century." *AJT* 13 (1908), pp. 86–91.

Grüneberg, Keith Nigel. *Abraham, Blessing, and the Nations: A Philological and Exegetical Study of Genesis 12:3 in its Narrative Context*. BZATW 332. Berlin: Walter de Gruyter, 2003.

Guilding, Aileen. *The Fourth Gospel and Jewish Worship*. Oxford: Oxford University Press, 1960.

Gundry, Robert H. "Recent Investigations into the Literary Genre 'Gospel,'" in *New Dimensions in New Testament Study*. Edited by Richard N. Longenecker and Merrill C. Tenney. Grand Rapids: Zondervan, 1974, pp. 97–114.

  Jesus the Word According to John the Sectarian: A Paleofundamentalist Manifesto for Contemporary Evangelicalism, especially Its Elites, in North America. Grand Rapids: Eerdmans, 2002.

Guelich, Robert. "The Gospel Genre," in *The Gospel and The Gospels*. Edited by Peter Stuhlmacher. Grand Rapids: Eerdmans, 1991, pp. 173–208.

Guijarro, Santiago. "Why Does the Gospel of Mark Begin as It Does?" *BTB* 33 (2003), pp. 28–38.

Gunkel, Hermann. *The Legends of Genesis: The Biblical Saga and History*. Translated by W. H. Carruth. New York: Schocken Books, 1964.

Gunton, Colin E. *A Brief Theology of Revelation: The 1993 Warfield Lectures*. Edinburgh: T. & T. Clark, 1995.

Gusfield, Joseph R. *Community: A Critical Response*. KCSS. Oxford: Blackwell, 1975.

Gutmann, Joseph, ed. *Ancient Synagogues: The State of Research*. Chico, Calif.: Scholars Press, 1981.

Güttgemanns, Erhardt. *Candid Questions concerning Gospel Form Criticism: A Methodological Sketch of the Fundamental Problematics of Form and Redaction Critics.* Translated by William G. Doty. 2nd edn. PTMS 26. Pittsburgh: Pickwick Press, 1979.

Habermas, Jürgen. *The Theory of Communicative Action. Vol. 1. Reason and the Rationalization of Society.* Translated by Thomas McCarthy. Boston: Beacon, 1984.

——— *Philosophical Discourses of Modernity.* Translated by Frederick G. Lawrence. Cambridge: Polity, 1987.

Hadas, Moses and Morton Smith. *Heroes and Gods: Spiritual Biographies in Antiquity.* RPS 13. London: Routledge & Kegan Paul, 1965.

Haenchen, Ernst. "Aus der Literatur zum Johannesevangelium 1929–1956." *ThR* 23 (1955), pp. 295–33.

——— "Neuere Literatur zu den Johannesbriefen." *ThR* 26 (1960), pp. 1–43, pp. 267–91.

——— "'Der Vater der mich gesandt hat.'" *NTS* 9 (1963), pp. 208–16.

——— *John: A Commentary on the Gospel of John.* 2 vols. Translated by Robert W. Funk. Philadelphia: Fortress, 1984.

Hägerland, Tobias. "John's Gospel: A Two-Level Drama?" *JSNT* 25 (2003), pp. 309–22.

Hagner, Donald A. *Matthew 1–13.* WBC 33a. Dallas: Word, 1993.

Halliday, Michael A. K. "Anti-languages." *AA* 78 (1976), pp. 570–84.

——— *Language as Social Semiotic: The Social Interpretation of Language and Meaning.* Baltimore: University Park, 1978.

Hampson, Norman. *The Enlightenment.* Harmondsworth: Penguin Books, 1968.

Hanson, K. C. and Douglas E. Oakman. *Palestine in the Time of Jesus: Social Structures and Social Conflicts.* Minneapolis: Fortress, 1998.

Hanson, Paul D. *The Dawn of Apocalyptic: The Historical and Sociological Roots of Jewish Apocalyptic Eschatology.* Philadelphia: Fortress, 1979.

Hanson, R. P. C. *Tradition in the Early Church.* London: SCM Press, 1962.

——— *Allegory and Event: A Study of the Sources and Significance of Origen's Interpretation of Scripture.* Louisville: Westminster John Knox, 2003. Repr. Richmond: John Knox, 1959.

Hare, Douglas R. A. *The Theme of Jewish Persecution of Christians in the Gospel According to St. Matthew.* Cambridge: Cambridge University Press, 1967.

Harland, Philip A. *Associations, Synagogues, and Congregations: Claiming a Place in Ancient Mediterranean Society.* Minneapolis: Fortress, 2003.

Harrington, Daniel J. "Sociological Concepts and the Early Church: A Decade of Research." *TS* 41 (1980), pp. 181–90.

——— "Second Testament Exegesis and the Social Sciences." *BTB* 18–19 (1988–89), pp. 77–85.

Harris, Marvin. *The Rise of Anthropological Theory: A History of Theories of Culture.* Rev. and enl. edn. Oxford: Altamira Press, 2001.

Harvey, Van A. *The Historian and the Believer: The Morality of Historical Knowledge and Christian Belief.* Chicago: University of Illinois, 1966. Repr. New York: Macmillan, 1996.

Hatch, Edwin. *The Organization of the Early Christian Churches.* 4th edn. Bampton Lectures for 1880. London: Longmans & Green, 1892.

Hatina, Thomas R. "Intertextuality and Historical Criticism in New Testament Studies: Is There a Relationship?" *BI* 7 (1999), pp. 28–43.

Hays, Richard B. *Echoes of Scripture in the Letters of Paul.* New Haven: Yale University Press, 1989.

"Can the Gospels Teach us to Read the Old Testament?" *PE* 11 (2002), pp. 403–18.

Heinrici, Georg C. F. "Die Christengemeinde Korinths und die religiösen Genossenschaften der Griechen." *ZWT* 19 (1876), pp. 464–526.

Der Zweite Brief an die Korinther. 7th edn. KEKNT 6. Göttingen: Vandenhoeck & Ruprecht, 1890.

Hendriksen, William. *Exposition of the Gospel According to John.* Grand Rapids: Baker, 1953.

Hengel, Martin. "Die Synagogeninschrift von Stobi." *ZNW* 57 (1966), pp. 145–83.

"Proseuche und Synagoge: Jüdische Gemeinde, Gotteshaus und Gottesdienst in der Diaspora und in Palästina," in *Tradition und Glaube: Das frühe Christentum in seiner Umwelt: Festgabe für Karl Georg Kuhn.* Edited by Gert Jeremias, Heinz-Wolfgang Kuhn, and Hartmut Stegemann. Göttingen: Vandenhoeck & Ruprecht, 1971, pp. 157–83.

"Die Ursprünge der christlichen Mission." *NTS* 18 (1971), pp. 15–38.

Judaism and Hellenism: Studies in their Encounter in Palestine during the Early Hellenistic Period. Translated by John Bowden. London: SCM Press, 1974.

Acts and the History of Earliest Christianity. Philadelphia: Fortress Press, 1979.

Studies in the Gospel of Mark. Translated by John Bowden. London: SCM Press, 1985.

The Johannine Question. Translated by John Bowden. Philadelphia: Trinity Press International, 1989.

"Literary, Theological, and Historical Problems in the Gospel of Mark," in *The Gospel and The Gospels.* Edited by Peter Stuhlmacher. Translated by John Bowden. Grand Rapids: Eerdmans, 1991, pp. 209–51.

Die Johanneische Frage: Ein Lösungsversuch. WUNT 67. Tübingen: J. C. B. Mohr, 1993.

The Four Gospels and the One Gospel of Jesus Christ: An Investigation of the Collection and Origin of the Canonical Gospels. Translated by John Bowden. London: SCM Press, 2000.

Hill, Charles E. *The Johannine Corpus in the Early Church.* Oxford: Oxford University Press, 2004.

Hilton, Michael and Gordian Marshall. *The Gospels and Rabbinic Judaism.* London: SCM Press, 1988.

Hirsch, E. D., Jr. *Validity in Interpretation.* New Haven: Yale University Press, 1967.

The Aims of Interpretation. Chicago: University of Chicago Press, 1976.

"Meaning and Significance Reinterpreted." *CI* 11 (1984), pp. 202–24.

Hobbs, Edward C. "Norman Perrin on Methodology in the Interpretation of Mark," in *Christology and a Modern Pilgrimage: A Discussion with Norman Perrin.* Edited by Hans Dieter Betz. Missoula, Mont.: Society of Biblical Literature, 1974, pp. 53–60.

Hock, Ronald F. *The Social Context of Paul's Ministry: Tentmaking and Apostleship*. Philadelphia: Fortress, 1980.

Hofrichter, Peter Leander. *Für und wider die Priorität des Johannesevangeliums*. TTS 9. Hildesheim: Georg Olms, 2002.

Holladay, Carl R. *Theios Aner in Hellenistic Judaism: A Critique*. SBLDS 40. Missoula, Mont.: Scholars Press, 1977.

Holliday, Michael A. K. "Anti-languages." *AA* 78 (1976), pp. 570–84.

Language as Social Semiotic: The Social Interpretation of Language and Meaning. Baltimore: University Park, 1978.

Holmberg, Bengt. *Paul and Power: The Structure of Authority in the Primitive Church as Reflected in the Pauline Epistles*. CBNTS 11. Philadelphia: Fortress, 1980.

Sociology and the New Testament: An Appraisal. Minneapolis: Fortress, 1990.

Holmes, Michael, ed. *Apostolic Fathers: Greek Texts and English Translations*. Rev. edn. Grand Rapids: Baker Books, 1999.

Hooker, Morna D. "On Using the Wrong Tool." *Theology* 75 (1972), pp. 570–81.

Horbury, W. "The Benediction of the Minim and the Early Jewish-Christian Controversy." *JTS* 33 (1982), pp. 19–61.

Horsley, Richard A. "Popular Prophetic Movements at the Time of Jesus: Their Principle Features and Social Origins." *JSNT* 26 (1986), pp. 3–27.

Sociology and the Jesus Movement. New York: Crossroad, 1989.

Hoskyns, Edwyn C. *The Fourth Gospel*. Edited by Frances Noel Davey. London: Faber & Faber, 1940.

Howard-Brook, Wes. *Becoming Children of God: John's Gospel and Radical Discipleship*. BLS. Maryknoll, NY: Orbis Books, 1994.

Huie-Jolly, Mary R. "Threats Answered by Enthronement: Death/Resurrection and the Divine Warrior Myth in John 5.17–29, Psalm 2 and Daniel 7," in *Studies in Scripture in Early Judaism and Christianity: Investigations and Proposals*. Edited by Craig A. Evans and James A. Sanders. JSNTSup 148. SSEJC 5. Sheffield: Sheffield Academic Press, 1997, pp. 191–217.

Hunsinger, George and William C. Placher, ed. *Theology and Narrative: Selected Essays*. Oxford: Oxford University Press, 1993.

Hurtado, Larry W. *Lord Jesus Christ: Devotion to Jesus in Earliest Christianity*. Grand Rapids: Eerdmans, 2003.

Ibuki, Yu. "'Viele glaubten an ihn' – Auseinandersetzung mit dem Glauben im Johannesevangelium." *AJBI* 9 (1983), pp. 128–83.

Instone-Brewer, David. "The Eighteen Benedictions and the *Minim* before 70 CE." *JTS* 54 (2003), pp. 25–44.

Isenberg, Sheldon R. "Millenarianism in Greco-Roman Palestine." *Religion* 4 (1974), pp. 26–46.

Iser, Wolfgang. *The Implied Reader: Patterns of Communication in Prose Fiction from Bunyan to Beckett*. Baltimore: Johns Hopkins University Press, 1974.

The Act of Reading: A Theory of Asthetic Response. London: Routledge & Kegan Paul, 1978.

"Interaction between Text and Reader," in *The Reader in the Text: Essays on Audience and Interpretation*. Edited by Susan R. Suleiman and Inge Crosman. Princeton: Princeton University Press, 1980, pp. 106–19.

Jacobson-Widding, Anita, ed. *Identity: Personal and Socio-Cultural: A Symposium*. Stockholm: Almquist & Wiskell, 1983.

Jarvie, Ian Charles. *The Revolution in Anthropology*. Chicago: Henry Regnery, 1967.

Jensen, Alexander S. *John's Gospel as Witness: The Development of the Early Christian Language of Faith*. Aldershot: Ashgate, 2004.

Jeremias, Joachim. *The Parables of Jesus*. Translated by S. H. Hooke. London: SCM Press, 1954.

Jerusalem in the Time of Jesus. Translated by F. H. Cave and C. H. Cave. London: SCM Press, 1969.

Jewett, Robert. *The Thessalonian Correspondence: Pauline Rhetoric and Millenarian Piety*. Philadelphia: Fortress, 1986.

Johnson, Benton. "On Church and Sect." *ASR* 28 (1963), pp. 539–49.

Johnson, Luke Timothy. "On Finding the Lukan Community: A Cautious Cautionary Essay," in *SBLSP*. Chico, Calif.: Scholars Press, 1979, pp. 87–100.

The Writings of the New Testament: An Interpretation. Rev. edn. London: SCM Press, 1999.

Jonge, Henk Jan de. "'The 'Jews' in the Gospel of John," in *Anti-Judaism and the Fourth Gospel*. Edited by Reimund Bieringer, Didier Pollefeyt, and Frederique Vandecasteele-Vanneuville. Louisville: Westminster John Knox, 2001, pp. 121–40.

Jonge, Marinus de. "Nicodemus and Jesus: Some Observations on Misunderstanding and Understanding in the Fourth Gospel." *BJTL* 53 (1971), pp. 337–59.

"Christology, Controversy, and Community in the Gospel of John," in *Christology, Controversy, and Community: New Testament Essays in Honour of David R. Catchpole*. Edited by David G. Horrell and Christopher M. Tuckett. NovTSup 99. Leiden: Brill, 2000, pp. 209–29.

Jonge, Marinus de, ed. *L'Evangile de Jean: Sources, rédaction, théologie*. BETL 44. Gembloux: Duculot, 1977.

Judge, Edwin A. *The Social Pattern of Early Christian Groups in the First Century: Some Prolegomena to the Study of New Testament Ideas of Social Obligation*. London: Tyndale, 1960.

"The Early Christians as a Scholastic Community," *JRH* 1 (1960), pp. 4–15.

"The Early Christians as a Scholastic Community: Part II," *JRH* 1 (1960), pp. 125–37.

"The Social Identity of the First Christians: A Question of Method in Religious History." *JRH* 11 (1980), pp. 201–17.

Rank and Status in the World of Caesars and St. Paul. Christchurch: University of Canterbury, 1982.

Käsemann, Ernst. *The Testament of Jesus: A Study of the Gospel of John in Light of Chapter 17*. Translated by Gerhard Krodel. London: SCM Press, 1968.

"The Beginnings of Christian Theology," in *New Testament Quotations of Today*. Edited by Ernst Käsemann. London: SCM Press, 1969, pp. 82–107.

Katz, Steven T. "Issues in the Separation of Judaism and Christianity After 70 CE: A Reconsideration." *JBL* 103 (1984), pp. 43–76.

Kazen, Thomas. "Sectarian Gospels for Some Christians? Intention and Mirror Reading in the Light of Extra-Canonical Texts." *NTS* 51 (2005), pp. 561–78.

Kea, Perry V. "Writing a *bios*: Matthew's Genre Choices and Rhetorical Situation," in *SBLSP*. Chico, Calif.: Scholars Press, 1994, pp. 574–86.

Keck, Leander E. "Mark 3:7–12 and Mark's Christology." *JBL* 84 (1965), pp. 341–48.

"On the Ethos of Early Christians." *JAAR* 42 (1974), pp. 435–52.

Kee, Howard Clark. "Aretalogy and Gospel." *JBL* 92 (1973), pp. 402–22.

Community of the New Age: Studies in Mark's Gospel. London: SCM Press, 1977.

Jesus in History: An Approach to the Study of the Gospels. 2nd edn. New York: Harcourt Brace Jovanovich, 1977.

Christian Origins in Sociological Perspective. London: SCM Press, 1980.

Knowing the Truth: A Sociological Approach to New Testament Interpretation. Minneapolis: Fortress, 1989.

"Synoptic Studies," in *The New Testament and its Modern Interpreters.* Edited by Eldon Jay Epp and George W. MacRae. Philadelphia: Fortress, 1989, pp. 245–89.

Who are the People of God? Early Christian Models of Community. New Haven: Yale University Press, 1995.

Keener, Craig S. *The Gospel of John: A Commentary.* 2 vols. Peabody: Hendrickson, 2003.

Kelber, Werner H. *The Kingdom in Mark: A New Place and a New Time.* Philadelphia: Fortress, 1974.

Mark's Story of Jesus. Philadelphia: Fortress Press, 1979.

The Oral and the Written Gospel: The Hermeneutics of Speaking and Writing in the Synoptic Tradition, Mark, Paul, and Q. Philadelphia: Fortress, 1982.

"Narrative as Interpretation and Interpretation of Narrative: Hermeneutical Reflections on the Gospels." *Semeia* 39 (1987), pp. 107–33.

Kennedy, George A. *New Testament Interpretation through Rhetorical Criticism.* SR. Chapel Hill: University of North Carolina Press, 1984.

Kermode, Frank. *The Genesis of Secrecy: On the Interpretation of Narrative.* Cambridge, Mass.: Harvard University Press, 1979.

Kilpatrick, G. D. *The Origins of the Gospel According to St. Matthew.* Oxford: Clarendon Press, 1946.

Kimmelman, Reuven. "*Birkat Ha-Minim* and the Lack of Evidence for an Anti-Christian Jewish Prayer in Late Antiquity," in *Aspects of Judaism in the Graeco-Roman Period.* Edited by E. P. Sanders and A. I. Baumgarten. London: SCM Press, 1981, vol. II, pp. 226–44.

King, K. "Kingdom in the Gospel of Thomas." *FFF* 3 (1987), pp. 48–97.

Kingsbury, Jack Dean. *Matthew as Story.* Philadelphia: Fortress, 1986.

"Reflections on 'The Reader' in Matthew's Gospel." *NTS* 34 (1988), pp. 442–60.

"Conclusion: Analysis of a Conversation," in *Social History of the Matthean Community: Cross-Disciplinary Approaches.* Edited by David L. Balch. Minneapolis: Fortress, 1991, pp. 259–69.

Kippenberg, Hans G. "Ein Vergleich jüdischer, christlicher und gnostischer Apokalyptik," in *Apocalypticism in the Mediterranean World and the Near East: Proceedings of the International Colloquium on Apocalypticism: Uppsala: August 12–17, 1979.* Edited by David Hellholm. Tübingen: Mohr, 1983, pp. 751–68.

Kirk, Alan. "The Johannine Jesus in the Gospel of Peter: A Social Memory Approach," in *Jesus in Johannine Tradition.* Edited by Robert T. Fortna and Tom Thatcher. Louisville: Westminster John Knox, 2001, pp. 313–21.

Klauck, Hans-Joseph. *Hausgemeinde und Hauskirche im Frühen Christentum.* Stuttgart: Katholisches Bibelwerk, 1981.

"Die Hausgemeinde als Lebensform im Urchristentum." *MTZ* 32 (1981), pp. 1–15.

"Community, History, and Text(s) – a Response." Paper presented at Life in Abundance: An International Conference on the Gospel of John: A Tribute to Raymond E. Brown. Baltimore, October 16–18, 2003.

Klijn, A. F. J. *Jewish-Christian Gospel Tradition.* SVC 17. Leiden: Brill, 1992.

Kline, Meredith G. "The Old Testament Origins of the Gospel Genre." *WTJ* 38 (1975), pp. 1–27.

Klink, Edward W., III. "The Gospel Community Debate: State of the Question." *CIBR* 3.1 (2004), pp. 60–85.

Kloppenborg, John S. *The Formation of Q: Trajectories in Ancient Wisdom Collections.* Philadelphia: Fortress, 1987.

Knierim, Rolf. "Old Testament Form Criticism Reconsidered." *Interpretation* 27 (1973), pp. 435–68.

Knight, Douglas A. "The Understanding of '*Sitz im Leben*' in Form Criticism," in *SBLSP.* Chico, Calif.: Scholars Press, 1973, pp. 105–25.

Koehler, Ludwig. *Das formgeschichtliche Problem des Neuen Testaments.* Leiden: Brill, 1924.

Koch, Klaus. *The Growth of the Biblical Tradition: The Form-Critical Method.* Translated by S. M. Cupitt. London: Adam and Charles Black, 1969.

Koester, Craig R. *Symbolism in the Fourth Gospel: Meaning, Mystery, Community.* Minneapolis: Fortress, 1995.

"The Spectrum of Johannine Readers," in *"What is John?" Readers and Readings of the Fourth Gospel.* SBLSymS 3. Edited by Fernando F. Segovia. Atlanta: Scholars Press, 1996, pp. 5–19.

Koester, Helmut. "One Jesus and Four Primitive Gospels," in *Trajectories through Early Christianity.* Edited by James M. Robinson and Helmut Koester. Philadelphia: Fortress, 1971, pp. 158–204.

Introduction to the New Testament: History and Literature of Early Christianity. 2 vols. Translated by Walter de Gruyter. HFF. Philadelphia: Fortress, 1982.

Ancient Christian Gospels. London: SCM Press, 1990.

Köstenberger, Andreas J. *The Missions of Jesus and The Disciples According to the Fourth Gospel: With Implications for the Fourth Gospel's Purpose and the Mission of the Contemporary Church.* Grand Rapids: Eerdmans, 1998.

Kraeling, Carl H. *The Christian Building. The Excavations at Dura-Europos: Final Reports.* New Haven: Yale University Press, 1967, vol. VIII, pt. 2.

Kraft, Heinrich. "Die Evangelien und die Geschichte Jesu." *ThZ* 37 (1981), pp. 321–41.

Kreissig, Heinz. "Zur sozialen Zusammensetzung der frühchristlichen Gemeinde im ersten Jahrhundert u. Z." *ESGL* 6 (1967), pp. 91–100.

Kristeva, Julia. *Semiotiké: recherches pour une sémanalyse: extraits.* Paris: Seuil, 1969.

La Révolution du langage poétique: l'avant-garde à la fin du XIXe siècle: Lautréamont et Mallarmé. Paris: Seuil, 1974.

Kügler, Joachim. "Das Johannesevangelium und seine Gemeinde – kein Thema für Science Fiction." *BN* 23 (1984), pp. 48–62.

Kuhn, Karl Gustav. "Das Problem der Mission in der Urchristenheit." *EMZ* 11 (1954), pp. 167–68.

Kuhn, Thomas S. *The Structure of Scientific Revolutions.* 2nd and enl. edn. Chicago: The University of Chicago Press, 1970.

Kümmel, Werner G. *The New Testament: The History of the Investigation of its Problems.* Translated by S. McClean Gilmour and Howard C. Kee. London: SCM Press, 1973.

Introduction to the New Testament. Translated by Howard C. Kee Nashville: Abingdon, 1975.

Kurz, William S. "Intertextual Permutations of the Genesis Word in the Johannine Prologues," in *Studies in Scripture in Early Judaism and Christianity: Investigations and Proposals.* Edited by Craig A. Evans and James A. Sanders. JSNTSup 148. SSEJC 5. Sheffield: Sheffield Academic Press, 1997, pp. 179–90.

Kysar, Robert. *The Fourth Evangelist and His Gospel.* Minneapolis: Augsburg, 1975.

John, The Maverick Gospel. Louisville: Westminster John Knox, 1976.

"Community and Gospel: Vectors in Fourth Gospel Criticism." *Interpretation* 31 (1977), pp. 355–66.

"The Gospel of John in Current Research." *RSR* 9 (1983), pp. 314–23.

John's Story of Jesus. Philadelphia: Fortress, 1984.

"Coming Hermeneutical Earthquake in Johannine Interpretation," in *"What is John?" Readers and Readings of the Fourth Gospel.* SBLSymS 3. Edited by Fernando F. Segovia. Atlanta: Scholars Press, 1996, pp. 185–89.

"The Expulsion from the Synagogue: A Tale of a Theory." Paper Delivered at the annual meeting of the SBL. Toronto, Canada, November 25, 2002.

"The Whence and Whither of the Johannine Community." Paper Delivered at Life in Abundance: An International Conference on the Gospel of John: A Tribute to Raymond E. Brown. Baltimore, October 18, 2003.

"The Whence and Whither of the Johannine Community," in *Life in Abundance: Studies of John's Gospel in Tribute to Raymond E. Brown.* Edited by John R. Donahue. Collegeville: Liturgical Press, 2005, pp. 65–81.

Lampe, G. W. H. *A Patristic Greek Lexicon.* Oxford: Clarendon Press, 1961.

Langbrandtner, Wolfgang. *Weltferner Gott oder Liebe: Der Ketzerstreit in der johanneischen Kirche.* BBET 6. Frankfurt: Lang, 1977.

Lategan Bernard C. and Willem S. Vorster. *Text and Reality: Aspects of Reference in Biblical Texts.* SBLSS. Philadelphia: Fortress Press/Atlanta: Scholars Press, 1985.

LaVerdiere, E. A. and W. G. Thompson. "New Testament Communities in Transition: A Study in Matthew and Luke." *TS* 37 (1976), pp. 567–79.

Lee, David. *Luke's Stories of Jesus: Theological Reading of Gospel Narrative and the Legacy of Hans Frei.* JSNTSup 185. Sheffield: Sheffield Academic Press, 1999.

Lee, Dorothy A. *The Symbolic Narratives of the Fourth Gospel: The Interplay of Form and Meaning.* JSNTSup 95. Sheffield: Sheffield Academic Press, 1994.

Lemcio, Eugene E. *The Past of Jesus in the Gospels.* SNTSMS 68. Cambridge: Cambridge University Press, 1991.

Lenski, Gerhard. *Power and Privilege: A Theory of Social Stratification.* Chapel Hill: University of North Carolina Press, 1984.

Lenski, Gerhard and Jean Lenski. *Human Societies: An Introduction to Macrosociology*. 5th edn. New York: McGraw-Hill, 1987.

Léon-Dufour, Xavier. "Towards a Symbolic Reading of the Fourth Gospel." *NTS* 27 (1981), pp. 439–56.

Leroy, Herbert. *Rätsel und Missverständnis: Ein Beitrag zur Formgeschichte des Johannesevangelium*. BBB 30. Bonn: Hanstein, 1966.

"Das johanneische Missverständnis als literarische Form." *BL* 9 (1968), pp. 196–207.

Levine, Lee I., ed. *The Synagogue in Late Antiquity*. Philadelphia: American Schools of Oriental Research, 1987.

Lewis, I. M. *Ecstatic Religion: An Anthropological Study of Spirit Possession and Shamanism*. London: Penguin Books, 1971.

Liddell, Henry George. and Robert Scott. *A Greek-English Lexicon*. Rev. by H. Stuart Jones. 9th edn. Oxford: Clarendon Press, 1996.

Lieu, Judith M. *The Second and Third Epistles of John: History and Background*. SNTW. Edinburgh: T. & T. Clark, 1986.

"Anti-Judaism in the Fourth Gospel: Explanation and Hermeneutics," in *Anti-Judaism and the Fourth Gospel*. Edited by Reimund Bieringer, Didier Pollefeyt, and Frederique Vandecasteele-Vanneuville. Louisville: Westminster John Knox, 2001, pp. 101–17.

Neither Jew Nor Greek? Constructing Early Christianity. SNTW. Edinburgh: T. & T. Clark, 2002.

Lightfoot, Robert H. *History and Interpretation in the Gospels*. London: Hodder and Stoughton, 1934.

Lincoln, Andrew T. *Truth on Trial: The Lawsuit Motif in the Fourth Gospel*. Peabody: Hendrickson, 2000.

"The Beloved Disciple as Eyewitness and the Fourth Gospel as Witness." *JSNT* 85 (2002), pp. 3–26.

Lincoln, Bruce. "Thomas-Gospel and Thomas-Community: A New Approach to a Familiar Text." *NovT* 19 (1977), pp. 65–76.

Lincoln, Bruce. *Discourse and the Construction of Society: Comparative Studies of Myth, Ritual, and Classification*. Oxford: Oxford University Press, 1989.

Lindars, Barnabas. *Behind the Fourth Gospel*. SCC 3. London: SPCK, 1971.

The Gospel of John. Century Bible. London: Oliphants, 1972.

"The Persecution of Christians in John 15:18–16:4a," in *Suffering and Martyrdom in the New Testament*. Edited by William Horbury and Brian McNeil. Cambridge: Cambridge University Press, 1981, pp. 48–69.

John. NTG. Sheffield: Sheffield Academic Press, 2001.

Llewelyn, G. R. and R. A. Kearsley, eds. "Letter-Carriers in the Early Church," in *New Documents Illustrating Early Christianity*. Sydney: Macquarie University Press, 1994, vol. VII, pp. 50–57.

Lohfink, Gerhard. *Jesus and Community: The Social Dimension of Christian Faith*. Translated by John P. Galvin. Philadelphia: Fortress, 1984.

Loisy, Alfred. *Le quatrième évangile*. Paris: Picard, 1903.

Louth, Andrew. "Return to Allegory," in *Discerning the Mystery: An Essay on the Nature of Theology*. Oxford: Clarendon Press, 1983, 96–131.

Lubac, Henri de. "Spiritual Understanding," in *The Theological Interpretation of Scripture: Classic and Contemporary Readings*. Cambridge, Mass.: Blackwell, 1997, pp. 3–25.

Lührmann, Dieter. "Biographie des Gerechten als Evangelium." *WD* 14 (1977), pp. 23–50.

Luomanen, Petri. "The 'Sociology of Sectarianism' in Matthew: Modeling the Genesis of Early Judaism and Christian Communities," in *Fair Play: Diversity and Conflicts in Early Christianity: Essays in Honor of Heikki Räisänen*. Edited by Ismo Dunderberg, Christopher Tuckett, and Kari Syreeni. NovTSup 103. Leiden: Brill, 2002, pp. 107–30.

Luthardt, Christopher Ernst. *Der johanneische Ursprung des vierten Evangeliums*. Leipzig: Dörffling und Franke, 1874.

——. *St. John the Author of the Fourth Gospel*. Edinburgh: T. & T. Clark, 1875.

——. *St. John's Gospel Described and Explained According to its Peculiar Character*. Translated by Caspar René Gregory. CFTL 3. 3 vols. Edinburgh: T. & T. Clark, 1876–78.

Luz, Ulrich. *Matthew 1–7*. Translated by W. C. Linss. Edinburgh: T. & T. Clark, 1989.

——. "Fiktivität und Traditionstreue im Matthäusevangelium im Lichte griechischer Literatur." *ZNW* 84 (1993), pp. 153–77.

——. *The Theology of the Gospel of Matthew*. Translated by J. Bradford Robinson. NTT. Cambridge: Cambridge University Press, 1995.

MacDonald, Margaret Y. *The Pauline Churches: A Socio-historical Study of Institutionalization in the Pauline and Deutero-Pauline Writings*. Cambridge: Cambridge University Press, 1988.

MacDonald, Neil B. "Illocutionary Stance in Hans Frei's *The Eclipse of Biblical Narrative*: An Exercise in Conceptual Redescription and Normative Analysis," in *After Pentecost: Language and Biblical Interpretation*. SHS 2. Edited by Craig Bartholomew, Colin Greene, and Karl Möller. Grand Rapids: Zondervan, 2001, pp. 312–28.

Mack, Burton L. *The Myth of Innocence: Mark and Christian Origins*. Philadelphia: Fortress Press, 1988.

——. "Social Formation," in *Guide to the Study of Religion*. Edited by Willie Braun and Russell T. McCutcheon. London: Cassell, 2000, pp. 283–96.

MacMullen, Ramsey. *Roman Social Relations 50 B.C. to A.D. 284*. New Haven: Yale University Press, 1974.

——. *Paganism in the Roman Empire*. New Haven: Yale University Press, 1981.

MacRae, George W. "The Fourth Gospel and Religionsgeschichte." *CBQ* 32 (1970), pp. 13–24.

Malatesta, Edward, ed. *St. John's Gospel, 1920–1965: A Cumulative and Classified Bibliography of Books and Periodical Literature on the Fourth Gospel*. Rome: Pontifical Biblical Institute, 1967.

Malherbe, Abraham J. *Social Aspects of Early Christianity*. 2nd and enl. edn. Rockwell Lectures of 1975. Philadelphia: Fortress, 1983.

Malina, Bruce J. *The Gospel of John in Sociolinguistic Perspective*. Berkeley: Center for Hermeneutical Studies in Hellenistic and Modern Culture, 1985.

——. Review of Wayne A. Meeks, *The First Urban Christians: The Social World of the Apostle Paul*. *JBL* 104 (1985), pp. 346–49.

——. "Normative Dissonance and Christian Origins." *Semeia* 35 (1986), pp. 35–59.

——. "Reading Theory Perspective: Reading Luke-Acts," in *The Social World of Luke-Acts: Models for Interpretation*. Edited by Jerome H. Neyrey. Peabody: Hendrickson, 1991, pp. 3–23.

The New Testament World: Insights from Social Anthropology. Rev. and enl. edn. Louisville: Westminster John Knox, 1993.

"John's: The Maverick Christian Group: The Evidence of Sociolinguistics." *BTB* 24 (1994), pp. 167–82.

Malina, Bruce J. and Richard L. Rohrbaugh. *Social-Science Commentary on the Gospel of John.* Minneapolis: Fortress, 1998.

Mannheim, Karl. *Ideology and Utopia: An Introduction to the Sociology of Knowledge.* Translated by Louis Wirth and Edward Shils. London: Routledge & Kegan, 1960.

Manns, Frédéric. *John and Jamnia: How the Break Occurred Between Jews and Christians c. 80–100 A.D.* Jerusalem: Franciscan Printing, 1988.

Marcus, Joel. *Mark 1–8.* AB 27. New York: Doubleday, 2000.

Martin, Francis, ed. *Narrative Parallels to the New Testament.* SBLRBS 22. Atlanta: Scholars Press, 1988.

Martyn, J. Louis. "Source Criticism and *Religionsgeschichte* in the Fourth Gospel." *Perspective* 1 (1970), pp. 247–73.

"Glimpses into the History of the Johannine Community," in *L'Evangile de Jean: Sources, rédaction, théologie.* Edited by Marinus de Jonge. BETL 44. Gembloux: Duculot, 1977, pp. 259–99. Repr. in *History and Theology in the Fourth Gospel.* 3rd edn. Louisville: Westminster John Knox, 2003, pp. 145–67.

The Gospel of John in Christian History: Essays for Interpreters. New York: Paulist, 1978.

"A Gentile Mission That Replaced an Earlier Jewish Mission?," in *Exploring the Gospel of John: In Honor of D. Moody Smith.* Edited by R. Alan Culpepper and C. Clifton Black. Louisville: Westminster John Knox, 1996, pp. 124–44.

History and Theology in the Fourth Gospel. 3rd edn. NTL. Louisville: Westminster John Knox, 2003.

Marshall, I. Howard. "Luke and His 'Gospel,'" in *The Gospel and The Gospels.* Edited by Peter Stuhlmacher. Grand Rapids: Eerdmans, 1991, pp. 273–92.

Marxsen, Willi. *Mark the Evangelist: Studies on the Redaction History of the Gospel.* Translated by James Boyce, Donald Juel, and William Poehlamnn. Nashville: Abingdon, 1969.

Mason, Arthur J. "Conceptions of the Church in Early Times," in *Essays on the Early History of the Church and the Ministry.* 2nd edn. Edited by H. B. Swete. London: Macmillan, 1921, pp. 3–56.

Matson, Mark A. "Interactive Rhetoric in Matthew: An Exploration of Audience Knowledge Competency. Paper presented at the annual meeting of the SBL. Atlanta, November 22, 2003.

Matsunaga, Kikuo. "The Galileans in the Fourth Gospel." *AJBI* 2 (1976), pp. 139–58.

"Is John's Gospel Anti-Sacramental? A New Solution in Light of the Evangelist's Milieu." *NTS* 27 (1981), pp. 516–24.

Mattill, Andrew J. "Johannine Communities behind the Fourth Gospel: Georg Richter's Analysis." *TS* 38 (1977), pp. 294–315.

McCasland, S. Vernon. "Travel and Communication in the NT," in *The Interpreter's Dictionary of the Bible.* Edited by G. A. Buttrick. Nashville: Abingdon, 1962–77, vol. IV, pp. 690–93.

McDonald, Lee M. *The Formation of the Christian Biblical Canon*. Rev. and enl. edn. Peabody: Hendrickson, 1995.

McGaughy, Lane C. *Toward a Descriptive Analysis of EINAI as a Linking Verb in New Testament Greek*. SBLDS 6. Missoula, Mont.: Society of Biblical Literature, 1972.

McGrath, Alister E. *Christian Theology: An Introduction*. Oxford: Blackwell, 1994.

McGuire, Meredith B. *Religion: The Social Context*. Belmont, Calif.: Wadsworth, 1981.

McHugh, John. "In Him was Life," in *Jews and Christians: The Parting of the Ways, A.D. 70 to 135: The Second Durham-Tübingen Research Symposium on Earliest Christianity and Judaism*. Edited by James D. G. Dunn. Tübingen: J. C. B. Mohr, 1992, pp. 123–58.

McKnight, Edgar V. *What is Form Criticism?* GBSNTS. Philadelphia: Fortress, 1969.

McKnight, Scot and Matthew C. Williams. *The Synoptic Gospels: An Annotated Bibliography*. IBRB 6. Grand Rapids: Baker Books, 2000.

McPolin, James. "Mission in the Fourth Gospel." *ITQ* 36 (1969), pp. 113–22.

Meier, John P. "Matthew, Gospel of," in *The Anchor Bible Dictionary*. Edited by David Noel Freedman. 6 vols. New York: Doubleday, 1992, vol. IV, pp. 622–41.

Meeks, Wayne A. *The Prophet-King: Moses Traditions and the Johannine Christology*. NovTSup 14. Leiden: Brill, 1967.

"The Man From Heaven in Johannine Sectarianism." *JBL* 91 (1972), pp. 44–72.

"The Social Context of Pauline Theology." *Interpretation* 36 (1982), pp. 266–77.

"Social Functions of Apocalyptic Language in Pauline Christianity," in *Apocalypticism in the Mediterranean World and the Near East: Proceedings of the International Colloquium on Apocalypticism: Uppsala: August 12–17, 1979*. Edited by David Hellholm. Tübingen: Mohr, 1983, pp. 687–706.

The First Urban Christians: The Social World of the Apostle Paul. New Haven: Yale University Press, 1983.

"Breaking Away: Three New Testament Pictures of Christianity's Separation from the Jewish Communities," in *"To See Ourselves as Others See Us": Christians, Jews, "Others" in Late Antiquity*. Edited by Jacob Neusner and Ernest S. Frerichs. Chico, Calif.: Scholars Press, 1985, pp. 93–115.

"A Hermeneutics of Social Embodiment." *HTR* 79 (1986), pp. 176–86.

The Moral World of the First Christians. LEC 6. Philadelphia: Westminster, 1986.

Mercer, Calvin. "APOSTELLEIN and PEMPEIN in John." *NTS* 36 (1990), pp. 619–24.

Messick, David M. and Diane M. Mackie. "Intergroup Relations." *ARP* 40 (1989), pp. 45–81.

Metzger, Bruce M. *The Canon of the New Testament: Its Origin, Development, and Significance*. Oxford: Clarendon Press, 1987.

A Textual Commentary on the Greek New Testament. 2nd edn. New York: American Bible Society, 1994.

Meyer, B. F. "Objectivity and Subjectivity in Historical Criticism of the Gospels," in *The Interrelations of the Gospels*. Edited David L. Dungan. BETL 95. Leuven: Leuven University Press, 1990, pp. 546–65.

Miller, Donald E. "Sectarianism and Secularization: The Work of Bryan Wilson." *RSR* 5 (1979), pp. 161–74.

Miller, Edward L. *Salvation-History in the Prologue of John: The Significance of John 1:3/4.* NovTSup 60. Leiden: Brill, 1989.

"The Johannine Origins of the Johannine Logos." *JBL* 112 (1993), pp. 445–57.

Minear, Paul S. "The Audience of the Fourth Gospel." *Interpretation* 31 (1977), pp. 339–54.

"The Beloved Disciple in the Gospel of John: Some Clues and Conjectures," *NovT* 19 (1977), pp. 105–23.

"The Original Functions of John 21." *JBL* 102 (1983), pp. 85–98.

Minor, Earl, ed. *Literary Uses of Typology: From the Late Middle Ages to the Present.* Princeton: Princeton University Press, 1977.

Mitchell, Margaret M. "Patristic Counter-evidence to the Claim that the 'Gospels Were Written for All Christians.'" Paper presented at the annual meeting of the SBL. Atlanta, November 22, 2003.

"Patristic Counter-Evidence to the Claim that the 'Gospels Were Written for All Christians.'" *NTS* 51 (2005), pp. 36–79.

Mlakuzhyil, George. *The Christocentric Literary Structure of the Fourth Gospel.* Analecta Biblica 117. Rome: Editrice Pontificio Istituto Biblico, 1987.

Moberly, R. W. L. *The Bible, Theology, and Faith: A Study of Abraham and Jesus.* CSCD. Cambridge: Cambridge University Press, 2000.

Moessner, David P. "One Again Again, What Sort of 'Essence?' A Response to Charles Talbert." *Semeia* 43 (1988), pp. 75–84.

Moffatt, James. *An Introduction to the Literature of the New Testament.* 3rd edn. ITL. Edinburgh: T. & T. Clark, 1918.

Mol, Hans. *Identity and the Sacred: A Sketch for a New Social-Scientific Theory of Religion.* Oxford: Blackwell, 1976.

Moloney, Francis J. "From Cana to Cana (John 2:1–4:54) and the Fourth Evangelist's Concept of Correct (and Incorrect) Faith," in *Studia Biblica 1978: II: Papers on the Gospels.* Edited by E. A. Livingston. JSNTSup 2. Sheffield: JSOT Press, 1980, pp. 185–213.

"The Function of John 13–17 within the Johannine Narrative," in *"What is John?" Volume II. Literary and Social Readings of the Fourth Gospel.* Edited by Fernando F. Segovia. SBLSymS 7. Atlanta: Scholars Press, 1998, pp. 43–66.

Moo, Douglas J. *The Old Testament in the Gospel Passion Narratives.* Sheffield: Almond Press, 1983.

Moore, George Foot. *Judaism in the First Centuries of the Christian Era: The Age of the Tannaim.* 3 vols. Cambridge, Mass.: Harvard University Press, 1927.

Moore, Stephen D. *Literary Criticism and the Gospels: The Theoretical Challenge.* New Haven; Yale University Press, 1989.

Morgan, Robert with John Barton. *Biblical Interpretation.* OBS. Oxford: Oxford University Press, 1988.

Morris, Leon. *The Gospel According to John.* NICNT. London: Marshall, Morgan & Scott, 1972.

"The Gospels and the Jewish Lectionaries," in *Gospel Perspectives III: Studies in Midrash and Historiography.* Edited by R. T. France and David Wenham. Sheffield: JSOT Press, 1983, pp. 129–56.

Motyer, Stephen. *Your Father the Devil? A New Approach to John and 'the Jews.'* PBTS. Carlisle: Paternoster, 1997.

"Method in Fourth Gospel Studies: A Way Out of the Impasse?" *JSNT* 66 (1997), pp. 27–44.

"The Fourth Gospel and the Salvation of Israel: An Appeal for a New Start," in *Anti-Judaism and the Fourth Gospel.* Edited by Reimund Bieringer, Didier Pollefeyt, and Frederique Vandecasteele-Vanneuville. Louisville: Westminster John Knox, 2001, pp. 83–100.

Moule, C. F. D. "The Individualism of the Fourth Gospel." *NovT* 5 (1962), pp. 171–90.

The Phenomenon of the New Testament: An Enquiry into the Implications of Certain Features of the New Testament. SBT 2/1. London: SCM Press, 1967.

The Birth of the New Testament. 3rd edn. London: Continuum, 2002.

Moulton, J. H. and G. Milligan. *Vocabulary of the Greek New Testament.* Peabody: Hendrickson, 1997.

Moxnes, Halvor. "What is Family? Problems in Constructing Early Christian Families," in *Constructing Early Christian Families.* Edited by Halvor Moxnes. London: Routledge, 1997, pp. 13–41.

"The Social Context of Luke's Community." *Interpretation* 48 (1999), pp. 379–89.

Moyise, Steven. "Intertextuality and the Study of the Old Testament in the New," in *The Old Testament in the New. Essays in Honor of J. L. North.* Edited by Steven Moyise. JSNTSup 189. Sheffield: Sheffield Academic Press, 2000, pp. 14–41.

The Old Testament in the New: An Introduction. CBSS. London: Continuum, 2001.

Müller, Ulrich B. *Die Geschichte der Christologie in der johanneischen Gemeinde.* SB 77. Stuttgart: Katholisches Bibelwerk, 1975.

Murphy-O'Connor, J. *St. Paul's Corinth.* Collegeville, Minn.: Liturgical, 1983.

Myers, Ched. *Binding the Strong Man: A Political Reading of Mark's Story of Jesus* Maryknoll, NY: Orbis Books, 1988.

Neale, D. "Was Jesus a *Mesith*? Public Response to Jesus and his Ministry." *TB* 44.1 (1993), pp. 89–101.

Neibuhr, H. Richard. *The Meaning of Revelation.* New York: Macmillan, 1960.

Neill, Stephen and N. T. Wright. *The Interpretation of the New Testament, 1861–1986.* 2nd edn. Oxford: Oxford University Press, 1988.

Nereparampil, Lucius. *Destroy This Temple.* Bangladore: Dharmaran, 1978.

Netting, Robert M., R. R. Wilk, and E. J. Arnould. *Households: Comparative and Historical Studies of the Domestic Group.* Berkeley: University of California Press, 1984.

Neyrey, Jerome H. "John III: A Debate Over Johannine Epistemology and Christology." *NovT* 23 (1981), pp. 115–27.

An Ideology of Revolt: John's Christology in Social-Science Perspective. Philadelphia: Fortress, 1988.

"The Sociology of Secrecy and the Fourth Gospel," in *"What is John?" Volume II. Literary and Social Readings of the Fourth Gospel.* Edited by Fernando F. Segovia. SBLSymS7. Atlanta: Scholars Press, 1998, pp. 79–9.

Review of Richard Burridge, *What are the Gospels? A Comparison with Graeco-Roman Biography. Catholic Biblical Quarterly* 55 (1993), pp. 361–63.

Nicholas, Michel. *Études critiques sur la Bible: Noveau Testament.* Paris: Michel Lévy Frères, 1864.

Nicholson, Godfrey C. *Death as Departure: The Johannine Descent-Ascent Schema.* SBLDS 63. Chico, Calif.: Scholars Press, 1983.

Nicol, Willem. *The Semeia in the Fourth Gospel: Tradition and Redaction.* NovTSup 32. Leiden: Brill, 1972.

Nock, Arthur Darby. "The Historical Importance of Cult Associations." *CR* 38 (1924), pp. 105–109.

Norden, Eduard. *Die antike Kuntstprosa: vom IV. Jahrhundert v. Chr. Bis in die Zeit der Renaissance.* Leipzig: B. G. Teubner, 1898.

O'Day, Gail R. *Revelation in the Fourth Gospel: Narrative Mode and Theological Claim.* Philadelphia: Fortress, 1986.

"The Word Become Flesh: Story and Theology in the Gospel of John," in *"What is John?" Volume II. Literary and Social Readings of the Fourth Gospel.* Edited by Fernando F. Segovia. SBLSymS 7. Atlanta: Scholars Press, 1998, pp. 67–76.

"Response: 'The Expulsion from the Synagogue: A Tale of a Theory.'" Paper presented at the annual meeting of the SBL. Toronto, Canada, November 25, 2002.

Oehler, Wilhelm. *Das Johannesevangelium, eine Missionsschrift für die Welt, der Gemeinde ausgelegt.* Gütersloh: Bertelsmann, 1936.

Zum Missionscharakter des Johannesevangeliums. Gütersloh: Bertelsmann, 1941.

Das Johannesevangelium, eine Missionsschrift für die Welt. 3 vols. Württemberg: Buchhandlung der Evangelischen Missionsschule Unterweissach, 1957.

Oepke, Albrecht. "Das missionarische Christuszeugnis des Johannesevangeliums." *EMZ* 2 (1941), pp. 4–26.

Okure, Teresa. *The Johannine Approach to Mission: A Contextual Study of John 4:1–42.* WUNT 2. Reihe 31. Tübingen: J. C. B. Mohr, 1998.

Olhausen, William. "A 'Polite' Response to Anthony Thiselton," in *After Pentecost: Language and Biblical Interpretation.* Vol. 2. SHS. Edited by Craig Bartholomew, Colin Greene, and Karl Möller. Grand Rapids: Zondervan, 2001, pp. 121–30.

Olsen, Marvin E. *The Process of Social Organization.* New York: Holt & Rinehart, 1968.

Olsson, Birger. *Structure and Meaning in the Fourth Gospel: A Text-Linguistic Analysis of 2:1–11 and 4:1–42.* Translated by Jean Gray. CB 6. Lund: CWK Gleerup, 1974.

Onuki, Takashi. "Zur literatursoziologischen Analyse des Johannesevangeliums: auf dem Wege zur Methodenintegration." *AJBI* 8 (1982), pp. 162–216.

Gemeinde und Welt im Johannesevangelium: Ein Beitrag zur Frage nach der theologischen und pragmatischen Funktion des johanneischen "Dualismus". WMANT 56. Neukirchen-Vluyn: Neukirchener Verlag, 1984.

Orchard, Helen C. *Courting Betrayal: Jesus as Victim in the Gospel of John.* JSNTSup 161. CGT 5. Sheffield: Sheffield Academic Press, 1998.

Osborne, Grant R. "Redaction Criticism," in *Interpreting the New Testament: Essays on Methods and Issues.* Edited by David Alan Black and David S. Dockery. Nashville: Broadman & Holman, 2001, pp. 128–49.

"History and Theology in the Synoptic Gospels." *TJ* 24 (2003), pp. 5–22.

Osborne, Robin, Jr. *Classical Landscape with Figures: The Ancient Greek City and its Countryside.* Dobbs Ferry: Sheridan, 1987.

Osiek, Carolyn. "The Family in Early Christianity: 'Family Values' Reconsidered." *CBQ* 58 (1996), pp. 1–24.

Osiek, Carolyn and David L. Balch. *The Family in the New Testament: Households and House Churches.* FRC. Louisville: Westminster John Knox, 1997.

O'Toole, Robert F. "Luke's Position on Politics and Society in Luke-Acts," in *Political Issues in Luke-Acts.* Edited by R. J. Cassidy and P. J. Scharper. Maryknoll, NY: Orbis Books, 1983, pp. 1–17.

"The Parallels between Jesus and Moses." *BTB* 20 (1990), pp. 22–29.

Overbeck, Franz. "Über die Anfänge der patristischen Literatur." *HZ* 12 (1882), pp. 417–72.

Overman, J. Andrew. *Matthew's Gospel and Formative Judaism: The Social World of the Matthean Community.* Minneapolis: Fortress, 1990.

Church and Community in Crisis: The Gospel According to Matthew. NTC. Valley Forge, Pa.: Trinity Press International, 1996.

Paget, James Carleton. Review of David C. Sim, *The Gospel of Matthew and Christian Judaism: The History and Social Setting of the Matthean Community. RRT* 7 (2000), pp. 48–51.

Painter, John. *John: Witness and Theologian.* London: SPCK, 1975.

"The Farewell Discourses and the History of Johannine Christianity." *NTS* 27 (1981), pp. 525–43.

The Quest for the Messiah: The History, Literature and Theology of the Johannine Community. Rev. and enl. edn. Edinburgh: T. & T. Clark, 1993.

"The Point of John's Christology: Christology, Conflict and Community in John," in *Christology, Controversy, and Community: New Testament Essays in Honour of David R. Catchpole.* Edited by David G. Horrell and Christopher M. Tuckett. NovTSup 99. Leiden: Brill, 2000, pp. 231–52.

Palmer, Humphrey. *The Logic of Gospel Criticism: An Account of the Methods and Arguments used by Textual, Documentary, Source, and Form Critics of the New Testament.* London: Macmillan, 1968.

Palmer, Richard E. Review of E. D. Hirsch, Jr., *Validity in Interpretation. JAAR* 36 (1968), pp. 243–46.

Pancaro, Severino. *The Law in the Fourth Gospel: The Torah and the Gospel, Moses and Jesus, Judaism and Christianity According to Jesus.* NovTSup 42. Leiden: Brill, 1975.

Patterson, S. J. *The Gospel of Thomas and Jesus.* Sonoma, Calif.: Polebridge, 1993.

Paulus, Heinrich E. G. "Bretschneider de Origine Ev. Et Epist. Joann." *HJL* (1821), pp. 112–42.

Pearson, Birger A. "1 Thessalonians 2:13–16: A Deutero-Pauline Interpolation." *HTR* 64 (1971), pp. 79–94.

Peterson, Dwight N. *The Origins of Mark: The Markan Community in Current Debate.* BIS 48. Leiden: Brill, 2000.

Peterson, Norman R. *Rediscovering Paul: Philemon and the Sociology of Paul's Narrative World.* Philadelphia: Fortress, 1985.

The Gospel of John and the Sociology of Light: Language and Characterization in the Fourth Gospel. Valley Forge, Pa.: Trinity Press International, 1993.

"The Reader in the Gospel." *Neotestamentica* 18 (1994), pp. 38–51.

Perrin, Norman. *What is Redaction Criticism?* London: SPCK, 1970.

"The Literary *Gattung* 'Gospel' – Some Observations." *ExpT* 82 (1970), pp. 4–7.

"Historical Criticism, Literary Criticism, and Hermeneutics." *JR* 52 (1972), pp. 361–75.

A Modern Pilgrimage in New Testament Christology. Philadelphia: Fortress, 1974.

The New Testament: An Introduction: Proclamation and Parenesis, Myth and History. New York: Harcourt Brace Jovanovich, 1974.

Piper, Otto A. "Unchanging Promises: Exodus in the New Testament." *Interpretation* 11 (1957), pp. 3–22.

Piwowarcyzk, Mary Ann. "The Narratee and the Situation on Enunciation: A Reconsideration of Prince's Theory." *Genre* 9 (1976), pp. 161–77.

Plantinga, Alvin. *Warranted Christian Belief.* New York: Oxford University Press, 2000.

Plett, Heinrich F., ed. *Intertextuality.* RTT 15. Berlin: Walter de Gruyter, 1991.

Plummer, A. *The Gospel According to St. John.* Cambridge: University Press, 1892.

A Critical and Exegetical Commentary on the Gospel According to St. Luke. 4th edn. Edinburgh: T. & T. Clark, 1901.

Porter, Stanley E. *Verbal Aspect in the Greek of the New Testament, with Reference to Tense and Mood.* SBG 1. New York: Peter Lang, 1993.

"The Use of the Old Testament in the New Testament: A Brief Comment on Method and Terminology," in *Studies in Scripture in Early Judaism and Christianity: Investigations and Proposals.* Edited by Craig A. Evans and James A. Sanders. JSNTSup 148. SSEJC 5. Sheffield: Sheffield Academic Press, 1997, pp. 79–96.

Porter, Stanley E., ed. *Reading the Gospels Today.* MNTS. Grand Rapids: Eerdmans, 2004.

Porter, Stanley E. and Craig A. Evans, eds. *The Johannine Readings.* BS 32. Sheffield: Sheffield Academic Press, 1995.

Powell, Mark Allan. *What is Narrative Criticism?* GBS. Minneapolis: Fortress, 1990.

"What is 'Literary' about Literary Aspects?," in *SBLSP.* Chico, Calif.: Scholars Press, 1992, pp. 40–48.

Chasing the Eastern Star: Adventures in Biblical Reader-Response Criticism. Louisville: Westminster John Knox, 2001.

Prince, Gerald. *Narratology: The Form and Function of Narrative.* Berlin: Mouton, 1982.

Pritz, R. A. *Nazarene Jewish Christianity.* SPN 37. Leiden: Brill, 1988.

Purvis, J. D. "The Fourth Gospel and the Samaritans." *NovT* 17 (1975), pp. 161–98.

Quast, Kevin. *Peter and the Beloved Disciple: Figures for a Community in Crisis.* JSNTSup 32. Sheffield: JSOT Press, 1989.

Rabinowitz, Peter. "Truth in Fiction: A Reexamination of Audiences." *CI* 4 (1977), pp. 121–41.

Rajak, Tessa. "Jews and Christians as Groups," in *"To See Ourselves as Others See Us": Christians, Jews, "Others" in Late Antiquity.* Edited by Jacob Neusner and Ernest S. Frerichs. SPSH. Chico, Calif.: Scholars Press, 1985, pp. 247–62.

Rawson, Beryl. *The Family in Ancient Rome: New Perspectives.* Ithaca: Cornell University Press, 1987.

Reicke, Bo. *Diakonie, Festfreude, und Zelos in Verbindung mit der altchristlichen Agapenfeier.* UUA 1951, 5. Uppsala: Lundequist, 1951.

Reinhartz, Adele. *The Word in the World: The Cosmological Tale in the Fourth Gospel.* SBLMS 45. Atlanta: Scholars Press, 1992.

    "The Johannine Community and its Jewish Neighbors: A Reappraisal," in *"What is John?" Volume II. Literary and Social Readings of the Fourth Gospel.* Edited by Fernando F. Segovia. SBLSymS 7. Atlanta: Scholars Press, 1998, pp. 111–38.

    "'Jews' and Jews in the Fourth Gospel," in *Anti-Judaism and the Fourth Gospel.* Edited by Reimund Bieringer, Didier Pollefeyt, and Frederique Vandecasteele-Vanneuville. Louisville: Westminster John Knox, 2001, pp. 213–27.

    "Women in the Johannine Community: An Exercise in Historical Imagination," in *A Feminist Companion to John.* Edited by Amy-Jill Levine. FCNT 5. London: Sheffield Academic Press, 2003, vol. II, pp. 14–33.

Remus, H. E. "Sociology of Knowledge and the Study of Early Christianity." *SR* 11 (1982), pp. 45–56.

Renan, Ernest. *Vie de Jésus.* 9th edn. Paris: G. Paetz, 1864.

Rensberger, David. *Johannine Faith and Liberating Community.* Philadelphia: Westminster, 1988.

    1 John, 2 John, 3 John. ANTC. Nashville: Abingdon, 1997.

    "Sectarianism and Theological Interpretation in John," in *"What is John?" Volume II. Literary and Social Readings of the Fourth Gospel.* Edited by Fernando F. Segovia. SBLSymS 7. Atlanta: Scholars Press, 1998, pp. 139–56.

Reploh, Karl-Georg. *Markus, Lehrer der Gemeinde.* Stuttgart: Katholisches Bibelwerk, 1969.

Rhoads, David and Donald Michie. *Mark as Story: An Introduction to the Narrative of a Gospel.* Philadelphia: Fortress, 1982.

Rhoads, David and Kari Syreeni. *Characterization in the Gospels: Reconceiving Narrative Criticism.* JSNTSup 176. Sheffield: Sheffield Academic Press, 1999.

Rich, J. and A. Wallace-Hadrill, eds. *City and Country in the Ancient World.* London: Routledge, 1991.

Richard, E. "Expressions of Double Meaning and their Function in the Gospel of John." *NTS* 31 (1985), pp. 96–112.

Riches, John K. "The Birth of Christianity," in *Early Christianity: Origins and Evolutions to A.D. 600.* Edited by Ian Hazlett. London: SPCK, 1991, pp. 28–39.

"The Synoptic Evangelists and Their Communities," in *Christian Beginnings: Word and Community from Jesus to Post-Apostolic Times*. Edited by Jürgen Becker. Louisville: Westminster John Knox, 1993, pp. 213–41.

Richter, Georg. "Präsentische und futurische Eschatologie im 4. Evangelium," in *Gegenwart und kommendes Reich*. Edited by Peter Fiedler and Dieter Zeller. SBB. Stuttgart: Katholisches Bibelwerk, 1975, pp. 117–52.

Ricoeur, Paul. *Interpretation Theory: Discourse and the Surplus of Meaning*. Fort Worth: Texas Christian University Press, 1976.

Time and Narrative. 3 vols. Translated by Kathleen Blamey and David Pellauer. London: University of Chicago Press, 1988.

"Historiography and the Representation of the Past," in *2000 Years and Beyond: Faith, Identity, and the "Common Era."* Edited by Paul Gifford with David Archard, Trevor Hart, and Nigel Rapport. London: Routledge, 2003, pp. 51–68.

Riddle, Donald Wayne. "Early Christian Hospitality: A Factor in the Gospel Transmission." *JBL* 57 (1938), pp. 141–54.

Riesenfeld, H. "Zu den johanneischen ἵνα–Sätzen." *ST* 19 (1965), pp. 213–20.

Robbins, Thomas, Dick Anthony, and Thomas E. Curtis. "The Limits of Symbolic Realism: Problems of Emphatic Field Observation in a Sectarian Context." *JSSR* 12 (1973), pp. 259–71.

Robbins, Vernon K. *Jesus the Teacher: A Socio-Rhetorical Interpretation of Mark*. Philadelphia: Fortress, 1984.

"The Social Location of the Implied Author of Luke-Acts," in *The Social World of Luke-Acts: Models for Interpretation*. Edited by Jerome H. Neyrey. Peabody: Hendrickson, 1991, pp. 305–32.

Robinson, James M. *A New Quest for the Historical Jesus*. SBT 25. London: SCM Press, 1959.

"The Problem of History in Mark, Reconsidered." *USQR* 20 (1965), pp. 131–47.

"The Johannine Trajectory," in *Trajectories through Early Christianity*. Edited by James M. Robinson and Helmut Koester. Philadelphia: Fortress, 1971, pp. 232–68.

The Problem of History in Mark and Other Marcan Studies. Philadelphia: Fortress, 1982.

Robinson, John A. T. "Elijah, John and Jesus: An Essay in Detection." *NTS* 4 (1958–59), pp. 263–81.

The Priority of John. Edited by J. F. Coakley. London: SCM Press, 1985.

Robertis, Francesco M. de. *Storia delle corporazioni e del regime associativo nel mondo romano*. 2 vols. Bari: Adriatica editrice, 1973.

Roberts, J. J. M. "Myth *Versus* History." *CBQ* 38 (1976), pp. 1–13.

Robertson, Roland. *The Sociological Interpretation of Religion*. Oxford: Oxford University Press, 1972.

Rodd, Cyril S. "Max Weber and Ancient Judaism." *SJT* 32 (1979), pp. 457–69.

"On Applying a Sociological Theory to Biblical Studies." *JSOT* 19 (1981), pp. 95–106.

Rohde, Joachim. *Rediscovering the Teaching of the Evangelists*. Translated by Dorothea M. Barton. London: SCM Press, 1968.

Rohrbaugh, Richard L. "Methodological Considerations in the Debate over the Social Class Status of Early Christians." *JAAR* 52 (1984), pp. 519–46.

"'Social Location of Thought' as a Heuristic Construct in New Testament Study." *JSNT* 30 (1987), pp. 103–19.

"The Pre-Industrial City in Luke-Acts: Urban Social Relations," in *The Social World of Luke-Acts: Models for Interpretation.* Edited by Jerome H. Neyrey. Peabody: Hendrickson, 1991, pp. 125–49.

"The Social Location of the Markan Audience." *Interpretation* 47 (1993), pp. 380–95.

"The Gospel of John in the Twenty-first Century," in *"What is John?" Volume II. Literary and Social Readings of the Fourth Gospel.* Edited by Fernando F. Segovia. SBLSymS 7. Atlanta: Scholars Press, 1998, pp. 257–63.

Rohrbaugh, Richard L., ed. *The Social Sciences and New Testament Interpretation.* Peabody: Hendrickson, 1996.

Rostovtzeff, Mihail. *The Social and Economic History of the Roman Empire.* 2 vols. 2nd edn. rev. by P. M. Fraser. Oxford: Clarendon Press, 1957.

Roth, Wolfgang. *Hebrew Gospel: Cracking the Code of Mark.* Oak Park, Ill.: Meyer-Stone Books, 1988.

"To Invert or Not to Invert: The Pharisaic Canon in the Gospels," in *Studies in Scripture in Early Judaism and Christianity: Investigations and Proposals.* Edited by Craig A. Evans and James A. Sanders. JSNTSup 148. SSEJC 5. Sheffield: Sheffield Academic Press, 1997, pp. 59–78.

Rowland, Christopher. *Christian Origins: An Account of the Setting and Character of the Most Important Sect of Judaism.* London: SPCK, 1985.

"Reading the New Testament Sociologically: An Introduction," *Theology* 88 (1985), pp. 358–64.

Runciman, W. G. "Class, Status and Power," in *Social Stratification.* Edited by J. A. Jackson. Cambridge: Cambridge University Press, 1968, pp. 25–61.

Russell, D. A. *Criticism in Antiquity.* London: Gerald Duckworth, 1981.

Russell, David S. *The Method and Message of Jewish Apocalyptic, 200 BC–AD 100.* London: SCM Press, 1964.

Saldarini, Anthony J. *Matthew's Christian-Jewish Community.* CSHJ. Chicago: University of Chicago Press, 1994.

Sanders, E. P. *Jewish Law from Jesus to the Mishnah. Five Studies.* London: SCM Press, 1990.

Sanders, E. P. and Margaret Davies. *Studying the Synoptic Gospels.* London: SCM Press, 1989.

Sanders, James A. "Intertextuality and Dialogue." *BTB* 29 (1999), pp. 35–44.

Sandmel, Samuel. *Philo of Alexandria: An Introduction.* Oxford: Oxford University Press, 1979.

Schäfer, Peter. "Die sogenannte Synode von Jabne: Zur Trennung von Juden und Christen im ersten/zweiten Jh. n. Chr," in *Studien zur Geschichte und Theologie des Rabbinischen Judentums.* AGAJU 15. Leiden: Brill, 1978, pp. 45–64.

Schiffmann, Lawrence H. *Who Was a Jew? Rabbinic and Halakhic Perspectives on the Jewish-Christian Schism.* Hoboken, NJ: Ktav Publishing House, 1985.

Schille, Gottfried. *Anfänge der Kirche: Erwägungen zur apostolischen Frühgeschichte.* Munich: Kaiser, 1966.

Schillebeeckx, Edward. *Revelation and Theology.* Translated by N. D. Smith. New York: Sheed & Ward, 1967.

Schmidt, Karl L. *Der Rahmen der Geschichte Jesu*. Berlin: Trowitzsch & Sohn, 1919.

"Die Stellung der Evangelien in der allgemeinen Literaturgeschichte," in *EUCHARISTION: Studien zur Religion und Literatur des Alten und Neuen Testaments: Hermann Gunkel zum 60*. Edited by Hans Schmidt. Göttingen: Vandenhoeck und Ruprecht, 1923, vol. II, pp. 50–134.

"ἐκκλησία," in *TDNT*. Edited by Gerhard Kittel. Translated and edited by Geoffrey Bromiley. Grand Rapids: Eerdmans, 1964–76, vol. III, pp. 501–36.

Schnackenburg, Rudolf. *The Gospel According to St. John*. 3 vols. Translated by Cecil Hastings *et al*. HTCNT. London: Burns and Oates, 1968–82.

The Johannine Epistles: Introduction and Commentary. Translated by Reginald and Ilse Fuller. Tunbridge Wells: Burns & Oates, 1992.

Schneemelcher, Wilhelm. *New Testament Apocrypha. Volume One: Gospels and Related Writings*. Rev. edn. Translated by R. McL. Wilson. Louisville: Westminster John Knox, 1991.

Schnelle, Udo. *Antidocetic Christology in the Gospel of John: An Investigation of the Place of the Fourth Gospel in the Johannine School*. Translated by L. M. Maloney. Minneapolis: Fortress, 1992.

Schniewind, Julius. "Zur Synoptiker-Exegese" *ThR* 2 (1930), pp. 129–89.

Schreiber, Johannes. *Theologie des Vertrauens: Eine redaktionsgeschichtliche Untersuchung des Markusevangeliums*. Hamburg: Furche-Verlag, 1967.

Schuchard, Bruce G. *Scripture within Scripture: The Interrelationship of Form and Function in the Explicit Old Testament Citations in the Gospel of John*. SBLDS 133. Atlanta: Scholars Press, 1992.

Schürer, Emil. *The History of the Jewish People in the Age of Jesus Christ*. Rev. and enl. edn. Translated by Geza Vermes, Fergus Millar, and Matthew Black. Edinburgh: T. & T. Clark, 1979.

Schwartz, T. "Cultural Totemism: Ethnic Identity Primitive and Modern," in *Ethnic Identity: Cultural Continuities and Change*. Edited by D. De Vos and L. Romanucci-Ross. Palo Alto: Mayfield, 1975, pp. 106–31.

Schweitzer, Albert. *The Quest of the Historical Jesus: A Critical Study of Its Progress from Reimarus to Wrede*. Translated by W. Montgomery. London: Adam & Charles Black, 1910.

Scroggs, Robin. "The Earliest Christian Communities as Sectarian Movement," in *Christianity, Judaism and Other Greco-Roman Cults. Studies for Morton Smith at Sixty*. Edited by Jacob Neusner. SJLA 12. Leiden: Brill, 1975, vol. II, pp. 1–23.

"The Sociological Interpretation of the New Testament: The Present State of Research." *NTS* 26 (1980), pp. 164–79.

Searle, John. *Speech Acts: An Essay in the Philosophy of Language*. Cambridge: Cambridge University Press, 1979.

Segal, Robert A. "The Social Sciences and the Truth of Religious Belief." *JAAR* 48 (1980), pp. 403–13.

Segovia, Fernando F. "The Love and Hatred of Jesus and Johannine Sectarianism." *CBQ* 43 (1981), pp. 258–72.

"The Theology and Provenance of John 15:1–7." *JBL* 101 (1982), pp. 115–28.

"John 13:1–20, the Footwashing in the Johannine Tradition." *ZNW* 73 (1982), pp. 31–51.

Love Relationships in the Johannine Community. SBLDS 58. Chico, Calif.:
Scholars Press, 1982.

The Farewell of the Word: The Johannine Call to Abide. Minneapolis: Fortress,
1991.

"Reading Readers of the Fourth Gospel and Their Readings: An Exercise in
Intercultural Criticism," in *"What is John?" Readers and Readings of the
Fourth Gospel*. SBLSymS 3. Edited by Fernando F. Segovia. Atlanta: Schol-
ars Press, 1996, pp. 237–77.

"Reading Readers Reading John: An Exercise in Intercultural Criticism," in
*"What is John?" Volume II. Literary and Social Readings of the Fourth
Gospel*. Edited by Fernando F. Segovia. SBLSymS 7. Atlanta: Scholars
Press, 1998, pp. 281–322.

Seitz, Christopher. *Figured Out: Typology and Providence in Christian Scripture*.
Louisville: Westminster John Knox, 2001.

Seton-Watson, Hugh. *Nations and States: An Inquiry into the Origins of Nations
and the Politics of Nationalism*. Boulder, Colo.: Westview Press, 1977.

Shim, Ezra S. B. "A Suggestion about the Genre or Text-Type of Mark." *Scriptura*
50 (1994), pp. 69–89.

Shuler, Philip L. *A Genre for the Gospels: The Biographical Character of
Matthew*. Philadelphia: Fortress, 1982.

"The Genre of the Gospels and the Two Gospel Hypothesis." *Jesus, the Gospels,
and the Church: Essays in Honor of William R. Farmer*. Edited by E. P.
Sanders. Macon, Ga.: Mercer University Press, 1987, pp. 69–88.

"The Genre(s) of the Gospels," in *The Interrelations of the Gospels*. Edited
David L. Dungan. BETL 95. Leuven: Leuven University Press, 1990,
pp. 459–83.

Sim, David C. *The Gospel of Matthew and Christian Judaism: The History and
Social Setting of the Matthean Community*. SNTW. Edinburgh: T. & T. Clark,
1998.

"The Gospels for All Christians? A Response to Richard Bauckham." *JSNT*
84 (2001), pp. 3–27.

Simonetti, Manlio. *Biblical Interpretation in the Early Church: An Historical
Introduction to Patristic Exegesis*. Translated by John A. Hughes. Edinburgh:
T. & T. Clark, 1994.

Smalley, Stephen S. *John: Evangelist and Interpreter*. Exeter: Paternoster, 1978.

1, 2, 3, John. WBC 51. Waco, Tx.: Word Books, 1984.

The Revelation to John: A Commentary on the Greek Text of the Apocalypse.
Downers Grove, Ill.: Intervarsity, 2005.

Smith, D. Moody. *Johannine Christianity: Essays on Its Setting, Sources, and
Theology*. Edinburgh: T. & T. Clark, 1984.

"The Contribution of J. Louis Martyn to the Understanding of the Gospel of
John," in *The Conversation Continues: Studies in Paul and John*. Nashville:
Abingdon Press, 1990, pp. 275–94. Repr. in *History and Theology in the
Fourth Gospel*. 3rd edn. Louisville: Westminster John Knox, 2003, 1–19.

John Among the Synoptics: The Relationship in Twentieth-Century Research.
Minneapolis: Fortress, 1992.

"John and the Synoptics and the Question of Gospel Genre," in *The Four
Gospels 1992*. Edited by F. Van Segbroeck *et al.* BETL 100. Leuven: Leuven
University Press, 1992, vol. II, pp. 1783–97.

The Theology of the Gospel of John. Cambridge: Cambridge University Press, 1995.

"Prolegomena to a Canonical Reading of the Fourth Gospel," in *"What is John?" Readers and Readings of the Fourth Gospel*. SBLSymS 3. Edited by Fernando F. Segovia. Atlanta: Scholars Press, 1996, pp. 169–82.

John. ANTC. Nashville: Abingdon, 1999.

"When Did the Gospels Become Scripture?" *JBL* 119 (2000), pp. 3–20.

"Response to Robert Kysar, 'The Expulsion from the Synagogue: The Tale of the Theory.'" Paper presented at the annual meeting of the SBL. Toronto, Canada, November 25, 2002.

Smith, Jonathan Z. "When the Bough Breaks." *HR* 13 (1973), pp. 342–71.

"The Social Description of Early Christianity." *RSR* 1 (1975), pp. 19–25.

"Too Much Kingdom, Too Little Community." *Zygon* 13 (1978), pp. 123–30.

Imagining Religion. Chicago: Chicago University Press, 1982.

"What a Difference a Difference Makes," in *"To See Ourselves as Others See Us": Christians, Jews, "Others" in Late Antiquity*. Edited by Jacob Neusner and Ernest S. Frerichs. Chico, Calif.: Scholars Press, 1985, pp. 3–48.

To Take Place: Toward Theory in Ritual. Chicago: Chicago University Press, 1987.

Drudgery Divine: On the Comparison of Early Christianities and the Religions of Late Antiquity. JLCR 14. CSHJ. Chicago: The University of Chicago Press, 1990.

"Classification," in *Guide to the Study of Religion*. Edited by Willi Braun and Russell T. McCutcheon. London: Cassell, 2000, pp. 35–44.

Smith, Morton. "Prolegomena to a Discussion of Aretalogies, Divine Men, the Gospels and Jesus." *JBL* 90 (1971), pp. 74–99.

Smith, T. C. *Jesus in the Gospel of John*. Nashville: Broadman, 1959.

Sommer, Benjamin D. "Exegesis, Allusion and Intertextuality in the Hebrew Bible: A Response to Lyle Eslinger." *VT* 46 (1996), pp. 479–89.

Soulen, R. Kendall. "The Believer and the Historian: Theological Interpretation and Historical Investigation." *Interpretation* 57 (2003), pp. 174–86.

Sproston North, Wendy E. "Witnesses to what was ἀπ'ἀρχῆς: 1 John's Contribution to our Knowledge of Tradition in the Fourth Gospel," in *The Johannine Readings*. Edited by Stanley E. Porter and Craig A. Evans. BS 32. Sheffield: Sheffield Academic Press, 1995, pp. 138–60.

"John for Readers of Mark? A Response to Richard Bauckham's Proposal." *JSNT* 25 (2003), pp. 449–68.

Staden, Piet Van. *Compassion – the Essence of Life: A Social-scientific Study of the Religious Symbolic Universe Reflected in the Ideology/Theology of Luke*. HTSS 4. Pretoria: University of Pretoria, 1991.

Staley, Jeffrey Lloyd. *The Print's First Kiss: A Rhetorical Investigation of the Implied Reader in the Fourth Gospel*. SBLDS 82. Atlanta: Scholars Press, 1988.

"What Can a Postmodern Approach to the Fourth Gospel Add to Contemporary Debates About its Historical Situation?," in *Jesus in Johannine Tradition*. Edited by Robert T. Fortna and Tom Thatcher. Louisville: Westminster John Knox, 2001, pp. 47–57.

Stambaugh, John E. and David L. Balch. *The New Testament in its Social Environment*. LEC 2. Philadelphia: Westminster Press, 1986.

Stanford, Michael. *An Introduction to the Philosophy of History.* Oxford: Blackwell, 1998.

Stanton, Graham N. "Matthew as a Creative Interpreter of the Sayings of Jesus," in *The Gospel and The Gospels.* Edited by Peter Stuhlmacher. Grand Rapids: Eerdmans, 1991, pp. 257–72.

A *Gospel for A New People: Studies in Matthew.* Edinburgh: T. & T. Clark, 1992.

"Revisiting Matthew's Communities," in *SBLSP.* Chico, Calif.: Scholars Press, 1994, pp. 9–23.

"The Fourfold Gospel." *NTS* 43 (1997), pp. 317–46.

"The Early Reception of Matthew's Gospel: New Evidence from Papyri?," in *The Gospel of Matthew in Current Study.* Edited by David E. Aune. Grand Rapids: Eerdmans, 2001, pp. 42–61.

Stanton, Vincent Henry. *The Gospels as Historical Documents.* 3 vols. Cambridge: Cambridge University Press, 1920.

Stark, Rodney. "The Class Basis of Early Christianity: Inferences from a Sociological Model." *SA* 47 (1986), pp. 216–25.

The Rise of Christianity: A Sociologist Reconsiders History. Princeton: Princeton University Press, 1996.

Stark, Werner. *Sociology of Religion: A Study of Christendom.* London: Routledge & Kegan Paul, 1967, vol. II.

Stark, Rodney. "The Class Basis of Early Christianity: Inferences from a Sociological Model." *SA* 47 (1986), pp. 216–25.

Stegemann, Ekkehard W. and Wolfgang Stegemann. *The Jesus Movement: A Social History of Its First Century.* Translated by O. C. Dean, Jr. Minneapolis: Fortress, 1999.

Stegner, William Richard. "The Use of Scripture in Two Narratives of Early Jewish Christianity (Matthew 4.1–11; Mark 9.2–8)," in *Studies in Scripture in Early Judaism and Christianity: Investigations and Proposals.* Edited by Craig A. Evans and James A. Sanders. JSNTSup 148. SSEJC 5. Sheffield: Sheffield Academic Press, 1997, pp. 98–120.

Stein, Robert H. "Is Our Reading the Bible the Same As the Original Audience's Hearing it? A Case Study in the Gospel of Mark." *JETS* 46 (2003), pp. 63–78.

Steinmetz, David C. "The Superiority of Pre-Critical Exegesis," in *The Theological Interpretation of Scripture: Classic and Contemporary Readings.* Cambridge, Mass.: Blackwell, 1997, pp. 26–38.

Stendahl, Krister. *The School of St. Matthew.* ASNTU 20. Lund: C. W. K. Gleerup, 1954.

Sterling, Gregory E. "Luke-Acts and Apologetic Historiography," in *SBLSP.* Chico, Calif.: Scholars Press, 1989, pp. 326–42.

Historiography and Self-Definition: Josephus, Luke-Acts and Apologetic Historiography. Leiden: Brill, 1992.

Sternberg, Meir. *The Poetics of Biblical Narrative: Ideological Literature and the Drama of Reading.* ISBL. Bloomington: Indiana University Press, 1985.

Stibbe, Mark W. G. *John as Storyteller: Narrative Criticism and the Fourth Gospel.* SNTSMS 73. Cambridge: Cambridge University Press, 1992.

John's Gospel. NTR. London: Routledge, 1994.

Stibbe, Mark W. G., ed. *The Gospel of John as Literature: An Anthology of Twentieth-Century Perspectives*. NTTS 17. Leiden: Brill, 1993.

Stiver, Dan R. "Ricoeur, Speech-act Theory, and the Gospels as History," in *After Pentecost: Language and Biblical Interpretation*. SHS 2. Edited by Craig Bartholomew, Colin Greene, and Karl Möller. Grand Rapids: Zondervan, 2001, pp. 50–72.

Stowers, Stanley Kent. "The Social Sciences and the Study of Early Christianity," in *Approaches to Ancient Judaism: Studies in Judaism and Its Greco-Roman Context*. Edited by William S. Green. BJS 32. Atlanta: Scholars Press, 1985, vol. V, pp. 149–81.

Strachan, R. H. *The Fourth Gospel: Its Significance and Environment*. London: Student Christian Movement Press, 1941.

Strauss, David Friedrich. *Das Leben Jesu für das deutsche Volk bearbeitet*. Leipzig: F. U. Brodhaus, 1864.

A New Life of Jesus. 2 vols. Authorized Translation. London: Williams & Norgate, 1865.

Strecker, Georg. *History of New Testament Literature*. Translated by Calvin Katter. Harrisberg, Pa.: Trinity Press International, 1997.

Streeter, Burnett Hillman. *The Four Gospels: A Study of Origins, Treating of the Manuscript Tradition, Sources, Authorship, and Dates*. London: Macmillan, 1924.

The Primitive Church: Studied with Special Reference to the Origins of the Christian Ministry. London: Macmillan, 1930.

Strimple, Robert B. *The Modern Search for the Real Jesus*. Phillipsburg, NJ: P. & R, 1995.

Stuhlmacher, Peter. "The Genre(s) of the Gospels: Response to P. L. Shuler," in *The Interrelations of the Gospels*. Edited by David L. Dungan. BETL 95. Leuven: Leuven University Press, 1990, pp. 484–94.

Suleiman, Susan R. "Introduction: Varieties of Audience-Oriented Criticism," in *The Reader in the Text: Essays on Audience and Interpretation*. Edited by Susan R. Suleiman and Inge Crosman. Princeton: Princeton University Press, 1980, pp. 3–45.

Swain, Simon. "Biography and Biographic in the Literature of the Roman Empire," in *Portraits: Biographical Representation in the Greek and Latin Literature of the Roman Empire*. Edited by Mark J. Edwards and Simon Swain. Oxford: Clarendon Press, 1997, pp. 1–37.

Swancut, Diana M. "Hungers Assuaged by the Bread from Heaven: 'Eating Jesus' as Isaian Call to Belief: The Confluence of Isaiah 55 and Psalm 78 (77) in John 6.22–71," in *Studies in Scripture in Early Judaism and Christianity: Investigations and Proposals*. Edited by Craig A. Evans and James A. Sanders. JSNTSup 148. SSEJC 5. Sheffield: Sheffield Academic Press, 1997, pp. 218–51.

Swartley, Willard M. *Israel's Scripture Tradition and the Synoptic Gospels: Story Shaping Story*. Peabody: Hendrickson, 1994.

Swete, Henry Barclay. *The Gospel According to St. Mark*. 3rd edn. London: Macmillan, 1909.

Talbert, Charles H. *Literary Patterns, Theological Themes, and the Genre of Luke-Acts*. SBLMS 20. Missoula, Mont.: Scholars Press, 1974.

What is a Gospel? The Genre of the Canonical Gospels. Philadelphia: Fortress, 1977.

Reading Luke: A Literary and Theological Commentary on the Third Gospel. New York: Crossroad, 1982.

"Once Again: Gospel Genre." *Semeia* 43 (1988), pp. 53–73.

Talmon, Yonina. "Pursuit of the Millennium: The Relation between Religious and Social Change," in *Reader in Comparative Religion: An Anthropological Approach.* Edited by W. A. Lessa and E. Z. Vogt. 2nd edn. New York: Harper & Row, 1965, pp. 522–37.

Tate, W. Randolph. *Biblical Interpretation: An Integrated Approach.* Peabody: Hendrickson, 1991.

Taylor, Vincent. *The Formation of the Gospel Tradition.* London: Macmillan, 1933.

Teeple, Howard M. *The Mosaic Eschatological Prophet.* JBLMS 10. Philadelphia: Society of Biblical Literature, 1957.

Temple, Sydney. *The Core of the Fourth Gospel.* London: Mowbrays, 1975.

Thatcher, Tom. *The Riddles of Jesus in John: A Study in Tradition and Folklore.* SBLMS 53. Atlanta: Society of Biblical Literature, 2000.

"The Riddles of Jesus in the Johannine Dialogues," in *Jesus in Johannine Tradition.* Edited by Robert T. Fortna and Tom Thatcher. Louisville: Westminster John Knox, 2001, pp. 263–77.

Theissen, Gerd. "Sociale Integration und sakramentales Handeln: Eine Analyse von 1 Cor. XI 17–34." *NovT* 24 (1974), pp. 179–205.

"Soziale Schichtung in der korinthischen Gemeinde," *ZNW* 65 (1974), pp. 232–72.

"Die Starken und Schwachen in Korinth: Sociologische Analyse eines theologischen Streites." *EvT* 35 (1975), pp. 155–72.

"Die Soziologische Auswertung religiöser Überlieferungen: Ihre methodologicshen Probleme am Beispiel des Urchristentums." *Kairos* (1975), pp. 284–99.

Soziologie der Jesusbewegung: Ein Beitrag zur Entstehungsgechichte des Urchristentums. TEH 194. Munich: Christian Kaiser Verlag, 1977.

The First Followers of Jesus: A Sociological Analysis of the Earliest Christianity. Translated by John Bowden. London: SCM Press, 1978.

Studien zur Soziologie des Urchristentums. WUNT 19. Tübingen: Mohr Siebeck, 1979.

The Social Setting of Pauline Christianity: Essays on Corinth. Edited and translated by John H. Schütz. Philadelphia: Fortress, 1982.

The Gospels in Context: Social and Political History in the Synoptic Tradition. Minneapolis: Fortress, 1991.

Theobald, Michael. "Schriftzitate im 'Lebensbrot' – Dialog Jesu (Joh 6). Ein Paradigma für den Schriftgebrauch des vierten Evangelisten," in *The Scriptures in the Gospels.* Edited by Christopher M. Tuckett. BETL 131. Leuven: Leuven University Press, 1997, pp. 327–66.

Thiemann, Ronald F. *Revelation and Theology: The Gospel as Narrated Promise.* Notre Dame: University of Notre Dame Press, 1985.

"Radiance and Obscurity in Biblical Narrative," in *Scriptural Authority and Narrative Interpretation: Essays on the Occasion of the Sixty-fifth Birthday of Hans W. Frei.* Edited by Garrett Green. Philadelphia: Fortress, 1987, pp. 21–41.

Thiselton, Anthony C. *New Horizons in Hermeneutics: The Theory and Practice of Transforming Biblical Reading.* Grand Rapids: Zondervan, 1992.

'"Behind' and 'In Front Of' the Text: Language, Reference and Indeterminacy," in *After Pentecost: Language and Biblical Interpretation.* SHS 2. Edited by Craig Bartholomew, Colin Greene, and Karl Möller. Grand Rapids: Zondervan, 2001, pp. 97–120.

Tholuck, Augustus. *Commentary on the Gospel of St. John.* Translated by Charles P. Krauth. Edinburgh: T. & T. Clark, 1860.

Thompson, B. C. *Making Sense of Reification: Alfred Schultz and Constructionist Theory.* London: Macmillan, 1982.

Thompson, James M. "An Experiment in Translation," in *The Expositor.* Eighth Series. vol. 16. London: Hodder and Stoughton, 1918, pp. 117–25.

Thompson, Marianne Meye. "After Virtual Reality: Reading the Gospel of John at the Turn of the Century," in *"What is John?" Volume II. Literary and Social Readings of the Fourth Gospel.* Edited by Fernando F. Segovia. SBLSymS 7. Atlanta: Scholars Press, 1998, pp. 231–38.

Thompson, Michael B. "The Holy Internet: Communication between Churches in the First Christian Century," in *The Gospels for All Christians: Rethinking the Gospel Audiences.* Edited by Richard Bauckham. Grand Rapids: Eerdmans, 1998, pp. 49–70.

Thrupp, Sylvia L., ed. *Millennial Dreams in Action: Studies in Revolutionary Religious Movements.* New York: Schocken, 1970.

Thyen, Hartmut. "Aus der Literatur zum Johannesevangelium." *ThR* 39 (1974), pp. 1–69.

"Aus der Literatur zum Johannesevangelium." *ThR* 39 (1974), pp. 222–52.

"Aus der Literatur zum Johannesevangelium." *ThR* 39 (1974), pp. 289–330.

"Aus der Literatur zum Johannesevangelium." *ThR* 42 (1977), pp. 211–70.

Tidball, Derek. *An Introduction to the Sociology of the New Testament.* Exeter: Paternoster, 1983.

Tiede, David L. *The Charismatic Figure as Miracle Worker.* SBLDS 1. Missoula, Mont.: Society of Biblical Literature, 1972.

Tilly, Charles. *As Sociology Meets History.* SSD. New York: Academic Press, 1981.

Timasheff, Nicholas S. *Sociological Theory: Its Nature and Growth.* 3rd edn. New York: Random House, 1967.

Todorov, Tzetan. "Reading as Construction," in *The Reader in the Text: Essays on Audience and Interpretation.* Edited by Susan R. Suleiman and Inge Crosman. Princeton: Princeton University Press, 1980, pp. 67–82.

Tolbert, Mary Ann. *Sowing the Gospel: Mark's World in Literary-Historical Perspective.* Minneapolis: Fortress, 1989.

Tomson, Peter J. "'Jews' in the Gospel of John as Compared with the Palestinian Talmud, the Synoptics, and Some New Testament Apocrypha," in *Anti-Judaism and the Fourth Gospel.* Edited by Reimund Bieringer, Didier Pollefeyt, and Frederique Vandecasteele-Vanneuville. Louisville: Westminster John Knox, 2001, pp. 176–212.

Torrey, Charles C. *The Lives of the Prophets: Greek Text and Translation.* JBLMS 1. Philadelphia: Society of Biblical Literature and Exegesis, 1946.

Tovey, Derek. *Narrative Art and Act in the Fourth Gospel.* JSNTSup 151. Sheffield: Sheffield Academic Press, 1997.

Treier, Daniel L. "The Superiority of Pre-Critical Exegesis: Sic Et Non." *TJ* 24 (2003), pp. 77–103.

Trobisch, David. *The First Edition of the New Testament*. Oxford: Oxford University Press, 2000.

Troeltsch, Ernst. *Die Soziallehren der christlichen Kirchen und Gruppen*. Tübingen: J. C. B. Mohr, 1912.

   The Social Teachings of the Christian Church. Translated by Olive Wyon. London: George Allen & Unwin, 1931.

Tuckett, Christopher M. *Reading the New Testament: Methods of Interpretation*. London: SPCK, 1987.

   "Introduction," in *The Scriptures in the Gospels*. Edited by Christopher M. Tuckett. BETL 131. Leuven: Leuven University Press, 1997, pp. xiii–xxiv.

Turner, Victor W. *The Forest of Symbols*. Ithaca: Cornell University Press, 1967.

   The Ritual Process: Structure and Anti-Structure. London: Routledge and Kegan Paul, 1969.

   Dramas, Fields, and Metaphors: Symbolic Action in Human Society. Ithaca: Cornell University Press, 1974.

Twelftree, Graham H. *Jesus the Miracle Worker*. Downers Grove, Ill.: Intervarsity, 1992.

Tyson, Joseph B. *A Study of Early Christianity*. New York: Macmillan, 1973.

van Belle, Gilbert. *Johannine Bibliography, 1966–1985: A Cumulative Bibliography on the Fourth Gospel*. BETL 82. Leuven: Leuven University Press, 1988.

van Eck, Ernest. "A Sitz for the Gospel of Mark? A Critical Reaction to Bauckham's Theory on the Universality of the Gospels." *HTS* 56 (2000), pp. 973–1008.

Van der Watt, Jan G. "The Dynamics of Metaphor in the Gospel of John." *SNTU* 23 (1998), pp. 29–41.

   "Community in Conflict: The History and Social Context of the Johannine Community." *Interpretation* 49 (1995), pp. 379–89.

van Tilborg, Sjef. *Reading John in Ephesus*. NovTSup 83. Leiden: Brill, 1996.

van Unnik, W. C. "The Purpose of St. John's Gospel," in *Studia Evangelica I*. Edited by Kurt Aland *et al*. TU 73. Berlin: Akademie, 1959, pp. 382–411.

Vanhoozer, Kevin J. *Biblical Narrative in the Philosophy of Paul Ricoeur: A Study in Hermeneutics and Theology*. Cambridge: Cambridge University Press, 1990.

   "The Reader in New Testament Interpretation," in *Hearing the New Testament: Strategies for Interpretation*. Edited by Joel B. Green. Grand Rapids: Eerdmans, 1995, pp. 301–28.

   Is There a Meaning in This Text: The Bible, the Reader, and the Morality of Literary Knowledge. Grand Rapids: Zondervan, 1998.

   "From Speech Acts to Scripture Acts: The Covenant of Discourse and the Discourse of Covenant," in *After Pentecost: Language and Biblical Interpretation*. SHS 2. Edited by Craig Bartholomew, Colin Greene, and Karl Möller. Grand Rapids: Zondervan, 2001, pp. 1–49.

   First Theology: God, Scripture and Hermeneutics. Downers Grove, Ill.: Intervarsity, 2002.

Vermes, Geza. *The Dead Sea Scrolls: Qumran in Perspective*. Rev. and enl. edn. London: SCM Press, 1994.

Verner, David C. *The Household of God: The Social World of the Pastoral Epistles.* Chico, Calif.: Scholars, 1983.

Via, Dan O. *The Ethics of Mark's Gospel: In the Middle of Time.* Philadelphia: Fortress, 1988.

Viviano, Benedict T. "Peter as Jesus' Mouth: Matthew 16:13–20 in the Light of Exodus 4:10–17 and Other Models," in *The Interpretation of Scripture in Early Judaism and Christianity.* Edited by Craig A. Evans. JSPSSup 33. SSEJC 7. Sheffield: Sheffield Academic Press, 2000, pp. 312–41.

von Harnack, Adolf. *The Expansion of Christianity in the First Three Centuries.* Translated by J. Moffatt. 2 vols. London: Williams & Norgate, 1904.

Bible Reading in the Early Church. Translated by J. R. Wilkinson. London: Williams & Norgate, 1912.

Die Entstehung des Neuen Testaments und die wichtigsten Folgen der neuen Schöpfung. BENT 6. Leipzig: J. C. Hinrichs, 1912.

von Soden, Hermann F. *Die Schriften des Neuen Testaments.* 4 vols. Berlin: Dunckler, 1902.

von Wahlde, Urban C. "The Terms for Religious Authorities in the Fourth Gospel: A Key to Literary Strata?," *JBL* 98 (1979), pp. 231–53.

"The Johannine Jews: A Critical Survey." *NTS* 28 (1982), pp. 33–60.

Vorster, Willem S. "Kerygma/History and the Gospel Genre." *NTS* 29 (1983), pp. 87–95.

"Gospel Genre," in *The Anchor Bible Dictionary.* Edited by David Noel Freedman. 6 vols. New York: Doubleday, 1992, vol. II, pp. 1077–79.

Votaw, Clyde Weber. *The Gospels and Contemporary Biographies in the Greco-Roman World.* FBBS 27. Philadelphia: Fortress, 1970.

Wagner, Günter, ed. *An Exegetical Bibliography of the New Testament: John and 1, 2, 3, John.* Macon, Ga.: Mercer University Press, 1987.

Walker, Norman. "The Reckoning of Hours in the Fourth Gospel." *NovT* 4 (1960), pp. 69–73.

Wall, Robert W. "Community," in *The Anchor Bible Dictionary.* Edited by David Noel Freedman. 6 vols. New York: Doubleday, 1992, vol. I, pp. 1099–110.

Wallace, Daniel B. *Greek Grammar Beyond the Basics.* Grand Rapids: Zondervan, 1996.

Walsh, Michael J. Review of David C. Sim, *The Gospel of Matthew and Christian Judaism: The History and Social Setting of the Matthean Community. HJ* 41 (2000), pp. 334–36.

Wansbrough, Henry. "The New Israel: The Community of Matthew and the Community of Qumran." *SNTU* 25 (2000), pp. 8–22.

Ward, Timothy. *Word and Supplement: Speech Acts, Biblical Texts, and the Sufficiency of Scripture.* Oxford: Oxford University Press, 2002.

Warner, Martin. "The Fourth Gospel's Art of Rational Persuasion," in *The Bible as Rhetoric: Studies in Biblical Persuasion and Credibility.* Edited by Martin Warner. London: Routledge, 1990, pp. 153–77.

Watkins, J. W. N. "Ideal Types and Historical Explanation," in *The Philosophy of Social Explanations.* Edited by Alan Ryan. Oxford Readings in Philosophy. Oxford: Oxford University Press, 1973, pp. 82–104.

Watson, Francis. *Paul, Judaism, and the Gentiles: A Sociological Approach.* Cambridge: Cambridge University Press, 1986.

Text, Church, and World: Biblical Interpretation in Theological Perspective. Edinburgh: T. & T. Clark, 1994.

Text and Truth: Redefining Biblical Theology. Edinburgh: T. & T. Clark, 1997.

"Toward a Literal Reading of the Gospels," in *The Gospels for All Christians: Rethinking the Gospel Audiences.* Edited by Richard Bauckham. Grand Rapids: Eerdmans, 1998, pp. 195–217.

Watty, William W. "The Significance of Anonymity in the Fourth Gospel." *ExpT* 90 (1979), pp. 209–12.

Weaver, P. R. C. *Familia Caesaris: A Social Study of the Emperor's Freedman and Slaves.* Cambridge: Cambridge University Press, 1972.

"Social Mobility in the Early Roman Empire: The Evidence of the Imperial Freedman and Slaves," in *Studies in Ancient Society.* Edited by Moses I. Finley. London: Routledge and Kegan Paul, 1974, pp. 121–40.

Weber, Max. *The Methodology of the Social Sciences.* Translated and edited by Edward A. Shils and Henry A. Finch. New York: Free Press, 1949.

The Sociology of Religion. Boston: Beacon Press, 1964.

Weeden, Sr., Theodore J. *Mark – Traditions in Conflict.* Philadelphia: Fortress, 1971.

Weiss, Herold. "Footwashing in the Johannine Community." *NovT* 41 (1979), pp. 298–325.

Weiss, Johannes. *Earliest Christianity: History of the Period A.D. 30–150.* 2 vols. Translated by Frederick C. Grant. New York: Harper & Brothers, 1959.

Weisse, C. Hermann. *die evangelische Geschichte kritisch und philosophisch bearbeitet.* 2 vols. Leipzig: Dörffling und Franke, 1838.

Weizsäcker, Carl H. v. *Untersuchungen über die evangelische Geschichte ihre Quellen und den Gang ihrer Entwicklung.* 2 vols. 2nd edn. Tübingen: J. C. B. Mohr, 1901.

Wellek, René and Austin Warren. *Theory of Literature.* London: Jonathan Cape, 1949.

Wellhausen, Julius. *Prolegomena to the History of Israel.* Translated by J. Sutherland Black and Allan Menzies. Edinburgh: Adam and Charles Black, 1895.

Das Evangelium Marci. Berlin: Georg Reimer, 1903.

Das Evangelium Matthaei. Berlin: Georg Reimer, 1904.

Das Evangelium Lucae. Berlin: Georg Reimer, 1904.

Das Einleitung in die drei ersten Evangelien. Berlin: Georg Reimer, 1905.

Das Evangelium Johannis. Berlin: Druck und Verlag von Georg Reimer, 1908.

Wendland, Paul. *Die urchristlichen Literaturformen,* 2nd edn. Tübingen: J. C. B. Mohr, 1912.

Wengst, Klaus. *Bedrängte Gemeinde und verherrlichter Christus: Der historische Ort des Johannesevangeliums als Schlüssel zu seiner Interpretation.* BTS 5. Neukirchen-Vluyn: Neukirchener Verlag, 1981.

Wenham, John. *Redating Matthew, Mark, & Luke.* Downers Grove, Ill.: Intervarsity, 1992.

Westcott, Brooke Foss. *The Gospel According to St. John.* London: John Murray, 1882.

Westermann, Claus. *The Gospel of John in the Light of the Old Testament.* Translated by Siegfried S. Schatzmann. Peabody: Hendrickson, 1988.

Whitacre, Rodney A. *Johannine Polemic: The Role of Tradition and Theology.* SBLDS 67. Chico, Calif.: Scholars Press, 1982.

White, L. Michael. "Shifting Sectarian Boundaries in Early Christianity." *BJRL* 70 (1988), pp. 7–24.

"Finding the Ties that Bind: Issues from Social Description." *Semeia* 56 (1991), pp. 3–22.

"Social Networks: Theoretical Orientation and Historical Applications." *Semeia* 56 (1991), pp. 23–36.

Wiarda, Timothy. "Scenes and Details in the Gospels: Concrete Reading and Three Alternatives." *NTS* 50 (2004), pp. 167–84.

Wiefel, Wolfgang. "Die Scheidung von Gemeinde und Welt im Johannesevangelium." *ThZ* 35 (1979), pp. 213–27.

Wilder, Amos. *The Language of the Gospel: Early Christian Rhetoric*. London: SCM Press, 1964.

Wiles, Maurice. "Scriptural Authority and Theological Construction: The Limitations of Narrative Interpretation," in *Scriptural Authority and Narrative Interpretation: Essays on the Occasion of the sixty-fifth Birthday of Hans W. Frei*. Edited by Garrett Green. Philadelphia: Fortress, 1987, pp. 42–58.

Wilkin, Robert L. "Toward a Social Interpretation of Early Christian Apologetics." *CH* 39 (1970), pp. 1–22.

"Collegia, Philosophical Schools, and Theology," in *The Catacombs and the Colosseum: The Roman Empire as the Setting of Primitive Christianity*. Edited by Stephen Benko and John J. O'Rourke. Valley Forge: Judson, 1971, pp. 268–91.

Wilkens, Wilhelm. *Zeichen und Werke. Ein Beitrag zur Theologie des 4. Evangeliums in Erzählungs- und Redestoff*. ATANT 55. Zurich: Zwingli, 1969.

Williams, Rowan. "Does it Make Sense to Speak of a Pre-Nicene Orthodoxy?," in *The Making of Orthodoxy: Essays in Honour of Henry Chadwick*. Edited by Rowan Williams. Cambridge: Cambridge University Press, 1989, pp. 1–23.

"Westcott to Robinson: Some Anglican Readings of the Fourth Gospel." Paper presented at the St. Andrews Conference on the Gospel of and Christian Theology. St. Andrews, Scotland, July 3, 2003.

Wilson, Bryan R. "An Analysis of Sect Development." *ASR* 24 (1959), pp. 3–15.

Sects and Society: A Sociological Study of Three Religious Groups in Britain. London: Heinemann, 1961.

Patterns of Sectarianism: Organization and Ideology in Social and Religious Movements. London: Heinemann, 1967.

"A Typology of Sects," in *Sociology of Religion*. Edited by Roland Robertson. Baltimore: Penguin Books, 1969, pp. 361–83.

Religious Sects: A Sociological Study. London: Weidenfeld & Nicolson, 1970.

Magic and the Millennium: A Sociological Study of Religious Movements of Protest among Tribal and Third-world Peoples. New York: Harper & Row, 1973.

Religion in Sociological Perspective. Oxford: Oxford University Press, 1982.

"Methodological Perspectives in the Study of Religious Minorities." *BJRL* 70 (1988), pp. 225–40.

Wimbush, Vincent L. "'... Not of this World ...' Early Christianities as Rhetorical and Social Formation," in *Reimagining Christian Origins: A Colloquium Honoring Burton Mack*. Edited by Elizabeth A. Castelli and Hal Taussig. Valley Forge, Pa.: Trinity Press International, 1996, pp. 23–36.

Winch, Peter. *The Idea of A Social Science and Its Relation to Philosophy.* London: Routledge, 1958, Repr. SPP. London: Routledge & Kegan Paul, 1988.

Windisch, Hans. "Der johanneische Erzählungsstil," in *EUCHARISTERION: Studien zur Religion und Literatur des Alten und Neuen Testaments: Hermann Gunkel zum 60.* Edited by Hans Schmidt. Göttingen: Vandenhoeck und Ruprecht, 1923, vol. II, pp. 174–213.

Winter, Paul. *On the Trial of Jesus.* 2nd edn. Berlin: Walter de Gruyter, 1974.

Wisse, Frederik. "Historical Method and the Johannine Community." *Arc* (1992), pp. 35–42.

Witherington, Ben, III. *Jesus the Sage: The Pilgrimage of Wisdom.* Edinburgh: T. & T. Clark, 1994.

John's Wisdom: A Commentary on the Fourth Gospel. Cambridge: Lutterworth Press, 1995.

Wrede, William. *Charakter und Tendenz des Johannes-evangeliums.* SVSGTR 37. Tübingen: Mohr, 1933.

The Messianic Secret. Translated by J. C. G. Greig. London: James Clark, 1971.

Wolf, Eric R. *Peasants.* FMAS. Englewood Cliffs: Prentice-Hall, 1966.

Woll, D. Bruce. *Johannine Christianity in Conflict: Authority, Rank, and Succession in the First Farewell Discourse.* SBLDS 60. Chico, Calif.: Scholars Press, 1981.

Wolterstorff, Nicholas. "The Migration of the Theistic Arguments: From Natural Theology to Evidentialist Apologetics," in *Rationality, Religious Belief, and Moral Commitment.* Edited by Robert Audi and William J. Wainwright. Ithaca: Cornell University Press, 1986, pp. 38–81.

Divine Discourse: Philosophical Reflections on the Claim that God Speaks. Cambridge: Cambridge University Press, 1995.

"The Promise of Speech-act Theory for Biblical Interpretation," in *After Pentecost: Language and Biblical Interpretation.* SHS 2. Edited by Craig Bartholomew, Colin Greene, and Karl Möller. Grand Rapids: Zondervan, 2001, pp. 73–89.

Wood, Charles M. "Hermeneutics and the Authority of Scripture," in *Scriptural Authority and Narrative Interpretation: Essays on the Occasion of the Sixty-fifth Birthday of Hans W. Frei.* Edited by Garrett Green. Philadelphia: Fortress, 1987, pp. 3–20.

Worsley, Peter M. *The Third World.* London: Weidenfeld & Nicholson, 1964.

The Trumpet Shall Sound: A Study of "Cargo" Cults in Melanesia. 2nd edn. London: Paladin, 1970.

The Three Worlds: Culture and World Development. London: Weidenfeld & Nicholson, 1984.

Wright, N. T. *The New Testament and the People of God.* Minneapolis: Fortress, 1992.

Wright, N. T. and Marcus Borg. *The Meaning of Jesus: Two Visions.* London: SPCK, 1999.

Wuthnow, Robert, James D. Hunter, Albert Bergesen, and Edith Kurzweil. *Cultural Analysis: The Work of Peter L. Berger, Mary Douglas, Michel Foucault, and Juergen Habermas.* London: Routledge & Kean Paul, 1987.

Yaghjian, Lucretia B. "Ancient Reading," in *The Social Sciences and New Testament Interpretation.* Edited by Richard L. Rohrbaugh. Peabody: Hendrickson, 1996, pp. 206–30.

Yoder, John Howard. *The Priestly Kingdom: Social Ethics as Gospel.* Notre Dame: University of Notre Dame Press, 1984.

Young, Frances M. "Exegetical Method and Scriptural Proof: The Bible in Doctrinal Debate." *SP* 19 (1989), pp. 291–304.

 "Allegory and the Ethics of Reading," in *The Open Text: New Directions for Biblical Studies?* Edited by Francis Watson. London: SCM Press, 1993, pp. 103–20.

 Biblical Exegesis and the Formation of Christian Culture. Cambridge: Cambridge University Press, 1997. Repr. Peabody: Hendrickson, 2002.

Zander, Alvin. *Motives and Goals in Groups.* Orlando: Academic Press, 1971.

 The Purposes of Groups and Organizations. San Francisco: Jossey-Bass, 1985.

INDEX

Non-biblical references